THE PETRINE
REVOLUTION
IN RUSSIAN
ARCHITECTURE

t the University of Illinois at Chicago, and a
niversity. His other books include *The Church
Great: The Works of Thomas Consett, 1723–*

m the
Fine Arts.

ta

.

Church of Sts. Peter and Paul, Peter-Paul fortress, Leningrad. Detail of the iconostasis, 1722–1726; designed by D. Trezzini.

JAMES CRACRAFT is a professor of Russian history
fellow of the Russian Research Center, Harvard U
Reform of Peter the Great and *For God and Peter the*
1729.

The University of Chicago Press, Chicago 60637
The University of Chicago Press, Ltd., London
© 1988 by The University of Chicago
All rights reserved. Published 1988
Printed in the United States of America

97 96 95 94 93 92 91 90 89 88   5 4 3 2 1

This publication has been supported by a grant fro
Graham Foundation for Advanced Studies in the

Library of Congress Cataloging-in-Publication Da

Cracraft, James.
    The Petrine revolution in Russian architecture.

    Bibliography: p.
    Includes index.
    1. Architecture, Baroque—Russian S.F.S.R.
2. Neoclassicism (Architecture)—Russian S.F.S.
3. Architecture—Russian S.F.S.R. 4. Peter I,
Emperor of Russia, 1672–1725—Contributions in
architecture. I. Title.
NA1186.C73 1988 720'.947 87-34293
ISBN 0-226-11664-6

For
E. A. W. C.

Contents

Church of Sts. Peter and Paul, Peter-Paul fortress, Leningrad. Detail of the iconostasis, 1722–1726; designed by D. Trezzini.

THE PETRINE REVOLUTION IN RUSSIAN ARCHITECTURE

James Cracraft

The University of Chicago Press
Chicago and London

JAMES CRACRAFT is a professor of Russian history at the University of Illinois at Chicago, and a fellow of the Russian Research Center, Harvard University. His other books include *The Church Reform of Peter the Great* and *For God and Peter the Great: The Works of Thomas Consett, 1723–1729.*

The University of Chicago Press, Chicago 60637
The University of Chicago Press, Ltd., London
© 1988 by The University of Chicago
All rights reserved. Published 1988
Printed in the United States of America

97 96 95 94 93 92 91 90 89 88   5 4 3 2 1

This publication has been supported by a grant from the Graham Foundation for Advanced Studies in the Fine Arts.

Library of Congress Cataloging-in-Publication Data

Cracraft, James.
  The Petrine revolution in Russian architecture.

  Bibliography: p.
  Includes index.
  1. Architecture, Baroque—Russian S.F.S.R.
2. Neoclassicism (Architecture)—Russian S.F.S.R.
3. Architecture—Russian S.F.S.R. 4. Peter I,
Emperor of Russia, 1672–1725—Contributions in
architecture. I. Title.
NA1186.C73 1988 720'.947 87-34293
ISBN 0-226-11664-6

For
E. A. W. C.

Contents

Figures

Photographs not otherwise credited were taken by the author. In addition: C. A. = Carol Anderson; W. C. B. = William Craft Brumfield; K. B. = Kathleen Buckalew; J. E. K. = Jack E. Kollmann.

Plates

The plates are arranged by building type, in chronological order of construction, as follows: (I) masonry ecclesiastical architecture, (II) wooden ecclesiastical and domestic architecture, (III) fortification, (IV) masonry domestic and official architecture. All photographs were taken 1979–1985 by William Craft Brumfield.

I

II

III

IV

Abbreviations

The full titles and other details of all works cited anywhere in this book in short-title form will be found in the Bibliography. In addition:

AKh	Akademiia Khudozhestv (Academy of Fine Arts), Leningrad
AN	*Arkhitekturnoe nasledstvo*
BL	British Library, London
Ezhegodnik III	*Ezhegodnik Instituta istorii iskusstv*
GMA	Gosudarstvennyi Muzei Arkhitektury im. A. V. Shchuseva (Shchusev State Museum of Architecture), Moscow
GME	Gosudarstvennyi Muzei Ermitazh (State Hermitage Museum), Leningrad
HCL	Harvard College Library
HL	Houghton Library, Harvard University
JGO	*Jahrbücher für Geschichte Osteuropas*
L.	Leningrad
LC	Library of Congress
MiIA SSSR	*Materialy i issledovaniia po arkheologii SSSR*
M.	Moscow
Opis. I	T. A. Bykova and M. M. Gurevich, *Opisanie izdanii grazhdanskoi pechati (1708–1725)* (M./L., 1955)
Opis. II	T. A. Bykova and M. M. Gurevich, *Opisanie izdanii, napechatannykh kirillitsei (1689–1725)* (M./L., 1958)
PiB	*Pis'ma i bumagi imperatora Petra Velikogo*, 12 vols. (SPb./L., 1887–1975)
PSZ	*Polnoe sobranoe zakonov rossiiskoi imperii s 1649 goda*, 1st ser., 46 vols. (SPb., 1830–43)
RL	Regenstein Library, University of Chicago

SCR   Society for Cultural Relations with the U.S.S.R., London

Soobshchen. III *Soobshcheniia Instituta istorii iskusstv*

SPb.   St. Petersburg

TsGADA   Tsentral'nyi Gosudarstvennyi Arkhiv Drevnikh Aktov (Central State Archive of Historical Documents), Moscow

TsGIA   Tsentral'nyi Gosudarstvennyi Istoricheskii Arkhiv (Central State Historical Archive), Leningrad

ZAP   *Zakonadatel'nye akty Petra I*, ed. N. A. Voskresenskii (M./L., 1945)

Preface

This volume forms part of a more extended study of the cultural revolution in Russian history that is inseparably linked with the person and policies of Peter I "the Great." It recounts in detail how modern standards of architecture supplanted traditional building norms in Russia following a massive injection of European expertise and indicates how, in consequence, the modern Russian built world came into being. The volume also sets the stage—almost literally so—for others to come, which will deal with the concurrent rise in Russia of the modern visual arts, with the emergence there of science and modern literature, and with the cumulative impact of the Petrine revolution on the development of the Russian language and the Russian way of life. Thus together the volumes will provide a comprehensive and detailed account of the Petrine revolution in Russian culture in its wider political, economic, and social setting.

I should perhaps stress that although it is offered as a self-contained work in Russian architectural history, this book was written by a general historian, not by a specialist in architecture. The book grows out of an interest in the overriding question of how Russia became Russia—medieval Muscovy became modern Russia—and hopes to be judged as a work primarily of history, secondarily of architectural history. But readers may view it the other way around, in which case I apologize in advance for its technical deficiencies, which could only be excused by reference to the overall project outlined above and the great question that it hopes to help resolve. On the other hand, the subject itself of this volume, the breadth and detail of its treatment of same, its theme of architecture as a paradigm of larger historical developments, and its modicum of technical language may well attract readers not normally drawn to architectural history in the more restricted or specialized sense of the term. In any event, that has been my intention in writing it.

The book draws on several years of library, archival, and picture research as well as extensive on-site inspection of architectural monuments, work that was greatly facilitated by various people and grants. The International Research and Exchanges Board and the Soviet Academy of Sciences supported my research in the Soviet Union in 1979 and 1981, while a fellowship from the National Endowment for the Humanities enabled me to spend the academic year 1979–1980 writing the first draft of the text. Much rewriting and further research were supported by the Russian Research Center of Harvard University, where I also benefited from the advice of many colleagues and friends. Scholars who read the manuscript in whole or in part and commented very helpfully include Walter B. Denny, Jack E. Kollmann, Lindsey A. J. Hughes, and William C. Brumfield. My deep gratitude to Professor Brumfield for supplying the plates for this book will be shared by every reader.

A grant from the Research Board of the University of Illinois at Chicago paid for most of the figures; many of these photographs were taken by Kathleen Buckalew and by Carol Anderson, both of whom I sincerely thank. The staffs of the Lenin Library in Moscow, the Regenstein Library of the University of Chicago, and several of the libraries of Harvard University were particularly helpful. But this is not to slight the assistance received at libraries where I spent less time, including those of the Metropolitan Museum of Art, New York, and of the Art Institute of Chicago; the library of the Hoover Institution, Stanford, California; the British Library, London; and the State Public Library, Leningrad. My concluding work at the Library of Congress in the spring of 1985 was pleasantly facilitated by the Kennan Institute for Advanced Russian Studies, Wilson Center for International Scholars, Smithsonian Institution, Washington, D.C.

Lastly, I must thank my wife, Caroline Pinder Cracraft, who "not only edits his works, but edits him."

In this book, transliterations from the Russian follow the modified Library of Congress system used by the *Slavic Review,* the journal of the American Association for the Advancement of Slavic Studies. Soft signs are dropped in the text in Russian proper names (e.g., Grabar, not Grabar') or when Russian words are anglicized (e.g., *Posol'skii prikaz* becomes Posolskii Prikaz; *Vasil'evskii ostrov,* Vasilevskii Island), but elsewhere they are retained; and common English equivalents of Russian names and other terms are used whenever possible. Dates are given in accordance with the Julian calendar adopted in Russia by decree of Peter I on January 1, 1700, thereby abandoning the tradition of calculating time "from the creation of the world." At that point the Julian calendar was eleven days behind the Gregorian calendar (twelve days in the nineteenth century, thirteen in the twentieth) which was gradually superceding it in Europe and beyond—to be adopted in Russia, in connection with another revolution, early in 1918.

J. C.
Chicago
May 1987

THE PETRINE
REVOLUTION
IN RUSSIAN
ARCHITECTURE

Arctic

Atlantic
Ocean

White Sea

S W E D E N

FINLAND

Lake
Onega

KIZHI

VYTEGORSK

ARCHANGEL

STOCKHOLM

*Lake
Ladoga*

R. Neva

BELOOZERO

R. Sheksna

VOLOGDA

COPENHAGEN

Gulf of Finland

R. Narova

ST. PETERSBURG

R U S S

DENMARK

*Baltic
Sea*

COURLAND

LITHUANIA

POLOTSK

W. Dvina

R. Kliazma

MECKLEN
-BURG

HANOVER

PRUSSIA

DANZIG

BELORUSSIA

SMOLENSK

MOSCOW

R. Moskva

BERLIN

Niemen

MINSK

R. Oka

DRESDEN

WARSAW

NEZVIZH

MOGILEV

KOZLOV

BREST

TAMBOV

POLAND

CHERNIGOV

VORONEZH

R. Danube

U K R A I N E

BELGOROD

VIENNA

KIEV

R. Don

MOLDAVIA

POLTAVA

R. Dniester

R. Pruth

R. Dnieper

IAROSLAVL'

KOSTROMA

T a t a r s

AZOV

TVER'

PERESLAVL'-ZALESSKII

ROSTOV VELIKII

*Sea of
Azov*

ALEKSANDROV

SUZDAL'

ZAGORSK

VLADIMIR

CRIMEA

ISTRA

ZVENIGOROD

MOSCOW

VIAZ'MA

KOLOMNA

PEREIASLAVL'-
RIAZANSKII

Black Sea

SERPUKHOV

RIAZAN'

CONSTANTINOPLE

KALUGA

A G P

TURKEY

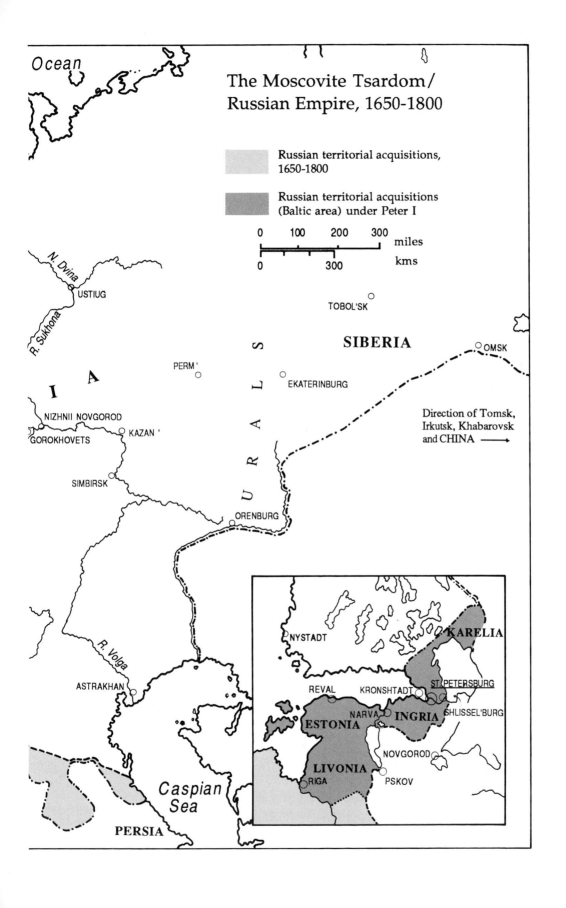

The Moscovite Tsardom/
Russian Empire, 1650-1800

Russian territorial acquisitions,
1650-1800

Russian territorial acquisitions
(Baltic area) under Peter I

0	100	200	300	
miles

| 0 | | 300 | | |
kms

Ocean

N. Dvina

USTIUG

R. Sukhona

TOBOL'SK

SIBERIA

OMSK

PERM'

EKATERINBURG

I   A

NIZHNII NOVGOROD

GOROKHOVETS

KAZAN'

SIMBIRSK

U R A L S

Direction of Tomsk,
Irkutsk, Khabarovsk
and CHINA ⟶

ORENBURG

R. Volga

ASTRAKHAN

NYSTADT

KARELIA

REVAL

KRONSHTADT

ST. PETERSBURG

NARVA

INGRIA

SHLISSEL'BURG

ESTONIA

NOVGOROD

LIVONIA

RIGA

PSKOV

*Caspian
Sea*

PERSIA

Figure 1   Peter I "the Great," tsar and first Russian emperor (1672–1725). Portrait in oil on canvas attributed to Andrei Matveev and supposedly painted in Amsterdam (1724–1725?) from an original (since lost) done from life by his teacher, Karl Moor (Carel de Moor), at The Hague in 1717, during Peter's second trip to Holland (see V. G. Andreeva, "Andrei Matveev," in Alekseeva, *Russkoe iskusstvo* [1974], pp. 141–44).

1
Introduction

> He transformed the existing architecture, [which was] coarse and
> deformed in the utmost degree; or rather, he caused architecture
> to be born in his country.
> —Fontenelle, eulogy of Peter I, 1725

"THE BIRTH OF ARCHITECTURE IN RUSSIA"

The proposition that the reign of Peter I witnessed the birth of architecture in Russia, as Fontenelle put it, was virtually self-evident to a literate European of the day. Fontenelle spoke before a public meeting of the Paris Academy of Sciences in 1725, eulogizing the recently dead tsar-emperor, who had been an honorary member of the academy since 1717; and there is no indication that anything he said provoked disagreement. Just as Russia before Peter—"Russia or Muscovy," Fontenelle called it, a little unsure—had not been part of Europe, so its buildings—"coarse and deformed in the utmost degree"—were not yet truly architecture. It had been precisely Peter's achievement to lead Russia into Europe, to begin civilizing it in accordance with European norms, and thus to bring about the birth in his homeland of architecture as such.[1]

Fontenelle's view of "Muscovy or Russia" in relation to Europe is amply reflected both in contemporary European literature and in later European histories. Livet and Mousnier, for example, point out (1980) that European dictionaries and geographies published before the eighteenth century "exhibit great hesitation in placing Muscovy in Europe," a hesitation which is evident in their own *Histoire générale de l'Europe*.[2] Yet if today historians can agree that the reign of Peter I "the Great" (1682–1725) marked the decisive onset of "Europeanization" in Russia, meaning by the term a political and an economic as well as a cultural process, there is no clear consensus as to how and why this took place and with what specific results, especially in the field of culture. The overall purpose of this book is to provide a case study of cultural Europeanization in seventeenth- and eighteenth-century Russia in just such concrete terms.

We began with Fontenelle, who never actually traveled to Russia but could readily have discovered the state of its buildings from various of the eyewitness accounts, many of them illustrated, that had been published by 1725. In asserting that Peter I had caused architecture to be born in his country, what did Fontenelle, speaking for his educated contemporaries, mean by "architecture"? If we look, in reply, to that characteristic product of early modern Europe, the comprehensive dictionary or "encyclopedia," we find that in relating the history of the building art and in describing the latter's qualities the commitment is entirely to Classical standards. Whether it is the detailed and illustrated exposition located in successive editions of the *Encyclopaedia Britannica,* first published at Edinburgh in 1768, or the entries to be read in shorter works, the view is the same. Here slightly condensed is what a *Dictionary of Arts and Sciences, Comprehending All the Branches of Useful Knowledge* published mid-century in London has to say under "Architecture":

> the art or science of erecting edifices, subdivided into civil, military, and naval. Civil Architecture, called absolutely, and by way of eminence, architecture, teaches how to make any kind of buildings, as palaces, churches, private houses, etc.; and the rules to be observed in it are solidity, convenience, and beauty; order, disposition, proportion, decorum, and economy. Solidity implies the choice of a good foundation, and sound materials; convenience consists in so ordering the parts of an edifice that they may not embarrass one another; beauty is that agreeable form and pleasing appearance which it exhibits to the eye of the spectator; and disposition is the agreeable union of all the parts. Proportion is the relation that all the work hath to the whole; decorum teaches to have regard to design, custom, and nature; and economy to consider the expenses, in order to regulate the form and magnitude of the fabric.

The key passage follows:

> With respect to the several periods and states of architecture, it is distinguished into antient, gothic, and modern. The Greeks and Romans were so happy in adjusting the various proportions of an edifice that any neglect of their rules has been found to be a deviation from proportion and beauty itself. It is for this reason that the moderns have retrieved the primitive simplicity of antient architecture, which upon the decline of the western [Roman] empire was lost in the general confusion of arts and sciences.

And thus:

> The manner of the antients being reputed the standard of beauty and grandeur, another division of architecture arises from the different proportions observed by them in different buildings, according to the bulk, strength, delicacy, richness, or simplicity required. This consists of five orders, all invented at different times, viz. Tuscan [also Etruscan], Doric, Ionic, Corinthian, and Composite.

With these we may compare identical sentences in the *Encyclopédie* of Diderot and D'Alembert, first published in 1778, where the alleged evil of Gothic architecture, apart from its excess of ornament, lay in its neglect of "la justesse des proportions, la convenance et la correction du dessein" as these had been prescribed first in Greece and then in Rome, only to be lost to the world until rediscovered in fifteenth-century Italy. Modern architects were to study closely "the plans and designs of the antique monuments of Greece and Rome" in order to acquire "the good taste of the ancients."[3]

There were no two ways about it. Whether it assumed forms that scholars would later classify as Renaissance, Baroque, or Neoclassical, architecture at its reputed best in early modern Europe conformed basically to Classical norms of proportion and decoration and particularly as these were embodied in the five architectural orders: the four established in antiquity (see Vitruvius) and a fifth, the Composite, in sixteenth-century Italy (by Sebastiano Serlio and others). Each order, it will be remembered, is a column-and-beam unit regulated by a proportional rule and garnished by a set repertory of ornament and moldings; and notwithstanding successive attempts to increase the repertory, these five orders remained the essential elements of architectural composition throughout the European world from the beginning of the sixteenth century to the end of the nineteenth, and even into the twentieth.[4] Much of the burden of this book is to show that building in this sense first came to Russia, fully and to stay, in the time of Peter I, when the very word *arkhitektura,* signifying precisely building in a would-be Classical mode, first gained currency in Russian.[5] Indeed, it is indicative of the eventual success of this revolution that by the end of the eighteenth century the terms *arkhitektura* and *arkhitektor* (architect) had become generally synonymous in Russian with the older *zodchii* (builder) and its derivative, *zodchestvo* (the art of building), as an inspection of Russian dictionaries printed then and later—to this day—will confirm.

But the Petrine revolution in Russian building was not only a matter of style. The qualities of early modern European architecture at its reputed best—the proportions and ornaments enacted in the five orders, the "convenient bigness" and "good foundations" just referred to, the "agreeable union of all the parts," and so forth—made technical demands which contemporary Russian builders, trained in the traditional local ways, could not meet. What then was to be done when the rulers of state and society conceived a desire for building in the "new style," for "architecture," as Peter I and his associates would learn to say? There followed in the space of less than thirty years an invasion of the building trades in Russia by literally thousands of European experts, the establishment of regular training in architectural theory as well as practice, and the naturalization in Russian of a whole new technical vocabulary of Italian, French, Dutch, English, German, and Latin terms. In short, in a fundamental technical sense, too, the reign of Peter I witnessed the birth—or a rebirth—of architecture in Russia.

Third, the Petrine revolution in Russian building was a matter simply of volume. The number and variety of structures erected and more, of projects undertaken or considered, were entirely unprecedented in Russia over any comparable span of time. Equally, in their scale both of labor employed and of capital invested the public works of the Petrine period, above all the construction of St. Petersburg, would remain unrivaled in Russia until the nineteenth century.

The Petrine revolution in Russian architecture would eventually transform the entire Russian built world, giving it, in the words of Catherine II (1762–

1796), Peter's deliberate successor in this as in other endeavors, a "more European appearance." But before proceeding something should be said about the revolution's larger historical context.

THE LARGER HISTORICAL CONTEXT

The Petrine revolution in Russian architecture was closely linked with certain political developments in both Russia and Europe and with certain European developments in architecture itself. The latter include postmedieval changes in construction and design, in the training and status of builders, in town planning and architectural taste, as well as an expanding range of building materials. The political developments in question encompass Russia's quite sudden emergence in the Petrine period as a European power and Peter I's concurrent efforts to transform his tsardom into a richer, stronger, more effective state.

The rise to dominance of Classical standards in sixteenth- and seventeenth-century European architecture was alluded to above, as were the new technical demands that came with it. This epochal development began in Italy late in the fourteenth century and was greatly facilitated by the "discovery" of Vitruvius's *De architectura,* a treatise in ten parts or "books" on all aspects of architecture dating to about 25 B.C. The numerous editions and translations of Vitruvius's treatise printed in Europe after 1486 allowed builders to imbibe the principles of Classical architecture without actually seeing the surviving examples available in Rome to Filippo Brunelleschi (1377–1446) and the other early exponents of the revived style. In fact, it was not long before ancient precedent became the rule for processes of actual construction as well as for design and ornament. Vitruvius's treatise in one form or another became a kind of "architect's bible" to which one turned for guidance on the burning of lime or the seasoning of timber or the painting of stucco with the same complete confidence that was accorded its pronouncements in matters of taste.[6]

From the ancients, in sum, Renaissance architects acquired a taste for round arches, barrel vaults, and flat ceilings as well as for the beauties of the several orders, which now were to serve more a decorative than a functional purpose; and with imitation and experiment came the technical means of constructing them. Renaissance architects built newly light and spacious palaces for rich and noble families and great domed churches for the pope and other ecclesiastical dignitaries (although the Renaissance double dome—steeply curved outside, hemispherical within—owes as much to other developments as it does to Classical prototypes). From the baths and villas of Imperial Rome were derived notions of splendor and formality unknown in the Middle Ages; a demand arose for suites of magnificent apartments, elaborate gardens, formalized townscapes, and planned cities, all to reflect Classical norms. Rome in particular underwent a complete transformation from the reign of Pope Sixtus IV (1471–1484), when the city's first master plan was prepared, through that of Sixtus V (1585–1590), when the architect Domenico Fontana transformed the layout of the principal streets and piazzas, to that of Alexander VII (1655–1667), when Bernini's colonnaded Piazza of St. Peter was completed. Meanwhile the technical knowledge thus gained was being recorded: in Alberti's *De re aedificatoria,* first published in 1485; in Leonardo da Vinci's writings; and in Galileo's exposition of the problems of mechanics and statics, published in 1638, the first such work known to historians.[7]

From Italy the revolutionary new architecture—secular (or palace), dome (or ecclesiastical), landscape (or garden)—spread to Switzerland and Germany, the Netherlands and England, Poland and the Austrian dominions, and, with special force, to France; as did the new theories of town planning and, closely related, of fortification. Both French and Italian architects as well as German and Swiss would figure prominently in the planning and building of St. Petersburg: in bringing the architectural revolution to Russia. Yet Peter I, as we shall see, seemed to prefer building as it was practiced in London and especially in Amsterdam, with its concentric plan (dating to 1610) based on a series of canals. The terrain on which St. Petersburg was to stand, Peter would observe, was like that of Amsterdam, necessitating both canals and sluice works; but he also seemed to prefer the more muted or limited use of Classical motives, the greater profusion of decorative detail, the more gadgety gardens and generally more modest scale of building that he found in Amsterdam to anything that he saw in Paris. London, he would learn during a four-month stay in 1698, was a huge, sprawling old city that had undergone, like Moscow itself, frequent and devastating fires. Indeed the Great Fire of London of 1666, which had raged for five or six days, destroying the greater part of the inner "City," afforded an opportunity for planning such as had never occurred in England: "a great opportunity to substitute a dignified, planned and healthy city for the unsanitary chaos that London had become."[8]

Architectural developments in London in the seventeenth century prefigured in many ways developments that were shortly to take place in Russia, particularly in Moscow. Medieval planning in London, by contrast to what came later, had been a matter of laying out streets and walls for convenience and security rather than purposefully grouping structures so as to produce both a rational distribution of functions—administrative, residential, industrial, commercial—and the impression of a harmonious whole. Well into the seventeenth century, in London as in Moscow, houses were hastily constructed primarily if not exclusively of wood; and starting as early as 1593 the English authorities attempted to deal with the ensuing dangers of fire and pestilence by restricting the erection of new houses, by requiring the use of brick and stone instead of timber, and by forbidding protrusions that broke the line of the street or diminished its width. Repeated efforts were made under Elizabeth I and James I to restrict the uncontrolled growth of London beyond the old city walls; and attempts at formal planning, by Inigo Jones, who had studied in Italy, date to 1618 (Lincoln's Inn Fields) and 1631 (Covent Garden).

In the wake of the Great Fire of 1666 Christopher Wren was ready with a scheme that might have made London the finest capital in the world, with its public buildings so arranged as to be easily seen and admired and with its chief streets, up to sixty feet wide, radiating from the heart of the City. For various reasons Wren was unable to carry out his plan fully. But a statute was passed whereby at least the outsides of all buildings were to be constructed of brick or stone, provisions for an increased supply of the latter were made, the building trades were reorganized, and funds were raised for widening and replanning the streets, among other measures. And Wren himself, who had studied in France and later designed fifty-two churches in London alone (half of them still standing, including the magnificent domed cathedral of St. Paul), created a vogue for Renaissance architecture in England that permanently altered English taste. "Our English Vitruvius," contemporaries called him. His basic ideas were to be magnified or exaggerated in the succeeding "English Baroque" of Hawksmoor and Vanbrugh.[9]

This was the architectural world in which, in 1698, the young Peter I spent four months. If the English could do it, he might well have reasoned, why not the Russians? There is no direct evidence that the similar regulations governing building which he soon introduced in Moscow, initially for the control of fire and then also for aesthetic purposes, were inspired by what he had seen or heard in London. Nor do we know for certain that it was in London that he first saw, and operated, a fire engine: an affair of portable cylinder and piston pump brought over from Nuremburg in 1625 to which had been added leather pipes and iron-wired hose, greatly increasing its efficiency. Was it seeing Wren's churches and other buildings, as Peter most certainly did, that confirmed his taste for architecture in the "new style"? Was it in England that Peter came to understand how the knowledge and skills of an architect like Wren (whom he may well have met) went beyond, or were other than, those of a traditional builder? It does not matter that we lack definite answers to these questions. Whether it was owing to observations made during his ostensibly diplomatic travels of 1697 and 1698 in England and Holland and also, for shorter periods of time, in north Germany, Austria, Poland, and, later (1716–1717), Denmark and France; whether it was a matter of the knowledge and impressions acquired in perusing his growing collection of European architectural books and prints; whether it was under the influence of his European friends or of any of the numerous European builders whom he hired for his service: whether it was owing to all of these factors and perhaps others that we have yet to mention, Peter proved determined to implant the new architecture, in all of its major manifestations, in Russia. This point will be extensively documented in the chapters to follow, particularly Chapters 5 and 6.

The preconditions for Peter I's program of intensive Europeanization in Russia, it is clear in retrospect, were by his time firmly in place. Beginning in the fifteenth century the Europe of the Roman inheritance, capitalist and overpopulated, had been experiencing an enormous outward expansion, one that was to culminate in the nineteenth century in Europe's domination of the world. This was the central development, no less, of an entire age in human history. And it meant that by the 1690s, when Peter I assumed full power, Russia had felt the pressure of Europe's expansion for a century or more, to the point where its ruler now had to choose: either Russia would respond to the challenge effectively and thus survive as a sovereign state and largely autonomous society, or it would suffer decline, colonization, and possible dismemberment. At the same time, the success of Russia's response hinged to a considerable extent on learning to live by Europe's rules, particularly in the military sphere. It was a dilemma that had to be faced at one time or another by all of the non-European peoples and states of the world.

Russia under Peter I became enmeshed in European politics as much by the pull of competing European interests as by the push of its own, more local and traditional concerns (retention of Ukrainian and Belorussian territories taken from Poland between 1654 and 1667, irredentist claims against Sweden on certain Baltic lands, a desire for allies against the Turks and Tatars). Peter I was encouraged by various European princes to launch a campaign against Sweden, then a formidable military power, which precipitated a long and, for Russia, nearly disastrous war for preeminence in northeastern Europe. Moreover, it was the Prussian ruler who in the course of this "Great Northern War" (1700–1721) opened the way for Russian troops to march into Mecklenberg and Holstein, two minor German states with which Russia became dynastically linked for decades to come. And after Russia's victory over Sweden, an alliance with the new power was sought by several of the established European states in a bid to outflank their rivals. By 1728, with the convening of the Congress of Soissons, the first European peace conference with full Russian participation, the Russian Empire *(Imperiia)*, as it now called itself, had become a permanent part of the European state system.[10]

In the meantime, Russian raw materials were increasingly sought by Danish, Dutch, German, French, and especially British merchants, a commerce that Peter I encouraged for his own political and military purposes and soon directed, against the wishes of all concerned, away from the secure but extreme northern haven of Archangel to his new Baltic port of St. Petersburg. By the end of his reign Russian trade with Europe had expanded greatly, while remaining largely in the hands of European merchants and shippers. Similarly, it was with the help of European experts and in pursuit of his military aims against Sweden that Peter modernized his army, created a navy, and built up the necessary supporting industries in metallurgy and armaments, textiles and shipbuilding. He also struggled to reform the Russian administrative and tax systems in accordance mainly with Swedish models, and again with the help of foreign experts.[11]

Indicative of Russia's growing economic and political importance in Europe was a new attitude toward Russia among European intellectuals. Here is Leibniz, the great philosopher, writing to Peter I in 1712:

> It seems to be God's will that the sciences encircle the earth and now arrive in Scythia [Russia], and that Your Majesty is now chosen as the instrument because you are able to select the best from Europe on one side and from China on the other, and to improve on that which both have accomplished by means of wise measures. Since almost everything concerning the sciences in your Empire is new and blank, as it were, innumerable mistakes that have gradually and in an unnoticed way gained currency in Europe may be avoided. . . . I would deem it the greatest honor, privilege, and pleasure to serve Your Majesty in an undertaking so praiseworthy and agreeable to God, for I am not one of those who cling to the fatherland alone, but look to the advantage of the whole human race . . . ; I would rather accomplish much good among the Russians than a little among the Germans or other Europeans.[12]

Leibniz's view of Russia in relation to Europe, past and future, closely resembles that of Fontenelle, quoted at the beginning of this chapter. Russia was a great *tabula rasa* on which Peter I would carve a new civilization with the help of European specialists, thus transforming both his own country and Europe itself, whose boundaries would now extend to China.

That Peter I had the power to work such a transformation in Russia was never doubted: certainly not by Europeans who omitted to go there themselves and perceived him, from afar, as more nearly absolute in his authority than any European ruler. Among those who did make the journey, however, and have left us their impressions, the actual limitations on the tsar's power were sometimes noticed. Particularly to have been noticed was the widespread opposition, both active and passive, aroused by Peter's "reforms" among his own countrymen: an opposition that was almost invariably seen by European observers as the product of ignorance, sloth, or plain barbarism. Less clearly observed was Peter's personal ambivalence in the face of wholesale Europeanization, an attitude that seems to have been rooted not only in patriotic sentiment but in his perception of European notions of the "well-regulated police state."[13] Their moral or spiritual justifications aside, these notions called for the supervision and control of all aspects of public life in the name of political and economic self-sufficiency. The well-being of the state had become the highest good for all of society; and European states sought to maximize their advantages in geography, population, or natural resources and to avoid enhancing those of their neighbors in a perpetual contest for ever greater power, wealth, and glory waged both within Europe and beyond: a contest that was only mitigated by the participants' more or less voluntary acceptance of an international "balance of power." Such was the world that Russia, under Peter I, would join.[14]

In any event, wielding the huge power that was his by inheritance, pure chance, and his own strenuous efforts Peter I pursued over a period of nearly thirty years a program of intensive Europeanization, one that sooner or later affected virtually all spheres of Russian life. The conception and implementation of this program, as well as its immediate and longer-term consequences, in all of their variety and interconnections, have yet to be either comprehensively or systematically studied by historians. Yet its most tangible achievement, indisputably, was the creation of the new capital, St. Petersburg, which became the principal site and then the embodiment of the Petrine revolution in Russian architecture. The latter, to repeat, affords both an excellent case study of cultural Europeanization in early modern Russia and a paradigm of that wider process, at once political and economic as well as cultural, whereby the Muscovy of Peter's fathers was transformed into the Empire of his successors.

The bulk of this book is concerned to document how the man-made environment of modern Russia—the distinctively "modern" Russian built world—came into being. But first, certain historiographical problems must be aired. Some of these problems involve Russian architectural history as a whole, and others are peculiar to the period before us; some are to be encountered in the history of building elsewhere, while others are unique to Russia. In any case, their existence will complicate in varying degrees the task ahead, a fact to be faced at its outset.

PROBLEMS

In 1979 the director of the Shchusev State Museum of Architecture in Moscow reminded an international conference of architectural historians that during the Second World War over 70,000 cities and towns, townships and villages were ruined or deliberately destroyed on the territory of the Soviet Union. Elsewhere it has been estimated that in the Moscow region alone 2,240 villages were severely damaged or destroyed and some 42,000 dwellings burnt to the ground. Still other estimates put the wartime destruction of urban housing at one-sixth of all such space, with a further one-sixth, at the least, badly damaged; and the destruction of outstanding architectural monuments, partial or complete, at about 3,000.[15] To this wholesale wartime destruction must be added the damage done to individual monuments or sites as a result of official Soviet neglect or programs of "urban renewal." The situation has recently shown marked signs of improvement. Still, in general it must be said that the principles of architectural restoration and, still more, of historic preservation have enjoyed only sporadic and limited support among Soviet planners and policymakers, support that has alternated with the deliberate destruction particularly of ecclesiastical monuments.[16]

It is estimated, for instance, that during the antireligious campaign of the Khrushchev years (1959–1964) about 10,000 churches were shut in the Soviet Union, many to be demolished. In the 1930s, just in Moscow, some 150 churches were destroyed and another 300 converted to other purposes without concern for architectural preservation. The former included, in the Kremlin itself, the church of the Savior in the Wood (na Boru)—the oldest building (1330), by over a century, then standing in the city—and the historic Ascension and Miracles monasteries; most of the mighty Simonov monastery, one of the old guardians of the city, dating back to the fifteenth century; the Kazan cathedral, on Red Square (1630s); the huge, ornate cathedral of Christ the Redeemer (1837–1880), built as a memorial to the victory over Napoleon; and the Assumption church on Pokrovka street (1696–1699), an outstanding example of "Moscow Baroque," which is the subject of a later chapter. By one reckoning, of fifty churches in Moscow outside the Kremlin rated architectural masterpieces early in this century, eighteen now survive; by another, of eighteen churches located in and around the Kremlin in 1930, only nine still stand. Similarly, most of Moscow's city walls (mainly of the sixteenth and seventeenth centuries) and both the Golitsyn palace and the Sukharev tower (important, again, in our story) have vanished under Soviet power.[17]

Tourists today in both Moscow and the provinces, knowing only their *Baedeker's Russia* of 1914, will sense the extent of the devastation to the built environment that has occurred in this century; just as a glance at the scholarly literature will reveal how frequently historians have had to rely for illustration on old photographs and conjectural reconstructions. But the history of destruction as well as neglect antedates the Soviet era, to be sure (nor is it a uniquely Soviet phenomenon!). Students of the architectural heritage of earlier centuries will know that apart from destroying countless individual monuments the large-scale rebuilding of more than 400 Russian cities and towns undertaken in the later eighteenth century—Catherine II's grand *pereplanirovka*—all but obliterated any surface evidence of their previous layout.[18] Indeed, it appears that any serious interest in the architectural heritage especially of pre-Petrine Russia, and consequently any serious effort to promote its values or to preserve its monuments, are scarcely a century old; and thus postdate by as much as a hundred years the beginnings of the related movement in Europe.[19] Until well into the Soviet era, it would seem, the more usual attitude toward Old-Russian architecture even among educated Russians was one of indifference if not contempt. This attitude can be traced back to the Petrine revolution in Russian building norms, and to the radical shift in aesthetic perspective that took root in Russia then.

The relative scarcity of evidence in Russian architectural history is not simply the result of disasters of human invention, of course. The ravages of a severe climate have also taken, and continue to take, their toll. Equally, the fact that until the present century the great bulk of Russian buildings was still put up in wood exposed Russian settlements, much more than was the case in Europe or even in North America, to periodic destruction by fire. Still, wartime destruction and official neglect, as much if not more than fire or weather, would seem to explain why the oldest surviving wooden structures in Russia, with but a few possible exceptions, date only to the seventeenth century; this by contrast to the situation in nearby Norway and Sweden, where some fifty-six wooden or "stave" churches of the twelfth to the early fifteenth centuries have been pre-served.[20] The striking disparity here evokes another comparison: between the roughly 11,000 medieval masonry churches preserved in England (267 from Anglo-Saxon—early medieval—times),[21] and the few hundred pre-Petrine ma-sonry churches to be found (my estimate), often in a very dilapidated state, in Russia.

The shortage of surviving examples especially of pre-Petrine secular architec-ture has compelled historians to rely heavily on paper evidence for their knowl-edge even of basic building techniques.[22] These written sources, scarce enough in their turn, can be supplemented by graphic and archaeological material, an example of the latter being the evidence unearthed in the famous digs at Nov-gorod.[23] Yet archaeological investigation in the Soviet Union has tended to concentrate on prehistoric and medieval sites, while the documentary sources so far in evidence are overwhelmingly official in character and include only a few actual building contracts. At the same time, the usefulness of any graphic material in question—material that is not the work of European visitors—is severely limited by the fact that before Peter I both cartography and architec-tural drawing in Russia were in a state of infancy. And it will be seen shortly that the graphic works done by foreign visitors, usually to illustrate accounts of their voyages and often the product of memory, are not always as reliable as once was thought. In short, as well as a scarcity of representative buildings to study historians particularly of sixteenth- and seventeenth-century Russian ar-chitecture are faced with documentary, graphic, and archaeological evidence that is exceedingly fragmentary or lacunal in nature, crude or careless in design, and biased in favor of officials and their concerns as against builders and theirs.[24]

One or two examples of the technical problems under review might be wel-come.

Among the most important governmental buildings in the Moscow Kremlin of the seventeenth century was the *Posol'skii prikaz*—"Ambassadorial Office" or department of foreign affairs. Early in this century the building was dated to 1591 and described by Igor Grabar—the pioneering historian of Russian art and architecture whose work is frequently cited in this book—as one of several structures in the Kremlin "created under the influence of the architectural in-novations that had arrived with 'German' builders from the West at the end of the sixteenth century." Grabar's main source for thus describing the Posolskii Prikaz was a "most curious representation" of the building drawn by a Swedish visitor, Erich Palmquist, in 1674.[25] "Most curious," indeed. Only a few years after Grabar wrote, and unfortunately for his description, it was revealed by careful comparison with other contemporary pictures that Palmquist's "repre-sentation" (fig. 2) was little more than "fanciful": the building itself was grossly out of perspective and its facade, with its greatly exaggerated frieze and Vene-tian arcade, evoked a work of the "Swedish Renaissance" rather than anything

Figure 2   View of *Posol'skii Prikaz*, Moscow Kremlin, drawn by Erich Palmquist, 1674.

built in Moscow (in 1565, in fact, not 1591). In Palmquist's drawing, evidently completed in Sweden from rough sketches done earlier in Moscow, only the building's windows approximated reality.[26]

But more, since Grabar wrote it has also been shown that the Posolskii Prikaz, together with the row of governmental buildings erected under Tsar Boris Godunov (1598–1605) adjacent to it, had become decrepit as well as overcrowded by 1670, and over the next ten years were pulled down to make way for another, much larger official ensemble.[27] Some idea of the appearance of the new Posolskii Prikaz (the structure that Palmquist sought to depict?) can be gained from an architectural design of 1703 showing the facade with a dominating pediment as it had been very recently reconstructed following a fire (fig. 3). This design of 1703 is doubly interesting to students of the Petrine revolution since before 1926 it was erroneously dated—in ignorance of certain archival material—to 1675, thus antedating the distinctly Petrine decoration of this second Posolskii Prikaz by more than a quarter of a century:[28] a crucial difference in time, as we shall see (Chap. 4). Later, following Peter I's removal of the central government to St. Petersburg, the second Posolskii Prikaz with adjacent offices fell into ruin and eventually disappeared, leaving us, in sum, with

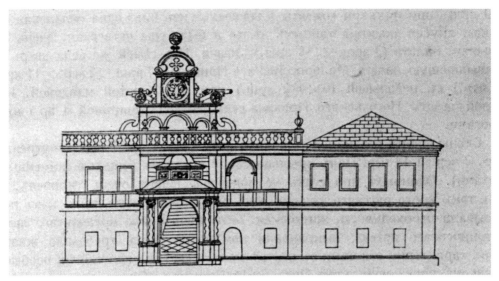

Figure 3   Sketch of *Posol'skii Prikaz*, Moscow Kremlin, 1703.

a meager collection of graphic and documentary evidence from which to recon-
struct the buildings that once housed the central government of the Muscovite
state. No wonder even scholarly accounts of the matter remain confused.[29]

The church of the Archangel Gabriel at Clear Pond (*Chistii prud*) in Moscow, more usually known as the Menshikov Tower after the grandee who commissioned it (A. D. Menshikov, favorite of Peter I), provides a second case in
point. In 1909 Grabar described this church, supposed to be the work of I. P.
Zarudnyi (sometimes also, in the sources, Zarudnev), as a "brilliant monument
of the combined, neo-Moscow Baroque," a style he saw expressing simultaneously an indigenous "Moscow Baroque" of the later seventeenth century and
the imported European (or Petrine) Baroque of the earlier eighteenth; in 1954,
when the term "Baroque" had disappeared from Grabar's Russian architectural
vocabulary (following the current Soviet fashion), he simply described the
church as "one of the greatest works of Russian architecture of all time."[30] But
more recently it has been argued, as a result (in part) of further research, that
the church was begun not in 1705, as Grabar had thought, but in 1701, thus
complicating its attribution to Zarudnyi; that if Zarudnyi was still its most probable builder, the influence of G. M. Fontana, an Italian who received several
other commissions from Menshikov, cannot be ruled out; and that in its original appearance, before the fire of 1723 and the rebuilding of the 1770s, the
church reflected the style of the "Petrine Baroque"[31] (figs. 4A–B, pl. 23). It
has also been shown that the celebrated interior sculptures of this church (fig.
5), whose design Grabar attributed (in 1954) to Zarudnyi and whose execution
he considered mainly the work of local artisans, were the work instead of a

A

B

Figures 4A–B Church of Archangel Gabriel at Clear Pond (Menshikov Tower), Moscow, begun 1701(?), damaged by fire 1723, rebuilt 1770s. A, Reconstruction "as of 1707" by I. E. Grabar'. B. Reconstruction of "original appearance" by A. I. Akselrod based on documentary evidence neglected by Grabar'.

Figure 5 Church of Archangel Gabriel at Clear Pond (Menshikov Tower), Moscow, 1701(?)/1770s; detail of interior sculpture.

group of Swiss-Italians imported, like Fontana, by Peter I.[32] Thus architecturally as well as chronologically the Menshikov Tower is a monument of the Petrine period, and its links with previous Russian building remain problematical.

The case of the Menshikov Tower introduces still further problems for students of Russian architectural history. I refer in the first place to the practice, widespread in the literature, of attributing buildings to particular builders primarily or even exclusively on stylistic grounds, and even in instances where a building's original structure and appearance cannot be definitely established. In his study of the builder Bukhvostov (active in the later seventeenth century), Teltevskii lists some eight churches and one monastic refectory that have been attributed to him by scholars on the basis of stylistic analysis alone; and he points out that documentary evidence of Bukhovostov's participation in the construction of any of these buildings has yet to be found. Knowing the large number of buildings for which there is some such evidence of Bukhvostov's "authorship," Teltevskii doubts that in seventeenth-century conditions he could have directed the construction of so many more. In any case, he remarks, few buildings of this period are "definitely attributable to one master," a chief reason being the "collective character of the work of builders" at the time.[33] This "collective character" of Russian building practices before the Petrine period will be discussed later (Chap. 3). Now it should be emphasized that the notion itself of "authorship" was as foreign to pre-Petrine Russia as it was to medieval Europe, and that searching for "architects" among Russian builders before the concept or even the term had arrived in their homeland is anachronistic at best. At its worst, indeed, the exercise has generated serious historical distortion.[34]

A related and more pervasive problem, one also suggested by the case of the Menshikov Tower, involves the nationalist bias of so much Soviet scholarship. This problem is familiar to readers of Soviet works in every branch of Russian history and is often, perhaps because it is so very familiar, passed over in silence. In the matter of architectural history, however, the influence of Soviet Russian nationalism is such as to warrant advance and explicit warning.

Here is an example, admittedly extreme, of what is at issue. The introduction to the first number (1953) of *Arkhitekturnoe nasledstvo* (*Architectural Heritage*), the leading journal in the field of Russian architectural history, asserts that Russian architecture of the eighteenth and nineteenth centuries (the centuries of Europeanization par excellence) is at once "penetrated by the most profound originality and organically linked with the national life"; hence, it is the duty of Russian architectural historians to "refute" any "tendency to minimize the role of our native builders and to ascribe their creations to foreign architects."[35] But the question of foreign versus native elements in individual architectural monuments, like that of external versus indigenous factors in architectural development more generally, is legitimately raised in any branch of architectural history; and such questions are of course always to be resolved, when resolved they can be, on due consideration of all available evidence. Moreover, with respect to the eighteenth and nineteenth centuries in Russian architectural history (as in, say, American architectural history of the same period), these questions repeatedly arise, making their proper resolution particularly important. In fact, the approach adumbrated in the remarks just quoted has promoted confusion both in the Soviet Union and in the West, where Russian architectural history—the little that there is—has tended to be written in uncritical dependence on the standard Soviet works.

Here is another, more immediately relevant example of what is at stake. In the introduction to a major and putatively revisionist history of architectural developments in the Petrine period produced by Grabar and others in 1954, the "complete misunderstanding" and even "direct falsification" of the subject by unnamed "bourgeois" historians are once more denounced while asserting that "only in Soviet times has in-depth work begun to reveal the genuine creators of Russian art, hitherto hidden behind the names of foreigners." Among previous studies devoted to this period (the introduction continues), only the "incomplete" work of Grabar himself and associates published in 1909 exhibits a "correct understanding of the value of eighteenth-century Russian art"; while in Soviet times it was only recently that "scholars discovered the deeply progressive elements" of this art, its "patriotism" not only of a "class character" but of a "wider and progressive national character" as well. Furthermore, the "link between the new art and that of pre-Petrine times lies mainly in the fact that the high level of Old-Russian art prepared and facilitated the rapid and brilliant flowering of the new." Similarly, a "large role in the enrichment of professional art was played by its direct link with peasant art, which was in the strict sense *the* national art and which throughout the eighteenth century as well as later remained the fruitful subsoil of professional art." It was "precisely for these reasons that the first Russian architects of the Petrine era, Zarudnyi and [M. G.] Zemtsov, yield nothing in their work to their foreign contemporaries." Indeed, already in the second half of the eighteenth century "Russian architecture was assuming a leading position in world art," although it was to be regretted that the "victory of national principles was far from complete; the dominance [*sic*] of foreigners continued, at this time and later."[36]

Such views would no longer merit attention were it not for the fact that they governed the research to a greater or lesser degree of a whole generation and more of Soviet architectural historians, whose works remain on the shelves to mislead the unwary. Even the work of Grabar, pioneer and giant in the field that he was, was not immune to their influence: his emphasis in 1909 or in 1911 on the decisive role of foreign architects in Petrine Russia, for instance, contrasts sharply with his insistence in 1954 on the superiority of the "native cadres."[37] More recently, to be sure, as references above to the case of the Menshikov Tower will have indicated, the power of such "national principles" in Soviet architectural historiography appears to be on the wane—no doubt a result, at least in part, of our burgeoning empirical knowledge. Yet a related provincialism of outlook continues to mark Soviet architectural scholarship, a provincialism made manifest by the practice of disregarding the non-Russian careers of foreign architects who worked in Russia, of largely ignoring links between developments in Russian architecture and international trends, and of avoiding almost completely the methods—and the standards—of comparative history. It will be necessary from time to time in the chapters that follow to return to this point.

A last problem to be considered here is that of periodization, which unavoidably raises several other vexing questions. Customarily, and certainly implicitly if not always explicitly, Russian architectural history is divided overall into two great periods—"Old-Russian" (drevnerusskii) and "modern" (novyi)—with the reign of Peter I providing the "break" (perelom) between the two. But this division suffers from having been initially determined by a preestablished view of the general course of Russian history rather than by architectural criteria as such, which presumably might have produced a scheme of successive dominant styles and related technical innovations comparable to the familiar sequence of Romanesque, Gothic, Renaissance, Baroque, and so forth in European architectural history. Moreover, the very simplicity of the customary scheme, its enveloping vagueness ("Old-Russian" to encompass seven centuries of building), has permitted specialists to subdivide the field without much regard to the whole. Geographical, political, simple chronological, or (but rarely) architectural criteria—or some combination thereof—have been employed to this end, the subperiods varying from one scholarly study to another. In short, Russian architectural history has yet to be periodized in accordance with a coherent and widely accepted scheme reflecting major changes in building styles and techniques.[38]

To some extent, it must be said, the fault lies less with the historians than in the subject itself. From its beginnings in the tenth century of the Christian calendar until late in the seventeenth century surviving Russian architecture exhibits, by comparison with contemporaneous European architecture, a certain homogeneity of style and, even more, continuity of technique. Development in Russian architecture in these centuries was mainly a matter of multiplying conventional forms in both structure and ornament, of what can be called stylistic agglomeration and the additive method in the organization of space. Technical breakthroughs were relatively rare; wood remained the dominant building material; the growth of towns was spontaneous rather than planned. Pre-Petrine Russian architecture was a largely autarkic phenomenon; external architectural influences were thoroughly rusticalized. There are of course geographical, economic, cultural, and political factors that explain why this should have been so. Yet the fact remains that until late in the seventeenth century, and by comparison with European architectural development over the same span of time, Russian architecture appears to have undergone few major changes.

To point out the predominance of continuity over change in pre-Petrine Russian architecture, however, does not altogether excuse the failure of historians to periodize either earlier or later Russian architectural history in a generally useful and acceptable way. Nor can the problem be wished away. The historical significance of the Petrine revolution in Russian architecture can only be determined by reference to both preceding and subsequent developments, and we must have some means to hand of facilitating such reference.

Accordingly, while retaining the customary overall division of Russian architectural history into "Old-Russian" and "modern" periods, this book assumes that the former is subdivided into an early Old-Russian or East-Slavic phase (tenth to fourteenth centuries), a middle Old-Russian or Muscovite phase (fifteenth and sixteenth centuries), and a late Old-Russian or national phase (seventeenth century). The modern period in turn may be subdivided into the Baroque, Neoclassical, and Empire phases—taking the story no further than the nineteenth century. The latter designations are, of course, essentially stylistic, and are meant to imply that the Europeanization of Russian architecture, a process decisively set in motion in the Petrine era, is the preeminent feature of the modern period. My periodization of Old-Russian architectural history, on the other hand, is meant to emphasize the largely autarkic as well as relatively indeterminate nature of pre-Petrine architectural development. But the rationale of this scheme, which seeks to overcome the deficiencies of previous attempts at periodization, will emerge as we proceed, it is hoped, and prove both clear and acceptable.

So much for the more technical problems to be encountered in studying the Petrine revolution in Russian architecture. Forewarned is forearmed. Now it might be observed that the birth of the new architecture in Russia necessarily entailed the rejection, above all by Peter I, of the Old-Russian—his own—architectural heritage. The next two chapters examine this heritage from the viewpoint first of contemporary European visitors, representatives if not agents of what was to come in Russia, and then of historians. These chapters seek to establish, in other words, the architectural context in which the Petrine revolution took place.

2

The Heritage in Contemporary European Eyes

Like all Russian towns Moscow is on the whole a mess, built without any architectural order or art.
—G. A. Schleussing, Moscow, 1687[1]

MOSCOW

Moscow in the second half of the seventeenth century was a city of perhaps 200,000 inhabitants, the seat of both tsar and patriarch, and a flourishing center of trade. Baron Mayerberg, the Austrian emperor's envoy in 1660–1661, marveled at the "great abundance of everything" to be found in its markets and at such low prices that there was "no place in the world which it could envy." Mayerberg also admired the city's natural setting—the "freshness of the air," the "fertility of the countryside"—and particularly its river connections, which enabled it, though situated far from the sea, to maintain a "very rich commerce in the most remote realms."[2]

Moscow's physical extent as well as its natural setting, the volume and variety of its commerce and especially its skyline were favorably to impress virtually every European visitor of the time. "The cupolas of the Kremlin churches are overlaid with a smooth, thick layer of gold leaf which sparkles brilliantly in bright sunshine, and from afar gives the entire city a beautiful appearance": so wrote Adam Olearius, who visited Moscow in the 1630s and again in 1643 on mission from the duke of Holstein.[3] "A splendid show altogether," exclaimed Samuel Collins, the tsar's English physician between 1660 and 1669, describing a view of the Kremlin's "churches and chapels," with their "gilded cupolas and great crosses."[4] "An infinity of towers and lofty churches which from a distance make a very fine sight," observed Jan Struys, a Dutch traveler and explorer who spent several months in Moscow in 1668–1669.[5] Similarly, a French missionary who passed through the city in 1685 and 1689, Phillipe Avril, found that when viewed from a distance Moscow presented "one of the most beautiful spectacles I have ever seen."[6]

Jan Struys heard in Moscow that there were as many as 95,000 houses and 1,700 bell towers within the city walls exclusive of the Kremlin.[7] A few years later a nephew of the tsar's Danish physician, Jacob Reutenfels, recorded being struck by Moscow's "nearly 2,000 churches, almost all of stone, which give the city a splendid appearance"—an "external beauty" that was enhanced by the hills on which the city stood; and by this visitor too Moscow was accounted one of the "greatest cities in the world" because of its physical extent and probable number of inhabitants.[8] "Urbs Moscua est amplissima," begins the description of the city by a Czech priest who was resident there from 1686 to 1689, and who reported that its churches numbered—"according to some"—as many

19

as 1,740.[9] The French king's agent in Moscow in 1689 estimated the city's population at between 500,000 and 600,000, the number of its masonry churches at 1,200, and the number of its masonry houses, all "newly built," at 3,000—a number that he did not consider large in proportion to the city's size.[10] The Austrian secretary of legation in Moscow in 1698 found the city to be both large—some fifteen miles in circumference, a figure repeated by other visitors—and "grandly adorned" as well as "fair to behold, with its more than two hundred goodly churches and multitudinous variety of towers"[11] (fig. 6).

Yet as impressive as Moscow might have seemed to these European observers, the view was far from uniformly positive. Dr. Collins noted that the city's outermost defense was a "wooden wall filled up with earth" which had been "made up" some years before "in four or five days." Jan Struys complained that its streets were "wide but uneven, and never paved [in stone], which causes great inconvenience, particularly in times of thaw and rain, when the mud reaches to one's knees, the logs and little bridges thrown here and there not-withstanding." Moscow's streets, as Reutenfels described them, were "surfaced not with stone but with wooden logs or timbers, which are laid in rows and constantly covered with mud or a thick layer of dust, being reasonably smooth only in winter, when snow and ice level things up." The Kremlin's masonry buildings, in the eyes of the Czech resident, were "old-fashioned, crudely con-structed, gloomy and dark." With a few "elegant" and very recent exceptions, Rev. David continued, Moscow's numerous masonry churches were built "in the old Greek style, circular and dark, and were surmounted by five towers with

Figure 6   View of Moscow from the south, ca. 1702, drawn by C. de Bruyn.

cupolas" from each of which rose a "ponderous cross held up by stays against the wind." With the exception of certain domestic structures recently erected by nobles and merchants, David found the city's masonry houses to be "dark" as well, this owing "in part to the thickness of the walls, in part to the disproportionately small windows."[12]

Adam Olearius left the most extended of the earlier seventeenth-century descriptions of Moscow, a description containing the famous remark that the city "shines like Jerusalem from without, but is like Bethlehem within." Here is more of what he had to say:

> The houses in the city (except for the stone residences of the boyars [high nobles], some of the wealthiest merchants, and the Germans) are built of pine and spruce logs laid one on top of another and crosswise [at the ends]. The roofs are shingled and then covered with birch bark or sod. For this reason they often have great fires. Not a month, not even a week goes by without some houses or, if the wind is strong, whole streets going up in smoke. Several nights while we were there we saw flames rising in three or four places at once. . . . The streets are broad, but in the fall and in rainy weather they are a sea of mud. For that reason, most of the streets are covered with round logs laid parallel to one another, so that one can walk across them as on a bridge. [Fig. 7]

Figure 7 View of a street in Moscow, ca. 1640; engraving in Adam Olearius, *Vermehrte Newe Beschreibung der Muscowitischen und Persischen Reyse*. Olearius notes (Baron edition, p. xii) that most of his illustrations were drawn from life by himself or by another member of the embassy.

Figure 8 Plan of Moscow engraved before 1646 by Matthaus Merian. This is a better version of the same plan printed in the first (1647) and subsequent editions of Olearius's account of his travels in Muscovy, and it evidently derives from a plan done in Moscow itself—the so-called Petrov plan—in or before 1605 by order of Tsar Boris Godunov. Note the Moscow river entering the city bottom center; the Iauza river, entering lower right; and the Neglinnaia, entering upper right. Also: the triangular Kremlin, center left, marked A, adjoined by Kitai-gorod, marked B; Tsar'-gorod (or Belyi-gorod), surrounding both, upper center left and right, marked C; the outermost district, Skorodom or Zemlianoi gorod, upper left and right and lower right, marked D; and, lower left, marked E, Zamoskvorech'e, or the town "Across the Moscow river," which in Olearius's time was inhabited mostly by the tsar's musketeers—*strel'tsy*—and their families.

Olearius proceeded to the topography of the city with reference to an accompanying "map" (fig. 8). He found that the first of Moscow's four main sections, called Kitai-gorod,* was surrounded by a thick stone wall (fig. 8, B) and dominated by the Kremlin (fig. 8, A), whose walls in turn and "deep moat" en-

---

*In Russian, *gorod* means "burg" or "fortified town [center]"; *Kitai* probably derives from the Old-Russian word *kita*, referring to the wattle and earthen walls that once enclosed this section, and not from the Russian word for China, as is often suggested, which would make little sense. Chinese were never numerous, or prominent, in Moscow.

closed "many magnificent stone palaces, churches, and other buildings, [including] a splendid palace in the Italian style": part of this palace, which indeed was built, late in the fifteenth century, under Italian supervision, survives today as the so-called *Granovitaia palata* (pl. 49). Within the precincts of the Kremlin (from Russian *kreml'*, meaning castle or citadel), and also in striking contrast to the ordinary—largely wooden—districts of the city, Olearius found no less than "two cloisters and fifty stone churches," each of the latter boasting "five white cupolas topped by a triple eight-ended cross and overlaid with a smooth, thick layer of gold leaf which sparkles brilliantly in bright sunshine." In the middle of the Kremlin stood "the highest tower of all, the bell tower of Ivan the Great" (pl. 4). Like the "splendid palace" just mentioned as well as two of the Kremlin's main churches and most of its fortified towers and walls, it too had been built, early in the sixteenth century, under Italian supervision.

Leaving the Kremlin by "the great gates [of Savior's Tower]," Olearius emerged into Red (*Krasnaia*, or "Beautiful") Square,

> the largest and best market square in the city. All day long it is full of tradespeople, both men and women, and slaves and idlers [fig. 9]. . . . In the square and in the neighboring streets, the wares and craft articles are displayed in stalls in specific locations, so that articles of one kind are found concentrated in one place. . . . Also near the Kremlin, in a street to the right, is their icon [holy picture] market, while further along is a special place where, in good weather, the Russians sit in the open having themselves shaved and their hair cut. They call it the louse market. . . . In this section of the city live most of the *gosti* or leading merchants, and also some Muscovite princes.

Figure 9 View of Red Square, Moscow, ca. 1640; engraving in Olearius, *Vermehrte Newe Beschreibung*. Tsar Mikhail Fedorovich (grandfather of Peter I) is seen in procession on Palm Sunday, while Olearius's embassy observes from lower left. Note the wooden house or shop to the right; the church of the Intercession on the Moat (or Basil the Blessed) to the left; and, center left, the Kremlin's main gate under the Spasskaia—or Savior's—Tower, with its celebrated clock (by Christopher Holloway, from England) dating to the 1620s.

So much for Kitai-gorod or the most central part of Moscow, some of whose place names today still evoke the serried traders' stalls of Olearius's time, as in "Fish" or "Crystal" street (*Rybnyi* or *Khrustal'nyi pereulok*) or the *Zariad'e* district (the district "Beyond the [trading] rows" in Red Square).

Next came the second main section of Moscow, which was called *Tsar'-gorod* or "Tsar's City" (fig. 8, C).

> It is laid out like a half-moon and is surrounded by a strong stone wall which, because of its color, they call the White Wall. The Neglinnaia river [now completely submerged] flows through its center. Here reside many magnates and Moscow princes, noblemen, notable citizens, and merchants who conduct their commerce hither and yon out in the country. Many artisans, especially bakers, also live here. In Tsar-gorod are located the bread and flower stalls, the butchers' blocks, the cattle market, and taverns selling beer, mead, and vodka. His Tsarish Majesty's stable is also in this section. Here, as well, is a casting works where many metal guns and large shells are made. Hans Falck, a very experienced master from Nuremberg, works here.

Moscow's third or outermost section, Olearius reported, was called *Skorodom*, meaning "Quick-house," probably because here were "located the wood market and the house market, where one may purchase a house that can be built in another part of the city in just two days" (fig. 8, D). We know from other sources that this section was also called *Zemlianoi gorod* after the earthen wall erected around it, just as Tsar-gorod, owing to its white wall, was also called *Belgorod* (or *Belyi-gorod*), that is, "White City."

Lastly, Olearius described a fourth section of Moscow lying south of the Moscow river and "surrounded by a barrier of timbers and wooden fortifications" (fig. 8, E). The section was called *Streletskaia sloboda*, meaning the "Liberty" or privileged settlement of the tsar's *strel'tsy* ("musketeers"), as Olearius noted; but the area was known more generally as *Zamoskvorech'e* or the town "Across the Moscow river." Olearius also noted that in this and the other main sections of the city were located "more than two thousand churches, monasteries, and chapels."[13]

The basic layout of seventeenth-century Moscow as described by Olearius should for future reference be borne in mind.

As for the interior furnishings of the typical wooden house of seventeenth-century Moscow, an embassy companion of Olearius discovered that there were

> seldom more than three or four pots and as many earthen or wooden dishes; some few of the better sort have pewter, but scarce any silver except some drinking cups, and those so ill kept that the tsar's plate looks like our tavern pots, being cleaned but once a year and that after a very slovenly manner. They also sometimes hang their rooms with mats and adorn them with a few images [icons] miserably painted. Some persons of quality use featherbeds, the

rest use quilts, and the common people chaff or straw . . . [or] they make use of their clothes, which they lay upon a bench or table in the summer and upon their stoves, which are flat, in the winter. The whole family is squeezed together in the same room; nay, in the country the poultry and pigs are quartered in the same place with the master and family of the house.[14]

The disdain with which on close inspection Europeans viewed most building in Moscow is equally plain in this half-facetious dialogue written in 1687 by an educated and much-traveled German named Schleussing.[15] Schleussing lived in Moscow between the spring of 1684 and the end of 1686—initially, like Olearius, as a member of a Saxon embassy and then, apparently, in temporary service to the tsar. In the dialogue, his imaginary questioner asks him if "Moscow, the chief city, is large and well built," to which Schleussing replies:

> Yes, large and extensive enough to comprise its own little world. It appears beautiful, indeed exquisite thanks to its numerous monasteries and churches. But come closer and enter the town itself, and you'll see that like all Russian towns it is on the whole a mess, built without any architectural order or art. For example, the streets are not paved in stone but only covered with wood; I might better call them village lanes. When it rains, even lightly, they become impassable because of the mud, and one can hardly proceed on horseback, especially in autumn.

Schleussing then stated that most of Moscow's houses were built of wood, "and in no particular order; only certain magnates and rich merchants have houses of stone." Did this mean that "great fires" frequently occurred?

> Oh yes, especially on their holidays, because of the lighted wax candles. They light these candles around their holy pictures day and night. . . . I often heard their night-time festivities interrupted by the ringing of the alarm bell, and such a barbarous hue and cry went up that I was frightened to death, thinking a rebellion had begun. I could never get used to these diversions and would jump from my bed and ask the servants, "Where's the fire?" But they would reply, "Oh, it's nothing, far away. Go back to bed, German, nobody will barge in on you tonight." And then they'd laugh, saying: "Look at our German! When he goes back he'll say he saw Moscow on fire." Well, last year [1686] the Lord God sent Moscow such a fire that I dare say nobody's laughing now!

The incidence of fire in Moscow struck every European visitor forcefully, and Schleussing was pressed by his questioner for details:

> Every section of the city has a certain number of musketeers assigned to it who are supposed to put out the fires with long hooks. The minute the alarm goes up they must run to it. But in hot weather the fire is frequently the victor. It is often so strong that although they quickly tear down the burning houses, the neighboring ones immediately burst into flames, which spread so fast that the fire can scarcely be contained. Only those who live in stone houses can find shelter and save their property.

So in Moscow there must be many a vacant and burnt-out lot, the questioner concluded. No, came Schleussing's reply, for at the wood and house market (confirming Olearius) "there are always many thousands of ready-made houses available at a very reasonable price," houses that could be "taken apart and then carried, ready to rebuild, to any point in Moscow." But this surely meant that Muscovites "must suffer great losses in household goods." No, again; for "the Russian has few household goods," a fact that Olearius's embassy companion had also noted—"hardly more than a couple of bowls, a few knives, a pot for boiling, a box or chest where unneeded clothing is put: all their wealth is in cash, which in the event of fire they snatch up to save with themselves." And their commercial goods? "These are not kept at home but in a special commercial building called a *gostinitsa*, which is solidly built of stone."

Schleussing went on in the dialogue to describe Moscow's layout and appearance in much the same terms as those used by Olearius about forty years earlier. The tone of the questions remains incredulous, that of the answers somewhat jocular. But the basic message conveyed is both unmistakable and familiar. It became a constant refrain, in fact, among contemporary European observers of the Old-Russian built world.

THE PROVINCES

Nor did the view improve as one moved from Moscow to the provinces. "Very few of their towns are worthy an exact description," observed Guy Miege, a member of the English embassies of 1663 and 1664, recounting their descent from Archangel to the capital. Vologda was a partial exception—"considerable both in respect of its size and of a strong stone wall which surrounds it"—and so was Iaroslavl, "the handsomest we saw in this journey. . . ; no very great town but remarkable for that the Volga runs by it, rendering it a place of good trade and populous."[16] It was a typical reaction.

Entering the country from the West, in 1661, Patrick Gordon's first impression of Pskov

> made a glorious show, being environed with a stone wall with many towers. Here are many churches and monasteries, some whereof have three, some five, steeples or towers whereon are round globes of six, eight, or ten fathomes circumference; which being covered with white iron or plate, and thereupon great crosses covered with same, make a great and pleasant show. One of these globes [cupolas], being the biggest, is all gilt.[17]

Yet up close "the view was pitiful," in the words of Jan Struys, who visited Pskov only a few years later: "the houses [were] nothing but bits and pieces of wood all huddled together in a haphazard manner." Pskov's inhabitants professed to prefer wood in building, Struys recorded, "wood being healthier than stone; and as for the workmanship, they allege that it is done by ancient custom, theirs from time immemorial—that in truth their houses are neither fine nor agreeable, but that they are comfortable and convenient nonetheless."

Struys also found that Pskov's walls of wood and stone were "fitted up with a few wretched towers" and were "neither crenelated nor [fixed with] platforms, and lacked bastions, redoubts, and every other [modern] defense." Novgorod, further down the road to Moscow, was only a shadow of its former self, its "suburbs almost as large as the town," its walls "in ruins." Struys was affronted by the "miserable cabins" that he saw in the countryside between Novgorod and the capital, whose inhabitants seemed to be "half buried" within them. Kolomna was merely a "village," albeit "one of the prettiest" on route; the walls and towers of Tver were wooden, its armament consisting of four old cannon.[18]

The city of Novgorod, medieval if not earlier in origin, elicited comment from every visitor entering the country from the west. Olearius noted that "from a distance," like Moscow, "the city makes a fine appearance, owing to the many monasteries, churches, and cupolas; but as in most cities all over Russia," he added, "the houses as well as the [outer] city walls and fortifications are built only of spruce timbers or logs" (fig. 10). About sixty years later the Hanoverian secretary of legation, F. C. Weber, similarly remarked that while Novgorod was "a city of great extent, fortified with old walls and deep ditches, almost all the houses are like wretched peasant cottages, built altogether of wood."[19] The rustic, wooden simplicity of the architecture of the Novgorod region was graphically recorded by the official artist in Baron Mayerberg's embassy (1660–1661), one of whose sketches is reproduced here (fig. 11).

Figure 10 View of Novgorod, ca. 1640; engraving in Olearius, *Vermehrte Newe Beschreibung.* The kremlin is lower right; the monastery of St. Andrew, lower left; and the main town, built largely of wood, lies across the Volkhov river from the kremlin.

Figure 11 View of the village of Edrovo (or Iadrovo), east of Novgorod, ca. 1660; engraving in *Al'bom Maierberga*.

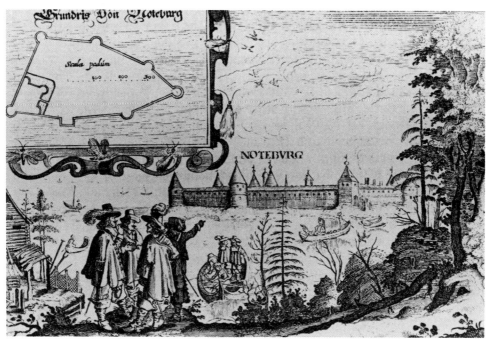

Figure 12 Plan and view of fortress of Noteborg, ca. 1640; engraving in Olearius, *Vermehrte Newe Beschreibung*.

Also regularly remarked on by European visitors was the poor or simply obsolete state of Russian fortification. The antiquated features of the Russian-built fort of Noteborg (called Oreshek in Russian, in both cases referring to the nutshaped island on which it stood) were duly noted by Olearius (fig. 12), who also observed that elsewhere in the country fortresses were "built of timbers and beams laid upon one another, which makes them vulnerable to fire."[20] In fact, as a masonry structure Noteborg/Oreshek was rare among Russian fortresses— as was Ivangorod, which was also located on Muscovy's western frontier and in 1669 was described by a German officer in Swedish service as a monster of essentially medieval design.[21] In the following chapter we will see that Ivangorod, which was built by the Muscovite government at the end of the fifteenth century, probably under Italian direction, had been rendered obsolete in the seventeenth century by the new-style Swedish fortifications erected at Narva just across the river from it.

Reutenfels, the Danish visitor quoted early in this chapter, went so far as to say (about 1671) that "the Muscovites have few places that are well fortified," a situation he attributed to their "ignorance of military architecture." For

> if fortifications are constructed anywhere, they will be for the most part either huge and clumsy, altogether lacking in finesse and solid reinforcement, or they will be built mainly of wood, flimsily, with thin walls, and from the first unable to withstand either cannon or fire. Fortifications of brick are built, but usually only before a very few towns, where [earthen] ramparts, ditches, and wooden palisades still constitute the main defense.[22]

Equally summary is this analysis:

> Stone being a rarity in Muscovy, and wood so plentiful, there are few houses but what are built of wood, which I observed to have two conveniences: one is that they are warmer than [houses of] stone, the other is that they are cheaper. But withal, they have this disadvantage, that they are more obnoxious to the element of fire, which is so outrageous that it sometimes devours a whole town at a blow. And hence it is that their houses are very rude, without any fashion or art, being only so many pieces of fir piled up one above another and moss stuffed in betwixt them, their windows very small and their roofs of barks of trees covered over sometimes with turf. . . . They are generally low, and those of the peasants not above one or two rooms at the most, in which the father, mother, children, hogs and hens lie all together. They have for the most part no chimneys, so that when they make use of their stoves the smoke goes out the windows. Another remedy the Muscovites have against the mischief of fire is the miserable furniture of their houses, which is so contemptible that in any such accident they can lose nothing with their lodgings but their dishes and spoons; so that they comfort themselves in their losses by the facility of their reparations.

This was written by Guy Miege, the English visitor of 1663–1664, who on his journeys from Archangel down to Moscow "never saw a town considerable enough to have any particular description. Ustiug is the greatest we saw, but it is built of wood, as the rest are, and paved only with piles of fir."[23]

Archangel on the White Sea had been Russia's chief link with Europe since the middle of the sixteenth century; convoys of merchantmen arrived there every summer and official embassies, like those of the earl of Carlisle (recorded by Miege), regularly put to shore. Balthasar Coyet, an official of the Dutch embassy of 1675–1676, records how the port was fortified by a "dry ditch and wooden walls topped here and there with towers" and opened by "two sets of gates, each guarded by two or three metal cannon." Inside this "Castle" were located shops and warehouses storing all kinds of goods, a wooden church, and a "large jail built of heavy wooden beams, all very high and standing upright very close to one another, with a small low entrance." The governor's house was "quite large, but wooden and not very well built." A few years before "great damage was done by a fire," for which reason a "fine quadrangular *Hof*" had been built with "watch-towers suitable for armament": this was the "*Duitsche Gasthof* or German covered market," which housed storage rooms and lodgings as well as the counters or stalls used by European merchants. Coyet's further remarks describe what was definitely a commercial town, one that virtually closed down for the long winter and retained much of a temporary appearance. It was also definitely marked by the presence of German, Dutch, and English merchants, whose warehouses as well as new commercial headquarters were among the most prominent structures in town.[24]

Yet the European presence in Archangel had not notably influenced its architecture. Twenty-five years later Coyet's compatriot, Cornelis de Bruyn, would find that in spite of Archangel's commercial importance all of its houses were still built of wood "or, to speak plainer, of vast pieces of timber joined together, and look odd enough from without." Bruyn would also observe that the town's streets were "covered with broken timbers, and so dangerous to cross that a man continually runs the hazard of falling down and doing himself a mischief; besides that they are full of the rubbish of houses, which in many places looks like the ruins of a fire."[25]

Coyet's embassy left Archangel for the journey south to Moscow in September 1675, and his reactions to the architecture seen on route were somewhat more positive than those of other European visitors. The town of Vologda, for instance, boasted "several fine masonry churches" as well as a "wooden church and bell tower built, they say, in a day; still, it is very fine, in the usual local style." Here too was a "most handsome monastery, splendidly constructed," and, in the center of town, "handsome houses belonging to both German and Russian merchants, with gardens of ornamental trees." Yet in Moscow, once again, it was the omnipresent building in wood and the consequent conflagrations that proved most remarkable. "Their houses for the most part are wooden, with masonry stoves, which get very hot and cause frequent fires, whence many hundreds, even thousands of houses burn down at times." On one of Coyet's first days in Moscow "fires burned in four parts of town, and the alarm sounded ceaselessly." He records the outbreak of four major fires in April 1676 alone, one of which destroyed some 200 houses "counting those that were pulled down," another about 300 houses, and a third two whole streets. In one case, "we began to look to our own things, since the fire was so close."[26]

In short, every seventeenth-century European visitor of whom we have record reacted negatively to Muscovite methods of fortification, to the extensive use of wood in building, and, not surprisingly, to the continual fires. "I shall say nothing about this town," wrote Neuville, the French agent, referring to his stay in Smolensk, in the west, in 1689, but that "it is built only of wood, like all the towns of this country, and surrounded by a simple stone wall." Novgorod was the first main stop in 1697 of the new Danish envoy to the Muscovite court, Poul Heins, who also reported that it was "built for the most part in wood" and "very badly fortified; the bastions are made of wood—not at all suitable for defense." Moreover, as Heins learned, "the entire lower town was consumed by fire a year and a half ago, and its inhabitants, as a result, were quite ruined."[27]

In the matter of design or style, however, the European reaction to building in Russia was less consistently negative. Indeed, as the seventeenth century wore on a positive note was occasionally struck by some of these observers of the Russian scene. Yet in doing so they tended to link such positive elements to direct or indirect European influence, and to treat them as signs of progress. Already in the 1660s Dr. Collins recorded that Tsar Aleksei Mikhailovich (father of Peter I), having "been in Poland"—he meant parts of Belorussia and the Ukraine until recently under Polish control—"and seen the manner of the princes' houses there . . . begins to model his court and edifices more stately." In 1669 Jan Struys found that some of the houses of the grandees located within the Kremlin were "fine and regular, comformably with the climate," and that the practice of cultivating decorative gardens was beginning to take hold: a practice "learned from the Germans" that had become widespread in parts of the city by the late 1680s, according to our Czech witness. The French agent in Moscow in 1689 discovered that a "splendid college in stone" and a "prodigiously high" stone bridge of twelve arches had recently been built under Polish supervision and with the patronage of Prince V. V. Golitsyn, who also saw to it that some of the main streets were paved in stone and whose own house, with its copper roof, was as "magnificent" as any in Europe (we will return to Golitsyn, who was an early "Europeanizer"). Kolomna, only a "village" in the eyes of Struys, in 1668, was described by his compatriot, Bruyn, stopping there in 1703, as a "town surrounded by a good stone wall" whose cathedral and episcopal palace were "well built in stone" (fig 13).[28] Apparently the architecture had improved in Kolomna between 1668 and 1703.

Balthasar Coyet, as indicated, was generally the most positive of these visitors. Yet his firmest praise was also reserved for buildings or details showing European influence. A "lovely church and monastery" in Archangel had a "tower with clock built by a Dutch master, and telling the time in both German and Russian letters." The "handsome houses" he saw in the center of Vologda belonged to "both German and Russian merchants, with gardens of ornamental trees." The audience hall in the tsar's palace of Kolomenskoe, outside Moscow, was "very splendid, complete with its tapestries and two French

Figure 13   View of Kolomna, ca. 1701, drawn by C. de Bruyn.

paintings." Patriarch Nikon's church of the Resurrection at the New Jerusalem monastery at Istra, northwest of Moscow, which was built to Italian designs and with the help of Belorussian craftsmen (Chap. 3), was

> a handsome structure, though unfinished. . . . They led us to the crypt, which is very fine and constructed in all particulars in accordance with the description in Holy Scripture, as is the entire church. Everything was splendid, with precious images of the saints. Then they took us to where we saw a full-length portrait of Patriarch Nikon, very well painted by a German.

Moreover, like Georgius David, the Czech priest, Coyet found the streets and houses and gardens of the suburban German Settlement by far the most spacious and beautiful in all of Moscow and its suburbs. This was the famous *Nemetskaia sloboda* or "the Sloboda of the Strangers," as Patrick Gordon called it, which at the time constituted a special enclave inhabited chiefly by German, Dutch, and British merchants and soldiers, the latter in Russian service. By contrast, the French agent Neuville was decidedly unimpressed by the suburban residences of the tsars, having been built of wood, as he points out, and "improperly called pleasure palaces; for they have neither gardens nor promenades and are surrounded by [fortified] walls."[29]

And reactions were the same, at best, still further afield. Bruyn's positive remarks about Kolomna were just quoted; but its walls and towers, he went on to say, were "not adapted for cannon" and on one side were "almost all fallen down" (obviously not the side he sketched in fig. 13); while within the town, apart from the cathedral and episcopal palace, "the rest is ordinary enough." Similarly, the important town of Nizhnii Novgorod, on the Volga, was "begirt with a fine stone wall" and possessed an imposing cathedral and episcopal palace; but all of its official buildings, including the governor's residence, were built of wood; indeed, in Bruyn's judgment, there was "no great sight to be seen in this city." Astrakhan, at the mouth of the Volga, was defended by a "good stone wall with ten gates." Yet apart from its cathedral, which was under construction, and one other church, everything else that Bruyn saw there was built of wood, including the governor's palace. Less than twenty years before Phillipe Avril had been struck by the international character of Astrakhan, and especially by its extensive Armenian and Tatar suburbs, the latter by itself having "the air of a town," with its ramparts and mosques and some 2,000 wooden houses. But in 1702, Bruyn learned, "one half of this town was reduced to ashes, and many ruins are still [1703] to be seen."[30]

Thus the exceptions to the generally negative reaction of seventeenth-century European visitors to architecture in Russia prove to be just that: exceptions, or isolated instances of praise for individual buildings or ensembles or details all of which tended to be linked, at the same time, to direct European influence. The more typical European view of the Russian-built world was decidedly critical as well as condescending, and would remain so well into the reign of Peter I.

FINAL IMPRESSIONS

F. C. Weber was secretary of legation for the elector of Hanover (who was also King George I of England) and then minister-resident in Russia from 1714 to 1719. His detailed and well-informed memoirs of his five-year stay include a description of Moscow as it appeared in Peter's reign, one that essentially repeats seventeenth-century views while making significant exceptions. Thus,

> The city makes a fine show at a distance by reason of its great extent and so many hundreds of steeples gilt all over, which when the sun shines upon them cast a brightness that pleases the eye. But within it falls very short of its outward appearance. It is divided in four districts, each of which is surrounded with a wall and a deep ditch, which, however, would prove but a poor defense against a regular attack. All the buildings in the Kremlin are of stone, and very durable, and for the greater part sumptuous, which would make a fine city if they stood regularly together.

Weber's reference to the Kremlin, although qualified in its praise, indicates that much new construction had taken place within its walls since Peter's accession

(Chap. 5). Regarding the masonry buildings to be seen elsewhere in Moscow, however, Weber confirmed that

> they lie dispersed up and down between thousands of wooden houses, besides which they do not face the streets but are hid in yards and surrounded with walls to secure them against fire and thieves. The streets are not regular, and paved but in few places, which renders the passage exceedingly difficult. The sort of building of which the greatest part of Moscow is made up consists of timber joined together in a square figure, after which the chinks are stopped with moss and a roof made over it of thin planks. Most of the houses in Moscow differ little or nothing from those in the villages.[31]

Weber was dismayed at the susceptibility of the Russian built environment to sudden destruction by fire, as so many visitors before him had been, including Korb, the Austrian diplomat on mission in Moscow in 1698. Korb's diary is replete with entries recording yet another terrible fire—fires that were "all the more disastrous because they mostly break out in the night time, and sometimes utterly consume to ashes some hundreds of wooden houses."[32] Similarly, in a single dispatch from Moscow dated September 10, 1707, the English envoy, Charles Whitworth, reported that the night before "a very terrible fire happened here, which burnt about 1,500 houses, and amongst the rest one where the English Consul lived. The Tsar by this accident has lost above 100,000 rubles worth of tobacco. . . . Today another fire has burnt down a church and cloister."[33] The problem seems to have worsened if anything in the half-century or more since Olearius's visit.

And thus the economy of housing in Muscovy, as Jan Struys observed in 1668–1669, continued to be such that "the best craftsmen are the carpenters, who make everything in this country, and are so adroit that they require only twenty-four hours to build a house." Bruyn made the same discovery in Moscow in 1702 and went on to record that "nothing surprised me more than the houses or rooms they sell here at market. These houses or rooms are framed of timber or trees, which you may take to pieces and carry to where you please, and set them up again presently." Olearius too had been amazed by Moscow's prefabricated housing industry, as was Neuville, the French agent, and, finally, Weber, who describes the "large markets where wooden houses stand by the hundreds ready made, and put up for sale; if a buyer is found for one, it is taken to pieces and carried to the place where he wants to have it set up, which is done in a few minutes."[34]

The state of the builder's art in Russia in the earlier years of Peter I's reign, as judged by European standards, is perhaps best conveyed by John Perry. Perry was hired by Peter in 1698 in England and spent most of the next fourteen years in the tsar's dominions directing the construction of canals, an undertaking without precedent in Russia. He also found time to observe local building projects, and he did so with the exacting eye of an experienced engineer. Thus at Voronezh, on the Don, in 1702, and "notwithstanding all my representations," the Russian official in charge of constructing a new shipyard "was pleased to let the work go on in their own way," with this result:

The houses of the Tsar and several of the lords (being framed of wood, to take down at pleasure, as is the way of Russia) with all the houses of the master-builders, artificers, and labourers, were carried thither [to the site of the new yard], and a large fortification with regular bastions was with all expedition made round this new place; which, after the expence of many hundred thousand rubles and above three years wearied experiments and endeavours to maintain the same, they were at last obliged to quit and lay it wholly aside; by reason that the floods still undermined the foundation, and came in upon them. . . .

all as Perry had tried to warn them it would happen.

The same thing occurred in Moscow, as Perry also tells it. Fearing imminent invasion by the Swedes, Peter ordered the city's fortifications to be strengthened and put two Russian officers in overall charge of the work. Several of the new bastions had to be built on marshy ground as well as to a considerable height. Perry observed that the foundations were being improperly laid and, happening to meet one of the officers in charge, pointed this out to him: "The foundation of these bastions would never be sufficient to secure and bear the great weight of earth that was to come upon them," he said, "but would settle out at the foot and tumble down before they were half finished." Not content with trying to explains things to the officer, Perry drew up a proposal in writing and sent it on to higher authority, eager to prove his "readiness for his Tsarish Majesty's service." But "the work went on as it was begun, and within six weeks after my said writing several of the bastions began to give way at the foot, settled one part from another, and tumbled down before they were half built; and three of them which happened to be in the worst ground, tumbled down a second time the same year [1708]; and though again built up the third time, yet to this day [1714] are not secured at the foundation nor raised to the proper height required for it" (fig. 14).

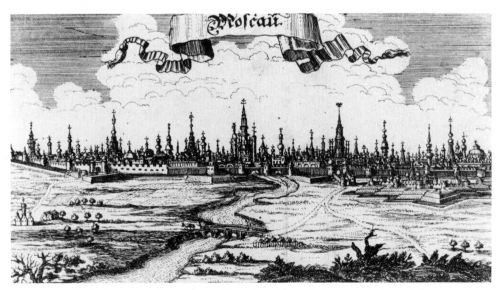

Figure 14   View of Moscow, ca. 1710, showing new fortifications in front of the old walls; contemporary engraving.

Perry's view of Moscow itself, which he first saw in 1698, recapitulates much of what his predecessors had seen. In his own words,

> Whenever any traveller comes within a fair view of the city, the numerous churches, the monasteries, and noblemen and gentlemen's houses, the steeples, cupolas and crosses at the tops of the churches, which are gilded and painted over, makes the city look to be one of the most rich and beautiful in the world, as indeed it appeared to me at first sight coming from the Novgorod road, which is the best view of it; but upon a nearer view, you find yourself deceived and disappointed in your expectation. When you come into the streets, the houses, excepting those of the boyars and some few rich men, are everywhere built of wood, after a very mean fashion. The walls or fences between the streets and the houses are made of wood, and the very streets, instead of being paved with stone, are lined or laid with wood, being done with fir baulks of about 15 or 16 foot long laid one by the side of another across the street upon other baulks that lie underneath them lengthways.

The pervasive use of wood in building prompted Perry, yet again, to speak of the "frequent and destructive fires in this country." In the course of nearly fourteen years he had worked in various and widely separated parts of Russia; but it was in Moscow particularly that fire was to be feared, no doubt because of the city's larger size and relatively greater density of building in wood. In Moscow, Perry duly noted, it was common in dry weather for a fire to spread rapidly,

> and burn so furious that there is no standing before it; and in this extremity it is the way of the Russes, in hopes to put a stop to the fire, to pull down the houses and fences that are made of wood; but they often have not time to carry [one] off, and as it lies upon the ground together with the wood with which the streets are lined, gives a train to the fire; so that I have known it in less than half a day's time, when there has been a gale of wind, burn above a Russ mile in length and destroy many thousand houses before it has been quenched, and often without giving the inhabitants an opportunity to carry off the tenth part of their goods.

Perry saw dire economic as well as architectural consequences deriving from the situation he so well described, for such fires had

> often brought many people to the last degree of poverty, when all that they have has been burnt; and it is one great cause that the houses appear so poor in Moscow, when they cannot raise money to build them better, and by reason of their being very often, as soon as they are built up, burnt down again to the ground. . . . Indeed the Tsar [Peter I] as well as his subjects suffers extremely by those general conflagrations; particularly once I remember when I was in Moscow there was in one warehouse near the river about 100,000 rubles worth of tobacco which belonged to the Tsar burnt [as Ambassador Whit-

worth, quoted above, also reported]; besides, his subjects are often rendered by those fires unable to pay the duties and taxes. It is certain that during the time I was in Russia, the city of Moscow in particular has suffered five times more by the accidents of fire than by all the taxes and charges of the war [against Sweden, begun in 1700]. Further, these repeated losses and destructions by fire are so great that I believe in twenty years' time they are more than would have rebuilt the city of Moscow with stone or brick.

The problem Perry raises here was to be addressed in various ways by the government of Peter I. But Perry also noticed that "some few houses in Moscow are lately covered with tiles" to help secure them against fire, while "others of the great boyars [were roofed] with sheets of iron."[35] In this remark, as in other of these "final impressions," signs of the Petrine revolution in Russian architecture begin to appear.

In Retrospect

The views of the Russian built world and particularly of Moscow quoted in this chapter were supplied by some twenty different observers, observers whose outlook had been formed by their experiences of living in Vienna, London, Amsterdam, Paris, Copenhagen, Leipzig, Marseilles, Venice, Naples, and Rome—not to mention such lesser European cities as Anhalt, Hanover, Olomouc, or, in some cases, the cities of the Near East. Yet their views are remarkably, even strikingly, convergent. And on their basis we in turn can picture a superficially splendid but comparatively primitive urban scene, a relatively few, usually quite recent, buildings excepted. The overall picture is one of a comparatively small number of crudely designed masonry churches and houses scattered among a dense but haphazard concentration of readily collapsible wooden structures liable at any moment to catch fire, the whole intersected irregularly by streets surfaced in wood—when surfaced at all—and surrounded on all sides by equally crude defense works. Suburban royal residences, built, again, of wood, were lacking in civilized prospects: were still enclosed by fortified walls. Moscow differed from the other cities and towns of Russia by reason of its size rather than its architectural qualities. Beneath its countless gilded crosses Moscow had an air of confusion, inconvenience, impermanence, if not of decay. The impression of a "medieval" townscape is conveyed, and of a largely destitute rural architecture: impressions that are strengthened on turning to the graphic representations some of these same visitors left behind.

These contemporary European observers of the Old-Russian architectural heritage have been quoted at length in part as a matter of emphasis and in part as a matter of record, since their testimony has been almost entirely ignored by Russian architectural historians. Yet we must proceed with caution. The nexus linking the frequency of destructive fires with the widespread use of wood in building—a practice based on habit, comfort, and convenience as well as the availability of building materials—was readily perceived by European visitors. So were the connections between both of these factors and a certain simplicity, even coarseness, of design. The influence of climate on architecture, presumably profound, was generally not as clearly perceived, however—even by visitors who remained to experience, and to comment on, the rigors of a Russian winter. Nor was any connection usually made between the state of Russian fortification and the country's actual defensive requirements, whether as perceived by its rulers or by anybody else. Nor was much thought given to cultural factors, for example, in the designing of churches; nor to broader economic considerations (John Perry was concerned with the economic consequences of those "dreadful fires," not with any economic factors that might have inhibited architectural development as such). Nor were aesthetic (or any other) standards of comparison ever made explicit.

Nevertheless, in depicting for ourselves the state of the man-made environment and of the building art in Russia on the eve of the Petrine revolution, these accounts of contemporary European observers remain valuable in two important respects. First, they provide an abundance of data—everything from general perspectives and precise measurements to details of design, ornament, and construction—with which to flesh out or refine the often meager physical and documentary evidence. But second, these contemporary European impressions of Russian architecture of the period under review, and especially any value judgments expressed, add a vital subjective dimension to the study of a phenomenon—the Petrine revolution—whose essence lay in a change of attitude. For by the end of the seventeenth century, it will be seen presently, an elite of Russian society—the decisively influential elite—had come to share these largely negative views of their own architectural heritage. A convergence of values had begun to take place.

These contemporary European accounts of the Russian built world constitute, in sum, a uniquely valuable as well as neglected source of both fact and motive in clarifying the historical context of the Petrine revolution in Russian architecture.

3

An Architecture in Crisis

The architecture of both town and cloister remained primitive
right to the end of the seventeenth century.
—N. Brunov, *Geschichte der Altrussischen Baukunst*

Brunov suggests that the powerful, disproportionate verticality dominating Russian architecture until the end of the seventeenth century exemplifies its primitiveness, a feature that he finds particularly characteristic of the contemporary wooden churches of the north. His point of view is obviously historical (and classicist); and it aims at distinguishing Russian architecture of the fifteenth, sixteenth, and seventeenth centuries both from an earlier architecture that was more definitely shaped by Byzantine norms and from the Europeanized architecture of post-Petrine Russia. Brunov's notion of the primitiveness of Old-Russian architecture of the centuries in question bears at the same time a universalist (or synchronic) aspect, since he also seems to have in mind the Gothic silhouette of medieval western Europe as well as monuments of still earlier ages. But whether historical or synchronic in nature, Brunov's view is clear: in 1700 or so Russian architecture was still on the whole "primitive."[1]

By contrast, the dominant nationalist tendency in Russian architectural historiography insists that in addition to its complete originality and unbroken, "organic" continuity Old-Russian architecture is distiguished by its generally high standards, both aesthetic and technical. The qualitative as well as the quantitative superiority of wooden over masonry construction is also asserted. These views go back to the very beginnings of Russian architectural scholarship, as is reflected for instance in a work published in 1889 by V. Suslov, Academician of Architecture. "Appointed by the Imperial Academy of Fine Arts to study monuments of our old art," Suslov reported back to the Academy, he turned first to the wooden churches of the north, since he considered them to embody not only beauty and a technical sophistication but an "immediate expression of the national genius."[2] It might be noted that the Academy by which Suslov was trained and of which he was later a member as well as the (classicist) standards against which he now rebelled—standards upheld, implicitly, by Brunov—derived from a common source: the Petrine revolution in Russian architecture.

Nobody disputes the fact—virtually certain for earlier periods, fully demonstrable for later—that wood was by far the most widely used building material in Russia until well into the twentieth century. In the seventeenth century, as contemporary European descriptions make clear, whole towns—Moscow itself—continued to be built almost entirely of wood, usually fir or pine, oak being reserved for defense works. The rough-hewn timber house of the ordinary town dweller remained largely identical to the rural *izba;* Moscow's streets, where surfaced at all, were surfaced for the most part in wood. Even churches, fortifications, official buildings, and the dwellings of grandees, structures in which masonry architecture first appeared on Russian territory, were still put up mainly in wood. But the nationalist school asks us to believe not only that timber predates masonry architecture in Russia, and that later examples in wood preserve unspoiled earlier and often uniquely Russian forms, but that masonry architecture itself frequently reflects the influence of building in wood and that it is seldom, if ever, the other way around. We are asked to believe, more specifically, that any foreign stylistic norms imported with the techniques of masonry construction in the eleventh century were more or less promptly domesticated under the impact of flourishing local traditions of building in wood; that the distinctive pyramidal roof *(shatër)* which began to be used in Muscovite masonry architecture in the sixteenth century was adapted from the local wooden architecture, where its origins are lost in the mists of time; and that the increasingly profuse ornamentation and growing compositional complexity of seventeenth-century masonry churches in Russia were a result, once again, of the influence of building in wood.[3] But none of this can be proven.

In fact, any properly historical discussion of the matter must begin by acknowledging that while masonry structures dating back to the eleventh century still stand on Russian territory, the oldest surviving wooden structures, with but a few possible exceptions, date only to the seventeenth. Already in the 1880s Suslov was lamenting the ruination "with each passing year" of the older wooden churches of the north, where virtually all surviving examples have been found; and practices since his time in architectural restoration—particularly that of creating, far from their original sites, open-air museums of extensively rebuilt wooden monuments—have done little to enhance the latter's historical value.[*] To be sure, the record is filled out to some extent by the graphic memorials of European visitors dating back to the sixteenth century; by modern photographs and drawings of wooden buildings that no longer exist; and by some, usually very limited, archaeological, iconographic, and literary evidence. It remains a fact, however, that very little is definitely known about wooden architecture in Russia before the seventeenth century.[4]

What is more, the traditions of wooden church building that appear to have flourished in central and then in northen Russia from the fifteenth century can

[*]See, for example, Filippova, *"Vitoslavlitsy,"* pp. 30–36, for a discussion with photographs of the monastic church of the Nativity of the Mother of God from the village of Peredki, the "oldest and most important [wooden] monument to have survived in the Novgorod region"; hypothetically dated to 1539 or "even earlier," it is known to have been "altered and rebuilt" in 1699, 1886, 1891, 1894, 1897, and at the beginning of this century, which alterations "completely changed its original appearance." Yet somehow this original appearance was completely restored between 1967 and 1971, when the church was moved to the Vitoslavlitsy open-air museum of wooden architecture outside Novgorod (pl. 36).

be traced back to Novgorod, whose *rubleniki*—builders or, literally, "choppers"—were famous for their craft alike in medieval Kiev and in seventeenth-century Moscow. Novgorod was in comparatively close cultural contact with Europe throughout the Middle Ages and particularly with Germany, Scandinavia, and Poland, from any of whose Romanesque or Gothic architecture the Old-Russian *shatër* might well have derived. Equally, the elaborate decorative carving and the multiplication of external or subsidiary structures that typify surviving seventeenth- and eighteenth-century north Russian wooden churches are also typical of surviving Scandinavian churches in wood dating to much earlier times. In other words, migrating Novgorod "choppers" were bearers as arguably as not of external as well as local traditions; so that no more than in the case of masonry architecture can it fairly be claimed, in light of what is definitely know, that Old-Russian building in wood was purely indigenous in its forms or that it represents, preeminently, the national tradition in Russian architecture.[5]

Then too, Voronin has pointed out that from a technical point of view the wooden architecture of seventeenth-century Russia was remarkably conservative by comparison with contemporary building in brick or stone; indeed, that as late as the middle of the nineteenth century the wooden building industry in Russia remained "among the most backward" in the country. The sawmill was introduced only in about 1676, in connection with one of the tsar's building projects; and wooden construction, unlike masonry, largely escaped governmental regulation until quite recent times. In fact, during the seventeenth century, as both before and after, construction in wood in Russia remained overwhelmingly in the hands of peasant carpenters, who continued to build with their simple tools—primarily the short axe or hatchet—and their "primitive" techniques, the latter well exemplified by the enduring preference for log as against frame construction. Such technical conservatism strongly militates against the notion of major structural or even decorative innovations arising first in Old-Russian wooden architecture.[*6]

---

*Filippova indicates that saws were used in Novgorod in medieval times but only in cabinetry, and that they came into general use in building only in the nineteenth century ("Vitoslavlitsy," p. 9). C. Norberg-Schulz, in his "Introduction" to M. Suzuki and Y. Futagawa, *Wooden Houses* (New York, 1979), emphasizes that Russian timber architecture relative to that of various parts of Europe always remained "primitive, in spite of its many fascinating manifestations"; for "log construction obviously does not offer the possibility of structural variation that the frame does. When horizontal logs are laid one above the other, the structure is fixed, and variation can be obtained only through detailing and combination with other types of construction." Thus "in the primitive Russian type, which employs round trunks everywhere, even for sills, the only structural 'refinement' found is a slight cantilever formed by the two or three top logs of the side walls, which serves to carry the projecting roof over the gable walls. The decoration which gives the Russian houses their lively, fairy-tale appearance is *applied* on windows, doors, and cornices, and its forms have no direct relationship to the wooden structure" (pp. 12–13).

Lastly, while building in wood might well have contributed any number of lesser structural and especially decorative features to Old-Russian masonry architecture, specific and equally if not more probable instances of the opposite occurring can also be adduced. A conspicuous example is the famous multicupolar "tower" church of the Transfiguration of the Savior built in wood on the island of Kizhi, in Lake Onega, about 1714 (fig. 15); it appears to have been inspired by the very similar masonry church—similar in structure if not in decorative detail—built at nearby Vytegorsk in 1708 (since destroyed) and indeed ultimately evokes such a major monument as the sixteenth-century church of Basil the Blessed in Moscow (pl. 6). Another example involves the use of glass in building. Glass first appeared in *masonry* construction; and as it became cheaper and more plentiful toward the end of the seventeenth century it began to be used in building in wood—leading there, as it had in masonry architecture, to the introduction of more and larger windows with associated decorative forms. Just this one innovation, Ilin remarks, "gave a completely different appearance, both inside and out, to building in wood."[7] One is tempted in the end to follow Nekrasov, who argued that seventeenth- and eighteenth-century Russian wooden architecture at its best was emphatically neither popular nor original. On the contrary, he urged, most of the houses that scholars regularly refer to in this connection reflect urban norms that were penetrating the north especially from the Petrine period; the seventeenth-century wooden tent-roof (*shatër*) churches of the north are reflections of a declining style in masonry architecture of the central regions; and the multicupolar churches at both Kizhi and Vytegorsk bear little or no relation to peasant art but are rather naive imitations by local burghers of what by now was conservative grandee architecture.[8]

We must reject, in sum, any assertion of the qualitative primacy of wooden over masonry construction in the development of Old-Russian architecture as untenable with respect to the evidence and unlikely as a matter of logic. Rather, it is safer to conclude that the relationship between the two was generally reciprocal, with the nature and extent of the influence expended varying from time to time and/or place to place.[9] In the seventeenth century, in the central regions of Russia, their relationship was closely interrelated—this being one major reason why the architecture of the period may be described as "national" in character. But it should also be noted that in the course of the century wooden architecture definitely became subordinate, qualitatively if not yet quantitatively, to masonry, a development that appears to have occurred everywhere in Russia except, not surprisingly, the far north, where building in wood retained its traditions until well into the eighteenth century. And this growing subordination of wooden to masonry construction is one major reason why we may think of the seventeenth century as witnessing the final phase in the history of Old-Russian architecture.

It is time to come clean. A national architecture, national in its scope and distinctiveness and centuries in the making, had reached a point of crisis: such is the thesis to be argued in this chapter as we consider successively domestic

Figure 15 Church of the Transfiguration of the Savior, island of Kizhi, Lake Onega, ca. 1714.

and ecclesiastical construction, fortification and town planning, the activities of the tsar's building department, Old-Russian building techniques, and one or two final case histories. In thus proceeding, however, it is hoped to avoid bias, whether of a classicist, nationalist, or any other kind. Hence Brunov's term "primitive" with respect to Old-Russian architecture is supplanted hereafter, depending on context, by the more neutral designations of "medieval," "conservative," or "traditional." Nor will the concepts of complete originality or of complete independence in architectural development, or of "organic" continuity, gain admittance in the pages that follow. Rather, Old-Russian architecture especially in its middle and late phases (fifteenth to seventeenth centuries) will be seen as a largely autarkic phenomenon: one whose originality lay in its singular blend of external and indigenous elements, whose independence was an aspect of its isolation from the main currents of world (particularly European) architecture, and whose development was no more "organic" than its buildings were alive.

Churches and Houses

There is little to add to what was said just above or in Chapter 2 about Old-Russian domestic building in wood. Contemporary representations both graphic and verbal of Russian urban scenes, later photographs as well as scholarly reconstructions of older Russian settlements, and archaeological evidence such as that unearthed at Novgorod all indicate that by the end of the seventeenth century Russian towns—Moscow included—were still made up predominantly of simple wooden houses (singular, *dvor*). These were one- to three-story structures, loosely rectangular in plan, with a total floor space of between 126 and 238 square meters, including sheds and various other attachments. Larger houses or mansions *(khoromy)*, averaging several thousand square meters of floor space, differed from this basic model mainly by reason of their larger number of rooms. Indeed, each room of that vast maze of rooms which comprised the royal palace at Kolomenskoe (1667–1681), the largest and most spectacular example of Old-Russian domestic architecture in wood that is known to us in any detail (before being pulled down in 1767 a miniature wooden replica was made), reflects the design of the traditional rural *izba* (figs. 16A–B). At work here was the ancient additive method in the organization of space, a method whereby the area needed for living or working or storage was expanded or diversified simply by the addition of new spatial cells to the original cellular nucleus. Similarly, the techniques by which such wooden houses or mansions or palaces were built or expanded remained simple and few, as did the tools employed. Surviving building contracts, in which *rubleniki* are instructed to build "in accordance with [*protiv*]" an existing structure or "as is done [*kak voditsia*]," clearly suggest that the conservative taste of clients was an additional factor inhibiting the development of Old-Russian domestic architecture in wood (a factor noted by contemporary European visitors, too). Apart from the as yet infrequent use of glass in building, also mentioned above, no signs of progress are visible here.[10]

A

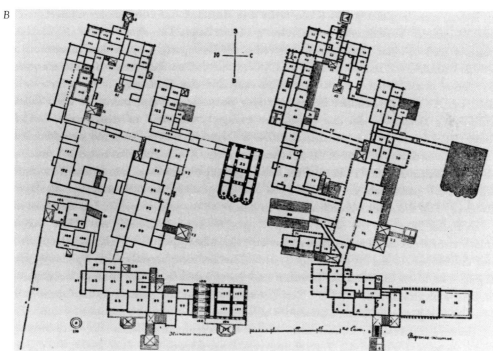

B

Figures 16A–B Palace at Kolomenskoe, ca. 1667–1681. A, Artist's depiction. B, Plans of first and second stories.

Much the same must be said regarding the state of domestic architecture in brick and/or stone in Russia by the end of the seventeenth century.[11] Two basic types of masonry dwelling can be distinguished here: the *palaty* (literally, chambers) of nobles and senior clergy, striving to imitate, as best they could, the palaces of the tsars; and the houses (singular, *dom*) of merchants and wealthier tradesmen, which reveal an effort to escape the customary forms of timber construction and to rid themselves of wooden lean-tos and attics. The most widespread type of bourgeois *dom* was a three-part mainly brick structure consisting either of two rooms separated by a central passageway or of three stories, the first a semibasement used for storage, the second for living, the third an attic (fig. 17). Such a house was based on wooden prototype which in turn was based on the old *izba*. Another type of brick house appeared in Moscow only at the very end of the seventeenth century, to be adopted by people of modest means in response to decrees of Peter I prohibiting wooden construction particularly in the city's central districts (Chap. 5). This was a one-room structure, often with an attached wooden entryway or passage, which has aptly been called a masonry *izba*.

As for the "chambers" of the notables, the humblest appear to have differed little from the better bourgeois house, which exhibited a tendency to become wider and more compact, almost regular in plan, as well as multiroomed (fig. 18, pl. 50). Grander establishments (figs. 19, 20) combined a variety of structures in domestic ensembles whose asymmetrical, picturesque composition and often elaborate decoration readily evoke contemporary royal or official ensembles (figs. 21, 22). Yet here too we can speak only of a tendency in masonry building to lessen its dependence on traditional forms; and here too grander houses differed from their humbler neighbors mainly by having more rooms, with the bigger room or rooms in either case used for dining or receiving guests, the smaller for sleeping.

The chambers of Averkii Kirillov have been offered as an example of the grander type of seventeenth-century Moscow domestic establishment (pls. 53A–B). But in the form in which they survive, the result of extensive rebuilding between 1705 and 1709, they represent rather an accommodation in an older building of principles—here mainly decorative—associated with the Petrine revolution in Russian architecture (Kirillov, who was a *dumnyi d'iak*, one of the four highest ranks of the Muscovite nobility, actually died in 1682, when his house passed to persons unknown).[12] Similarly, the chambers or palaces built in and around Moscow between the 1680s and the first years of the eighteenth century for various intimates of Peter I and his family (for his aunt Tsarevna Maria Alekseevna, for instance, or for his favorite, F. A. Golovin) signal the beginnings of a marked transition from the free, asymmetrical, fully traditional composition of seventeenth-century grandee building to the regularized architecture of the Petrine period (pl. 51, fig. 23; cf. pls. 50 and 56, figs. 20 and 94, etc.).

Figure 17 Reconstruction of the Belov house, Gorokhovets, later seventeenth century.

Figure 18 Reconstruction of the Rabotnikov house, Iaroslavl', end of seventeenth century.

Figure 19 Reconstruction of the Bishop's Chambers *(Palaty)*, Suzdal', 1682–1707.

Figure 20 Mansion of the Boyar Romanov family, Kitai-gorod, Moscow, sixteenth and seventeenth centuries, restored 1858–1859.

Figure 21   Terem palace, Moscow Kremlin, 1630s, rebuilt in the nineteenth century.

Figure 22   Ambassadorial palace complex, Kitai-gorod, Moscow; view from the inner courtyard, ca. 1660; engraving in *Al'bom Maierberga*.

Figure 23   Palace of F. A. Golovin, suburban Moscow, ca. 1700; engraving by Henryk de Witte and (?) G. M. Fontana, before 1706. Located across the Iauza river from the German Settlement, the palace and its grounds were frequently the site of elaborate festivities staged by the youthful Peter I and his friends.

In fact, apart from the growing number of houses being built—particularly in Moscow—and the use of more elaborate decoration, we find little that was essentially new in masonry domestic architecture in Russia at the end of the seventeenth century: little that is not more properly connected with the history of the Petrine revolution. Conservatism in design went hand in hand with simplicity of technique. Builders eschewed the use of any sort of architectural drawing, for example, and continued instead to "draw" the plan of a house on the ground by means of sticks and cord.[13] Rooms and external structures—entryways, passages, staircases, attics, sheds—continued to be added to the central building, were usually made of wood, and were usually attached without regard to overall symmetry of design: indeed, without regard to any overall design. The results generally speaking were the crudely constructed, thick-walled, small-windowed, crazily encumbered houses described by contemporary European visitors and pictured from various sources both here and in the previous chapter.

A good deal more is known about ecclesiastical architecture in seventeenth-century Russia, since here stone and especially brick were much more widely used and many more monuments survive (the deliberate destruction referred to above, in Chapter 1, notwithstanding). We even have some numbers. Rough estimates based on official and other sources put the total number of churches standing on Russian territory in about 1700 at approximately 15,860. The bulk of these, or as many as 10,000 churches, had been completed, rebuilt, or built anew since the 1620s; and the bulk of those that remained dated most probably to the sixteenth century, when more masonry structures—mainly churches— were constructed on Russian territory than in all of the preceding centuries of Old-Russian architectural history combined.[14]

With respect to Moscow itself, the contemporary estimates quoted in Chapter 2 range from the "nearly 2,000 churches, almost all of stone" reported by a Danish visitor in 1671, to the 1,740 churches—"according to some"—reported by Rev. David in the late 1680s, to the 1,200 masonry churches mentioned by Neuville in 1689, to the 200 "goodly churches" mentioned by Korb in 1698; Perry, writing after 1698, confined himself to "numerous churches." The larger numbers must be greeted with the skepticism implied by David. Cornelis de Bruyn, far more concerned than the others to describe the Russian built environment in detail, both verbally and graphically, offered a total as of June 1702 of 679 "churches and monasteries, including chapels," in Moscow and its environs. Recent scholarly estimates indicate that some 288 masonry churches were built in and around the city in the seventeenth century.[15]

But we must restrain our delight in numbers lest we lose sight of the main point. A boom in masonry church construction in the sixteenth century resumed by all indications with ever greater force in the seventeenth, following the disturbances and destruction of the so-called Time of Troubles (1598– 1613). And a relative abundance of monuments of both centuries survives to help us in assessing the state not only of ecclesiastical architecture in Russia on the eve of the Petrine revolution, but of Old-Russian architecture more generally.

In Chapter 1, the sixteenth century together with the fifteenth were classed as the middle or Muscovite phase in Old-Russian architectural history, a phase in which church building revived in central Russia (northeastern *Rus'*) in connection with the rise of the rulers of Moscow. In fact, several new types of church were produced in these centuries which, with their variants, may be said to exemplify a distinctive Muscovite style.[16]

The church of the Savior in the Andronikov monastery (1420s) represents the first of these types to emerge: its cross-in-square plan with a single dome, four piers, and three apses reflects prototypes to be found in twelfth- and thirteenth-century Vladimir and Suzdal; its stepped vaulting and roof derive from the traditions of Chernigov and Smolensk (and of Novgorod and Pskov); while its high socle and crown of ascending tiers of ogee arches were the product of more recent and quite local developments (pl. 1). Recessed doorways of ogee archivolts, ultimately Romanesque in inspiration, are another prominent feature of churches of this first type, all of which were once surrounded by elevated open galleries on all but their east sides. The premier example of a second type of Muscovite church is the pentacupolar Dormition cathedral; rectangular in plan, with six piers and five apses, it was erected in the Kremlin between 1475 and 1479 and originally stood on a socle more than three meters high (pl. 2). A third type to appear in Moscow by the end of the fifteenth century was the small "pier-less" church with a single apse and dome notable also for its combined domical and groin vaulting. And the fourth and decidedly monumental if not triumphal type of church to arise in this period is well illustrated by the church of the Ascension at Kolomenskoe (1530–1532). Some sixty-six meters high, taller than any earlier building in Russia, its massive central cube set atop a high socle and crowned by a thickset octagon followed by an elongated pyramidal roof, its every detail both inside and out serves to emphasize its upward thrust (pl. 5). An equally striking example of this fourth type is the church of the Intercession on the Moat (or of Basil the Blessed, as it is popularly called) in Red Square (1555–1560/1588). With its central "tower church" surrounded by nine subsidiary chapels and its complex, fanciful decoration (some of it added in the seventeenth century, as were the external galleries and various other attachments), the church of Basil the Blessed is the most famous in Russia (pl. 6).

But here it is less important to classify and describe the churches of the Muscovite period than it is to emphasize the dynamic and expansive development of Old-Russian architecture that these churches represent. Indeed, the effort to classify is in some degree futile, since variants and combinations of established types seem to have proliferated in the sixteenth century in unprecedented profusion. The tower church of the Crucifixion at Aleksandrov (1570s) immediately comes to mind (pl. 7) as does the older church of the Mother of God in Moscow's Monastery of the Don (1591–1593), a variant of the pier-less church whose tiers of purely decorative semicircular arches form a kind of pedestal for its single, elongated cupola (pl. 8). It should also be stressed that builders in and around Moscow in this period drew on traditions that had been established elsewhere in Russia (the lands of *Rus'*) as well as on local ways; that churches built in and around Moscow became models for churches built everywhere else in the expanding Muscovite realm, the last of the independent schools of Old-Russian architecture, that of Novgorod, now falling victim to the process; and that this dynamic and expansive development of architecture, with two discernable yet only partial exceptions, remained a largely autarkic phenomenon.

The exceptions are the two churches erected in the Kremlin under the direction of Italian masters. The first of these is the Dormition cathedral, which has suffered relatively few major alterations since it was built (1475–1479; pl. 2). Ivan III had originally commissioned some local masters to demolish the tumbledown limestone church dating back to 1326 that stood on the site and to replace it with a building modeled on the twelfth-century Dormition cathedral in Vladimir, the most imposing church—and the only pentacupolar one—in his dominions. But in 1474 the new building, somewhat larger than its model, collapsed. Builders summoned from Pskov judged that the mortar had been mixed improperly. This assessment was accepted by Aristotele Fieravanti (or Fioravanti), who with his son and an assistant had arrived in Moscow in March 1475, having been hired in Italy by Ivan's ambassador to undertake the work of rebuilding that the Pskov masters refused to do. Fieravanti decided to make a fresh start, although he was constrained by Ivan and the head of the church to follow the Vladimir model—a church in which, quoting a contemporary Russian chronicle, Fieravanti was said to have decried "something of our own masters."[17] He referred no doubt to the influence of the builders from Lombardy who are thought to have worked in Vladimir in the twelfth century.

It is clear that in building the new Dormition cathedral for Ivan III Fieravanti made two lasting contributions to Old-Russian architecture. The first was the structure itself, which, with its exceptionally light and spacious interior and its many new and original features, was thereafter widely imitated (the Dormition cathedrals of Rostov-the-Great and of the Trinity-St. Sergius monastery at Zagorsk [pl. 46], for example, or the cathedrals of St. Sophia in Vologda and of Sts. Boris and Gleb in Novgorod, etc.). The second was technical in nature. Fieravanti built his own brickworks so as to produce better—harder—bricks; prescribed a high quality mortar, to be handled with trowels; filled up inner wall spaces with brick and cement instead of loose gravel and sand; reinforced walls and vaults with iron rather than wooden girders and ties; and greatly impressed his local assistants, contemporary sources suggest, by his use of level, compass, and drawings.[18]

The application by Russian builders of some of these new techniques was crucial to the boom in masonry construction of the sixteenth century. Voronin notes that this certainly was so with respect to brickmaking, for instance, and urges that the same could be said for the working of limestone and the mining of lime, where Fieravanti's methods of cutting stone and making mortar provided new possibilities for more sturdy construction.[19] All the same, Fieravanti's Dormition cathedral does not mark the sharp break in Russian architectural history that some scholars have claimed for it, since it so obviously accommodated itself to local tastes and traditions while remaining unique in points of both structure and ornament. It proved beyond the competence of Old-Russian builders to reproduce Fieravanti's cathedral in anything like its entirety.

Similarly, the cathedral of the Archangel Michael built in the Kremlin under Aloisio Novi (or Alevisio Novy) between 1505 and 1509 is distinguished for its incorporation of Renaissance motives in a building that still strongly reflects local traditions.[20] The cathedral's appearance today, unlike that of the Dormition cathedral (on whose plan and structure it may have drawn), is the outcome of numerous later alterations. Yet we can be certain that in contrast to the Dormition cathedral, whose Renaissance influence is to be seen primarily in its symmetry of composition, its geometrical regularities of structure, and its column-like internal supports (originally crowned with capitals), the Renaissance features of the Archangel cathedral were confined to the decoration of its external facades, particularly the north and the west, which look on Cathedral Square (pl. 3). Here the horizontal division into two zones by a broad entablature running around the building about halfway up its walls is cut vertically by a double row of pilasters whose capitals consist of volutes, acanthus leaves, and flowers. The upper row of pilasters supports a second, more strongly defined entablature, which in turn gives way to a series of semicircular shell gables terminating the vertical sections of the walls (each gable topped originally by an ornamental pyramid). The doorways in the west and north walls are decorated with carved arabesques; the latter also with flowers, fabulous beasts, candlesticks, and urns. Blind arches and smaller pilasters ornament the lower walls and arched rectangular niches in molded surrounds, the upper. The scheme is entirely in the style of the northern Italian Renaissance; and various of its details—the circular windows in the central gable of the west front, the scallops in the other gables, its pilasters and entablatures—were widely imitated by Russian builders and craftsmen in the sixteenth and seventeenth centuries. But it must be emphasized that the Archangel cathedral in Moscow remained the only Old-Russian building in which Renaissance ornamental forms were applied consistently, indeed correctly.

In fact, if the development of ecclesiastical architecture in the sixteenth century was a largely autarkic phenomenon, so it remained in the seventeenth, which in Chapter 1 was classed as marking the final or national phase in Old-Russian architectural history.[21] Now, a tendency to multiply subsidiary structures and to complicate the decorative program, already pronounced in churches of the later Muscovite period, becomes predominant. Here we find, increasingly as we move forward in time, churches of an unprecedented variety, complexity, ornateness, and, in some instances, size. In the seventeenth century, even the structurally simple churches of an earlier age became asymmetrical in composition or "picturesque" (a favorite adjective of commentators), the result of adding chapels with apse and cupola, vestibules or a narthex, a bell tower topped by a pyramidal roof. Such was the fate of the church of the Mother of God in Moscow's Monastery of the Don (fig. 24, pl. 8). In the seventeenth century, decorative details became smaller but were applied in far greater quantity; doors and especially windows—larger and more numerous than ever before—acquired richly worked casings; while exterior surfaces assumed an intensely polychromatic as well as varied appearance, the result of a widening use of ceramic tiles, faience paneling, and brick patterns (pl. 6). Interior wall paintings, shrinking individually in size as they grew richer in detail, and multiplying in horizontal rows, took on the appearance of carpets completely and evenly covering the walls. Roofs of decorative arches were surmounted by five or more cupolas, the drum of only the central cupola admitting any light. A good example in all respects of the tendencies under review is the church of the Trinity built for the merchant Nikitnikov in the heart of commercial Moscow, which was begun in 1634 and completed about twenty years later (fig. 25, pls. 9A–B). But even the churches built in a revival of Fieravanti's Dormition cathedral, with their properly windowed drums and relatively open, spacious

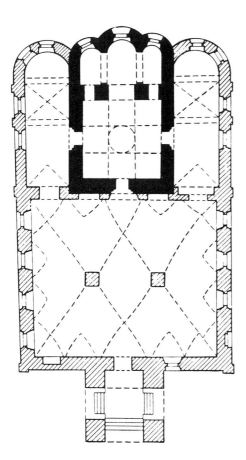

Figure 24 Church of the Mother of God, Monastery of the Don, Moscow, 1591–1593; plan, showing the original church in bold with seventeenth-century additions.

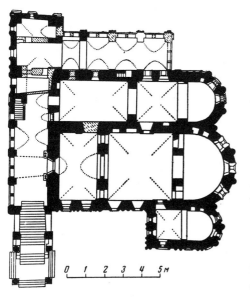

Figure 25 Church of the Trinity in Nikitniki, Moscow, 1634–ca. 1653; plan.

0 1 2 3 4 5 M

interiors, took on narthex, galleries, and bell tower in addition to new or enlarged decorations.

Ecclesiastical architecture of the seventeenth century, in short, differs from
that of the preceding period in its more frequent or more inventive combination of established styles, its multiplication of enveloping attachments, and its
greater profusion of decorative detail (fig. 26, pls. 10–12). It may be that the
close interrelation of developments in wooden and masonry architecture, mentioned above, was one factor at work here. Another, certainly, was the migration and interaction of regional styles increasingly evident in the buildings of
these years, a process that promoted architectural agglomeration and/or diver-
sity not only in Moscow itself and its environs but in the regional centers
increasingly tied to Moscow. At any event, these tendencies led in numerous
individual churches not just to an agglomerative complexity and asymmetry of
composition, but to that overloading of ornament and fragmentation or degeneration of form which even sympathetic students of this architecture—Nekrasov
was not one—have criticized. Nekrasov went so far as to suggest that seventeenth-
century churches are the "most primitive in all of Old-Russian architecture."[22]

Thus for all of its obvious vigor, numerically speaking, its stylistic variety and
exuberance, masonry church construction in Russia had entered a critical
phase. Ilin refers to the "unfinished quality of the decoration" that is characteristic of buildings of the seventeenth century.[23] Elsewhere he points out that
in this century more than in the preceding period "qualitative differences of
architectural production" are to be noticed, a phenomenon he attributes to the
"attraction to building of inadequately experienced architects lacking extensive
previous training." Ilin also emphasizes the "conservative attitude of the client"
as a factor inhibiting development in ecclesiastical as well as domestic architecture.[24] I might only add that this conservatism and greater incidence of technical deficiency are common rather than occasional features of Old-Russian
church architecture in what proved to be its final phase; and that, like the
overloading of ornament and degeneration of form just noted, they are indicative of architectural stagnation if not decline. In fact, the only categorical exception to this general rule are the late seventeenth-century churches typed
"Moscow Baroque," whose special historiographical as well as historical qualities will be discussed in Chapter 4.

FORTIFICATION AND TOWN PLANNING

The sixteenth and seventeenth centuries in Russian history were also a period
of extensive military construction. Once again, however, our knowledge of
structures built of wood is extremely limited. As one authority observes, echo-
ing earlier scholars, not a single major example of Old-Russian fortification in
wood has survived, leaving us with some "insignificant" physical remains and a
few "often very problematic and sometimes quite inaccurate" written sources

Figure 26 Church of St. John the Baptist, Tolchkovo (Iaroslavl'), 1671–1687.

from which to attempt reconstructions.[25] On the other hand, our knowledge of sixteenth- and seventeenth-century masonry fortification has been steadily improving, a development that is owed in part to archaeology, in part to intensive archival work, and in part to careful study of the enduring remains, which are sometimes quite extensive. Even the great earthen and wooden defensive lines erected south of Moscow to ward off Tatar raiders, and which long ago had disappeared from surface view, are becoming better known.

The oldest such line (*zaseka*) goes back to the fifteenth century and linked such urban centers as Kaluga, Serpukhov, Kolomna, and Pereiaslavl-Riasanskii. These defenses were strengthened and extended in the sixteenth century, when governmental offices specifically charged with constructing and maintaining fortifications—the *Zasechnyi* and *Gorodovoi prikazy*—first appeared in Moscow (1570s). By the end of the century, moving steadily south as well as outward east and west, marking the expansion of the Muscovite state, more barriers or lines had been built and the whole costly system had become known as the *cherta*. In the 1630s, when it was extensively renovated, the *cherta* included more than forty fortresses, each with a garrison of between ninety-seven and 1,450 men armed with up to thirty-seven pieces of artillery. Then, between 1645 and 1653, a vast new system of defenses was erected still further south, from deep in Ukrainian territory in the west through Belgorod and on to Tambov in the east—the so-called Belgorod *cherta*—and thence to the Middle Volga (the Simbirsk *cherta*).[26]

The Belgorod system has been closely studied on the basis of archival material from the directing government office in Moscow (the *Riazriadnyi prikaz*, particularly its Belgorod section or *stol*).[27] It was some 800 kilometers long, more than 100 kilometers of which were earthen ramparts thrown across the customary routes of Tatar incursion. The ramparts south of Kozlov, at the eastern end of the system, were forty kilometers in length and two-and-a-half meters high, with four strong points (*gorodki*) and several dozen towers, some made of wood, the others of earth (fig. 27). These ramparts were put up in six months (1636) by 950 men working under a Dutch engineer (Jan Cornelis van Rodenburg) at a cost to the treasury of about 8,000 rubles; a French engineer, David Nichol, directed 3,744 men in the construction of another crucial section in 1647 and the rebuilding of Belgorod itself in 1650. The rest of the system consisted of deliberately preserved forest zones, hundreds of ditches, and vertical or slanting wooden palisades formed of stakes up to seven meters long driven into the ground. Twenty-five fortified towns in addition to Belgorod were located at various points along the line—fortified, again, almost entirely in wood.

Yet if the Belgorod *cherta* fulfilled its original purposes of encouraging settlement and thwarting Tatar invaders, and was an impressive engineering, even logistical achievement, clearly it cannot be considered one of the great walls of architectural history. Conceived and for the most part executed along wholly traditional lines, it would soon be made obsolete by further Russian expansion south and by the state's new defensive requirements.

Figure 27 *Ostrog* from Il'inskii, near Perm', 1668; restored and now located at the open-air Museum of Old-Russian Architecture near Irkutsk.

In the west, by contrast, where Russians were opposed at one time or another by the relatively well-armed forces of the Livonian (German) Knights of the Sword, Poland-Lithuania, and the Swedish monarchy, strong masonry fortifications had long been a necessity. Kostochkin is the leading authority here.[28] His period is delimited, at one end, by the "decisive step forward" in Old-Russian military architecture that took place at the turn of the fifteenth century (meaning construction of the rectangular fortress of Ivangorod at Narva, on what was then the Livonian border) and, at the other, by developments that took place at the beginning of the eighteenth century, when defense works arose which had "almost nothing in common with Old-Russian forts and castles."[29] Indeed they had not, as we shall see (Chap. 5). Kostochkin's studies are notable for their imaginative use of both graphic and written sources in reconstructing fortifications most of which have completely disappeared. But his work is marked at the same time by an approach to the subject which considers developments on Russian territory in isolation from parallel and even earlier developments in Europe, an approach which is especially misleading when discussing the rise of new fortifications on Russia's western frontiers.

Thus Kostochkin insists, for example, that the appearance on Russian territory of the "rectilinear, quadrangular or, as we say, regular [*reguliarnaia*] fortress was an independent [wholly indigenous] phenomenon in Old-Russian military construction" (fig. 28).[30] But this is highly unlikely. Indeed, it is probable that the castle itself of Ivangorod (begun in 1492), a structure much discussed if not vaunted by Kostochkin, was built under Italian supervision. Similarly, Kostochkin almost completely ignores the rebuilding of the Moscow Kremlin undertaken by Italian masters, on commission from Ivan III, beginning in 1485. Other specialists, on the contrary, have urged that the Kremlin's Italianate fortifications—with their distinctive swallowtail or "ghibelline" merlons and wide semicircular arches supporting thicker walls (permitting lower embrasures) (pl. 42)—set a pattern that would frequently be followed in Old-Russian fortress construction (figs. 29, 30).[31]

The basic point is indisputable. Russian military architecture of the seventeenth century, as compared with that of contemporary Europe, was essentially "medieval" in character or, at its best, "transitional" as between "medieval" and "modern."[32] We might recall here the critical remarks of various seventeenth-century European observers of Muscovite fortification quoted in Chapter 2. The relative ease with which Ivangorod fell to Swedish forces in 1581 also tends to prove the point, as does the fall of the immense new Russian fortress of Smolensk (1586–1602) to Polish attackers in 1611. Seventeenth-century Russian fortifications reveal a preference for decoration as well as for archaic forms. Nekrasov points to the "picturesque decorativeness" of the Kremlin's new towers and roofs (1670s; pl. 42) or of the gates and towers of the royal residence at Kolomenskoe (1672–1673; pl. 44); to the "exclusively decorative," even "fantastical" character of the Rostov kremlin (1670–1683), which expresses principles "quite contrary to the idea of strength required in a fortress" (fig. 31); and to monastic fortifications put up in the provinces well into the eighteenth century which were "completely in the style of sixteenth-century Russian building."[33] Historians agree, even Kostochkin would concede, that at the end of the seventeenth century masonry defenses were being built or rebuilt in Russia using methods adopted in the later fifteenth and the sixteenth centuries, and mainly for the purposes of prestige and internal security (pls. 43–46). On a comparative European basis, it bears repeating, "Muscovite military architecture was imposing rather than advanced."[34]

The contrast between "medieval" Muscovite fortifications and their "modern" European counterparts could not be more clearly seen than in the graphic material showing the towering Russian castle of Ivangorod (destroyed in World War II) as it faced, directly across the river Narova, the strikingly horizontal defenses of Narva, with their projecting triangular bastions.[35] The latter were

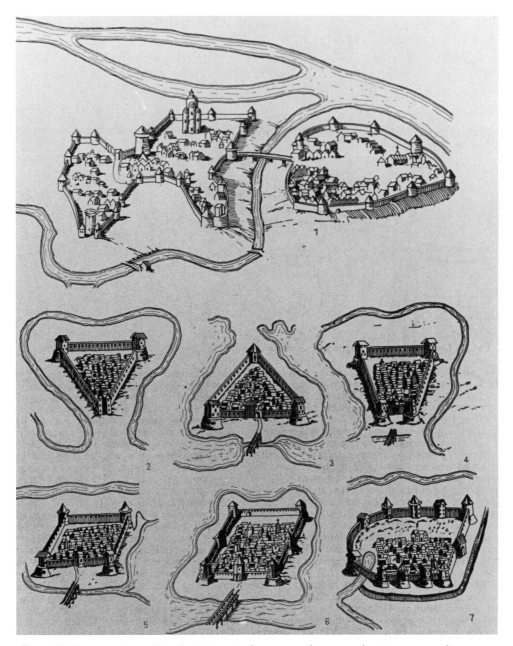

Figure 28 Reconstructions of "regular" Muscovite fortresses on the western frontier, seventeenth century.

built by the Swedes in the seventeenth century, and in 1700 utterly defeated the siege of a large Russian army under Peter I. In fact, such modern defenses as were erected in pre-Petrine Russia—parts of the Belgorod *cherta* in the 1630s and 1640s, elements of a new masonry fortress at Archangel (1670s–1680s), the bastioned earthern ramparts around Moscow (1618, 1639) and Novgorod (1632)—were invariably built under the direction of specially hired European experts. It was a job that only they, as of then, could do.

Figure 29 Remains of the fortress of Smolensk, 1586–1602.

Figure 30   Monastery of the Don, Moscow; fragment of the eastern wall with tower, 1686–1711.

Figure 31 Main or "Holy" gates, kremlin of the town of Rostov-the-Great (Rostov Velikii), 1670–1683, with church of the Resurrection (1670).

The function and design of fortifications are of course closely bound up, historically, with concepts of town planning. In the Russian case, indeed, it could be argued that military considerations played an exceptionally important part in determining the pattern of urban growth. This fact is reflected in the now standard Russian words for "city" (*gorod*), which originally meant a fortified enclosure or settlement, or simply a fort or fortress, and for "town planning" (*gradostroitel'stvo*), an obviously related word that originally meant "fortification-building." The point is repeatedly stressed in the growing literature on Old-Russian town planning.

Virtually all of the cities and towns of seventeenth-century Russia had begun life as princely fortresses, acquiring in time a marketplace outside the walls and then a permanent commercial-residential district (*posad*) that in turn was enclosed by walls: the pattern is clear in the plan of Moscow, as we saw in Chapter 2 (fig. 8). The whole complex eventually incorporated various suburban settlements, namely, the tax-exempt *slobody* or "liberties" (singular *sloboda*) and the military and other *sotni* or "hundreds" (singular *sotnia*), many of whose inhabitants gradually became part of the tax-paying urban population or *posadskie liudi*. But as late as 1652 some 30 to 40 percent of Russian towns were primarily or even exclusively military settlements located, for the most part, along the eastern and southern frontiers. In the sixteenth and seventeenth centuries, by another calculation, as many as 50 percent of the total urban population of Russia were military or governmental personnel.[36]

It has been suggested that in these same centuries (if not still earlier) towns were built or rebuilt in Russia following certain definite principles. Such "planning," it seems, consisted of giving some thought to the distribution of towns in relation to one another, to the choice of specific sites for new towns, and to the location within them of fortified centers, which in turn determined the disposition of the main streets; in the case of certain new settlements in Siberia, apparently, it was also a matter of building in conformity with a preconceived plan reflecting geometric motives.[37] But such "town planning," overwhelmingly strategic in character when not simply natural or inevitable, was a far cry from the principles to be introduced under Peter I. Indeed one scholar, Chiniakov, would go further. Stressing the peculiar prominence of the Old-Russian town's fortified center—*detinets, gorod,* or *kreml'*—by comparison with the contemporary cities of either Europe or Asia, Chiniakov makes clear the "medieval" nature of town planning in Russia until well into the seventeenth century.[38] His points accord closely with the findings of another investigator: namely, that with respect to population aggregates and to the level of its administrative and commercial development, Russia's "urban network" in the later seventeenth century resembled China's in the late fourteenth and those of Japan, England, and France in the late fifteenth or early sixteenth centuries.[39] In other words, seventeenth-century Russian "urban communities in many respects were little more than overgrown villages: the continuum between town and countryside was not only social and legal, but economic as well."[40]

It is not surprising, therefore, that outside of Moscow seventeenth-century European visitors found little that was remarkable in Russian towns. It was a matter of their relatively small size, physical homogeneity, and lagging architectural as well as social, political, and economic development.

BUILDING AND BRICKMAKING

The chief agency of such technical innovation as took place in Russian building in the sixteenth and seventeenth centuries, most notably in fortification, appears to have been the tsar's Department of Masonry Affairs (*Prikaz kamennykh del*). The department's archives were almost completely destroyed in the Moscow fire of 1737, but its operations have been reconstructed to some extent from the archives of the other offices with which it had dealings.[41]

Already in the later sixteenth century the department was attracting the best builders in Russia to the tsar's service, where they assumed in due course the rank and pay of royal masters or assistant masters (*gosudarevia mastera* or *podmastera*) in their trades of stonemason or bricklayer (*kamenshchik*), brickmaker, or—the more skilled—kilner (*kirpichnik* or *obzhigal'shchik*). Most masters before that time had remained in the employ of their ecclesiastical or local secular lords. By the later seventeenth century large numbers of builders were more or less permanently employed by the department, as were hundreds and even thousands of contract laborers, in an ever growing volume of major construction projects. The department was also setting building standards. For instance, the direct use of design sketches in building seems to have been introduced by the department in the 1630s, in response to the exigencies of renovating and extending the fortified lines to the south; there the need of an overall plan as well as plain drawings, to give the local workers a better idea of what the foreign experts had in mind, was pressing. At about the same time, and under a similar impetus, the use of the scale model was introduced. Dutch engineers in the department's pay, having been commissioned to design new ramparts for Moscow and Rostov, constructed either a full-size sample or section of the works in mind or a portable model in wood or clay. In either case, the model was intended both to show to the authorities for their approval and to provide the builders with a practical guide.

Yet the use of such scale models seems to have been confined in the seventeenth century, even among royal projects, to the fortifications that were built under foreign supervision. Meanwhile the architectural sketches that were drawn in the Department of Masonry Affairs reveal the severe limitations, as yet, of the native assistants. As Voronin points out, the draftsmen, engravers, and icon painters who were put to the task, diverted temporarily from their usual work of decorating tableware and arms for the tsar and his court, painting portraits and holy pictures, or sketching maps and illustrating storybooks, produced architectural drawings, even when ruler and perhaps compass had been used, that were flat, one-dimensional, crudely representational, "iconographic," and altogether lacking in scale (fig. 32). Such drawings were capable of serving

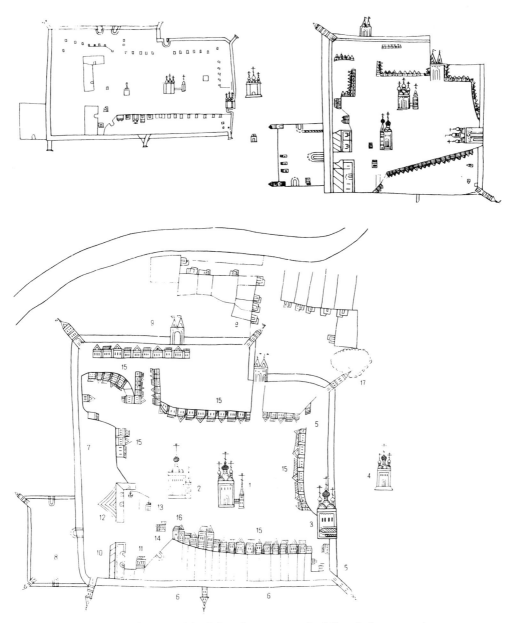

Figure 32 Russian drawings of the Pokrovskii monastery, Suzdal', end of seventeenth century.

only as a rough guide to the natural terrain of a projected site or to the relative disposition of the individual parts of a building or ensemble of buildings. Moreover, the drawings themselves soon became stylized: abstract, static, simple signs. In the words of another specialist, such efforts were "far removed from the architectural drawings which appeared in Russia at the beginning of the eighteenth century," and resembled rather the builders' sketches of medieval Europe.[42]

The Department of Masonry Affairs also acted to standardize building materials. The seventeenth century witnessed an enormous expansion in the production of bricks in Russia, and brickworks, no longer confined to the main towns, sprang up on private and especially monastic estates as well as on state lands. In Moscow itself the department maintained several permanent works; elsewhere, while a project was under construction, it operated temporary facilities. The dimensions of the "great royal brick," approximately twenty-five by twelve by six centimeters, came to be widely accepted. But the quality of the bricks produced and the techniques of production had not kept pace with European norms; in fact, they had not changed since the days of Fieravanti, at the end of the fifteenth century. To remedy this situation, and with military needs again uppermost in mind, two Dutch masters were hired in 1630 to make bricks in one of the tsar's Moscow works "in conformity with their German model," as their contract stated. Their methods of more rapid production of harder bricks of more uniform size were fairly soon adopted by local manufacturers, for example by the "stoveman" (pechnik) Aleksei Kondratev, who in 1647 at the tsar's Danilovskie works (also in Moscow) produced 34,000 bricks "on the German model."

We may wonder how quickly or widely these latest techniques were spread, however, and the new standards established. As the century wore on, the Department of Masonry Affairs increasingly bought bricks from outside manufacturers—one result, evidently, of the growing demand for bricks from all sides, the government's included. Another consequence of this growing demand, it seems, was an increasing shortage of skilled brickmakers; while the difficulties of transport meant that brickworks were dispersed all over the country, in close proximity to building sites, where they were only seasonally operated and often very small. In short, for various reasons the production of building materials in Russia—of lime and limestone, too, but especially of bricks—would continue until late in the eighteenth century to employ the techniques developed and to exploit the quarries first mined in the sixteenth and seventeenth centuries. The architectural revolution of Peter I did not intrude here: not in the short run.[43]

The Department of Masonry Affairs was liquidated in or about 1700, when its remaining functions and personnel were transferred to other offices, including those charged with the construction of St. Petersburg. Both as an employer of builders and as a supplier of building materials, the department had played an exceedingly important part in the development of Old-Russian architecture, especially between the 1580s and 1670s. In particular, thanks to the virtually permanent employment the department provided, craftsmen could develop their skills and become "professional" masons or masters. Yet, as Voronin points out, given the fact that the department did not have exclusive control of building even in Moscow, such opportunities were not limited to workers living in the capital or engaged on the tsar's projects. Rather, throughout the seventeenth century skilled craftsmen might emerge in Russia wherever extensive building took place. And for both governmental and private projects master builders continued to be drawn from certain regional centers—Kostroma, notably, or Beloozero—as well as from Moscow.[44]

This last point is worth stressing, since it touches on several others of interest here. The typical construction team in seventeenth-century Russia was made up mostly of peasants working under the direction of one or two master masons who had been certified as such, at one time or another, by the Department of Masonry Affairs. This was the case at the Kirillov monastery in the far north (Kirillo-Belozerskii monastery) in the late 1650s and 1660s, for instance, where as many as 2,000 workers labored in a single season on an extension of the monastery's fortifications. Of a team of twenty-three builders working at the royal estate of Izmailovo in 1667, sixteen were peasants (twelve, monastic peasants) from the Kostroma district and four were Moscow residents; the team was directed by a royal master assisted by two apprentices, his nephews. The team engaged in building the Main Pharmacy in Moscow in 1674 included thirty-nine peasants from the Iaroslavl and Kostroma districts (thirty-seven from private estates) and six townsmen (three from Moscow), all of them working under two brothers who had been trained by their father, also a royal master mason.[45] We notice in these and similar data that could be adduced not only the rural origins of most builders in Muscovite Russia but also the hereditary nature of their trade, the on-site apprenticeship that was their training, and what all of this suggests about their building techniques and about their attitudes toward their work.

Indeed, basic building techniques appear scarcely to have changed in Russia since medieval times, when an existing structure or, less often, a rough wooden model served as the illiterate builder's guide.[46] From such structures or models he took his measurements and hence the term *sorazmernost'*—"proportionality" in the sense of corresponding measurements or dimensions—as distinct from the more abstract, theoretical, and now standard *proportional'nost'*, a term of obvious Latin origin introduced in the Petrine period. The Old-Russian builder understood proportion not according to the Classical norms of harmony, symmetry, order, and the like which had prevailed in European architecture since the sixteenth century, but in the simpler sense of spatial relations established by custom and practicality. He knew elementary arithmetic and practical geometry and how to use his few tools. He worked with a team all of whose members hailed from the same region if not from the same village and whose leader undertook to build a church or other structure in conformity, as mentioned, with an existing building or approved model. Seventeenth-century building contracts concluded between a master builder and his team, on the one side, and their client, on the other, contain the client's pointed description of what he had in mind, including instructions as to exactly what building or parts or details of existing buildings were to be copied. The breadth of the master builder's ensuing responsibilities—from selecting the exact site, calculating costs, and ordering materials to closely supervising if not directly participating in the actual work of construction—should also be borne in mind, since a preoccupation with design is the hallmark of the modern architect. In addition, such European architectural manuals or pattern books as were acquired in the seventeenth century by the Department of Masonry Affairs or by the tsar's Armory Chamber (which retained numerous artists and artisans for a variety of not always military tasks) were exploited by builders who had access to them only as a source of decorative detail.[47] And land surveying remained an "inexact science" in Russia—hardly a science at all—right to the end of the seventeenth century. Before Peter I and the work of European surveyors and cartographers in Russia, land surveying and hence mapmaking were based not on the universal system of astronomical points but on the local network of rivers and principal trade routes. The result was a very rough picture of the land in question, not an accurate depiction of either the distances involved or the land's topography.[48]

At the technical level, then, as in matters of style or design, Old-Russian architecture continued to be governed by tradition right to the end of the seventeenth century. It remained a craft based on custom, essentially, rather than an art based on science. This was as true in fortification and town planning as it was in domestic or ecclesiastical construction, a point that Kostochkin, writing in 1979, appeared willing to grant.[49] And exceptions to this generalization prove on inspection to be only partial or special exceptions,[50] something that must also be said of the churches of the so-called Moscow Baroque, a point brought out in the following chapter.

Similarly, any improvements in material production registered in the seventeenth century—the manufacture of more and better bricks, the quarrying of more limestone, and the production of more lime, more iron, and more glass—were essentially quantitative rather than qualitative changes, and constituted important prerequisites of the Petrine architectural revolution rather than major technical achievements as such. It should also be noted that the few genuine technical innovations to be observed in late Old-Russian architecture were introduced in the military sphere, in connection with the design and construction under foreign experts of various new defense works. Indeed, almost all of the thirty European builders known to have worked in Russia in the seventeenth century were so engaged—this at a time when the great majority of the approximately 100 native builders who have so far been identified were hired to build churches.[51]

CASE HISTORIES

The late Old-Russian or national phase in Russian architectural history came to an end in the Petrine period, when local builders proved unable to respond satisfactorily to the demands of the ruling elite. By way of illustrating this last point concretely, we might consider two case histories.

The first concerns the grandiose main church of the New Jerusalem monastery at Istra, some sixty kilometers west and north of Moscow, which was begun in 1658 under the patronage of Patriarch Nikon, the head of the Russian ecclesiastical establishment. Once it was thought that this strange church, called the church of the Resurrection, was built to conform with descriptions of the church of the Holy Sepulchre in Jerusalem that had been conveyed orally and perhaps with the aid of a model by one or more Russian pilgrims sent for that purpose to Palestine.[52] Now it is clear that the basic inspiration for the church came rather from a copy of Bernardino Amico's *Treatise on the Plans and Drawings of the Sacred Edifices of the Holy Land*, which was published at Florence in 1620. This was the second, augmented edition of a work first published in 1609; and it incorporated the observations, measurements, and drawings made by Bernardino in Jerusalem and elsewhere in Palestine in the 1590s, all with the object of providing models for builders in Europe who wished to replicate the shrines of the Holy Land. We notice that with respect to his drawings of the church of the Holy Sepulchre, however, Bernardino "frankly confesses" to having introduced various changes in order to "correct" or "beautify" the design of the building, which at base was a twelfth-century church built by Crusaders from Europe incorporating earlier Byzantine structures. And we have only to compare Bernardino's plan of the church of the Holy Sepulchre in Jerusalem with plans of the church of the Resurrection at Istra to see how closely the builders of the latter attempted to follow the outlines of the former (figs. 33A–B).[53]

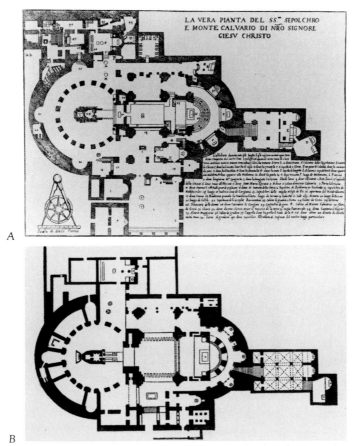

Figures 33A–B   A, Plan of the church of the Holy Sepulchre, Jerusalem, by Bernardino Amico, 1620. B, Plan of the church of the Resurrection, New Jerusalem monastery, Istra, 1658–1666.

The church of the Resurrection of the New Jerusalem monastery was thus one of the earliest nonmilitary structures in Russia—perhaps the earliest—to have been built following architectural drawings or plans. Its construction between 1658 and 1666 was closely supervised by Patriarch Nikon himself, who, dissatisfied with efforts to replicate the Bernardino plan, would order the work pulled down and the project started anew. He behaved similarly in connection with the main church of his new Iverskii monastery at Valdai (nearer to Novgorod than Moscow); and was so possessed by the notion that he ordered yet a third monastic church to be built after the Bernardino model, which in its turn inspired still further imitations.[54]

The builders of the Resurrection church at Istra, like those of Nikon's two other monastic churches mentioned, were stonemasons and bricklayers drawn most likely from Moscow and elsewhere in Russia. But the elaborate carved, brick, and ceramic decoration of these churches was definitely the work of Belorussian craftsmen—immigrants or internees following the recent Muscovite takeover of their homeland—and bore the marks of the European, particularly the Polish, Baroque. After the Resurrection church was ceremoniously dedicated, in 1685, various of its forms and decorative details were widely imitated by Russian builders, as in the multicupolar and many-windowed wooden churches erected by order of Metropolitan (senior bishop) Ioan Sysoevich of Rostov. These churches are thought by Ilin to have influenced in turn such a well-known surviving example of building in wood as the church at Kizhi (fig. 15).[55]

In 1723 the huge masonry pyramidal dome over the great rotunda of the Resurrection church at Istra collapsed, and in 1726 a fire at the monastery further damaged the building. It was rebuilt, now with a conical dome in wood, between 1752 and 1759 according to designs by Rastrelli (the subject of extensive comment in a later chapter) and under the direction of Karl Blank. The net effect of these renovations was to give the building a more regular—a more European—appearance (fig. 34). But we should remember that European influences were at work in its construction right from the start, however circuitous their route, however much they were localized, however bizarre—from a European perspective—their effect. Indeed, the fact of this intense localization—or rusticalization—of European forms also deserves emphasis, as the process was only further intensified in the influence that this church in turn exercised on Old-Russian building norms. The ambitious Patriarch Nikon and the Russians who followed him were reaching out to Europe; but they did so in a manner that was as yet tentative, naive, and, in varying degrees, both contradictory and unconscious (e.g., pl. 14).

The first walls of the New Jerusalem monastery at Istra, erected in 1656, were wooden. In 1690 a team of builders headed by Bukhvostov was commissioned to replace them with masonry structures, some of which survive. Bukhvostov's biographer attempts to account for their traditional and ornamental character by referring to contemporary Russian practices in monastic fortifica-

Figure 34 Church of the Resurrection, New Jerusalem monastery, Istra, 1658–1666, rebuilt 1752–1759. This photograph was taken before World War II, when the church was almost completely destroyed. It is now under restoration.

tion, which by and large had lost its strategic significance (as noted above) and now served only for ostentation and perhaps protection in times of civil disorder.[56] That such was the intention of patrons and builders cannot be proven, however; nor can it be proven that Bukhvostov and his team were capable of anything else. Rather, it might be stressed that the defenses of the New Jerusalem monastery erected in the 1690s were both typical of contemporary Russian military architecture and undeniably "medieval" in character, a term that also applies to the defenses put up at Tobolsk about the same time.

The architectural upgrading of Tobolsk, then the capital of Russian Siberia, offers a second case study of the state of the building art in Russia on the eve of the Petrine revolution. The first masonry structure erected in Tobolsk—the first ever built in Siberia—was the residence of the metropolitan (bishop) dating to 1674. This was in large part destroyed by a fire that devastated the city in 1677. In 1679 the new metropolitan petitioned the tsar for permission to build a masonry cathedral, which was granted by a charter of 1680 directed to the governor of Tobolsk, who was to see to the provision of funds, materials (a supply of iron was to be sent from Moscow), and labor (by local crown peasants, who were specifically not to be recruited in plowing time). The tsar's charter also specified which church in Moscow was to be copied and indicated that appropriate models, sketches, and estimates were being sent. The work began in earnest in April 1683 with the arrival of masons from Moscow and continued with interruptions owing to weather and building accidents until October 1686, when the cathedral was consecrated. It was a standard one-story pentacupolar church with two rows of windows (and, soon to be added, two side chapels). A massive bell tower (1683–1685), a new episcopal residence (1681–1690), and new gates (1685–1688) completed the cathedral complex of Tobolsk, which is considered to mark the real beginnings of masonry construction in Siberia.[57] Yet from what we know of its construction and appearance, the ensemble was decidedly conservative in any larger historical setting (fig. 35).

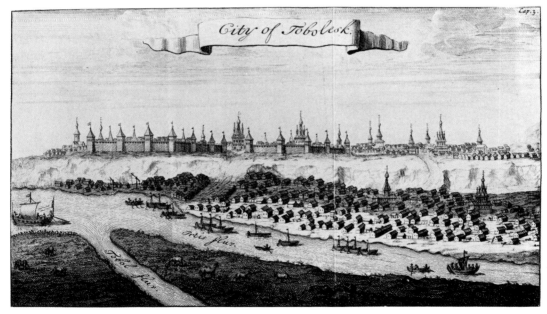

Figure 35 View of Tobol'sk, ca. 1692; contemporary engraving. Note cathedral complex in center—still with wooden walls—flanked by older wooden *gorod* (left) and commercial-residential districts *(posady)*, with their churches, all in wood (right and below).

Much the same can be said of the secular rebuilding that took place at this time in Tobolsk. In June 1697 orders went out from Moscow to replace the town's wooden fortifications with masonry ones for the purposes of both defense and fire prevention. Simion Remezov, a local government official with experience in drafting and cartography, was put in charge of the work.[58] Remezov drew up plans first of the existing town center and then of his projected *gorod*. Both drawings survive; both are crude pictures rather than architectural plans, giving a sort of bird's-eye view of the subject with structures flattened out so as to be seen from above. Moreover, the projected masonry *gorod* was only an extended version of the existing wooden one, with the placement and design as well as the names of existing towers simply transposed from one plan to the other. In the summer of 1698 Remezov visited Moscow, where at the Armory Chamber he was given an Italian architectural manual to study—a *friazhskaia kniga* as it says in the sources, the adjective referring customarily to people or things from the greater Italian (or Latin) world. Remezov himself later wrote about the influence on his work of his visit to Moscow and of the "Italian book," in which, as he said, he had to struggle with unfamiliar measuring systems, a Latin text, and both Arabic and Roman numerals (as opposed to the familiar—and soon obsolete—Slavonic numbering system). In Moscow Remezov also discovered that it was now official policy—Peter I's policy—to "send overseas to the European states for every kind of ingenious science," including the "knowledge of drafting and mapmaking [*karty*] . . . the compass [*kompas*], and other things . . . [such as] how to measure the land and the sea." Remezov went on to describe, with a touch of awe, the use and importance of the compass for builders, surveyors, and mapmakers.[*]

Soon after his return to Tobolsk Remezov again drew a plan of the *gorod*. Although nothing much has moved, by comparison with his earlier efforts this plan is much more finished in form. It is drawn roughly to scale, with plain two-dimensional shapes representing the buildings instead of little pictures; we might suspect Remezov of pride in his new knowledge since in the lower-left corner of his plan, following European usage, he has drawn an open compass over the key to his scale. Equally interesting are his successive design sketches for a new stone church at Tobolsk, which reveal a search for the right combination of structure and decorative detail, the latter evidently taken from buildings he had seen in Moscow and from the illustrations in his "Italian book." Remezov also designed the most important building of the new official ensemble, the *Prikaznaia palata* ("Office Chamber"), whose foundations were laid in May 1700. Here, the basic structure of the recently built Lefort palace in Moscow is loaded down with a profusion of ornament obviously collected from a

---

[*]Evidently the compass was not used in Russia before the late seventeenth century, and then only in mapmaking (see A. A. Tits, "Chertezh v russkoi stroitel'noi praktike XVII veka," in Lazarev et al., *Drevnerusskoe iskusstvo*, p. 217).

variety of later seventeenth-century buildings also to be seen in and around Moscow (fig. 36). It was the best that Remezov could have done—given the norms of prevailing fashion, his self-taught methods, and the conditions in which he worked. His trading center or covered market (gostinnyi dvor) at To-bolsk, which was begun in 1702 under a master mason sent from Moscow, its exact site selected by the central authorities contrary to all local advice, may similarly be judged a typical example of seventeenth-century Muscovite build-ing in which some features of the new Petrine architecture are nonetheless visible.

Remezov's work as a whole at Tobolsk is rightly considered typical of Old-Russian town planning, his greater reliance on drawings and more exact ren-dering thereof notwithstanding.[59] His name has also been cited in connection with his sketches of masonry and wooden plank houses for Tobolsk, which were done in 1700–1701 on orders from Moscow and have been characterized as an "early if admittedly very primitive example of the 'model house' scheme."[60] This is indeed a very primitive instance of the principle of the model house introduced by Peter I with reference to Moscow and first seriously applied in the construction of St. Petersburg; for here, again, longstanding Russian con-ventions prevail. Remezov ended his days in Omsk studying the fortifications erected there by Swedish prisoners-of-war.

Figure 36 Design by S. Remezov for the Pri-kaznaia palata (governmental Office Cham-ber), Tobol'sk, ca. 1700.

The history of the rebuilding of Tobolsk, like that of the building of the New Jerusalem monastery, reveals how firmly custom ruled in Russian architecture at the end of the seventeenth century despite manifest strivings for something that was new. And in this the two cases are typical. A recent study of the masonry construction carried out at Novgorod in the 1690s, following the devastating fire of 1686, shows the extent to which the basic layout of the city center, which dated to the fifteenth century, was preserved; also obvious is the utterly traditional nature of the new governor's compound, with its wooden roofs, towers, and fences (fig. 37). Like Remezov's official ensemble at Tobolsk, the compound in Novgorod was torn down less than a century later in connection with Catherine II's modernization of the Russian urban scene.[61] Or there is the example, equally telling in its way, of the new Dormition cathedral built at Riazan between 1683 and 1692. Its construction was supervised by a master mason and assistants sent from Moscow while its design was a matter of the usual detailed specifications laid down by the local bishop, who was inspired by the Resurrection church of the New Jerusalem monastery. But the cathedral was scarcely finished when it collapsed. The celebrated Bukhvostov was appointed to begin again, having already built two churches at Riazan, one of them for L. K. Naryshkin, an uncle of the young Tsar Peter.[62]

Bukhvostov's work at Riazan is better considered in the context of the so-called Naryshkin or Moscow Baroque, which is the subject of the following chapter. At this point the case for the generally "medieval" character of Russian building at the end of the seventeenth century, and for an overall crisis in Old-Russian architecture, might be considered closed.

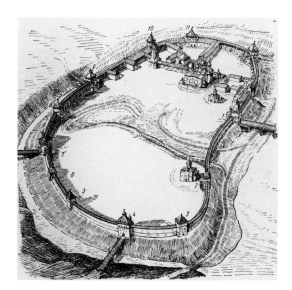
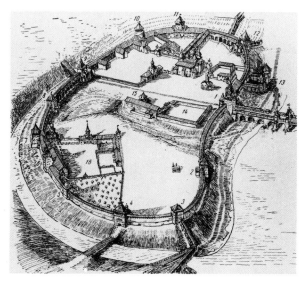

Figure 37 Reconstructions of the Novgorod kremlin in 1484–1492 (left) and ca. 1700 (right: no. *16*, lower left, is the new governor's compound, 1692–1696).

4
Moscow Baroque

Muscovite architecture of the seventeenth century can nowise
be identified with that stage in the development of European
architecture which is called the Baroque.
—B. R. Vipper, *Arkhitektura russkogo barokko*

Proponents of a "Moscow Baroque" in seventeenth-century Russian architecture point to the church of Josaphat the Tsarevich at Izmailovo (1678/1687–
1688) as the earliest known example of the type (fig. 38); to the church of the
Sign of the Most Holy Mother of God at Dubrovitsy (1690–1697/1704?), also
near Moscow, as the most remarkable of surviving specimens (fig. 39, pl. 17);
and to the church of the Intercession of the Mother of God at Fili (1690–
1693), now in Moscow, as the finest of the type (fig. 40, pl. 18). Because the
last of these churches as well as at least six others considered to be in the same
style were commissioned by members of the Naryshkin family (the family of
Peter I's mother), the type has also been called the "Naryshkin Baroque." But
under either name the buildings in question and more, the concept itself of a
Baroque period or style in pre-Petrine Russian architecture, have excited considerable controversy in the literature. The controversy is succinctly delimited
in the quotation above from B. R. Vipper,[1] a scholar who remains second in
the whole field of Russian art history only to I. E. Grabar, who virtually in-
vented the "Moscow Baroque."

The distinctive features of these churches include sanctuaries and apses or
side chapels of roughly equal size (hence a regular plan and symmetrical external appearance); towers composed of sharply delineated, progressively smaller
polygonal structures which either completely dominate the main structure or
form free-standing bell towers; their interior and exterior decoration, embracing
everything from elements of the Classical orders, pediments, and volutes to an
extensive use of sculpture (figs. 41, 42); and, in some instances, their ground
plans, which are either oval or of a fluid cruciform design (fig. 43). There is
not perfect agreement on which churches are to be included in the "Moscow
Baroque," however, and some of its proponents have argued that certain secular
as well as monastic buildings of the late seventeenth century can also lay claim
to the name (pls. 13, 16). Then too, another leading authority, M. A. Ilin,
points out that the basic composition of "Moscow Baroque" churches can be
traced back to much older churches in and around the city (cf. figs. 43 and 44
or pls. 16 and 4), and argues that their novelty lies rather in the wealth, fi-
nesse, and variety of their ornaments, some of which reflect Classical motives
not seen before in Russia. In Ilin's judgment, it is owing to the "abundance of
its decorative forms" that the church of the Trinity at Troitskoe-Lykovo (1698–
1704, pl. 22) may be classed as "an outstanding monument of this style."[2]

Figure 38 Church of Josaphat the Tsarevich, Izmailovo, 1678/87–1688; main tower.

Figure 39 Church of the Sign of the Mother of God at Dubrovitsy (near Moscow), 1690–1697/1704(?); detail showing transition from first to second tier.

Figure 40 Church of the Intercession of the Mother of God at Fili (now in Moscow), 1690–1693; detail of the upper tiers.

Figure 41 Alabaster relief "Golgotha," interior of the church of the Sign of the Mother of God at Dubrovitsy, 1690–1697/1704(?).

Figure 42 Church of the Trinity at Troitskoe-Lykovo, 1698–1704; crucifix above the iconostasis. A sculpted crucifix was extremely rare in Russian church art at this time, and here it is obviously a product of direct European influence.

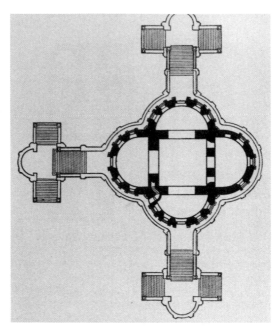

Figure 43 Church of the Intercession of the Mother of God at Fili, 1690–1693; plan.

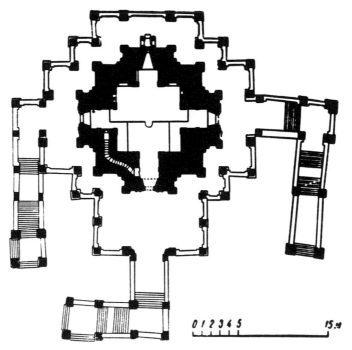

Figure 44 Church of the Ascension, Kolomenskoe (now in Moscow), 1530–1532; plan.

There can be no doubt that the churches under review represent something that was new in Russian architecture and that their influence can be detected in numerous churches and bell towers erected in Russia in the earlier eighteenth century (pl. 24).[3] But is the new type or style properly called Baroque? And can we therefore date the decisive Europeanization of Russian architecture to its appearance? If not, what is the significance of the "Moscow Baroque" in Russian architectural history?

MOSCOW BAROQUE?

The basic characteristics of Baroque architecture in Europe are fairly easy to define. Continuing the revolution which took place in Italy in connection with the Renaissance, and which had proclaimed a revival of the elements of Classical architecture together with the Classical system of proportions, leading Roman architects of the seventeenth century—Borromini, Bernini, Pietro da Cortona—now employed this heritage in newly profuse, plastic, and fluent ways. In contrast broadly speaking to their Renaissance predecessors, they and their followers or imitators built on a large scale, preferred irregular or complex forms, and sought movement in line, mass, and space (double-S curves, twisted columns, undulating walls, fluid or open ground plans). They fused painting and sculpture with architecture while making bold use of rich materials, directed light, illusionism, and dramatic action extended over space (sculpted and painted figures soaring upward into the dome, sweeping stairways). In describing this architecture scholars refer to its "spatial dynamism" and "pulsating juxtapositions"; adjectives like magnificent, exuberant, theatrical, emotional, and ostentatious are regularly employed. Yet an underlying integrity and harmony of both interior and exterior elements, an overall centralization and subordination of the various parts, are also present in Baroque buildings and projects for buildings, landscapes, and town plans. "We thus understand," Norberg-Schulz writes, "that the two seemingly contradictory aspects of the Baroque phenomenon, systematism and dynamism, form a meaningful whole."[4]

The Baroque style in architecture, it should be stressed, was a direct outgrowth by way of "Mannerism" of Renaissance architecture, and was first realized in buildings designed and put up in Rome between the 1620s and the 1660s. From there the new style soon spread to northern Italy, thence to Switzerland, Austria, Bavaria, Spain, and beyond, where it developed in sundry and sometimes novel ways, although always in the spirit of the Italian models. Indeed, the history of the Baroque affords an excellent instance of the process of cultural diffusion, with Rome as the "center of spread." For it quickly became an international style and one that by the beginning of the eighteenth century dominated European architecture.[5]

Had a variant of the new style emerged in Russia by that time? Early in the twentieth century, in their monumental *History of Russian Art,* Grabar and his colleagues argued that such had indeed taken place. In their view, the Baroque

> was perhaps the most international of any style that prevailed before or after
> it in Europe, for never were the national characteristics of the separate peoples
> effaced to such a degree, and reduced to naught, as in the two centuries of its
> domination. Everywhere it was one and the same manner, the same details,
> an invariable type.

Only in Russia, suggested Grabar and his colleagues, and only at first, in the
last years of the seventeenth century, were elements of the Baroque assimilated
and reworked into a wholly individual variant or "type." This could have happened in Russia, they urged, because there the Baroque was not the latest link
in a long chain of architectural development but rather a kind of explosion
which took Moscow "unawares." Moreover, in Russia Baroque motives did not
arrive directly from Europe but rather by way of the Ukraine, to which they
had come from Poland (to which they had come from Italy and Germany).
From the Ukraine, as well, came churches with staged towers composed of
progressively small octagonal structures, a type that had first appeared, supposedly, in the local wooden architecture. The application of Baroque decorative
elements—pilasters, capitals, cornices, columns, pediments, niches, and the
like—to staged-tower churches produced in Moscow and its environs an entirely new style. Contemporaries called it the "style of Tsars Peter and Ivan"
after the reigning monarchs (Peter I and his half-brother Ivan V, who died in
1696); later it was called the "Naryshkin style" or the "Naryshkin Baroque"
after the patrons of so many of its buildings. By 1897 the style was referred to
as the "Russian Baroque," a name that "better defines its essence and observes
its links with the Western Baroque," as Grabar put it. "But it would be still
more exact and correct," Grabar argued further, "to call it the Moscow Baroque
[*Moskovskoe barokko*] in order to distinguish it both from the Western variants
[of the Baroque] and from the St. Petersburg Baroque, which was, when all is
said and done, also Russian." This "Moscow Baroque" flourished in the last
quarter of the seventeenth century in secular as well as ecclesiastical architecture (although many fewer examples of the former survived, or were built),
leaving as its finest monument the church of the Intercession of the Mother of
God at Fili (figs. 40, 43; pl. 18).[6]

Yet even at this early date Grabar was not entirely consistent or clear in his
conception of the "Moscow Baroque." Elsewhere in this same monumental
work we read that "precisely because only bits and pieces of the Baroque
reached Moscow" in the seventeenth century "the new style was not adopted
as a ready-made, finished whole. . . . That is why the Moscow Baroque style
has so little in common with the Western European Baroque . . . why to foreigners, for all its elusive Baroque elements, a church like that of the Intercession at Fili seemed as Russian as the church of Basil the Blessed [pl. 6]."[7] As
indeed it still does. Furthermore, a close reading of Grabar's initial formulation

of the nature and derivation of the "Moscow Baroque" reveals both a dearth of documentary evidence to support it and a correspondingly heavy reliance on purely visual comparisons. This way of proceeding is attributable perhaps to the influence on Russian art scholarship of Wölfflin's seminal *Renaissance und Barock* (1888), a work Grabar called the "best exposition of the Baroque" in European art and architecture but which more recent students have criticized precisely for its visual bias.[8]

At any event, the notion of a "Moscow Baroque" in late seventeenth-century Russian architecture was soon invaded from two general directions. In a symposium of 1926 V. V. Zgura argued in favor of a more embracive use of the term and dated the birth of the phenomenon to the *first* quarter of the century[!]. But N. I. Brunov, in the same place, expressed considerable overall skepticism regarding the "so-called 'Russian Baroque' " and urged in particular that the much-vaunted tower of the church at Fili was "indisputably Western in origin," not at all Baroque, and not an essential element of late seventeenth-century Russian architecture. He compared it with Bukhvostov's pentacupolar Dormition cathedral at Riazan, a major monument of the 1690s (pl. 21), in clinching his case.[9]

Brunov's skepticism was to prevail. A few years later F. I. Shmit reviewed the arguments and decided, on putatively Marxist grounds, that there was no reason for describing Russian architecture at any point in the seventeenth century as "Baroque in essence." Baroque decorative details might have appeared here and there but Baroque architecture as such in Russia was an eighteenth-century phenomenon, one implanted by Peter I and his successors for the pleasure of ruler and court and an aspect of that quickening process of Europeanization whose reception had only been "slowly prepared for in the subconscious of the most progressive circles of seventeenth-century Moscow."[10] Nekrasov agreed. "It is perfectly clear that the notion once expressed concerning the Baroqueness [*barochnost'*] of Russian architecture of the seventeenth century is mistaken," he declared, a matter, now, of a more strict understanding of what constituted Baroque architecture in Europe itself and of observing the obviously Old-Russian elements of the buildings in question. Nekrasov accounted only a few churches put up in and around Moscow late in the seventeenth century, probably by European masters, partial exceptions to his rule—for example, the church of the Sign of the Mother of God at Dubrovitsy (pl. 17). But these churches were to be linked with the rise in Russia under Peter I in the first quarter of the eighteenth century of the "new" or "modern" architecture.[11]

And there, by the 1930s, the matter stood. It seemed clear that "Baroque" in the original European sense of the term could not properly be applied either to seventeenth-century Russian architecture as a whole or to any one phase or style within it. Yet the significance of the numerous "Baroque" ornaments observed on the buildings in question still needed clarifying. This problem among others was addressed in due course by B. R. Vipper.

Moscow Mannerism?

Vipper had the advantage, rare among his Soviet colleagues, especially those trained after the Bolshevik Revolution, of having studied and traveled extensively in Europe. He drew on this experience to good if not brilliant effect in an essay written between 1943 and 1945 but not published until much later, an essay in which he introduced the terms "rusticalization" and "Mannerism" into the discussion and gave new prominence to probable Dutch influence on seventeenth-century Russian architecture.[12]

The first of these terms Vipper had earlier employed in his fundamental study of Latvian architecture in the "Baroque epoch." In his words,

> Rusticalization of artistic forms occurs when the traditions and elements of style pass over from one nation to another whose culture is at an inferior level of development or from one stratum of society to another. Forms are then simplified and generalized, typical qualities are emphasized and spatial contrasts are replaced by surface rhythms. Yet although such a process certainly implies a deformation, even a distortion of the historical style [here, the Baroque], it can never be called a decline. The impact of a historical style creates in the store of provincial art a certain repertoire of methods and motifs, which in their turn, by amalgamating with the age-old traditions of folk crafts, gradually form a kind of national artistic dialect.

Vipper urged that within the boundaries of such a substyle or national artistic dialect—or "local provincial dialect"—the development of "original ornamental forms, a distinctive symbolism, and an independent artistic conception" might lead eventually to the emergence of a "complete and independent language . . . a new national style." Thus in Latvia (formerly Livonia with Courland) Baroque architecture flourished in the first half of the eighteenth century; but the way had been prepared by the emergence in the preceding decades of local "dialects of the Baroque style," a complex process of stylistic intermingling most closely linked in its genesis with East Prussia, "where the Baroque style flourished late, but gloriously." External and especially Prussian influences and individual architects played a catalytic and sometimes dominant role in the development of a mature Latvian variant of Baroque architecture; and the "Baroque wave, growing continually stronger, began to influence the methods of peasant carpentry" as well as grandee architecture.[13]

In the case of the "Moscow" or "Naryshkin Baroque," however, various factors worked to produce a style whose overall effect was "completely anti-Baroque." If anything, Vipper suggested, the so-called Naryshkin Baroque in Russian architecture corresponds rather to the "Mannerist" phase of the 1520s and the 1530s in European architecture. Of course, the concept of a distinct Mannerist phase in European art, distinct from either the (late) Renaissance or the (early) Baroque, is not universally accepted by scholars; and even its proponents have found Mannerism difficult to define, especially with respect to ar-

chitecture.* But in Vipper's hands the term helped to clarify the complex derivation as well as the belated and rusticalized character of the "Baroque"
ornaments that proliferated in late seventeenth-century Russian building.

In Vipper's view, this rich ornamentation reveals, apart from purely indigenous products, Mannerist motives derived predominantly both from East Prussia
and especially Holland (where they had already undergone rusticalization) and
from the Ukraine: which was to say, from Poland and East Prussia by way of
the Ukraine, or from Italy by way of Poland and then of the Ukraine. The
importance of the Ukrainian channel proved steadily greater as the century
progressed. It was for this reason that

> the treatment of decorative motives becomes more plastic, luxurious, with a
> rich play of light and shade, more dynamic; a medley of colors gives way to a
> simpler, monumental contrast of two tones (usually white ornament against a
> red background). But the motives themselves were borrowed as before mainly
> from the Mannerist repertoire. . . . Only at the very end of the century do
> the first symptoms appear approximating the Baroque, in the form of oval or
> polygonal windows, the complex curves of church cupolas, and the luxuriant,
> succulent acanthus.

Yet among external factors Dutch influence remained paramount, as witness

> a whole series of specific phenomena in Russian architecture at the turn of the
> seventeenth century, foremost among them the use of two colors—red and
> white—which is so typical of Russian building of this period. The source of
> this technique is to be traced, ultimately, to Holland (and partly to Denmark
> and North Germany) at the turn of the sixteenth century.

From sixteenth- and early seventeenth-century Dutch architecture also came
the steep roofs that appeared on Russian towers by the 1690s; and "no less
certain," Vipper urged, was the Dutch provenance of the stepped pediments
and cartouches that were common in late seventeenth-century Russian building. Meanwhile the growing penetration of southern influences is registered in
a group of buildings—the church at Dubrovitsy being one (pl. 17)—that were
put up in these years, "their profoundly Russian national character notwithstanding."[14]

---

*Cf. F. Wurtenberger, *Mannerism: The European
Style of the Sixteenth Century*, trans. M. Heron (New
York, 1963), pp. 82–101, where we read for example
that "Mannerism far surpassed former ages in the variety with which it organized and daringly combined
the orders of columns" (p. 97) while at the same
time "a tendency toward the dissolution of architectural features is evident in Mannerist architecture in
general" (p. 98). A standard reference work can say
only that Mannerism in architecture "denotes a style
current in Italy from Michelangelo to the end of the
sixteenth century. It is characterized by the use of
motifs in deliberate opposition to their original significance or context, but it can also express itself in
an equally deliberate cold and rigid classicism. The
term applies to French and Spanish architecture of
the sixteenth century as well, but how far it applies
to the northern [European] countries is controversial" (J. Fleming et al., *The Penguin Dictionary of Architecture* [Harmondsworth, 1966], p. 184).

What then is the "Naryshkin" or "Moscow Baroque" as an architectural style? In Vipper's formulation, it is a "concatenation [stseplenie] of the most opposite tendencies, currents, and influences." It is the resolution of interacting external norms—as mediated by Dutch and Ukrainian architecture—and indigenous precedents; and if it has a European analogue and/or ultimate source, it is the Mannerist, not the Baroque, style. In particular, the staged towers and polygonal apses of Naryshkin churches are neither Baroque nor, in principle, new to Russian architecture. Equally, their elaborate external staircases reflect the traditions of Russian wooden architecture and recall, if anything in Europe, Mannerist or Palladian examples (the Baroque preferred internal stairways). Again, the exterior decorative program of these churches, like that of certain other buildings in or near Moscow, evoke Mannerist prototypes here both rusticalized and merged with various features of a "vulgarized Baroque"; while their interior ornamentation blends traditional Russian with Baroque motives derived from Poland and East Prussia by way of the Ukraine. It is rather in their combination of these contradictory elements, in their pronounced verticality coupled with their flamboyant decoration, that Naryshkin churches offer anything that is essentially new by comparison with earlier or contemporary Russian churches.[15]

Vipper's remains the most sophisticated attempt in the literature both to define the "Moscow Baroque" by means of visual comparisons and to provide, in his application of the concept of rusticalization, a theoretical model with which to explain its rise. His essay concludes by identifying three "peculiarities" of the style, the first being its *ordernost'*, or idiosyncratic use of the Classical orders:

> But it is perfectly clear that precisely the tectonic essence of the system of orders, as a principle of wall division and as expressive of the static relationship of support and load, is completely foreign to Naryshkin architecture—as witness the absence in many buildings of the time of a sharp delineation of the stories (the Riazan cathedral [pl. 21]), the breaking up of cornices, the disposition of supports at corners or along edges, etc. Here if you will is to be seen more of the skeletal Gothic than of the musical, energetic Renaissance or Baroque.

Their duality of scale is a second peculiarity of many monuments of the "Naryshkin Baroque," in Vipper's view, citing the example, again, of Bukhvostov's cathedral at Riazan: "I have in mind the simultaneous presence in one and the same building of two completely different scales, the one grandiose, monumental, almost irrational in its immensity and verticality, the other miniature, ornate, detailed, and intimate, as in a fairytale." And the third peculiarity of this architecture, according to Vipper, resides in its interrelations of space and mass, and in the impression these give of a kind of ethereal fragility.

Vipper conceded that in the centralized and rounded plans of many of these same churches European influence can be detected. But their ultimate source, he insisted, was Dutch ecclesiastical architecture of the first half of the seventeenth century, which was only peripherally Baroque. Furthermore, the "Baroque symptoms" to be observed in the plans of various Naryshkin churches

> are completely devalued by the plainly anti-Baroque conception of space and mass: by the essential and stubborn adherence of Muscovite architecture of this period to the Old-Russian traditions of isolated, closed spaces lacking a clearly expressed direction. The circular proportions of Naryshkin churches (even of the church at Dubrovitsy) have nothing in common with the curvilinearity of Baroque masses and spaces.

In the end, Vipper declared, the "Moscow Baroque" is a "quite specifically Russian phenomenon, very complex in nature and without direct analogies not only in Baroque architecture, but in the history of architectural style more generally."[16]

NATIONALIST ASSERTIONS

When Vipper wrote the essay just discussed Soviet historical scholarship had already entered that phase of coarse Marxism and extreme Russian nationalism typical of the Stalin period, a fact that no doubt explains why, although the essay dates to between 1943 and 1945, it was not published until 1978. We need not dwell on the overall views of the "Moscow Baroque" publicly advanced in this period (it lasted until the end of the 1950s, with lingering traces thereafter). The buildings in question were hailed as the "brilliant culmination of the evolution of Old-Russian architecture"; as constituting, indeed, "one of the most brilliant pages in the history of Russian national architecture." The "Moscow Baroque" anticipated the "Russian Baroque" of the eighteenth century while both, to be sure, had little in common with the "Western Baroque," since the latter was "characterized by a narrow, closed circle of religious and court themes expressive of the ideology of Catholic reaction and the feudal aristocracy" and hence was "decadent" in its forms and images (the "Moscow Baroque" was "popular" or "national" in essence and so could not have been "decadent").[17] The eclectic, purely ornamental use of elements of the Classical orders by Russian builders—whereby, for instance, "columns were converted into a tectonic decoration of the facade"—was not a product of technical deficiency or inadequate training or poor taste (as might have been thought) but a matter of "creative adaptation" in accordance with the deep-rooted, "picturesque" norms of the national tradition.[18] Indeed, in the development of the "Moscow Baroque" the influence of popular art, with its "strength and vitality," its "love of the joyful, the colorful, and the picturesque," was fully revealed.[19] And so on. The effect of this putative revision was to convert the "Moscow Baroque" into a wholly indigenous product, to acclaim its works as paragons of architecture, and to suggest that the "progressive" tendencies which it embodied rendered the Petrine revolution inevitable, or even superfluous.

Whatever else the Stalinist phase in Soviet architectural historiography may have accomplished, the question of the "Baroqueness" of the "Moscow Baroque" was effectively closed. The legacy of this tour de force is reflected in numerous works by M. A. Ilin published between 1957 and 1979, works which also reflect an effort to resume the researches of earlier scholars. Thus in an essay of 1957 expressly devoted to the "problem of the 'Moscow Baroque,'" Ilin asserted that any affinities between the new types of churches appearing in and around Moscow from the 1680s and the Baroque style in Europe were a matter of a few decorative forms only. The "essence" of the Baroque "remained alien to Russian masters," and so "in speaking of the 'Moscow Baroque' the completely conditional sense of the term must be indicated." Ilin argued that the architecture in question was "completely original," meaning that it combined in entirely original ways compositional elements that were traditional in Old-Russian building—especially wooden building—with "quite singular" decorations having only "some" connection with the "Western Renaissance and Baroque."[20]

The main tendency of Ilin's approach, it is clear, was simultaneously to acknowledge and to minimize outside influences on the builders of the "Moscow Baroque." Accordingly, the "opinion that Russian architecture of the last two decades of the seventeenth century was dependent for both compositional forms and decorative principles on Ukrainian architecture, which in turn reflected elements of the Polish-Catholic Baroque," was not, in his judgment, "acceptable." Yet the influence from about 1655 of Belorussian craftsmen, if only on decorative develoments, *was* to be noticed. Before their arrival, Ilin pointed out, columns had appeared in Russian architecture lacking capitals and bases, or with capitals and bases reversed. In either case, they were utterly functionless and unconnected with the rest of the decorative scheme. But the Belorussian craftsmen changed all that, and particularly by their introduction of more elaborately carved iconostases replete with Classical motives, whose presence in Russian churches then inspired admiring Russian decorators to frenzies of imitation.[21]

Ilin went on to suggest that by the end of the seventeenth century, when the "Moscow Baroque" flourished, the Belorussian influence had been russified; that judging by visual comparisons alone it was rather Dutch "prototypes" that were now operative; but that, in any case, Russian architectural decoration of these years could not be considered a "provincial school of the European Baroque" since it only adapted Baroque forms and motives in the light of established and peculiarly Russian decorative principles. Indeed, it was "impossible to confuse a single Russian building of the late seventeenth century and its interior and exterior decoration with a contemporary structure of the European Baroque."[22] Finally, in 1979 Ilin proposed that the "Moscow Baroque" be called (again) the "Russian Baroque," evidently to stress its more general success. He now saw the "Russian Baroque" as at once the "basic tendency" in

Russian building between about 1675 and 1700 and the "culminating stage" of the ever more decorative architecture of the entire seventeenth century. It testified to the "impetuous activity" of Russian builders of the time and to the "vitality" of their art while making possible the "organic continuity of national forms in the architecture of the modern, post-Petrine period."[23]

In short, if the term "Baroque" in "Moscow" or "Russian Baroque" could not be eradicated, it was to be emptied of any very specific meaning and then, like the phenomenon itself, completely russified. The search for European sources or prototypes, models or influences, even parallels or analogues, was still in effect discouraged, if not foreclosed.

UKRAINIAN AND BELORUSSIAN BAROQUES

A process similar to the discovery, refinement, and ultimate rejection—or assimilation—of the "Baroque" in "Moscow Baroque" is characteristic of the historiography of the "Ukrainian Baroque." In its original formulation, again by Grabar, masonry architecture revived from its long decline and developed in seventeenth-century Ukraine in close dependence on the Baroque, especially the Polish Baroque. Numerous Roman Catholic churches and chapels erected in western Ukraine from early in the century and even in Kiev (at least two major churches) served as models facilitating the "penetration of Ukrainian architecture by the Baroque tradition." At the same time, a process of adaption, expressive of local tastes, took place—the elaborately carved iconostases of seventeenth-century Ukrainian Orthodox churches were an obvious instance. Working early in the twentieth century, when many more examples survived, Grabar divided all Ukrainian masonry churches into two main groups, to which he added a third or "mixed type." The first group derived from the traditional, strongly vertical wooden churches of the three- and five-cupola types which were then "dressed in Baroque finery . . . pilasters, capitals, corniches, pediments over windows, columns, polygonal or cruciform niches." Churches of the second group, much more dependent on Polish or Western models, were typically basilican in form complete with transept, polygonal apse, and, often, twin towers rising on the west front; while their decorative scheme, composed of curvilinear pediments and stone scutcheons, volutes and richly decorated pilasters, cartouches and an ever more profuse variety of other sculpted ornaments, was entirely Polish. Churches of the third or "mixed type" were neither one thing nor the other: traditional in structure, but with very extensive Baroque additions. Grabar also pointed to the extensive restoration and new decoration in the taste of the period of older churches in seventeenth-century Ukraine, where Baroque architecture flourished particularly during the reign of Hetman Ivan Mazepa (1687–1709) (figs. 45, 46).[24]

Figure 45 Church of the Dormition, Monastery of the Caves, Kiev; eleventh century, extensively rebuilt in the second half of the seventeenth century and again, following a major fire, in the 1720s. The church was destroyed in 1941.

Figure 46 Main church of the Brotherhood Monastery of the Epiphany, Kiev, 1690s; front and plan. The church was demolished in 1935.

Complementing and in some degree underlying Grabar's view of the masonry churches of the "Ukrainian Baroque" was Pavlutskii's interpretation of the wooden ecclesiastical architecture of the period.[25] Pavlutskii cautioned that none of the surviving examples of Ukrainian wooden architecture (this was in 1909) dated to before the beginning of the eighteenth century; yet enough graphic evidence had been preserved, in the form mainly of manuscript and printed book illustrations, to determine that "Ukrainian [wooden] architecture in all of its characteristic features existed already in the seventeenth century." Three main sources of this architecture were identified: (1) the indigenous stock of basic Old-Russian, ultimately Byzantine forms; (2) the Russian ("North Russian") and especially Old Believer influence, most noticeable in churches of the period located in northern and eastern Ukraine;* and (3) the Baroque, especially the Polish Baroque. Thus the traditional wooden churches with their steep four-sided roofs covering square main structures arranged either three in a row or five in a cluster were transformed under the impact of the Baroque into affairs of polygonal or round main structures surmounted by as many as nine staged towers with cupolas and adorned, inside, with elaborate iconostases. Elsewhere, the Russian influence altered the shape of roofs and cupolas in the direction of lower overall structures and more sinuous forms. But in either case, whether speaking of Ukrainian masonry or wooden architecture of the seventeenth century, the decisive influence of Baroque and particularly Polish Baroque models was highlighted by both Pavlutskii and Grabar.

This notion of a "Ukrainian Baroque" in seventeenth-century architecture, like that of a "Moscow Baroque," soon came under revision. Almost at once Lukomskii proposed broadening the term to include an earlier "Ukrainian Baroque proper . . . almost Catholic in feeling," the work largely of Italian and Polish masters; a later "Mazepite Baroque," Germanic in its decorative details, both European and local in its structural forms; a "Naryshkin Baroque" similar to that of the Moscow region, whence masters were known to have been sent to the Ukraine, but exhibiting at the same time local decorative features; and, finally, the Baroque of Rastrelli and his followers, emanating from St. Petersburg, which flourished between the 1740s and 1760s.[26] Yet Lukomskii himself later suggested that the major buildings of the "Ukrainian Baroque" which he discussed here were to be seen rather as the "richest and most precious monuments of the pure Ukrainian style."[27] And in this he foreshadowed the direction of more recent Soviet scholarship, where the "Ukrainian Baroque" in architecture has simply disappeared, to be replaced as it were by a new emphasis on Russian influence. In the most thorough treatment to date of Ukrainian architecture of the period (by Tsapenko) its interdependence with contemporary Russian architecture is emphasized and their gradual convergence, between

---

*The Old Believers were the dissident, conservative, populist faction in the Russian church schism of the later seventeenth century and, as such, often fled in search of religious freedom to the lands east and south of Russia proper, bringing with them, in this case, their traditional church architecture.

the 1670s and the 1770s, is stressed. Indeed, here the Pavlutskii-Grabar thesis of a "Ukrainian Baroque" is summarily rejected for its "one-sided picture of the development of Ukrainian architecture of this period as a simple borrowing of Western European Baroque architecture" (had that been said?). At the same time, the decidedly Baroque architecture of western Ukraine is entirely ignored by Tsapenko on the pretext that the territory was then dominated by Polish nobles.[28]

On the other hand, a "Belorussian Baroque" in architecture dating in its origins to the sixteenth century has become a fixture of Soviet scholarship. That this should be so, when the "Ukrainian Baroque" has been consigned to oblivion, is in part a matter of Soviet politics, to be sure, but also one of undeniable historical fact. In Belorussia, owing to its complete incorporation in the Polish-Lithuanian Commonwealth, the "basic trend" in seventeenth- and eighteenth-century architecture was undeniably Baroque, as a major work in the field makes clear.[29] Ecclesiastical building in Belorussia in this period was on the whole Catholic (fig. 47), although Orthodox architecture soon developed in tandem with it, producing in a number of lesser monuments a notable synthesis of East and West. At first Italianate in character (many architects of the period came from Italy, as was the case elsewhere in the Commonwealth), the Baroque in Belorussia assumed from the middle of the seventeenth century an increasingly distinctive aspect—the result also, it would seem, of Russian and Ukrainian influences. Surviving churches of the period in Mahilou (Mogilev), basilican in plan and often graced with twin west towers, testify unmistak-

Figure 47 Jesuit church in Nesvizh, Belorussia, 1584–1593; main facade.

ably to the dominance of the Polish Baroque (fig. 48); while the imposing external staircases, high staged tower, Classical window surrounds and other decorative details of the city's town hall (1679–1697) bear witness to the ubiquity in neighboring territories of architectural features once thought peculiar to the "Moscow Baroque" (fig. 49). Further, it is becoming increasingly clear that

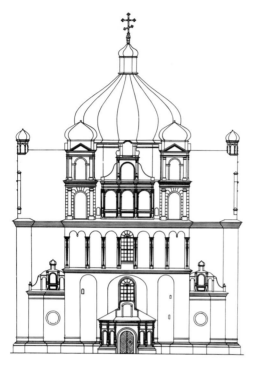

Figure 48 Nikolaevskii (Orthodox) church, Mogilev (Mahiloŭ), 1669; main facade.

Figure 49 Town Hall, Mogilev (Mahiloŭ), 1679–1697; facade.

dozens of Belorussian craftsmen—wood and stone carvers, ceramicists and tilers—brought Renaissance and Baroque motives together with their techniques to Moscow and other Russian centers, where they left their stamp on numerous major monuments of the second half of the seventeenth century.

We are back to Moscow, whose size and growing political as well as economic importance naturally attracted the cultural elite of both Belorussia and the Ukraine, countries long linked to Russia by geography, ethnicity, and the bond of their common Orthodox faith. Late in his career Grabar spoke of the "iconostazation [*obikonostasen'e*]" of later seventeenth-century Russian architecture, a remark quoted by a more recent student in explaining, after Ilin, the contribution made by the "typical Belorussian iconostasis" to the development of the "Moscow Baroque."[30]

Such an iconostasis is remarkable for its intricately molded naturalistic motives and for its use of the Classical orders, whereby the icons are framed by cornices and columns with bases and capitals all carved in high relief (fig. 50),

Figure 50 Iconostasis of the Nikolaevskii (Orthodox) church, Mogilev (Mahiloŭ), 1669; detail. The blank space at center is for an icon.

this in sharp contrast to the flat tracery of contemporary Russian work. The very terminology of the Classical order—cornice/*karniz*, base/*baza*, capital/*kapitel'*—first appeared in Russia in documents relating to the commissioning and production by Belorussian craftsmen of iconostases of this kind. Another of their contributions to Russian architecture was the use of glazed ceramic tiles to decorate both the exterior and interior of buildings, as may be seen not only in friezes around walls and under domes composed of simple triangular tiles but also in window surrounds, portals, and even inconostases constructed of polychrome ceramic and designed, once again, after the Classical orders. Extensive decorative schemes of colored tiles as well as elaborately carved iconostases were provided by Belorussians in the 1650s for Patriarch Nikon's monastic churches at Istra and Valdai, whence a taste for their work overtook, among others, the tsar. Numerous royal churches of the "Moscow Baroque" as well as royal residences (at Kolomenskoe, Izmailovo), we now know, were decorated by Belorussian craftsmen in the later decades of the seventeenth century—or by their Russian apprentices (fig. 51, pl. 20). What is more, Belorussian masters appear to have transmitted their practice of using pattern books to their Russian counterparts, who in the 1680s and 1690s began making regular use of European architectural manuals and prints in their search for new and more elaborate decorative forms.[31]

In fact, tracing the use made by Russian builders of European graphic material has opened a second verifiable path of diffusion with respect to the sources of the "Moscow Baroque."[32] Many of the growing number of European publications which entered Russia during the seventeenth century dealt with architecture and related matters or were illustrated with engravings of architectural interest. For example, inventories of the tsar's library indicate that by the latter half of the century it included one book "with illustrations of European [or "German": *nemetskie*] towns, fortifications, masonry buildings and models to teach draftsmanship"; another providing "instructions for the building of masonry palaces and churches"; a third illustrating the "masonry buildings of all the German states"; and still another offering "drawings of Holland." Illustrated descriptions of Amsterdam and Rome were also to be found in the royal library, as was a book on the construction of palaces (the inventories provide no further details). In the previous chapter we noted that around 1700 S. U. Remezov used an "Italian book" in designing buildings for Tobolsk, and that Patriarch Nikon's builders at the New Jerusalem monastery undoubtedly had a copy of Bernardino Amico's book of drawings of the churches of the Holy Land. Among other works available to Nikon's craftsmen, according to patriarchal inventories, were two illustrated manuals on carving, a book on Italy, an illustrated book on German architecture, and seven illustrated descriptions of various countries. A catalog of the library of the Ambassadorial Office (Posolskii Prikaz) in Moscow compiled in 1696 records that some seventy-seven books belonging to A. S. Matveev, head of the department from 1671 to 1676, were acquired by the office in 1677 after Matveev's banishment (the result of a po-

Figure 51 Iconostasis of the church of the Mother of God of Smolensk, Novodevichii convent, Moscow, 1683–1685; detail. Executed by local artists working under the Belorussian master Klim Mikhailov, who had been brought to Russia in 1657–1658 by Prince G. S. Kurakin and had worked for Patriarch Nikon at the New Jerusalem monastery (1659–1667) and then for Tsars Aleksei Mikhailovich and Fedor Alekseevich (father and half-brother of Peter I) at Kolomenskoe (1668–1683).

litical struggle): sixteen of the books, written in French, German, or Italian, were on architecture and allied subjects, such as woodcarving, landscape gardening, and the construction of fountains. These very same books, it seems, were later removed from the office's library by Prince V. V. Golitsyn, its head from 1682 to 1689.

This same Golitsyn commissioned or was otherwise directly involved in the construction of several buildings of the "Moscow Baroque," including his own Moscow residence and adjacent church, the church of Josaphat the Tsarevich at Izmailovo (fig. 38), and the churches of the Transfiguration and of the Intercession as well as the new bell tower at the Novodevichii convent in Moscow (pls. 15, 16). The convent was patronized by various members of the royal family, while the church at Izmailovo has been aptly described as the "court church" of Tsarevna Sophia, the half-sister of Peter I who ruled during his minority (1682–1689) and whom Golitsyn served as chief minister. At least a dozen churches clearly exemplifying characteristics of the "Moscow Baroque" were built between 1684 and 1707 or so under the patronage of members of the princely Golitsyn clan, including the celebrated church at Dubrovitsy (B. A. Golitsyn; see pl. 17); and to a degree not achieved in the churches put up by members of the Naryshkin family (maternal relations of Peter I), these "Golitsyn churches" can be said to have embodied "all that was new in Russian culture at the end of the seventeenth century."[33]

Indeed, it emerges on due investigation that all of the buildings associated by scholars at one time or another with the "Moscow Baroque" were built at the expense of representatives of the topmost Russian elite: were patronized by members of the innermost circles of power and prestige if not by the rulers themselves or their immediate relations. And in this fact, I will urge, lies the ultimate historical significance of the so-called Moscow Baroque.

CONCLUSIONS

A review of the historiography of the "Moscow Baroque" reveals, at a minimum, the limitations of the method of visual comparison in determining the nature and derivation of the architecture in question. An initial enthusiasm for the Baroque in European architecture as interpreted by Wölfflin and others led Russian scholars, notably Grabar and Pavlutskii, to define a Baroque in seventeenth-century Russian and Ukrainian architecture almost exclusively on the basis of visual similarities. Nationalist—or patriotic—considerations plainly were also involved: a movement in architecture that had swept Europe by the end of the seventeenth century could not have bypassed Russia; the "Ukrainian Baroque" was then important primarily as the proximate source of the "Russian" or "Moscow Baroque"; and it was in Russia, uniquely, that a wholly individual variant of the new international style emerged. Conversely, it was this very individuality of the "Moscow Baroque" that explained the still striking disparities between its monuments and those of the Baroque elsewhere.

By the 1930s, however, the impropriety of identifying as Baroque any one style or phase in seventeenth-century Russian architecture was generally accepted by scholars, a consequence, at least in part, of a better appreciation of what constituted Baroque architecture in Europe itself. Since then the term "Moscow Baroque," almost invariably placed in quotation marks, has nearly always been used in a highly conditional sense. Vipper's essay of the 1940s, which was only published in 1978, is the outstanding case in point. Still relying heavily on visual evidence, yet drawing on an exceptionally wide range of examples to illustrate his argument, Vipper insisted that the Baroque and the "Moscow Baroque" in architecture were essentially incompatible. He pointed up the potentially complex derivation of the latter's unmistakably Baroque (or Renaissance or Mannerist) decorative elements and introduced the concept of rusticalization in explaining their appearance. Vipper also emphasized the apparent Dutch affinities of the "Moscow Baroque" while upholding the thesis of substantial Ukrainian influence.

Vipper's emphasis on a pervasive Dutch influence in later seventeenth-century Russian architecture deserves attention, and for two reasons. Contacts with Holland—especially commercial contacts—were the most extensive of direct Russian contacts at this time with any part of Europe, a factor which suggests that further research in both Dutch and Russian collections might disclose evidence documenting a specifically architectural influence. Secondly, the development of architecture in Holland paralleled to a striking degree that which later took place in Russia, and thus might illuminate by comparison any underlying processes at work. We might briefly consider this second point.

In the Netherlands, a leading authority writes,

> the Renaissance, which was accepted from the sixteenth century, was above all a matter of externals, of decoration. . . . There was little basic development throughout the whole sixteenth century and the beginning of the seventeenth. . . . The very first specimens of Renaissance-like forms in building, as in painting, are merely bastards of Gothic and non-Gothic ornamentation . . . . It was particularly upon decorative sculpture that men expended their enthusiasm for what was new.

One could refer to broad historical developments—political, social, religious—inhibiting for a considerable time the acceptance of Renaissance and then Baroque architecture in Holland (or, say, in England), and to the simple fact of Holland's distance from Rome. But Ter Kuile points out, more specifically, that the first Italian builders active in the Netherlands in the early sixteenth century were not trained architects, and that as the century wore on their local followers were "everywhere busy with commissions for which correctness of style was considered less important than a fantastic variety of forms." It was a matter, in short, of ignorance—and taste. And the result was architecture that was "extravagant and unplanned, though very picturesque": an "uninhibited display of stone bands and blocks, window arches, volutes, obelisks, masks, cartouches, strapwork, and other decorative motifs enlivening the brick walls." In the seventeenth century, Ter Kuile goes on to say, Dutch ornamentation only increased "in richness and detail, from the bottom of the building to the top."[34] Indeed, the high staged towers of seventeenth-century Amsterdam and other of its buildings' decorative details, like the "gay pinnacles" newly added to the towers of its old fortifications, readily catch our interested eye, as they did Vipper's (fig. 52).

Equally, the concept of rusticalization deserves credit in interpreting the "Moscow Baroque" especially if it is understood somewhat more strictly, and applied more comprehensively, than Vipper was willing (or able) to do. According to Stech (in 1933), rusticalization (*Rustikalisierung*) is the "barbarization of form" or the "disintegration of style under the impact of new factors, whether aesthetic or sociological in nature"; and, as such, is a phenomenon repeatedly to be met with in art history. Stech identified three general characteristics of the process occurring when "primitive" art is suddenly penetrated by art of a higher order: a "disregard of proportion," "uncertainty with respect to spatial dispositions," and an "emphasis on accessories." Rusticalized art differs from "pure" primitive art by reason of its comparative lack of stylistic integrity or homogeneity, its attachment of new meaning to old motives, and its imita-

Figure 52 View of Amsterdam by A. Beerstraten, ca. 1660; painting in oil on canvas.

tion and incorporation of foreign forms, which induce a certain clumsy or awkward quality that is never present in truly primitive art.[35] The concept has wide application. In his discussion of sixteenth-century Dutch architecture, for instance, Ter Kuile refers to the "degeneration of style" that followed the introduction of Italian Renaissance forms and the consequent development of a "Dutch Mannerism" noteworthy for its exceedingly varied, fantastic, even grotesque ornamentation.[36] A similar tendency in seventeenth-century Russian architecture led, as we saw in the preceding chapter, to that overloading of ornament and fragmentation or degeneration of form which even sympathetic students of this architecture have observed.[37]

It suited the dominant nationalist school in Soviet historiography to minimize if not to deny any affiliation between the "Moscow Baroque" and Baroque architecture elsewhere. The adoption of this attitude had two positive results. One was to stress, more strongly than before, the essentially indigenous nature of the buildings in question while the other was to seek, with renewed vigor, documentary evidence in support of this view. Thus the careers of the leading native builders associated with the "Moscow Baroque"—Zarudnyi, Osip Startsev, Bukhvostov—underwent intensive study, albeit with limited results. Bukhvostov's biographer admits that next to nothing is known about his early life (including how and by whom he was trained) and that there is documentary evidence of his being in charge of constructing only a handful of buildings.[38] Thus too Grabar's conclusion, on the basis of fresh archival research, that at least three builders together with helpers and plans and prefabricated ornaments were dispatched from Moscow to Kiev in the 1690s, and that at least two Ukrainian builders in turn worked in Moscow in the first years of the eighteenth century: findings that tended to invalidate Grabar's earlier assertion of the dependence of the "Moscow Baroque" on Ukrainian prototypes. Indeed, until much more information is uncovered, Grabar now warned, "we are unable to establish a clear picture of . . . the architectural interrelations between Moscow and the Ukraine at this time."[39]

More recent research by Soviet scholars has continued to undermine various of the nationalist positions. The case of the putative architect Ivan Petrovich Zarudnyi was raised in Chapter 1. Writing in 1954, Grabar hailed Zarudnyi as the builder of the church of the Archangel Gabriel in Moscow (also known as the Menshikov Tower after the favorite of Peter I who commissioned it), which he acclaimed as "one of the greatest works of Russian architecture of all time." Here Grabar also attributed numerous other major monuments to Zarudnyi, including the church of the Sign at Dubrovitsy, the jewel of the "Moscow Baroque"; and stressed both the Russian roots and the "originality" of Zarudnyi's style as well as his "profound influence" on Russian builders down to the nineteenth century.[40] But it has since been confirmed that the church at Dubrovitsy (renovated in the 1840s) was built by Italian masters and that the influence of G. M. Fontana, an Italian architect recruited by Peter I, is to be detected in the Menshikov Tower; also, that the latter's original appearance, before the fire of 1723 and the rebuilding of the 1770s, was in the style rather of the "Petrine Baroque."[41] Similarly, the internal decoration and celebrated sculptures of both churches, like those of still a third example of the "Moscow Baroque," are now thought to have been done not by Zarudnyi or other local "innovators" (as Grabar had claimed) but by a group of Swiss-Italian artisans hired, again, by Peter I.[42] Among the many structures once attributed to Zarudnyi, in sum, only several iconostases and a few triumphal arches, all decidedly Petrine in character, survive critical scrutiny. Once held up as the outstanding exponent of an independent "Moscow Baroque" in Russian architecture, Zarudnyi is now classed as a skillful woodcarver and icon-painter in the employ of European masters imported by Peter I.[43]

A scholarly consensus regarding the nature and derivation of the "Moscow Baroque" in late seventeenth-century Russian architecture is at last emerging from the decades of research and debate. And among the most helpful contributions that have so far been published, it deserves repeating, are studies documenting both extensive Belorussian influence on many of the buildings in question and the use made by Russian builders of European graphic material.[44] As Hughes points out, it is a question not only of European publications dealing specifically with architecture but also of the numerous foreign books available in seventeenth-century Russia that were richly illustrated with both realistic and stylized architectural motives. Ilin is quoted in support of the view that the decorative details in "Moscow Baroque" architecture came primarily from books decorated with ornate title pages, headpieces, and tailpieces. Yet it was not a question solely of learned treatises or of their illustrations. The most easily obtainable material, especially for provincial Russian craftsmen, were the cheap European prints and broadsheets—*friazheskie* ("Italian") and *nemetskie* ("German") *listy*—which enjoyed increasing popularity in seventeenth-century Russia and could be bought in the streets of Moscow. Here again the concept of rusticalization readily applies for, in Hughes's words, given the "technical side of Russian architectural practice" it is likely that a "crudely executed column on a broadsheet provided the Russian craftsman with as much inspiration as a highly sophisticated diagram in a treatise." In fact, as she says,

> there is no evidence that seventeenth-century Russian builders grasped the theoretical implications of the Classical order system, still less the philosophical or mathematical aspects of Renaissance architecture; nor, indeed, is there much likelihood that they would have been able to read texts and captions in foreign languages. It is necessary to think in terms of the Russian craftsman deriving visual, rather than intellectual, stimulation from the books and drawings that may have fallen into his hands and incorporating those elements that pleased him into his own creations as naturally as he might copy features from a local building.

Similarly, Hughes argues, the most likely source of Ukrainian influence on the development of the "Moscow Baroque" lies in the stream of illustrated works—gospels, psalters, theses, collections of patristic homilies—issuing from Ukrainian presses in the seventeenth century and widely distributed in Russia, works in which Renaissance or Baroque architectural motives began to appear as early as 1624.[45]

The visual evidence advanced over the years by students of the "Moscow Baroque" to demonstrate its Baroqueness (or its Renaissance or Mannerist qualities) certainly testifies to the wide range of possible prototypes—Dutch, north German, Polish, Ukrainian, even Italian—reflected by various details or parts of these buildings. So does the growing body of evidence put before us by the progress of architectural history elsewhere, most particularly perhaps in Poland with respect to the lands of the Polish-Lithuanian Commonwealth of the sixteenth, seventeenth, and eighteenth centuries, lands that included Belorussia and much of the Ukraine (fig. 53).[46] But it must be emphasized that the documentary evidence so far adduced regarding the derivation of the "Moscow Baroque" points to two verifiable paths of diffusion, and only to two: first, the imported European and Ukrainian graphic material just mentioned; second, the work in Russia of Belorussian craftsmen, especially their elaborate iconostases. Moreover, this documentary evidence indicates what were at best indirect or tenuous processes of architectural diffusion, processes that only heightened the prospects for rusticalization; and even visual comparisons reveal—have always revealed—how limited are the similarities between the Muscovite buildings under review and their supposed counterparts in Europe. In short, most of these buildings constitute a highly ornate variant of late seventeenth-century Russian architecture, one that is distinguishable from the rest of contemporary Russian architecture by the more European character of various of its decorative features. In a few instances—the Menshikov Tower would seem to be one (pl. 17), the church at Dubrovitsy perhaps another (pl. 19)—these buildings represent very early examples of the new "Petrine Baroque" in Russian architecture, a style that displayed major structural as well as decorative innovations traceable directly to masters from Europe.

The haphazard, often profuse appearance of Classical decorative elements in buildings put up in and around Moscow in the 1680s and 1690s does not signify the advent of an original, independent, pre-Petrine Russian variant of European Baroque architecture. It signifies, rather, that in its architectural development as in other respects Russia's traditional isolation from the centers of European civilization was beginning rapidly to break down. The "Moscow Baroque" demonstrates, more clearly than anything we have so far observed, a striving for something new; just as it reveals, once again, an architecture in crisis. For a preference by the patrons of these buildings for European as distinct from Russian architectural forms is plain to see, a preference that can be taken to indicate a perception on their part of the comparative inferiority—aesthetic and/or

Figure 53 Town Hall, Chelmno, north-central Poland, 1567–1570.

technical—of Russian (Old-Russian) as against European (Renaissance, Mannerist, or Baroque) architecture. These patrons were members, as noted, of the topmost Russian elite, including the tsar himself, the youthful Peter I. And it is in the evidence thus provided of the changing taste of this elite that the ultimate historical significance of the "Moscow Baroque" surely lies: there, and in the role that it no doubt played in fueling the aspirations of those who would soon launch the Petrine revolution in Russian architecture.[47]

Nor should we forget, in moving on, the larger question before us. This book is concerned with the transfer to Russia not of a particular architectural style, call it the Baroque, but of a whole epoch in European architectural history in its major technical and material as well as aesthetic aspects, an epoch that began in Italy in the fifteenth century. The "Moscow Baroque" was a small, if significant, step on the way.

5
Revolutionary Transitions

But this is certain of them, they do not want a genius; besides
that, they are fond of imitation, let it be good or evil.
— Cornelis de Bruyn, Moscow, 1702[1]

The Petrine revolution in Russian architecture was prompted to a considerable
extent by pressing military needs, meaning the offensive and particularly the
defensive requirements of Peter I's campaigns against the Turks and especially
the Swedes. This aspect of the architectural revolution amounted in essence to
a revolution in Russian fortification and to the introduction of shipbuilding in
Russia. It was a revolution that saw the establishment in Russia of what contemporary Europeans already called—what Peter I and his associates would
learn to call—"military" and "naval" architecture.

"Modern" fortifications appeared in Europe itself following a revolution that
began, again, in fifteenth-century Italy. Responding to the growing range and
power of siege artillery, which rendered existing defenses obsolete, towers were
gradually reduced to wall-top level; the walls themselves were made lower and
thicker or set in wide, deep ditches from which only their upper parts projected;
and triangular or "arrowhead" bastions were pushed out from the walls to per-
mit defending artillery to sweep all approaches to the fort, which was now
preferably pentagonal in plan rather than square or rectangular (or irregular).
The guiding principle was one of horizontal rather than vertical defense, with
the bastion instead of the tower playing the key role: the batteries of up to four
cannon emplaced in each of the two flanks connecting the bastion's angular
head with the wall behind it—the curtain—protected both the curtain itself
and the slanting surfaces of the neighboring bastions. An entire city could be
ringed with bastions of the new type to provide a defensive system with no
blind spots. Then, the space beyond the ditch surrounding the bastioned enceinte or city wall might be invested with a long sloping glacis, tamped earth
ramparts, lunettes and ravelins: with outworks designed to protect additional
artillery emplacements and to provide a clear, ever longer and more sweeping
field of fire (fig. 54). Sieges again became lengthy, difficult, costly affairs. Warfare itself was now a series of sieges punctuated by battles between armies
brought face to face in the open only by some combination of maneuvering
skill, confidence, and logistical pressure.

Naturally, the revolution in fortification prompted a corresponding development of siegecraft. Vauban—Sebastien le Prestre de Vauban (1633–1707)—is
the leading figure here. Although he built or rebuilt several hundred strongholds for the French king and furnished his realm with a cordon of powerful
fortresses, Vauban's contemporary fame rested primarily on his achievements as

Figure 54 Fortified town of Gravelines, Flanders; engraving of 1699.

a specialist in sieges. It was said that no fortress could withstand an assault led by Vauban. His success in this field was owed mainly to his famous "system of parallels," whereby he advanced his troops and siege artillery in a series of carefully calculated and methodically executed movements under the protection of earthworks and trenches dug parallel to the defensive lines, until both troops and breaching batteries were securely established at the counterscarp or outer edge of the ditch surrounding the fortress under siege (fig. 55). As a designer of fortifications, in turn, Vauban's response to the greater firepower of siege artillery was to expand the ditch to 100 meters or more and fill it with enormous outworks, also built of brick, which dwarfed the bastions and assumed the chief burden of withstanding an assault. Following Vauban military architects especially in northern Europe—on the northern and northeastern frontiers of France—outdid one another in the invention of new and ever more complicated outworks. Hornworks and crownworks as well as the basic ravelins and lunettes, redans and demi-lunes, tenailles and double-tenailles sprouted around towns and fortresses in an ever greater profusion and near fantastical complexity. Sprawling fortification belts, many hundreds of meters wide, became a prominent feature of the eighteenth-century landscape.[2]

Positional or siege warfare thus came to rule military thinking in seventeenth-century Europe and permanent fortifications to replace provisional defenses, the latter usually a matter of earthen banks and wooden palisades. Even east of the Rhine and north of the Alps, areas where massive defenses were comparatively few and far between, the interlocked development of modern siegecraft and modern fortification gradually took hold. Here coastal positions were favored. The Polish-Swedish wars of 1626–1629 and 1655–1660 produced complete sets of bastioned defenses for the cities of Gdańsk (Danzig), Toruń, and Elbląg in Royal (Polish) Prussia, for instance.[3] Elsewhere in the Polish-Lithuanian Commonwealth, particularly in the Ukrainian lands vulnerable to Tatar or Turkish incursion, small forts of the new type arose; the hexagonal bastioned enceinte with outworks at Kodak on the Dnieper (fig. 56), built in

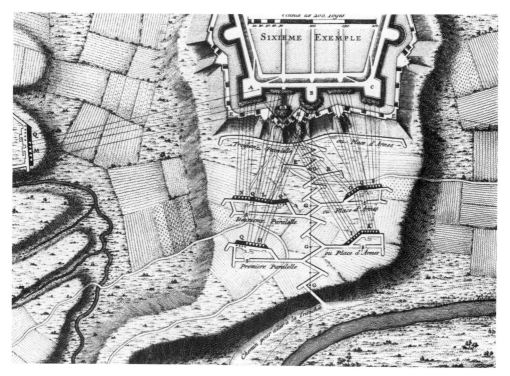

Figure 55 The "sixth example" from S. de Vauban, *De L'Attaque et de la défense des places.* Note defensive bastions A, B, C; a "petite demi-lune" at D and a "chemin couvert" at E; and, on the offensive side, breaching batteries at H, I, K, etc., as well as first, second, and third parallels, etc.

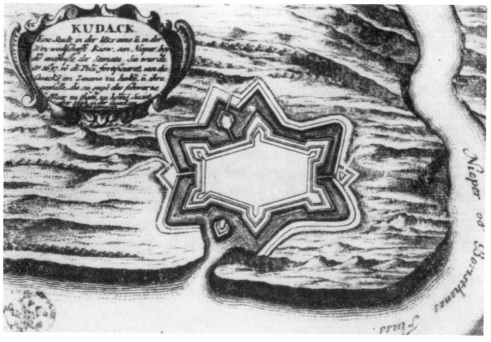

Figure 56 Fortress of Kodak on the Dnieper, 1638; drawing of 1652 by Beauplan.

1637 with the help of French engineers, is an example.[4] So too is the seventeenth-century Swedish fortress at Narva mentioned in Chapter 3, which in 1700 successfully withstood the siege of a large army under Peter I, turning the battle into a Russian rout.

Azov: New Fortification and Shipbuilding

Peter's ignominious defeat by the Swedes at Narva, entailing heavy losses of both men and materiel, impressed on him the necessity of mastering the techniques of modern warfare if he and his dynasty, and possibly even the Russian state, were to survive. The history of the rest of his reign, and particularly of the long "Swedish War" (1700–1721), as the Russians called it, amply bears this out. Yet Peter's personal interest in what he would learn to call "military" and "naval" as distinct from "civil" architecture went back to the 1680s, and was steadily strengthened by both success and adversity. In his preface to the *Naval Statute* of 1720 he recalled how as a youth he "eagerly undertook to learn geometry and fortification [*fortofikatsiia*]" from a Dutchman in his entourage;[5] while official records of the time indicate that between 1684 and 1687 funds were advanced for the construction of a miniature fortified town or "play citadel" at Preobrazhenskoe, the suburban royal estate where Peter spent much of his adolescence.[6] This was the "capital city of Pressburg [*Presshpurkh*]," as he called it,[7] a fort built for the purposes of his war games and designed, a contemporary drawing leaves no doubt (fig. 57), under direct European influence. A similar five-sided structure of earthen ramparts surrounded by ditch and outworks was constructed near the royal village of Kolomenskoe, the site of elaborate military exercises in the fall of 1694.[8] The design of these fortifications is usually attributed to General Patrick Gordon, a Scotsman hired many years before by Peter's father and the young Peter's closest military advisor. But Gordon himself, in a neglected account of the matter, says that Peter "had himself drawn out" the plan of the fort "and caused [it] to be built" in the fall of 1693; that under Peter's orders it was "fortifyed with all sort of newfang. outworks and things requisite for a defense" in the fall of 1694; and that the ensuing siege, directed by Peter and costing a number of casualties, was "looked upon as a preludium of some important business in hand."[9]

The "important business in hand" proved to be the Russian campaigns of 1695 and 1696 against Azov (in Turkish, Azak), an Ottoman town located at the mouth of the river Don close to the Ottoman-Russian frontier. Azov had been captured by a force of Russian (Don) and Ukrainian Cossacks in 1637 with the help of a German engineer and retaken by the Turks in 1642, since when it had been heavily refortified. On the basis of contemporary sources, including Gordon's published diary, the historian Bogoslovskii describes the fortifications at Azov as they stood in 1695:

> The main fortress was a quadrangular masonry structure with bastions and a separate masonry stronghold located within it. Beyond the walls Azov was

Figure 57 "Siege" of the "citadel" of "Presshpurkh," with the young Peter I (presumably) on horseback. From an early eighteenth-century manuscript.

protected by an earthen rampart with ditch and palisade. These were ringed at distances of 500 and 1,000 meters by two further earthen ramparts, the remains of earlier sieges. About three kilometers above Azov two masonry towers [kalanchi, from Turkish kalantsha] had been raised on either bank of the Don and armed with cannon. Joined by three thick iron chains stretched across the river's channel, these towers blocked the exit to the sea for any vessels descending the Don. Another masonry fort, called Liutik, had been built on the north branch of the river. It was a regular structure comprising masonry walls of from thirty-eight to forty-one meters in length, four octagonal towers roofed in wood, and corner doors plated in iron. A mosque and living quarters for the commandant and officers were located in the middle of Liutik, which was surrounded, on the three sides not facing the river, by earthen ramparts and a ditch filled with water. Both this fort and the *kalanchi*, General Gordon tells us, were built in 1663 on the sultan's orders to prevent the Don Cossacks from gaining access to the sea of Azov.[10]

From this description it appears that the Ottoman fortifications at Azov were more transitional than modern in structure and design, a case of older defenses being strengthened by more modern additions (fig. 58). General Gordon elsewhere reveals that on finally taking the town, in 1696, his engineers set about "fortifying the old wall in a more regular way, with a large ravelin before the gate."[11] Still, it is likely that the Ottoman fortifications at Azov were the most advanced that the young Tsar Peter had as yet seen. Less than a year later (1697), in recounting his victory to a merchant in Holland, Peter would sketch the Azov area calling special attention to the watchtowers—the *kalanchi*—above the town and to his new-style additions to them (fig. 59). And even twenty years later, in recording a dream of the night before, Peter would recall that during the siege of Azov he had "approached the *kalanchi*" and had found them to be built "in accord with [the principles of] good architecture [*po khorosheiu arkhitekturoiu*]."[12]

Peter's ambitious plans for Azov, which clearly reflect contemporary European architectural norms and were to be executed by hundreds of builders recruited in Europe, called for extensive renovation of the existing defenses and for the construction of wholly new fortifications in and around the town (fig. 60). Azov was to become a major Russian port and military base as well as the seat of a senior bishop (metropolitan)—a kind of second capital, it would seem. Moreover, Peter's legislation affecting Azov and particularly his correspondence with its newly appointed governor, I. A. Tolstoi, reveal his close personal supervision of all the new building there.[13] A certain Major "Iagan Breklin"—obviously German (Johann Bröklin?)—was put in charge of military construction, and Peter's instructions to him abound in such terms as *bastion, flank, ravelin,* and *kontro shkarp,* all in Russian (Cyrillic) script. To his orders to the major of April 10, 1706, Peter attached his own design sketch with the subscript, "Build the *sitadel* like this, in stone" (fig. 61).[14]

To be sure, as Peter became steadily more absorbed in his war against the Swedish king and then in the building of St. Petersburg, the projects at Azov and elsewhere on territory newly conquered from the Turks languished, and were abandoned altogether following the Russian defeat by the Turks at the battle near the river Pruth, in Moldavia, in 1711. Yet the Azov campaigns and building projects were of crucial importance in the architectural history of the period. For it was in the conquest and reconstruction of Azov that Peter first seriously utilized the techniques of modern siegecraft and fortification, and first faced the problems of modern town planning. And these were experiences he was later to draw on to good if not brilliant effect, particularly in the building of St. Petersburg.[15]

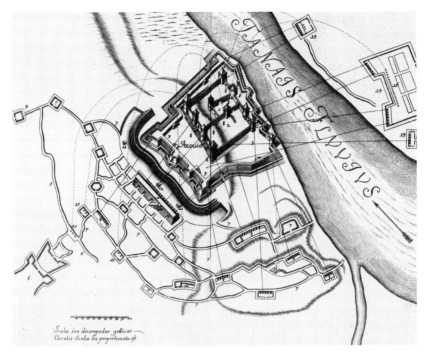

Figure 58 Russian siege of Azov, 1696; contemporary engraving. Note the inner, traditional (medieval) square fortress with high towers surrounded by modern bastioned walls and ditch and (out front) earthen rampart with ditch; the ensemble is surrounded in turn by modern Russian siege works.

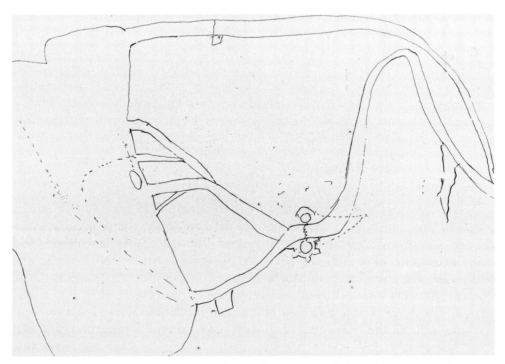

Figure 59 Drawing by Peter I of the Don river delta, indicating twin Turkish watchtowers above Azov taken by the Russians in 1696 and their projected new-style fortifications.

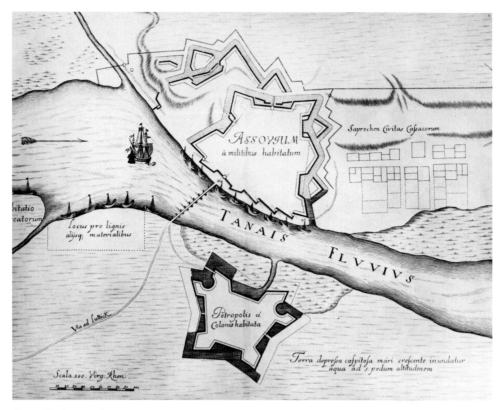

Figure 60 Projected Russian fortifications at Azov, ca. 1698; contemporary engraving. Note, center below, the new Russian settlement or "colony" to be called "Petropolis."

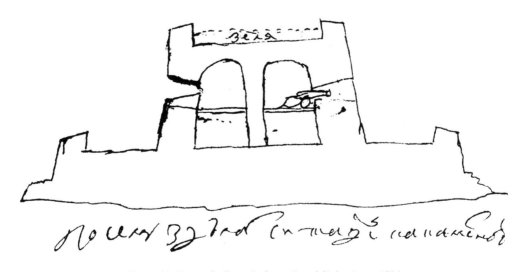

Figure 61 Design by Peter I of new "citadel" for Azov, 1706.

It was also in connection with the second Azov campaign that Peter first immersed himself in the problems of shipbuilding, or naval architecture—*ar-khitektura navalis*—as he would come to call it.[16] According to Patrick Gordon, who was in a position to know, the victory at Azov was owed primarily to the thoroughness of Peter's preparations in this regard: "A fleet built, fitted, manned and provided with all sorts of ammunition, artillerie, and provisions to superfluity was his Majesty's particular care, and incredible allmost . . . that they were built and ready in so little time"; indeed, "the building of galleys being a thing impracticable in this country and thought by many impossible to be brought to perfection, yet by the extraordinary care and indefatigable industry of his Czarish Majesty 20 to 30 galleys and lesser craft were in a short time in good forwardness": their hulls having been built "according to a modell brought from Holland" by carpenters "fetched up" from the Dutch merchant fleet wintering at Archangel.[17] Peter had earlier begun building ships with Dutch help at Archangel; but Voronezh, located east and south of Moscow on a tributary of the Don, was the site of the frenetic activity of the late winter and spring of 1696. As Peter himself would later record it, "skilled craftsmen from England and Holland were summoned" to Voronezh and in 1696 "a new thing began in Russia: the construction at great effort of ships, galleys, and other vessels." And to establish the business on a firm footing, Peter wrote further, he "purposed to introduce this art to his people," for which reason he sent "a large number of noblemen to Holland and other countries to study [naval] architecture and navigation [*arkhitektura i upravlenie korabel'noe*]."[18]

In 1696 and for several years thereafter the shipyards of Voronezh were the focus of a systematic effort to build a fleet of up-to-date warships for deployment on the sea of Azov and from there, perhaps, on the Black Sea itself (fig. 62). In December 1696 Peter appointed A. P. Protasev to the newly created post of *Admiralteits* (cf. Dutch *Admiraliteit* or German *Admiralität*, meaning Admiralty); his instructions were to organize in and around Voronezh, with "German" help, the construction of fifty-two warships and to establish to this end an "Admiralty Office [*Admiralteiskii dvor*],"[19] the first such office in Russian history. Meanwhile some 122 young Russians were sent to Europe to study navigation and ship-building (more than half of them to Venice, the rest to England and the Netherlands), and dozens of European shipwrights—Dutch, English, Danish, Swedish, Italian—were imported to work at Voronezh. But things did not go well. Owing to a shortage of skilled local labor, inefficient management (Protasev was soon cashiered), disputes among the foreign experts, and other factors, the ships produced at Voronezh were more or less unseaworthy. The English ambassador to Moscow blamed it all on the first batch of Italian and Dutch shipwrights, "who for want of experience, dry timber, and sufficient time, as well as for their private gain, ran up the vessels very slightly with green and bad stuff, so that they decay'd before they were finished, which the Czar perceived at his return from Great Britain" (in 1698), whereupon English shipwrights were put in charge.[20]

Figure 62 New Russian warships, ca. 1698; contemporary engravings. Note traditional dress of commanders and guards on the poop decks.

Be that as it may, the Dutch traveler Cornelis de Bruyn, visiting Voronezh in 1703, was impressed by the extent of its "conveniences for shipbuilding" and by the "great storehouse" there "full of all sorts of naval stores, each in a place apart, even to cloaths for the seamen, and everything else they can want." He recorded seeing fifteen ships in the water (including "four men of war, the biggest of 54 guns") and another twelve on shore ready to be launched ("five men of war after the Dutch fashion, from 60–64 guns; two after the Italian, from 50 to 54; a galeass after the Venetian, and four gallies"); and he counted seventeen galleys at a second yard near the town. "Besides all this," Bruyn reported further, "they were at work upon five men of war after the English built," one of which was named in honor of Peter I himself "because he had the direction of her upon the stocks"; while "ashore on the other side of the river were about 200 brigantines, most of them" also built at Voronezh.[21]

Peter I's lifelong interest in all aspects of shipbuilding; his close supervision of the shipyards he founded at Archangel, Voronezh, Kazan (on the Volga),

St. Petersburg, and elsewhere in his dominions; his heavy reliance in these matters on Italian, Dutch, and especially English shipwrights, craftsmen, and other experts: all this can be readily documented.[22] So could Peter's growing appreciation of the benefits of maritime trade and of the importance of a navy, and his ability to use a wide range of nautical terms of Italian, Dutch, and English provenance, terms that for the most part permanently entered the Russian language. But here it should be stressed that if today naval like military construction is considered a branch of engineering rather than architecture, the distinction was not so clear in Peter's time, as a glance at the fortifications of the period or at detailed drawings of contemporary warships and merchantmen readily confirms. Nor was any such distinction made at the time. Indeed, it was Peter's early attraction to shipbuilding as well as to siegecraft and fortification that first brought him into close contact with building as it was practiced in Europe, and with the language and techniques of the new architecture. The establishment under Peter I of naval architecture in Russia together with the creation of a Russian shipbuilding industry—and some 1,260 seagoing vessels were built in Russian shipyards between 1688 and 1725[23]—were among the outstanding achievements of the reign, a point that should not be lost sight of in our more extended discussion of related developments in military and especially civil architecture.

A Revolution in Military Architecture

Peter I's return to Moscow in 1698 from his lengthy stay in Europe was preceded by the arrival of hundreds of specialists whom he had hired there. A sense of the suddenness with which they arrived and of the numbers involved is reflected in the dispatches of the new Danish resident, Poul Heins. "Nearly 800 people of all sorts have come," he reported from Moscow on July 8, "for the most part sailors, cannoneers, and others whom the tsar took into his service in Holland." By July 29, "a quantity of all sorts of people whom the tsar has taken into his service in England and Holland" was arriving "every day—engineers, architects, bombardiers, officers"; indeed, "such a great quantity" had come that some of the experts had to be "sent back for lack of employment."[24] Hundreds of those who stayed, as indicated earlier, proceeded to Azov, to work on the various building projects there. Others, as Heins noted, were sent elsewhere—to Smolensk and Kiev, for example, to direct the construction of new fortifications; or further south, to build a canal linking the Volga with the Don, a scheme unprecedented in Russia in its technical (if not its imaginative) dimensions.[25]

In Moscow itself the most important military project of the earlier years of Peter's reign was the building of the "Tseikhgauz" (cf. German *Zeughaus*), a vast new arsenal for which a plan was drawn up in 1701.[26] The records of the responsible governmental office, the Armory Chamber, are instructive:

> On January 20 of this year 1702 all manner of supplies were brought into the Kremlin for the construction of this Tseikhous. . . . And from February 1 of this year 1702 it was ordered to level [certain] old stone buildings and to build anew on these sites, following the design of the said Tseikhous, under the supervision of Ivan Saltanov of the service-nobility and of the painter Mikhail Choglokov of the Armory Chamber. . . . And with them is to be, for [the making of] all architectural measurements in the construction of this house, and for the supervision of the stonemasons, the Saxon masterbuilder Kristofor Kundurat [Christopher Conrad].[27]

Conrad had been commissioned, it is clear, both to build the new arsenal and to instruct his Russian masons "in the German manner" of building. He did so until 1714, when he was sent to St. Petersburg, returning to his work in Moscow only in 1722. Conrad has been criticized as a "mediocre builder" whose mistakes had to be corrected by his more experienced Russian associates, particularly Choglokov; and it is now thought that the "Tseikhgauz" (modern Russian *Tseigauz* or *Arsenal*) was completed only in 1736, under the noted German architect, Shumacher[28] (its appearance today is the result of still later restorations). Whatever the truth of the matter, completing the project took second place to military construction elsewhere. As Weber, the German diplomat, would observe when in Moscow, in 1719: "Seventeen years ago an Arsenal of extraordinary bigness and strength was begun to be built by the Czar's orders, of which now appear only the foundations and the outwalls, the rest remaining unfinished, since the Czar set his mind upon the building of Petersbourg."[29] In fact, the only other major military project carried out in the old capital during the Petrine period was the erection in 1707–1708, in response to a sudden fear of Swedish invasion, of extensive earthen ramparts around the Kremlin and Kitai-gorod, a system dominated by eighteen modern bastions (fig. 14). The work of some 30,000 conscripted laborers, the design reflecting European direction, these fortifications constituted the single most ambitious defensive project as yet undertaken in Russia (they were pulled down between 1817 and 1823).[30]

A similar if much less extensive system of earthen ramparts and bastions was put up around the old castle of Noteborg soon after it was taken by Russian forces in the autumn of 1702. Noteborg—Oreshek (or Orekhov) in Russian—was located at the source of the Neva river, on Lake Ladoga, on the northwestern frontier of the tsar's dominions (fig. 12). Whether for lack of a foreign expert whom he could trust or of a Russian master who could do the job, Peter I himself initially designed the new fortifications there, as surviving graphic material shows (fig. 63). Peter also personally directed the taking of Noteborg, an event recorded in a detailed engraving by a Dutch artist in his service, A. Schoonebeeck. The engraving indicates among other things that Russian siegecraft continued to improve in accordance with contemporary European norms (cf. fig. 64).

Peter renamed the renovated fortress *"Shlissel'burg"* or "Key-stronghold" (German *Schlüssel* plus *burg*), no doubt to signify both its strategic importance

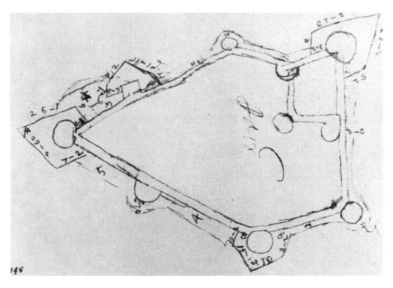

Figure 63 Design by Peter I of new fortifications for Noteborg/Shlissel'burg, 1702.

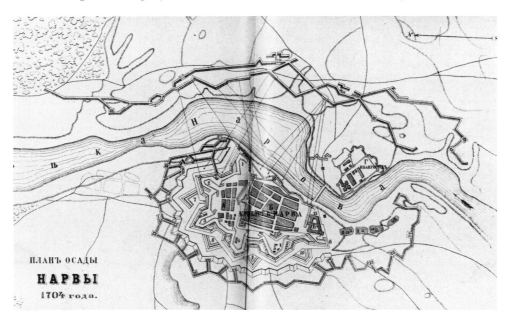

Figure 64 Plan of the successful Russian siege of Narva, 1704. The elaborate siegeworks (above) are shown across the river Narova from the complex Swedish defenses of the town. The old castle of Ivangorod is center right, again on the Russian side of the river.

and his overall policy of Europeanization. Wooden barracks, storehouses, a commandant's residence as well as walls and towers were put up by Russian builders at various times until 1716, when the foundations of permanent masonry structures were laid. In 1721 overall direction of construction was given to Trezzini, the first important architect of St. Petersburg, as we will see; and following his plans a barracks and treasury, a palace for Peter I, and a new commandant's house and bell tower were completed. And thus was completed the step-by-step transformation of the medieval castle of Noteborg into the new-style fortress of Shlisselburg. In this way, too, numerous other Swedish strongholds in the Baltic littoral were renovated in the first years of the eighteenth century, with or without expert foreign guidance.[31]

From an architectural point of view the most important fortifications erected under Peter I were located in and near St. Petersburg. Yet already it is clear that the renovations at Azov and at Noteborg/Shlisselburg, like the new fortifications at Moscow, Novgorod, Smolensk, and Kiev referred to above—like the fortress of the New Dvina built in these years to guard the harbor at Archangel (fig. 65)—all signaled the onset of a momentous change in Russian military construction. Defense works like these were to be found everywhere in the contemporary European world but not elsewhere in the tsar's dominions, where fortifications of the modern type were at best prefigured in those isolated works built in the seventeenth century under foreign experts that were mentioned in Chapter 3. The direct line of development in Russia of modern military architecture began with Peter I's "play fort" of the 1680s at Preobrazhenskoe and the similar structure of the early 1690s erected near Kolomenskoe; proceeded with the renovations undertaken most notably at Azov (after 1696) and Noteborg/Shlisselburg (from 1702); and thence gathered force, as later chapters will show, until by the middle of the eighteenth century it encompassed all military construction of any importance undertaken anywhere in the Russian Empire. The record—graphic, archaelogical, documentary—is remarkably clear.

To be sure, it was more than the accident of Peter I's personal interest in fortification that inspired this revolution in Russian military architecture. Es-

Figure 65 Fortress of the New Dvina, near Archangel, ca. 1703, drawn by C. de Bruyn.

pecially in view of the early course of the Russo-Swedish war, when, it bears repeating, the survival of Peter's monarchy and perhaps of the Russian state hung in the balance, upgrading the realm's defenses was an obvious and urgent priority. This fact has been emphasized by scholars—as has the fact that in the east and north, away from the "front lines," early Petrine fortification continued to reflect traditional Russian norms. Nor should it be difficult to see why Peter had recourse in this matter to European models and plans, to European specialists, to European terminology. Traditional Russian methods and designs would have been of little or no avail in the face of the Swedish threat (or at Azov); European expertise, unlike, say, Turkish or Chinese, was readily available; and there was, as we have seen, some precedent. While not denying the farsighted determination and astonishing energy of Peter himself, it can be said that the Petrine revolution in Russian military architecture was at bottom a matter of historical necessity.

NEW CURRENTS IN CIVIL ARCHITECTURE

The early years of Peter's reign also witnessed the construction of important civil buildings. Examples of such buildings in and around Moscow include, apart from various churches, the Main Pharmacy, the Sukharev Tower, the mansions of V. V. Golitsyn, M. P. Gagarin, B. P. Sheremetev, and F. M. Apraksin, and—in or near the German "Liberty" or Settlement—the palaces of F. A. Golovin and François Lefort, all of whom were leading officials or favorites of the young tsar. Among these buildings only Lefort's palace survives today, in much altered form, housing the historical archives of the Ministry of Defense. The Sukharev Tower and Golitsyn mansion survived until the 1930s and so could be photographed, as could the Main Pharmacy, which was pulled down in 1874. What little we know of the other buildings in question is owed to a few graphic or written references.

The building housing the Main Pharmacy was begun at Peter I's direction in 1699, in Red Square, on the site of the present Historical Museum (which dates to 1883). It was described by a Dutch observer in 1707 as "a large stone structure" and one that was, all considered,

> a very fine building, with a beautiful tower in front. . . . Its entryway lies through a large base court, at the end of which is a great staircase that leads to the first apartment, which is vaulted and very lofty. . . . There are also beautiful halls here, finely vaulted, and particularly two which are identical in structure, one of them serving as a laboratory and the other, as a library.[32]

Weber, the German diplomat, visiting the building in 1716, similarly found it "one of the most splendid in the city."[33] He also noted that the director of the Main Pharmacy at this time was a Scotsman, Dr. Areskine (or Ereskine), Peter I's personal physician, who no doubt influenced the design of the building or at least its internal layout and furnishings. Pictures of its exterior (fig. 66) present a central structure of three stories topped by a tiered tower in the Netherlandish style of the "Moscow Baroque" and flanked on either side by rectangular two-story wings. The walls were decorated with tiles, the rows of windows with pilasters and pediments, the facade with entablature and ornamental columns standing on high pedestals. In its use of these decorative elements the Main Pharmacy was a good example of late seventeenth-century Muscovite architecture; but in its scale and symmetry or regularity of design, and perhaps in the fineness of the vaulting, it was not.[34]

Much the same can be said (so far as anything definite can be said) of the original Lefort palace in Moscow's German Settlement, which inspired Remezov's governmental headquarters at Tobolsk (Chap. 3). The palace was built facing a tributary of the Moscow river, the Iauza, in 1697–1698, under D. V. Aksamitov, acting on orders from Peter I, who gave the building to Lefort; and its mixed, Muscovite-European (notably, -Dutch) character extended to the interior, where in spite of the European decorative details the layout of the main rooms with their large corner stoves and particularly the position in the banqueting hall of the head table—solitary, on a dais, off in one corner—reflected Russian custom. In 1706, Lefort having died, Peter gave the palace to Prince Menshikov, for whom it was greatly expanded and redesigned in 1707–1708, apparently under the direction of G. M. Fontana. And so began its transformation into the ponderous, oddly Classical structure to be seen today.[35]

Figure 66   Main Pharmacy, Moscow, 1699–1705; nineteenth-century drawing.

The Sukharev Tower, on the other hand, was essentially a late Old-Russian building, its European elements—"German Renaissance," in Grabar's telling phrase—reflecting thorough rusticalization (fig. 67). It was erected between 1692 and 1701 on Peter I's orders—he is said personally to have taken part in its construction—and under the overall direction, apparently, of Choglokov. It served primarily as a gatehouse in Moscow's outermost ramparts at the point where the main road down from the north, still the great trade route with Europe, entered the city; and it evidently took its name from the regiment of

Figure 67 Sukharev Tower, Moscow, 1692–1701; nineteenth-century drawing.

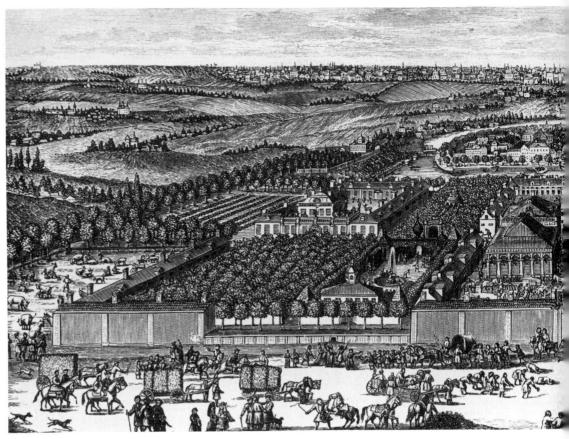

Figure 68 View of F. A. Golovin estate, suburban Moscow, ca. 1700; engraving before 1706 by Henryk de Witte and (?) G. M. Fontana. Moscow's skyline is visible in the far distance as is, middle distance, on the banks of the winding Iauza, the German Settlement with—large structure to the extreme right—the Lefort (later Menshikov) palace.

musketeers commanded by L. P. Sukharev who were responsible for maintaining this section of the city's defenses. The building's high, arcaded ground story or socle, through which the gateway itself ran, was surmounted by a two-story structure surrounded by an open gallery which connected to the ground by a wide, typically Old-Russian exterior staircase. This central structure was surmounted in turn by a multistoried polygonal tower complete with a clock and tent roof, making the whole building one of the two or three tallest in Moscow at the time. Its decorative program, evoking in places the "Moscow Baroque" (pl. 52), consisted of pilasters and pediments, columns and balustrades all carved in white stone, which contrasted sharply with the basic red brick of the building. In 1701 Peter established his new School of Mathematics and Navigation in the tower, whose premises had been specially expanded for the purpose.[36]

Very little is known about any of the other important secular buildings put up in and around Moscow in the earlier years of Peter I's reign. An engraving

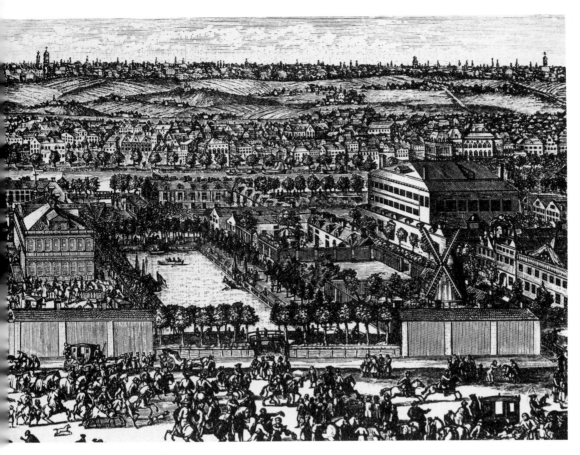

(Figure 68 continued)

from before 1706 pictures the handsome suburban estate, long since disappeared, of F. A. (later Count) Golovin, with its decidedly European or perhaps Dutch-style buildings and ornamental plantings, windmill (new to Russia), basin with balustrade, topiaries, and fountain (fig. 68; also fig. 23). The mansion in Kitai-gorod acquired by Field-Marshal B. P. Sheremetev in 1700 appears to have been built in the 1670s, a "typical boyar dwelling" of the day which Sheremetev then updated notably by the addition of extensive stucco molding in the new "Petrine" style.[37] The correspondence of another grandee, Admiral F. M. Apraksin, reveals that in 1712 a spacious and fireproof mansion was being built for him in Belyi-gorod (Moscow) in the "Prussian manner" after detailed drawings by a "fine Italian architect [G. M. Fontana?]."[38] It is not known whether the project was ever completed. Between 1705 and 1709 the house that had belonged to another senior official, Averkii Kirillov (died 1682), was rebuilt in an obvious attempt to incorporate newly fashionable forms, mainly by making the central facade symmetrical and by adding an attic adorned with dashing volutes (pls. 53A–B). The similarity of the ornamentation here with that of the so-called Menshikov Tower (pl. 23) once led scholars to attribute the rebuilding of Kirillov's house to I. P. Zarudnyi; but now it is accepted that the similarity points rather to the work of Italian masters.[39] It was mentioned earlier in this book that the Menshikov Tower's elaborate internal ornamentation in European and particularly Italian Baroque modes was almost certainly the work of Italian artisans led by G. M. Fontana.

Indeed, the increasingly European character of the decorative program of early Petrine buildings in Moscow, both secular and ecclesiastical, is striking. Ilin proposes that the root of the new trend is to be found in the triumphal arches erected in the city to celebrate Peter I's military victories, beginning with the conquest of Azov (1696). Fully Baroque in both form and detail, executed by skilled local carvers on the basis of European designs, and never before seen in Moscow, the successive triumphal arches marking Petrine victories (fig. 69) are thought to have inspired Muscovite builders of the early eighteenth century in the way that the Belorussian iconostases of the later seventeenth century inspired the builders of the "Moscow Baroque." It is a promising theory.[40]

Figure 69 Triumphal arch designed by I. P. Zarudnyi and erected in Moscow—in the German Settlement, near the Lefort/Menshikov palace—in 1709 in honor of the recent Russian victory over the Swedes at Poltava; contemporary engraving.

More to the point here, the secular buildings just discussed, like the contemporary churches of the "Moscow Baroque" discussed in the preceding chapter, were all closely connected with members of the topmost Russian elite if not with the tsar himself (in addition to the Sukharev Tower, Peter I personally helped to build at least two of these churches and endowed several others). The fact that Italian masters participated directly in the building or rebuilding of various of these structures should also be stressed, since this had not occurred in Russia for about 200 years. Finally, the 1680s and 1690s were a time of extensive masonry construction by the inhabitants of Moscow's German Settlement, a develpment that did not pass unnoticed by members of the Russian elite and particularly not by Peter I, who spent much of his time during these same years in the Settlement. We recall in this connection the Czech visitor's reference of the late 1680s to the "many large and beautiful stone houses recently built by Germans and Dutchmen for their habitation,"[41] and the impressive graphic evidence of De Witte's panoramic depiction of the Settlement and nearby Golovin estate of about 1700 (fig. 68).

In short, the striking European influence that can be observed and partly documented in Russian official and court buildings of the turn of the seventeenth century (including churches of the "Moscow Baroque") testifies unmistakably to a growing preference by Peter I and his relations, officials, and friends for European rather than local (or traditional) architectural forms. The evidence begins to suggest, indeed, that a definite movement was under way, a full-scale transition to something new. At the same time, naturally, their exposure in and around Moscow to architecture that was increasingly influenced by European norms conditioned the first direct experience by Peter and his associates of architecture in Europe, where their taste for what they were beginning to call the "new style [novaia moda]" was confirmed.[42]

A Convergence of Taste

In 1697 Peter I sent some 122 Russians to Europe to study navigation, shipbuilding, and related subjects—one party, comprising seventy-eight "volunteers," to Venice, the rest to England and Holland. The express purpose of their visit did not include study of civil architecture; and thus one of the volunteers, Prince B. I. Kurakin, recorded in his autobiography that in Venice between 1697 and 1699 he dutifully applied himself to the "mathematical arts" as well as *"fortofikatsii ofen'sivy* [and] *difensivy."*[43] Yet from the diaries of his later travels as an ambassador of Peter I it is clear that since his first trip to Europe Kurakin had developed a keen eye for civil as well as military architecture and that his standards in both respects, indeed his vocabulary, had been Europeanized. In various entries of 1705 for instance he notes that the old stone walls of Smolensk were now surrounded by newly built "earthen fortifications, counterscarp and ditch, and palisades [*fortetsa zemlianaia, kontra-shkarp i fossa, i s politsaty*]"; that the "old earthen castle" built under Peter I's father at Polotsk had required reinforcement "with fascines [*fashinami*]"; that in the suburbs of Vilnius were to be found numerous "fine houses" and notably the "splendid" new house of the governor, with its gardens and "fountains [*fontany*]"; that Königsberg was "exceeding well fortified [*ufortifikovano*]"; that the royal palace in Berlin, "though as yet unfinished, and not large, is regularly [*regularno*] built" while the newly erected Ritterakademie was "not very nice"; that the bridge across the Elbe at Dresden was "very fine, in stone"; and so on, repeatedly, often in some detail, at every stop on the way.[44]

Kurakin was not alone in this respect. Far and away the most revealing Russian account of traveling in Europe at the end of the seventeenth century was left by P. A. (later Count) Tolstoi, who had been sent by Peter I to Venice to learn navigation. Tolstoi was over fifty years old when he left Moscow in February 1697 (to return in November 1699), and his diary of his journey has an amplitude and attention to detail that make it unique among such documents (in its printed form it occupies some 300 pages). Most interesting here, of course, are Tolstoi's many and increasingly enthusiastic observations of the architecture he encountered on route.[45]

After leaving Moscow he stayed one night at Viazma, where he noted the "two wooden *goroda*, the big one with five masonry towers and within, two masonry churches; and beyond it, a monastery with wooden walls and masonry church." That was all. At Smolensk the "prodigious" fortifications were observed—the sole instance in Tolstoi's account of his travels of a positive adjective applied to building in Russia. The first city seen on Polish (Belorussian) territory, Mogilev (Mahiloŭ), was "much larger than Smolensk" but had only earthen walls and "no round towers." Minsk, traversed next, was "much smaller than Mogilev" and its governor's residence was "wooden", although some masonry houses were noted and the "fine vaults" and "marvelous construction" of two churches were admired. Approaching Warsaw by way of Slonim—"a sizable place, but no large fine buildings"—Tolstoi noticed the "wooden houses" in the capital's suburbs. Yet Warsaw itself, a "large place" dominated by its royal castle "well made of masonry" (fig. 70), had within it "many marvelous gardens" as well as "numerous masonry churches and cloisters" and "quite a few large senatorial houses of fine masonry construction"; in fact, "the houses in Warsaw and all the building in the castle are all masonry: the houses handsome and tall, many are four stories high, and all face the street." Outside Warsaw in a grandee's garden Tolstoi found a "large and most amazing structure spouting much water." It was essentially a "bath" surrounded by pavilions and "fountains [*fontany*] of wondrous and rich construction." The walls of the structure were "all of plaster beautifully worked like carved alabaster" and in many places were "decorated with shells and great mirrors" and furnished with "other wonderful things impossible to describe in detail—handsome stoves, a coffee-house trimmed in plaster of the most splendid craftsmanship, numerous fine ornaments, the finest tables, handsome chairs, magnificent paintings. . . ."

Already in Poland, in remarks for instance at the great monastery-shrine of

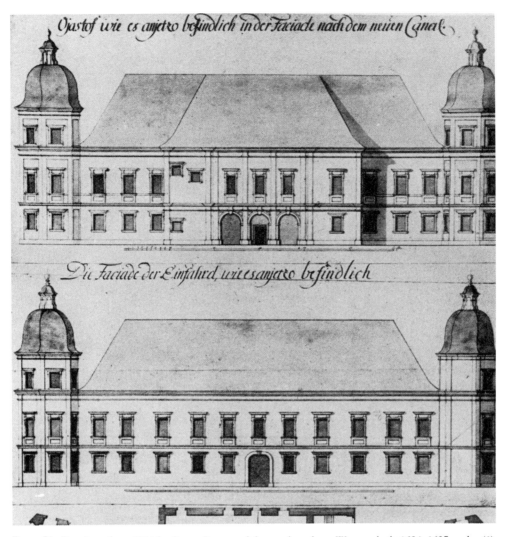

Figure 70 Drawing of ca. 1724 by Saxon Bauamt of the royal castle at Warsaw, built 1624–1627 under (?) Matteo Castelli, architect.

Częstochowa, Tolstoi was learning to distinguish a "fine Italian style" in architecture, a matter preeminently of marble construction or facing, great rounded arches and vaults, "most wondrous" plaster modeling, and "marvelous painting." In Vienna similarly he found much to admire, most especially the streetlights—"lanterns fixed along all the streets and alleys burning oil all night long"—and a "tall column of carved alabaster and modeled plaster of most wondrous Italian workmanship"; also, the public fountains flowing with "wondrously pure water" and, evidently another first for Tolstoi, a "*shpital*, that is, a kind of almshouse or sickhouse." The hospital is described in detail—"numerous beds of fine carpentry in an exceedingly long hall [where] the sick people lie," etc.—as is a skeleton "under glass in an icon-case": this an affair of "human bones arranged in an appropriate way and linked by copper wire." The "enormous and splendidly laid out" Imperial gardens outside Vienna excited Tolstoi's view, with their "wondrous things" holding various flowers and herbs, the great variety of fruit trees "planted in proportion [*po proportsii*]," and the lemon and pomegranate trees standing in rows in "fine great masonry pots," all providing a "most splendid perspective [*preshpektiva*]." Here too were "many copper columns fairly made like male and female humans." Indeed, this had all been done "architecturally [*arkhitektural'no*]" (figs. 71, 72).

Venice was "stupendous," its "domestic building all of the most marvelous masonry and great size, and of such rich and harmonious construction as can be found in few places in the world." The basilica of San Vittore in Milan (1560–1566) was of "miraculous workmanship . . . all of carved alabaster. Inside, one altar is most marvelously made of the most marvelous black marble." In another church in Milan the "wonderful paintings in the Italian style" were particularly noted; in the city's main library, it was the "images finely carved from alabaster and various materials and of modeled plaster"; also, the "human likenesses carved of white marble and various military things on a panel of such marvelous workmanship that nobody could describe the like." Milan had a "most excellent rampart around it, many fortifications, churches, monasteries, and houses of marvelous masonry construction and nothing built of wood.' Similarly, the town walls of Naples were of "handsome masonry construction, as are all the houses, and nothing is of wood." Outside Naples a Jesuit church was "handsomely decorated in various marbles and alabaster, with gilded vaults and walls, and two large and magnificent organs [*argany*]."

In Rome, seemingly everything that Tolstoi saw both pleased and amazed him. There was Bernini's "large and wide masonry bridge marvelously built" over the Tiber near the Castel S. Angelo, with its "most wondrously crafted masonry [balustrades] and iron railings on both sides, and with six columns to either [balustrade] atop which stand angels finely carved of alabaster." Palaces, libraries, academies, hospitals, public squares and fountains are described by Tolstoi, fountains "from which wonderfully clear and cool water constantly flows," fountains "equipped with such magnificent figures that for their multitude nobody could truly describe them; indeed, should someone want to see all the fountains in Rome he would have to stay two or three months and look at nothing else." Words began to fail him; repetitious superlatives abound. "In Rome there are two thousand churches and monasteries of the various [religious] orders and all are most splendidly built, with astonishing ornamentation inside and gloriously decorated externally with wondrously carved magnificent alabaster and marble floral ornaments." Here is the basilica of St. Peter, with Bernini's "fine great rounded *pliatsa* [piazza], around which stand masonry columns to the number of 576, extremely tall, large, and round, with fine promenades amidst them paved in stone, and with [balustrades] above on which

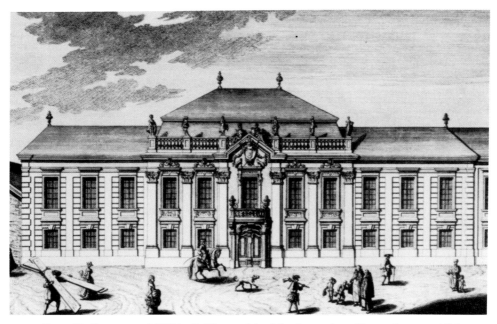

Figure 71 Engraving of 1737 by S. Kleiner of the Schönbrun palace, Vienna, begun in 1696; J. B. Fisher von Erlach, architect.

Figure 72 Engraving of 1737 by S. Kleiner of the Piarist church, Vienna, begun in 1698; v.-Hildebrandt, architect.

stand images of saints all most handsomely wrought of alabaster, each holding a cross. . . ." Tolstoi goes on:

> In the middle of the piazza stands a four-sided column made from one stone, below very thick and above, thin, very tall and splendidly made. On top of this column [obelisk] stands a four-pointed cross, and off to either side two large handsome fountains from which extraordinarily pure water shoots high in abundance. The Church of St. Peter is very large, larger than any to be found in the world, and most marvelously constructed. Before the church is a great [estrade] of such marvelous proportions as to be hard to describe. From here one enters the great porch, magnificently built. From this porch a row of five splendid great bronze doors opens into the church, whose vaults are supported by huge columns. Between the columns are fine altars in the Roman [Catholic] manner, and the decoration of the church is magnificent. In the middle stands the great altar, over which a canopy rests on four very high columns. The canopy and columns are carved in the most marvelous fashion, and on the columns at the corners stand wonderfully carved angels, all splendidly gilded. . . . The interior of this great church is all magnificently done in white marble, with the most wonderful alabaster carving in many places. . . . The paintings on the walls and ceilings are in the most magnificent, glorious Italian style.

The pope's garden nearby was "most fine, with numerous splendid fruit trees and flowers of various kinds all planted in wonderful proportion. In this garden are numerous glorious fountains from which flows the most wondrous clear water, and among them one miraculous thing made just like a great high hill, whence a great quantity of water flows into an enclosed place of white stone, where it forms a small pond in which sails a [model] ship of copper complete with masts and sails, cannon and all the necessary instruments. . . ." In Rome, too, Tolstoi noted, "fine illustrated architectural folios and books of houses and fountains and every other splendid thing are printed."

Early in his long journey home Tolstoi stopped in Florence, and the effect on him of his stay in Rome was telling. The walls of Florence were "old-fashioned" and its medieval houses were lacking in "proportion"; building in Florence generally, Tolstoi opined, was "not in accord with architecture [*ne po arkhitekture*]." But the newer houses on either side of one wide street were so built, being both large and tall, handsomely decorated and harmoniously ranged. And so were the city's (Renaissance and Baroque) churches, most notably Brunelleschi's princely chapel of San Lorenzo (designed 1418). The chapel was "large, eight-sided, all its walls even, its face of splendidly worked grey stone; in many places around the windows finely polished alabaster" had been installed. Inside, "the church is constructed of various marbles and with such craftsmanship as none better is to be found in the world. And in these marbles [marble walls and panels] are set colored Indian and Persian stones, shells and corals and pieces of amber and crystal, all in such exquisite fashion as to be impossible to describe . . . marbles glittering like mirrors . . . tombs of various marbles so superbly made as to be incomprehensible to the mind of man, and above which stand figures carved of alabaster which cannot be adequately described" (fig. 73).

Figure 73 Chapel of San Lorenzo (Medici chapel), Florence; designed 1418 by Filippo Brunelleschi; interior, monument of Grand Duke Ferdinand I.

So much for Tolstoi's observations of architecture in Italy (once he had left Italy, his diary has little more to say on the subject). Russians traveling in Europe at the end of the seventeenth century, to judge from their surviving letters and journals or memoirs, were both alert to the buildings that they saw and favorably impressed by monuments of civil more often than military architecture.[46] They were most often and most favorably impressed by the large scale, wealth of decoration, richness of materials, symmetrical proportions, and high quality of workmanship that they observed in Baroque and Renaissance buildings (as we would now call them) in Poland, Austria, Germany, and Italy. These buildings included churches and palaces, to be sure, but also villas with their parks and gardens, libraries and museums, academies, town halls, and hospitals. Such buildings in the "Italian style," as the Russians frequently termed it, corresponded with and indeed heightened their sense of what was noble, admirable, or beautiful in architecture: "marvelous," "amazing," "stupendous," "indescribable" in their Russian equivalents are characteristic adjectives, occurring especially often in descriptions of buildings in Italy. And in this the taste of Russians abroad coincided with that of contemporary European visitors to Moscow, who admired, if anything there, the few official and court buildings referred to above; admired them not alone for the familiarity of much of their decoration or for their relatively good design and workmanship but for their splendor, luxury, symmetry, and/or great size. A convergence of taste was obviously under way.

What is more, the first work on architecture ever written in Russian was compiled in 1699 by a cadet of the princely Dolgorukov clan while studying in Venice. His "Civil Architecture, Selected from the Famous Architect Palladio and from many other Famous Architects," a sort of introduction to European architectural theory and practice, is essentially a translation of a contemporary Latin edition of the first of Palladio's celebrated *Four Books on Architecture* (1570) supplemented by extracts from other Italian authorities and by the translator's own explanatory notes and personal observations of architecture in Venice and Poland.[47] Here Russian readers could discover the standard architectural orders, related technical terminology, and such basic principles as the importance of strict symmetry of proportion in building for both practical and aesthetic reasons: "*takoe zdanie budet krepko*" and "*tak stena . . . budet imet' izriadnuiu preportsiiu*" ("such a building will be strong" and "thus the wall . . . will have fine proportions"). The text is accompanied by seventy-three sketches, most of which were taken from the Italian manuals but a few of which were apparently drawn by the translator himself (fig. 74). Dolgorukov had been sent to Venice to study mathematics with a view to shipbuilding, not "civil architecture" as he says here, defining it as the "science which teaches how to make palaces and every sort of building." But he had not been able to restrain himself. And in Moscow his manuscript seems to have attracted the attention of builders anxious to satisfy the demand for building in the "new style." Details of Prince Menshikov's palace in the German Settlement—the former Lefort

Figure 74 Architectural sketches from the Dolgorukov manuscript, 1699.

palace that was entirely rebuilt in 1707 and 1708—correspond more or less closely with sketches in the Dolgorukov manuscript.[48]

The Petrine revolution in civil as distinct from military or naval architecture, it becomes increasingly clear, was initially a matter of preference rather than necessity: of a rapidly developing taste among members of the Russian elite for architecture in the "new" or the "Italian style." A determination to implant the new style in Russia and to import the necessary techniques naturally followed. We can sense as much in the record of Peter I's interview of October 4, 1700, with Patriarch Adrian, the current head of the Russian church. Peter urged that the Moscow academy, which was under patriarchal jurisdiction, needed upgrading so that it could produce graduates with a "knowledge of military affairs, of building, and of the physician's art."[49] It was as if building of the kind that Peter envisaged, like the desired military and medical expertise, was as yet unknown in Russia.

A first important step in this direction was the preparation of Russian editions of the standard European works on architecture. Dolgorukov's modest compilation of 1699, which was never printed, was one such effort. In 1700 Peter I's agent in Amsterdam was ordered to see to the printing of books "in Slavonic" on architecture, among other subjects;[50] and several manuscript Russian translations of architectural manuals printed in Amsterdam survive to show that the project got that far.[51] In 1709, at Peter's urgent instigation and under his personal supervision, and with the help of G. M. Fontana, an illustrated Russian edition of Vignola's *Regola delli cinque ordini d'architettura*, one of the most popular architectural textbooks in contemporary Europe, was published at Moscow in the new "civil" type (a streamlined, Europeanized version of the more elaborate and cumbersome "church" or "Cyrillic" type). The first work on architecture ever to be printed in Russia or in Russian, it appeared in a second edition in 1712 and in a third in 1722.[52]

The year 1709 also saw the publication in Russia of several translated works on fortification (e.g., of L. C. Sturm's *Architectura militaris hypotetica et eclectica*, Nuremburg, 1702) and on shipbuilding (C. Allard's manual in Dutch published at Amsterdam in 1705) as well as a third Russian edition of a German textbook on plane geometry.[53] In 1711 it was the turn of Blondel's *Nouvelle manière de fortifier les places* (Paris, 1683), with Peter I as editor; in 1724, of Vauban's *Manière de fortifier* (Amsterdam, 1689; Paris, 1692, 1694).[54] A Russian translation of the first chapter of Vitruvius's classic *De architectura libri X* was sent to Peter in 1715, evidently the work of a Russian student abroad;[55] other Russian manuscript translations of European architectural works as well as the numerous architectural engravings found among Peter's effects testify to a rising Russian interest in these years in French and especially Italian architecture, including landscape architecture, which was the subject of an album of engravings published at St. Petersburg in 1718.[56] In addition to the translated works, many of them copiously illustrated, the growing volume of works on architecture in original European editions collected by Russians at this time, most notably by Peter himself, must be counted.[57] Yet the importance of such works in the development of architectural theory and practice in Russia and in forming Russian taste cannot of course compare with that of the various Russian editions mentioned. The Russian edition of Vignola's textbook, in particular, became the single best known work on architecture in eighteenth-century Russia.[58]

A second major step in the process of implanting European architectural norms in Russia involved the importation, in wholly unprecedented numbers, of European masters. We noticed earlier that in order to carry out his shipbuilding program or to build up Azov Peter I hired hundreds of experts while traveling in Europe in 1697 and 1698. In July 1703 another such group arrived headed by Dominico Trezzini, who had been in the Danish king's service for about five years and was hired in Copenhagen by the Russian ambassador, Izmailov. The party of ten included a Danish engineer, a French plasterer, and four other Italian builders, one of whom was G. M. Fontana. Trezzini and the engineer were promptly dispatched to St. Petersburg, the former to play a critical role in the creation of the new capital; while Fontana, like the rest of the party, was at first put to work in Moscow. There as we saw he supervised the rebuilding of the Lefort/Menshikov palace and perhaps the completion of the Menshikov Tower and also probably built a house for the city's military commander, M. P. Gagarin. Later, as just indicated, he helped prepare the Russian edition of Vignola's textbook. In 1710 Fontana was transferred to St. Petersburg, where he built or at least assisted in building Menshikov's country seat at Oranienbaum as well as his palace in town.[59] That left in Moscow, among European builders whose names are known to us, only Christopher Conrad supervising construction of the new arsenal, which was halted in 1714 by the terms of a general prohibition on building shortly to be explained. In 1714, as we also saw, Conrad too was summoned to St. Petersburg.

Far and away the most important architectural projects undertaken by European masters in Russia in the earlier eighteenth century were sited in and around St. Petersburg. Nor were their efforts confined to the tasks of designing and building. For it was under Trezzini and other architects hired in Europe by Peter I that systematic training in architecture was first organized in Russia. This third important step in the Europeanization of Russian building norms, together with the related step of sending Russians to Italy or Holland for the express purpose of completing their architectural training, will be discussed in the following chapter. But before proceeding a final early initiative of the Petrine regime must be considered, namely, its direct and steadily more comprehensive regulation, beginning in Moscow in the last years of the seventeenth century, of both public and private construction.

REMODELING MOSCOW

Moscow at the end of the seventeenth century, as depicted in Chapter 2, was a thriving commercial and administrative city but architecturally, in the memorable words of a contemporary German visitor, it was "a mess." The clustered mansions of its grandees, like numerous of its churches and monasteries, were set deep in fenced-off yards and gardens while its meandering, largely unpaved streets and alleyways, like its irregular squares and open spaces, were crowded with countless stables and sheds, shops and stalls, and collapsible, one-room houses—cabins or even shacks, as we might call them. It was a city built for the most part of wood and, given its density, a city continually afflicted by fire. This fatal nexus of wood and fire early attracted Peter I's attention, who seems to have been equally concerned with appearances. In Europe in 1697 and 1698 he had spent anywhere from several days to several months in Riga, Mitau, Königsberg, Amsterdam, The Hague, London, Oxford, Dresden, Warsaw, and Vienna; and on his return to his capital in August 1698 the physical differences between it and a typical European city of the day would have been plain to him.

The typical European city of the end of the seventeenth century (as P. A. Tolstoi discovered) was built almost entirely of brick and stone, with its houses and shops directly facing the street and any appurtenances thereto confined to the rear of the lot; just as livestock and the essential vegetable gardens—and new graveyards—were confined to the city's outskirts. The streets of contemporary European cities were paved in stone and, if not always straight, were generally of a regular width. The main streets were illuminated at night by specially fixed lights and were kept relatively free of refuse. Broad avenues and carefully planned squares and townscapes afforded sweeping, harmonious, even dramatic views. It was these features of the typical European city of the day, as well as the architecture of many if not all of its buildings, that distinguished it more or less sharply from the Moscow of the 1690s; not its central fortress and market square, its few radial and circular thoroughfares, or its surrounding walls and ramparts, features that they shared.

Unlike his predecessors, Peter I did not attempt to prevent the recurrence of destructive fires in Russian towns simply by ordering devastated streets to be widened. As a series of instructions sent to provincial administrators in 1697 and 1698 indicates, his government now sought to forestall the outbreak of fires by regulating home heating practices, by controlling the use of cook stoves and steam baths, and above all by promoting exclusively masonry construction.[60]

The new regulations were applied in the first instance to such official and court buildings as the new administrative complex at Tobolsk, the new Lefort palace in Moscow's German Settlement, and the new arsenal in the Kremlin, which was to be built on a site recently wrecked by fire. But on January 17, 1701, Peter decreed that in "burnt-out places" everywhere in Moscow "people of means" were to build masonry houses and "people of no means, [houses] in wattle and daub [*mazankye*, or houses with walls of clay held up by wooden supports]." The latter were to be constructed in accordance with a specified model, and rebuilding in wood anywhere in Moscow was henceforth proscribed under pain of severe penalty.[61] This sweeping decree, vaguely provided and practically incapable of execution, was followed in 1704 by another requiring householders within the Kremlin and adjoining Kitai-gorod (together containing about 2 percent of registered households in Moscow) to build in brick or stone and to use good workmen. Here it was also required that houses were not to be located as formerly somewhere back in the lot but up front, facing the street or alley. The owners of lots in these central districts who could not afford masonry construction were to sell them forthwith.[62] In 1705, in order to hasten the prescribed rebuilding of houses in the Kremlin and Kitai-gorod, masonry construction elsewhere in Moscow was temporarily prohibited and householders or shopkeepers able and willing to build in the prescribed manner were encouraged to acquire lots in Kitai-gorod by purchase or exchange.[63] Peter repeated these various directives in an order of 1707, where he decreed that they were to remain in effect until masonry buildings were constructed "everywhere in the Kremlin and Kitai-gorod in accord with [the principles of] architecture [*po arkhitekturu*]";[64] until, in other words, at least these central districts of Moscow had been architecturally Europeanized.

The mixture of practical and aesthetic motives impelling Peter I's decrees of 1701 to 1707 regulating new construction in Moscow, their intention at once of preventing fire and of promoting the architectural Europeanization of the city, is clear enough. At the same time, a number of fiscal and administrative enactments—loosening up residency requirements, abolishing various restrictive trading practices, attempting to establish a form of home rule, among others—also worked to further these ends, if less directly so.[65] Still other measures of relevance include the installation in 1698 of eight streetlights burning hemp-seed oil (hemp being a Russian staple) at Peter's favorite suburban residence of Preobrazhenskoe, evidently the first streetlights ever to be seen in Russia.[66] Equally noteworthy are his repeated orders, beginning in 1700, providing for the paving of Moscow's streets in cobblestone and for—a complete innovation—their regular cleaning with water (at least in the German Settlement).[67] Meanwhile, as noted above, churches and official buildings as well as fortifications were being built in and around Moscow under the guidance of European masters or in ways that strove to reflect the "new style." Such construction did not come under the ban of 1705 on masonry building outside the Kremlin and Kitai-gorod, a ban that was strengthened in 1709 by a provision enforcing the sale of lots therein by persons who would not rebuild in brick or stone to persons who would.[68]

Yet fires continued to take a heavy toll. In August 1709 much of Moscow beyond Kitai-gorod was visited, and reconstruction, perforce, was done in wood. At the beginning of 1710 it was the turn of Kitai-gorod, which prompted a repeat of the ban on wooden construction and of the requirement to build facing the street.[69] A shortage of building materials later in 1710 evoked anew the ban on masonry domestic or commercial construction outside Kitai-gorod.[70] In 1712, once more to prevent fire, it was decreed that houses of both masonry construction and wattle and daub were to be roofed with tiles and that their roofs were not to be pitched.[71] The most devastating fire to hit Moscow during the whole Petrine period, by all accounts, occurred in May 1712, destroying some 4,543 buildings and causing an estimated 2,700 deaths.[72] Within a week the requirement of wattle-and-daub construction was extended to the whole of Belyi-gorod (surrounding the Kremlin and Kitai-gorod on three sides), leaving wooden construction legally permissible only in the outermost districts of the city (Zemlianoi-gorod).[73] Soon it was directed that all masonry and wattle-and-daub houses in Belyi-gorod were to be roofed in tile or, in view of a temporary shortage of tiles, in specially prepared wood.[74] Measures were also taken to increase the supply of building materials, since a scarcity of bricks, cut stone, and tiles had obliged Peter's government to ignore on occasion its own regulations.[75] But by this time, by 1713, Peter's own interest in such matters had shifted to St. Petersburg, where the resources of his realm were now being insistently drawn.

On October 9, 1714, in accordance with a decree of Peter I promulgated by the Senate and promptly printed for wide distribution, any further masonry building was prohibited for an indefinite time everywhere in the tsar's dominions except St. Petersburg.[76] The obvious intent of this decree, which was reprinted in 1718, 1719, and again in 1724,[77] was to speed up construction in the new capital. And with respect to Moscow, it appears to have been strictly enforced. Beginning in December 1714 it was legally permissible to build houses even in the central districts of the city only in wattle and daub, and in conformity with a prescribed model.[78] The effect of these and further measures was to bring masonry construction in Moscow to a complete halt. A survey conducted a few years later found that some twenty-eight major building projects—seventeen involving churches—had been suspended in 1714.[79]

The ban on masonry building in Moscow was lifted with respect just to the Kremlin and Kitai-gorod in 1718, when still further regulations were introduced and older ones reinstated. In the Kremlin and Kitai-gorod, came word from the tsar, who was temporarily in residence at nearby Preobrazhenskoe, all buildings were to be made of brick or stone and roofed with tiles. They were to face the street, which was to be paved in stone, as was done in "other European states." Householders who could not comply with these regulations were to change places with Muscovites who could. Elsewhere in the city churches and houses were to be roofed with tiles or shingles, and if built of wood were to be finished with plaster ceilings. The numerous provisions, enforceable under pain of severe penalties, were to be supervised in their implementation by Moscow's "Ober-Komendant" assisted by an "architect [arkhitektor] sent from Petersburg."[80] Indeed, this decree and subsequent ones confirming it,[81] like the related provisions of an "Instruksiia" sent to Moscow's "Ober-Politseimeister" in 1722,[82] serve to emphasize how in the matter of architectural advancement the old capital had yielded to the new.

Any further discussion of the effects of the Petrine architectural revolution on Moscow's fabric and plan will be left to the concluding chapter, so as to be seen in their proper context. But here it might be observed that the revolution whose beginnings we have traced could only have come to fruition, in the short time that it did, in the building of a completely new city. From the architectural point of view there is a compelling logic in Peter's ambition to proceed from the congestion of old Moscow and the abortive experiments at Azov to the construction of his "paradise" by the Baltic.

6

Revolution Embodied:
The Building of St. Petersburg

From paradise, that is, St. Petersburg.
—Peter I to A. D. Menshikov, 1706[1]

The city of St. Petersburg, renamed Petrograd in 1914 and Leningrad in 1924, has been one of the great cities of the modern world. As the capital of the Russian Empire for two centuries and still, today, the second city of the Soviet Union, its history has attracted considerable scholarly attention. But more to the point here, during the period of the Empire St. Petersburg was the trend-setter in Russian architecture, the source and arbitrator of architectural taste, an attainment it ultimately owed, as it did its very existence, to Peter I, tsar and first emperor. It was to an extraordinary degree Peter's city, the nick-name—"Peter" (or "Piter")—by which it is still popularly known.

The early history of St. Petersburg is examined in this chapter in connection with the Petrine revolution in Russian building norms. It is the scale of the architectural undertaking which it represented that is of concern and the extent to which it embodied a decisive change of direction in Russian architectural development. Equally, the contributions of European architects and craftsmen to the building of St. Petersburg will be highlighted, in part because of the intrinsic historical importance of these contributions, in part because they have been slighted in the historical literature. And in forwarding its aims the chapter will focus on Peter I, whose personal role in the architectural history of his period, hitherto clearly important, now becomes paramount.[2]

THE TSAR'S TASTE

Peter I grew up in Moscow, in the palaces of the Kremlin and on the suburban royal estates of Kolomenskoe, Izmailovo, and Preobrazhenskoe, following a pattern that was traditional for a Russian tsarevich. But owing to the early death of his father (in 1676, when Peter was four years old) and to the play of court politics, he was extraordinarily free as a youth to pursue his own affairs and interests. The latter included, above all, sailing on the lakes north of Moscow and eventually on the White Sea, and soldiering, which he pursued with a passion particularly at Preobrazhenskoe, where he established what became his personal headquarters in greater Moscow for the rest of his life. Both pursuits brought him into close contact with European specialists living in the German Settlement; for instance, with the Dutch shipwright Karsten Brandt, who taught him to sail, as mentioned earlier, and with the Scotsman, Patrick Gordon, and the Genevan, François Lefort, who became his military tutors and boon companions. And Peter maintained this relatively free, impulsive, and somewhat irresponsible way of life even after he and his party had assumed full power (in 1689)—as witness, most notably, the sixteen months he spent traveling incognito in Europe (1697–1698). He would have stayed longer had not units of his musketeers rebelled in Moscow, to be put down by General Gordon, but not before he was summoned home.

We can assume, accordingly, that Peter I's taste in "civil" architecture was initially formed by the churches and houses that were built in and around Moscow by members of his family and court, occasionally under his direct patronage if not with his personal participation, in the years of his childhood and youth; buildings whose structural regularities reflected European influence as did, still more, their decoration. This taste for architecture in the style of the so-called Moscow or Naryshkin Baroque (Naryshkin being his mother's family name) was then reinforced and refined as a result of the young tsar's travels in Europe, where a bias in favor of building on a grand scale, and against the use of wood, was also confirmed. In any event, this is what the later history of his reign would indicate.

More specifically, Peter I's architectural taste as it developed seems to have favored the Dutch. His first known discussion of architecture with an architect occurred in Amsterdam in 1697, with Simon Schijnvoet (also Schynvoet or Schynvaet), a master of the Dutch Baroque at least one of whose writings Peter at some point acquired; and it was in Amsterdam in 1697, as Peter later recalled, that he learned the basics of "naval architecture."[3] The log walls of his first house in St. Petersburg were planed flat and painted to resemble brickwork, the wooden shingles of its roof were made to resemble tiles, and its windows were mullioned and fitted with numerous small panes of glass all in a Dutch manner that departed smartly from traditional Russian norms (pl. 39). Moreover the buildings with which Peter was later most intimately associated—his Summer Palace in St. Petersburg (pl. 54A) or "Monplaisir" at suburban Peterhof, the "Little Dutch House [*Gollandskii domik*]" as he called it (pl. 59B)—present an unmistakably Dutch aspect, as numerous observers have noted.

The clearest statement of the mature Peter I's personal preferences in architecture is found in his letter of November 7, 1724, to "Architectural student [*uchenik Arkhitektury*] Ivan Korobov" in Antwerp:

> You write asking to go to France and Italy to train in civil architecture [*dlia praktiki arkhitektury tsivilis*]. I've been to France myself [in 1717], where there's no ornamentation in architecture, which they don't like, and build only in a plain and simple way, very thickset, and all in stone, not brick. I've heard a lot about Italy; also, we have three Russian people who studied there, and are well trained. But in both these places the building situation is very different from the one here [in St. Petersburg], [which is] more like the Dutch. Therefore it's proper for you to live in Holland and not Brabant, and to learn the manner of Dutch architecture, especially in foundations, which are needed

Figure 75 "House and Garden of a Gentleman's Estate" in Holland, by Jacob van der Ulft (lived 1627–1689); painting in oil on canvas.

here (for they have a similar situation regarding the base of walls), and in the proportions of gardens—how to lay them out and decorate them, both with trees and with all kinds of figures, which nowhere in the world do they know how to do so well as in Holland. It's also necessary to learn about sluices [*sliuznomu delu*], which are much needed here. Therefore put aside everything and do the aforesaid.[4]

Peter's dislike of French classicism is evident here as is his preference for the decorativeness of Dutch architecture, its use of brick (good stone anyway was hard to come by in the St. Petersburg area), and its way with a garden (fig. 75). No less clear is the practical side of his liking for Dutch building, a preference based on his awareness of the similarity in natural conditions between Holland and the St. Petersburg area. That same day—November 7, 1724— Peter also wrote to his agent in charge of the Russian students in Holland, instructing him to find work in building for Korobov and three compatriots and repeating that they were to learn the "manner of Dutch architecture and especially foundations [*fundamenty*], which are needed here," there being in Holland a "similar situation"; and again the students were specifically enjoined to study Dutch garden architecture.[5] A memorandum found among these papers indicates that a few years before Peter had sent two Russian students to Holland to learn "how to build both churches and houses."[6]

Peter also frequently hired or sought to hire Dutch builders to work in Russia. This policy is reflected in his correspondence over the years with Prince B. I.

Kurakin, whose charge as Peter's chief representative in western Europe (from 1711) included recruiting experts for the tsar's service. In one of these letters Peter advises Kurakin that a certain Dutch architect whom Kurakin had recruited was dead, "to our misfortune, since our need for such [people] is great. For God's sake look hard for another such as we urgently need; and if you find a good one, promise him even three thousand a year; just make sure he's good." On another occasion Peter ordered Kurakin to send him models and plans of Dutch fortifications and to hire two experienced military engineers in Holland.[7] In 1723 he ordered the Senate in St. Petersburg to draw up a project for building roads using Swedish models and another for building a canal, sluices, and towers "after the Dutch system."[8] We might remember here the many Dutch shipwrights hired by Peter to build his navy, as mentioned in Chapter 5.

Yet it would be wrong to represent the mature tsar as a determined partisan of Dutch architecture or, indeed, as a patron with any very fixed architectural tastes beyond a general preference for the "new style." As the letter to Korobov just quoted also indicates, Peter was well aware of the primacy in European architecture of Italy, where, but for the rebellion back in Moscow, he would have traveled from Vienna in 1698.[9] As late in his reign as June 1723 Peter personally instructed the director of building in St. Petersburg to send two advanced architectural students to Rome to replace two others who had just been summoned home to work.[10] In short, what information there is suggests that at least as many Russian architectural students were sent to Italy under Peter as to Holland, and that many more Italian builders of all kinds worked in Russia in these same years than Dutch.

And not just Italian. Frenchmen were prominent among the designers and decorators of early St. Petersburg, while it was Germans, numerically speaking, who made perhaps the greatest contribution to the building of the new city. Nor should we forget the work of Swedes (especially Swedish prisoners-of-war), Danes, Scotsmen, and Englishmen in connection with various building projects undertaken throughout Peter I's dominions. In fact, only one Dutch architect is known to have worked in St. Petersburg in the later and busiest years of the reign, Steven van Zwiedten, the designer of a palace known to us only from plans.[11] A list of some fifty "foreign masters" currently in its pay drawn up by the St. Petersburg Chancellery of Construction in November 1723 names only three Dutchmen apart from Van Zwiedten—one a "sluice master" engaged in building a windmill, another identified simply as a specialist in "cement matters."[12] Again the practical side of the Dutch contribution to the Petrine architectural revolution is emphasized.

The range of Peter I's architectural interests is readily gauged from a survey of his library.* More than half of the printed and manuscript works so far identi-

---

*E. I. Bobrova, *Biblioteka Petra I: ukazatel'-spravochnik* (L., 1978), is the indispensable guide and the following data are derived from it. Bobrova lists 1,663 books and manuscripts, but speculates that by the end of Peter's life his library might actually have contained as many as 2,000 titles (p. 11). Bobrova also indicates which of the works listed belonged to Peter personally, as distinct from a relative or associate; almost all of the architectural works are so indicated.

fied were in foreign languages, and a high proportion of those that remain were translations. More precisely, more than a fifth of the foreign—that is, European—books acquired by Peter particularly in his last years were on architecture, and about a third of these had to do with military and naval construction. Virtually every aspect of what in contemporary Europe was considered the "new" architecture was represented, as were all the standard authorities: Vauban on fortification (copies of four editions) and Sturm on Vauban (published in French at The Hague in 1708), Scamozzi on the principles of architecture (editions in Dutch, Italian, and German), Decker's *Architectura civilis* (three copies), Campbell's *Vitruvius Britannicus, or the British Architect, containing the plans, elevations and sections of the regular Buildings, both publick and private, in Great Britain* (London, 1715); copies of English, German, and Italian editions of Palladio; and French as well as German editions of the architectural course, based on Vignola, taught at the Royal Academy of Architecture in Paris. Peter had also acquired copies of the Latin and French editions of Vitruvius's *Ten Books on Architecture*, Sebastien LeClerc's *Traité d'architecture* (Paris, 1714), Rossi's *Studio d'architettura civile* (Rome, 1702), and works of Daniel Morot, an architect famous in contemporary Holland. Böckler's *Architectura curiosa nova* (Nuremburg, 1704), Blondel's manual on fortification (French and German editions), and Vignola's textbook on the five architectural orders (in Dutch, French, German, and several Italian editions) made their way into Peter's library as well as works on designing fireplaces and grills, on stucco ceilings, on vaulting, on decorating with tapestries and paintings, or with statuary. Descriptions of Versailles, of the "principal houses of Europe," of the palaces of Genoa, of both the ancient triumphal arches and the "modern" buildings of Rome catch our eye—as do surveys of the squares, gates, fountains, churches, houses, and palaces of Paris, or of the ancient architectural monuments of Europe as a whole. We notice copies of still other dictionaries, manuals, textbooks, and picture books of military, naval, civil, and landscape architecture published in the later seventeenth and very early eighteenth centuries. Indeed, there can have been few larger collections of printed books in the field—at least 150 titles—anywhere in Europe at this time.

Peter I's library also contained at least fourteen manuscript works on architecture in European languages, several if not all of which, like numerous of the printed works just mentioned, had been sent or formally presented to him by their authors—a fact that by itself testifies to the reputation he had gained in Europe as a patron of architecture. Yet Peter's purposiveness in acquiring a library of the best architectural works available deserves emphasis. In his correspondence of just a few months in 1706–1707, for instance, we find him instructing various officials or agents to send him from Amsterdam or Rome "books by every author on fortification" and "architectural books of various kinds in Latin, Dutch, and German," the languages he and his assistants could best contend with; or "books on fortification by every author . . . and architectural books from which this art can be learned from the beginning"; or again, "the new and best architectural books (best if in Latin, but if you can't find that, then in whatever)": instructions that were promptly carried out, as this correspondence also indicates.[13] The records of Peter's own travels in Europe in 1716 and 1717 show him stopping to buy architectural books and prints directly from local dealers.[14]

Further, four manuscript and six printed works in Russian translation on various aspects of building were found in Peter's library at the time of his death.[15] The manuscripts included the original translations with illustrations of the 1722 printed edition of Vignola's textbook and of the 1709 edition of Sturm's manual (both mentioned in Chapter 5). Peter had personally supervised the preparation of these works. The latter is based on the German edition of Sturm's *Architectura militaris* published at Nuremburg in 1702, a copy of which Peter had passed to A. G. Golovkin for translation sometime before the end of 1708, when he issued instructions for its printing and illustration and himself contributed both a note to the text and, it seems, an illustrative sketch. The manual consists of eighty-one dialogues in which a teacher acquaints his pupil with the methods of some thirty-nine experts on fortification.[16] Vignola's textbook on the architectural orders was also first published in Russian translation in 1709 but not before Peter himself, having commissioned the work, interrupted its printing: "We have inspected" the copy sent to him, he wrote in September 1709,

> and [find that] in certain places it is not correctly [done], on which we send herewith a list of notes. Order Architect Fantanna [G. M. Fontana] to correct these [mistakes] together with some Russian who might know architecture, however little [*s kem-nibud' ruskim, kotoroi by khotia nemnogo znal arkhitekturu*]. And having corrected [it], order a hundred copies of the book to be printed . . . and send us five or ten as soon as possible.[17]

In preparing the Russian edition of Vignola's textbook, to be sure, the basic problem lay in rendering the technical vocabulary of European (Classical) architecture—here in Italian—in ways accessible to a Russian reader; and the solution adopted by Fontana and the translator(s), not surprisingly, was in the main simply to transliterate, thus creating a whole new architectural vocabulary in Russian. Reprinted in Moscow in 1712 and again in 1722, the Petrine edition of Vignola's textbook was the first book on architecture ever published in Russia, where it remained the single best known work on the subject for nearly a hundred years.[18]

There is additional evidence of Peter I's concern to make basic architectural manuals available in Russian. In January 1722, in connection with preparing a history of his reign, a history in which his achievements as builder were to be given prominence, Peter noted that as early as 1699 he had initiated the translation of books on architecture—a reference no doubt to his patent to this effect granted to the Amsterdam merchant, Jan Tessing, that same year.[19] Other cases of his direct intervention in the matter include the publication in 1709 and again in 1710 of a Russian translation of the second (1702) edition of Koehorn's work in Dutch on the "new fortification," which Peter had gone to some trouble to acquire;[20] and the publication in 1711 of a Russian translation of Blondel's *Nouvelle manière de fortifier les places* (1683). In February 1709 Peter had written to the latter's translator, K. N. Zotov, stating that he had read over the translation and found parts of it "very well and clearly translated" but others "very obscurely and unintelligibly" done; therefore the work was to be translated again, in which undertaking, Zotov was advised by the tsar, it was "not necessary to translate word for word but rather the sense [*sens*] of the matter, so as to write in one's own language as clearly as possible."[21] Also remarkable in these projects is Peter's insistence that the translated works be properly illustrated, usually a question, especially in the earlier part of his reign, of redirecting the efforts of European engravers already in his pay. Nor did he ever consider the task of translation well enough done. A note in his own hand dating from 1723 stresses the necessity as he saw it of training translators both in the languages to be translated and in the subjects of translation, the latter to include *"arkhitektur"* both *"militaris"* and *"tsivilis."*[22]

Thus the catholicity of the mature Peter's interest in architecture is readily seen as well as its practical bent: the early and continuing emphasis on fortification, shipbuilding, and related affairs. One of the six printed works on architecture in Russian translation found in his library is a copy of the Moscow 1709 edition of Alard's *Niewe hollandse Scheeps-Bouw* (Amsterdam, 1705; *Novoe galanskoe karabelnoe stroenie* in the Russian edition) with numerous engraved illustrations, following those in the original, by Pierre Picart, the French Hugenot engraver in Peter's service whom he regularly employed for such purposes (also known as Pickaert, from his long residence in Holland). The book had been acquired by his representative at The Hague in 1705 and naturally it, too, gave rise to serious problems of translation.[23] A related work to be found in Peter's library is a copy of the Russian edition of an English manual on rigging published at St. Petersburg in 1716, complete with parallel lists of English and Dutch technical terms prepared under Peter's personal supervision and printed in Russian letters; and here again we have evidence of Peter's correcting the text before publication.[24] Still another such work is a copy of the Moscow 1708 translation of the Amsterdam 1696 edition of Bouillet's treatise in French on building canals, docks, and sluices, and on sailing on rivers. This work was reprinted in Moscow, presumably also by Peter's order, in 1713.[25]

The historical importance of Peter I's activities in collecting at least 164 European works on architecture, in commissioning Russian translations of some of them, in editing the translations and overseeing their publication, in press-runs of several hundred copiously illustrated copies each, will be obvious. Indeed, the dissemination in Russia of the new architectural knowledge—of *arkhitektura* itself, as Peter would have said—is scarcely conceivable without these efforts. But the contents of his library contain still further indications of the extent of his personal interest here: two manuscript works, evidently composed by Peter himself, on shipbuilding and fortification.[26] These are the only

Figure 76   Architectural sketch by Peter I relating to Peterhof.

works by a Russian on any aspect of architecture to be found in the tsar's library, just as they are among the very few Russian architectural works of any kind—none of them ever printed—dating from the entire period.

Still more, Peter I's efforts as an editor and even a writer of architectural works may be linked with his essays in drafting. In Chapter 5 it was noted that he drew up a plan for the play fort at Kolomenskoe in 1693, and sketched the fortifications near Azov in 1697 (fig. 59) as well as the new defenses for Noteborg in 1702 (fig. 63); also, that in 1706 he sent his design of a new "citadel" to the responsible official in Azov (fig. 61). It was mentioned just above that in 1708 he evidently contributed a sketch to the Russian edition of Sturm's *Architectura militaris*. In 1720 he sent Prince Kurakin a diagram of a ship he had drawn, noting that it was "out of proportion [*bez preportsii*]." At least five sketches done by Peter at various times in connection with planning the buildings and grounds at Peterhof survive to show how closely he followed that project (fig. 76). By the end, it would seem, Peter had become something of an architect himself.[27]

THE EUROPEAN MASTERS

It was not as an amateur architect or as an avid collector, editor, and publisher of books on architecture that Peter I most decisively influenced the development of building in Russia. More critical in this regard was his policy of hiring numerous European builders of all kinds for service in his dominions. In the preceding chapter it was suggested that the activity in and around Moscow, Azov, Voronezh, and elsewhere from 1698 of hundreds of Italian, German, English, and Dutch experts constituted a wholly unprecedented invasion of the building industry in Russia—if only in its volume. But the magnet, after 1703, was St. Petersburg, where still larger numbers of European builders of every description arrived to carry out an ever wider array of projects. Grabar esti-mates, no doubt conservatively, that in Peter's time more than a thousand Europeans were engaged in the construction of the new capital,[28] their living quarters soon occupying much of the left bank of the Neva; and by 1717 three Lutheran churches and one Roman Catholic, a large hostel for newcomers, and a large hall decked out to hold "assemblies" had also been built in this new "German Settlement."[29]

The most prominent European builders to work in and around St. Petersburg under Peter I were Dominico (or Domenico) Trezzini and G. M. (Giovanni Maria) Fontana, who have already been mentioned; Andreas Schlüter, the fa-mous sculptor and architect of the Prussian court who was hired in Berlin in 1713 after a long search and promptly named "Ober-Baudirektor" of St. Peters-burg;[30] Gottfried Schädel, who also entered Russian service in 1713, took charge of completing Menshikov's palace at Oranienbaum, and later worked on projects in Kiev, where he died (1752); Schlüter's assistant Johann Friedrich Braunstein, active between 1714 and 1724 mostly at Peterhof; and such other Germans as T. Schwertfeger (in Russia from 1713 to 1733), G. J. Mattarnowy (1714–1719), best known for designing the building called the *Kunstkamera*, and N. F. Harbel (1717–1724), who took part in various major projects. To these names should be added the Italians Gaetano Chiaveri (in Russia from 1718 to 1726) and Niccolo Michetti (1718–1724): the former is known to have designed a hospital and at least one church,[31] the latter to have been entrusted with still more important commissions (he acquired, by 1720 or so, the title of *General'nyi arkhitektor*).[32] Finally, Jean Baptiste Alexandre Le Blond, who in 1716 succeeded Schlüter in overall charge of planning for St. Petersburg and its environs, must be listed here.

The professional competence of these architects, indeed of all of the Euro-pean builders who worked on St. Petersburg in its early years, has been ques-tioned by some Russian scholars, as have their motives for coming to Russia. The criticism is curiously indignant, even bitter, in tone: as if, on the one hand, the greatest masters in Europe should have left work and home in a disinterested desire to promote an architectural revolution in distant Russia; or as if, on the other hand, the good will, industry, and native talent of their Russian pupils and assistants should somehow have made up for their lack of the desired expertise.[33] It is not a debate that we need to enter. The construc-tion of St. Petersburg as it stood in about 1725 and the architectural revolution which it embodied were essentially and undeniably the work of European mas-ters hired by Peter I, who obviously was motivated in this by a wish to build extensively in the "new style," a wish that could not have been accommodated by local builders employing the traditional methods described in Chapter 3.

Trezzini's is the most important name here—to be found as "Andrei Trezin" or "Tresin" or even "Druzin" in Russian documents but invariably "Dominico Trezzini" or simply "Dominico," in Latin letters, in his own signature.[34] Born about 1670 in Lugano, in that Italian region of Switzerland whose architects and other artists and craftsmen gave such a powerful boost to the development of Baroque architecture in south Germany,[35] his own work reflecting both this German or southern Baroque and the more restrained northern variant he knew from his years (1699–1703) in Copenhagen, Trezzini lived and worked in St. Petersburg continuously from his arrival in 1703 to his death in 1734. Lisaevich rightly stresses how strange the first buildings that he saw in Russia must have seemed to Trezzini: the overwhelmingly wooden structures and antique walls or earthen ramparts of the towns to be glimpsed on his way from Archangel down to Moscow late in the summer of 1703, and then from Moscow north again and west to the site only recently named St. Petersburg; the "medieval" medley of colors and shapes in the fortified monasteries on route; the chaos of Moscow itself. Yet adaptability, clearly, was one of Trezzini's strengths. "From 1703 to 1716," he later wrote, "I worked alone." By this he meant that until Le Blond's arrival, and under Peter I's overall supervision, he laid down the basic principles for the initial construction of the new city, provided on-site inspection of various building projects, and personally designed the most important structures. For his efforts he was named "Lieutenant-Colonel of Fortification and Architect" in 1710 with emoluments that were fairly generous by contemporary European standards, lavish by Russian.

Other signs of Peter's favor are not hard to find. In 1709 Trezzini married a woman from his hometown in Switzerland, and in 1710 the tsar stood godfather to their son. Having begun by building the bastioned fortress of Kronshlot (later Kronshtadt) on the island of Kotlin, at the mouth of the Neva, and the fortress of St. Petersburg itself (pls. 47, 48), with its church named after Sts. Peter and Paul, Trezzini went on to design Peter's Summer Palace (pl. 54A), the first Winter Palace, the building housing the new administrative colleges (pls. 58A–B), and the original Alexander-Nevskii monastery (pl. 26). The Peter-Paul church, which survives much as it was originally designed (pls. 25A–B), and which inspired numerous imitations, is today generally considered the city's most important architectural monument of the Petrine period.[36]

It was Trezzini and his assistants who first laid out the streets and squares of Vasilevskii Island, projected to be the city's central district, and drew up an overall plan for the island of Kotlin. In April 1714 Peter ordered that houses were to be built in St. Petersburg in accordance with plans by "Arkhitektor Trezin," an order that was repeated in September 1715 and in both instances was printed for wide distribution.[37] These plans specified one model house for ordinary tax paying citizens and another for "well-to-do persons," as can be seen in contemporary engravings of both structures (figs. 77A–B); the design of a third model house, for "grandees," once ascribed to Trezzini, is now attributed

A

B

Figures 77A–B Model houses designed for St. Petersburg by D. Trezzini: A "for taxpayers" and B "for well-to-do persons"; contemporary engravings by P. Picart (Pickaert).

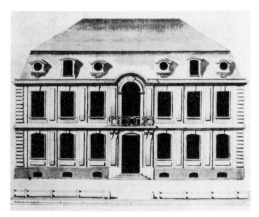

Figure 78 Design of a model St. Petersburg house for "grandees" attributed to J. B. A. Le Blond; contemporary engraving by A. Rostovtsev.

to Le Blond and dated to the end of 1716 (fig. 78).[38] Trezzini's own model house for "grandees" was in effect the Summer Palace. Designed for Peter I and begun in April 1710, it was the first masonry palace to rise in St. Petersburg; and it no doubt set the pattern for the many other mansions built by Trezzini both before and after 1716, the remains of one or two of which can still be seen on Vasilevskii Island. Indeed, panoramic views of St. Petersburg engraved in these early years indicate that all three of Trezzini's model houses promptly set the standards for domestic building in the new capital.

Many more buildings since destroyed issued from Trezzini's workshop, while the school that he established under the St. Petersburg Chancellery of Construction (and of which he was, in effect, the first director) provided the first systematic training in architecture ever to be offered in Russia. Mikhail Zemtsov, his best pupil, went on to train dozens of other native builders who in their turn perpetuated Trezzini's influence for decades to come.

Although Trezzini was made subordinate to the architects of greater reputation who came from Europe after him, he was never really displaced by them. Andreas Schlüter, with an annual salary (5,000 rubles) five times greater than his, produced newly elegant or at least more ornamental designs for projects at Peterhof and in St. Petersburg, where he finished the decoration of the Summer Palace for the tsar (pl. 54B); but he died, in 1714, after little more than a year on the job. A competition held in St. Petersburg to determine a design for the new administrative colleges—the first architectural competition ever to take place in Russia—was won by Trezzini. All the leading lights—Harbel, Schwertfeger, Michetti, Van Zweidten, C. B. Rastrelli, Trezzini himself—were invited in 1722 to submit designs, and in January 1724 the designs were presented to Peter I. Possibly Trezzini won the competition, at least in part, because his design reflected Muscovite precedent, namely, the attached, linear disposition of the governmental departments—*prikazy*—in the Kremlin at Moscow. At any rate, the exterior of Trezzini's building of the Twelve Colleges on Vasilevskii Island—the building is half a kilometer long—was largely completed in 1732, two years before his death; and the interior was finally finished, by Zemtsov, in 1742. It too remains, with later alterations, one of the architectural landmarks of the city (pls. 58A–B).

Trezzini's relationship with Le Blond, who is generally considered the ablest of the architects to have worked under Peter I, indicates his actual standing. Hired by Peter's agents in France in 1716, a pupil of Le Nôtre and a member of the Royal Academy of Architecture in Paris as well as an established authority on both town planning and landscape architecture, Le Blond greatly impressed the tsar at their first meeting, in June 1716 at Pyrmont (Piermont), where Peter had stopped to take the waters. "This master possesses extraordinary qualities and great talent," Peter wrote introducing Le Blond to Menshikov, now governor-general of St. Petersburg, adding that no further construction was to be undertaken without Le Blond's approval.[39] And for the next three years, until his sudden death from smallpox in 1719, Le Blond, as "General-Director" of all building in St. Petersburg and its environs, went about his grand commission. He designed in particular two suburban residential complexes for the tsar—at Strelna and at Peterhof—and a palace in town for Admiral F. M. Apraksin. Within months of his arrival he also drew up, with Trezzini's help, a grandiose plan for the development of St. Petersburg which focused on Vasilevskii Island (fig. 79). Later students have suggested that this very focus doomed the plan, since Menshikov regarded the Island as his personal preserve and wanted nothing of the scheme; but it has also been urged that Peter himself rejected Le Blond's plan as excessively elaborate and then

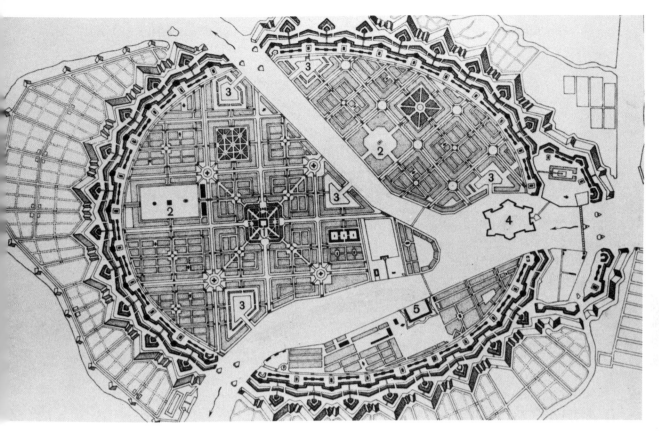

Figure 79 Projected plan of St. Petersburg, focusing on Vasil'evskii Island, by J. B. A. Le Blond, 1717. No. 1 in the plan = a palace for Peter I; 2 = market squares; 3 = harbors surrounded by warehouses; 4 = the fortress; 5 = the Admiralty. Churches terminate the diagonal streets emanating from the palace at 1.

confirmed his approval of Trezzini's earlier effort, which had been printed not long before Le Blond arrived.[*] In any event, while it too focused on Vasilevskii Island Trezzini's more modest project definitely carried the day, and remained influential in planning the Island's development for the rest of the century. It is equally clear that implementation of Le Blond's grandiose scheme, which circulated in various manuscript and printed copies, would have been far beyond the technical and financial resources at Peter's command. Its more lasting significance lies in the inspiration it gave to Russian planners of a later generation.[40]

[*]According to a contemporary source (the secretary of the Dutch envoy in St. Petersburg), "When Mons. Le Blond, the famous architect of Paris whom he had taken into his service, arrived at Petersburg, Peter took him to Wasili Ostrof [Vasilevskii Island], and after walking over the whole island with the plan [Trezzini's] in his hand, said to him, 'Well, Mons. Le Blond, what is to be done to carry my plan into execution?' 'Raze, Sire, raze,' answered Le Blond, elevating his shoulders; 'there is no other remedy than to demolish all that has been done and begin anew.' 'I thought so,' replied the Czar, and retired to his boat. He employed Le Blond to construct some handsome edifices at Peterhof and elsewhere, but never spoke to him again of Wasili Ostrof" (J. Staehlin, *Original Anecdotes of Peter the Great* [London, 1788], p. 202).

Trezzini was the most important of the architects who worked for Peter I, a question less of the monuments he left behind than of his ready compliance with the tsar's dictates, his influence on the overall shape of the nascent city, and the guidance he gave to countless Russian associates in the course of more than thirty years of teaching and building.

Masters and Students

The training in architectural theory as well as practice provided under the aegis of the St. Petersburg Chancellery of Construction constituted the first such training ever organized in Russia. The method was to form a team or "command [*komanda*]" under the direction of one of the architects recruited in Europe, the team to include, apart from the architect himself and his students, masters and apprentices in the various building trades. The first and most prominent "command" was that formed under Trezzini in 1707. Initially two youths from the Moscow School of Mathematics and Navigation, founded by Peter I only a few years earlier, were assigned to him. They were joined in 1710 by three students of foreign languages, including Mikhail Zemtsov, who had been sent to St. Petersburg from the Armory Chamber in Moscow. In 1711 a sixth Russian youth was assigned to Trezzini. As far as can now be determined, none of these youths had any actual building experience before joining the command; nor were any of them born into a building family, as might have been expected in view of local tradition. Rather, in addition to a presumed interest in the subject, their qualifications for studying architecture rested on a basic literacy in Russian and a demonstrated aptitude for mathematics and foreign (European) languages.[41]

The average age of this first group of architectural students in Russia was twenty (somewhat older than would be the case later), and their life as such was difficult at best. Not even paid by the chancellery until they had formally qualified as architectural students and begun to participate in the command's building projects (which for this group came in 1713), they were subject to the absolute authority of their masters, who were liable to treat their shortcomings with corporal punishment. Owing to these conditions, and perhaps to their own lack of experience, many of the students in the chancellery's commands quarreled with their masters, as the records show, or simply "fled from training."

In Trezzini's command the theoretical part of the course consisted basically—for most students, exclusively—of work in the new Russian edition of Vignola's textbook, a practice that became standard in eighteenth-century Russian architectural training. The aim was to assimilate the information concerning the five architectural orders and methods of building contained in the textbook especially by means of careful and repeated copying of its many illustrations (fig. 80). The most promising students moved from this to copying sketches by their teacher, and from that to free composition. On the practical side, students progressed by assuming ever greater responsibility in specific construction jobs. In Trezzini's command his senior students assisted him directly in the major projects assigned him by the tsar, sometimes going so far as to execute his plans—never very detailed—in his absence. In 1719, for example, Trezzini sent Zemtsov to Moscow to supervise the construction of certain new buildings there—buildings that were to "face the street," Zemtov's instructions read, "and not sit back in the lot, as was done in the old days."[42]

Mikhail Grigorievich Zemtsov was the "first Russian architect [*arkhitektor*]" in history.[43] Having joined Trezzini's command, as mentioned, in 1710, and learned Italian, which he could then interpret, he became his master's closest assistant, to the point of taking up residence in his house. By 1719 he had formally qualified as a student of architecture and in 1720, after the stint in

IONICK ORDER. 43

Figure 80 Two illustrations from the fourth English edition (London, 1694) of Vignola's textbook, entitled *Vignola, or the Compleat Architect. Shewing, in a plain and easie Way, the Rules of the Five Orders in Architecture.* The Russian 1722 edition of same also closely followed the original Italian text and illustrations.

Moscow, he joined Niccolo Michetti's command, whom he also assisted as interpreter. In 1721 Michetti sent him to work on the palace of Kadriorg in Reval (now Tallinn), commissioned by Peter I in 1718 for his wife Catherine (fig. 81); and from there Peter ordered him to travel to Stockholm, where he was to study the local architecture and to engage "two or more masters with skills we do not have, but of which we have need."[44] Zemstov hired eight craftsmen during his several months' stay in Stockholm, including, by his report, masters who could lay bricks in such a way as to be impervious to damp. By 1723 he was back in St. Petersburg, where he seems to have taken charge of landscaping Peter's residences in the city and suburbs, which in practice meant designing various structures for their extensive parks. A skilled draftsman, he was also commissioned by Peter I to copy the plates from Sebastien LeClerc's treatise on landscape architecture published at Paris in 1714.

Figure 81   Palace of Kadriorg, Tallinn (formerly Reval), Estonia, 1718–1727; N. Michetti, architect.

It was in 1723, too, that Zemtsov was certified by Michetti in the rank of *arkhitekturii gezel'* (from German *Geselle* or journeyman), which entitled him to work independently at an annual salary of 180 rubles (up from 120). The following year he petitioned Peter to be recognized as *arkhitektor* for his work "for the glory of the Russian nation [*natsii rossiiskoi*]." An examining committee was accordingly organized at the Chancellery of Construction comprised of Trezzini, C. B. Rastrelli, Van Zwiedten, and Chiaveri. The committee decided that for his accomplishments "in the architectural art and in the practice [thereof] with diligence in buildings for His Imperial Majesty" Zemtsov merited his promotion. This somewhat equivocal attestation was Trezzini's idea; Rastrelli had wanted to go further, and to certify Zemtsov as "architect full and actual [*arkhitektor polnii i deistvitel'nyi*]" with an annual salary comparable to Architect Michetti's (1,000 rubles) because he bore comparable responsibilities (at this time Trezzini's annual salary was also 1,000 rubles plus housing and other allowances, Chiaveri's 1,100, and that of a certain Dutch "sluice master" 1,540 rubles). But Van Zwiedten and Trezzini insisted that Zemstov's annual salary be set at 600 rubles, and the chancellery made it 550[45]—having decided, probably, and probably for financial reasons alone, that a Russian subject need not be paid as much as a foreigner.[*]

As early as 1722 Zemtsov had his own "architectural student" assisting him, and by 1723 he was in charge of his own command. In 1724 it was the largest architectural command in St. Petersburg, its fourteen students engaged at various stages in a course of arithmetic, geometry, Vignola on the architectural orders, drafting, and on-site instruction. The lessons were conducted in a special room of Michetti's house, where Zemtsov was again living; not long afterward the school, steadily growing, moved to more spacious quarters in the nearby *Pochtovyi dvor* (Post Office). Also living with Zemtsov at this time and assisting him in his school were two advanced architectural students recently returned from Italy, T. N. Usov and P. M. Eropkin.

Zemtsov's most important contribution to the architectural revolution of his time was as Peter I's collaborator in creating the royal parks in and around St. Petersburg, particularly the Summer Garden and the grounds at Peterhof. His only surviving building, the church of Sts. Simeon and Anna in Leningrad (pl. 27), is obviously modeled on Trezzini's work (cf. pls. 25A and 26). A so-called Italian palace that had been built in St. Petersburg in wood early in the 1720s according to plans by Michetti and landscaped by Zemtsov was rebuilt in brick and stone in 1725–1726 under Zemtsov's supervision, and in 1730 he designed

[*]Between 1716 and 1722 the annual salary of one of the most highly regarded native builders, Ivan Ustinov, son of Grigorii Ustinov, also a leading builder (and part-time typesetter) under whom Ivan had trained, was 180 rubles—up from the 136 rubles assigned to him annually from 1712 to 1716 (up in turn from the 36 rubles a year he was earning in 1712, when he was sent from Moscow to work in St. Petersburg) (see Mikhailov, *Arkhitektor Ukhtomskii*, pp. 12 and 333 [n. 9]). A hierarchy is clearly apparent in these pay scales: (1) European masters, (2) European-trained native masters, (3) locally (traditionally) trained native builders.

Figure 82 Anichkov palace, St. Petersburg; original design of the main facade by M. G. Zemtsov, ca. 1741.

an orangery for it. His sketch and plan of an elaborate pavilion or hall—"Zala" or "Sala"—erected in the Summer Garden in 1727 also survive. This appears to have been the first building actually put up following his designs. Various other surviving sketches and plans—of palaces, triumphal arches, churches, and church towers—testify to the leading role Zemstov played in the architectural embellishment of St. Petersburg in the 1730s and 1740s, where his activities included designing the Anichkov palace (fig. 82) and repairing the interiors of Trezzini's building of the Twelve Colleges. It is a more modest record, in sum, than Russian nationalist historians have tried to claim for him. Yet it shows both how well and how soon the principles of European architecture could be learned by a Russian without extensive study in Europe itself.[46]

By contrast, T. N. Usov and P. M. Eropkin, mentioned above, were among the first Russians sent to Europe by Peter I expressly for the purpose of studying architecture—"civil architecture"—rather than shipbuilding and navigation, mathematics with a view to practicing either, or any of the other arts and sciences. The idea of doing so may have been first put to the tsar by an officer in his service, Iurii Kologrivov, who in 1716 submitted a detailed proposal for improving the state in Russia of the "third element of architecture [*arkhitektura*], namely the civil [*tsivilis'*], the first two being the naval [*navalis*] and the military [*militaris'*]." Kologrivov pointed out that apart from arithmetic and geometry the "parts [*chasti*]" of architecture included "history, the pictorial arts, sculpture, optics, perspective, [and] mechanics [*gistoriia, piktura, skulptura, perspektiva, mekhanika*]," without a knowledge of which it was "impossible to be a good architect [*arkhitektor*]." He proposed that "two students, intelligent and of a good constitution, [and] already skilled in drawing—since in architecture nothing takes more time than drawing"—be selected to pursue a special three-year course of training. The first year would be devoted to theory, in which the students would attend to the subjects mentioned "and become adept at drawing, and learn such language and history as are appropriate"; while the next two years would consist of "practics [*praktika*]," in which they would study the construction of a large building from its foundations up. "And if possible," Kologrivov added, "such practical training should be done in Italy, for two years, which is like four years here." Kologrivov proposed himself to take charge of such students as the tsar might designate for further study in Italy or better, in Rome, "since I know the language and the city"; and he rounded off his proposal by outlining the costs involved in the venture and the itinerary to be followed.[47]

The proposal was accepted, and Kologrivov went to Rome. On his way he bought numerous paintings for Peter I (a total of 117 in Brussels and Antwerp) and, once in Rome (1718), hired builders for the Russian service (including Niccolo Michetti) and bought statuary for the Summer Garden. He returned to Russia only in the reign of Peter's grandson, Peter III (1727–1730), and practiced architecture in various, evidently minor capacities until his death in 1755.[48] Kologrivov's student charges went on to somewhat greater fame, if not to any greater fortune.

In 1716, as was mentioned earlier, Peter I ordered that twenty members of the noble class not less than seventeen years of age were to prepare to study architecture abroad. Eventually eight students were dispatched, four to train in Holland, four in Italy. The latter included Usov and Eropkin. They traveled overland to Amsterdam and by sea to Livorno (as Kologrivov had proposed), where they studied Italian while waiting some six months for their leader to join them. The whole party then proceeded to Venice and on to Rome, where Usov, Eropkin, and their two comrades studied for a time with Sebastiano Cipriani, an architect of some distinction and member of the famous Academy of St. Luke who had earlier, it seems, taught Kologrivov. They studied next at the still more illustrious Academy of Design in Florence, where Kologrivov had successfully sought the duke's protection. In June 1723 the four students received permission from the tsar to return to Russia. On their arrival in St. Petersburg he personally interviewed them and set them to work drawing up projects and models for houses and gardens at Preobrazhenskoe, his residence in suburban Moscow, and at Strelna, near St. Petersburg.

The following year Peter I commissioned Usov and Eropkin to design further projects and models for his palace and park at Strelna and, pleased with the results, ordered the Chancellery of Construction to examine and certify them. The examination was conducted by a committee composed of Trezzini, C. B. Rastrelli, and Zemtsov (only very recently certified himself), and took place on December 21, 1724. Rastrelli proposed to accord them the rank of *arkhitektor*, Trezzini and Zemtsov, the lesser status of *gesel'*, with annual salaries of 250 rubles, on the grounds that "although they have been in foreign states, and have been trained in theory, they are not so skilled in practice."[49]

Usov and Eropkin then took up residence with Zemtsov, who gave them a studio and the benefit of his advice while they in turn gave him books and prints brought from Italy. Sometime in 1725 Usov designed a palace for Strelna of much larger overall dimensions and much richer interiors than any so far seen in Russia. It also employed the enfilade system of aligning internal doors in sequence, usually close to the windows, so that a vista is obtained through the series of rooms when all the doors are open; Le Blond had introduced the system in Russia, where it came to be widely applied in palaces and great houses. For their work at Strelna, Usov and Eropkin were soon judged—by a committee composed this time of Trezzini, C. B. Rastrelli, Zemstov, and Chiaveri—worthy "to be inscribed in the rank of architect." They thus moved to the forefront of St. Petersburg builders at a time when, following Peter I's death (January 1725), any major building in the area had largely come to a halt. Usov, evidently the abler of the two, later tested the architectural qualifications of two of Van Zweidten's students, whom he judged to draw "very badly" and recommended that they be transferred to Zemstov's command. He died on May 13, 1728, at the age of twenty-eight, in Moscow, where he had been sent to remodel the former Golovin mansion. Eropkin, on the other hand, was appointed to the newly formed "Commission for the Construction of St. Petersburg" in 1737, where he seems to have taken the lead in drawing up a lengthy building code, in effect the first "treatise-codex on architecture and town planning" ever composed in Russia. He also translated an edition of Palladio before being banished from the capital for his alleged involvement in a political plot.[50]

The name Ivan Korobov came up early in this chapter, when discussing Peter I's taste in architecture. Korobov[51] was attending the Moscow School of Mathematics and Navigation when in May 1714 he and nineteen other students were transferred on the tsar's orders to St. Petersburg, there to take up places in Peter's new Naval Academy. In the fall of 1718 Korobov and I. A. Mordvinov were selected for further study in Italy, both youths having shown, as it was reported to Peter, exceptional aptitude in "architectural science [*arkhitekturnaia nauka*]." But eventually they were sent instead to the Netherlands, there to learn, in the words of Peter's supervising agent in Amsterdam, "civil architecture as well as how to make sluices, lay out gardens, and dig foundations."[52] It was from Antwerp that Korobov wrote to Peter in July 1724 requesting that he be allowed to proceed to France and Italy, the letter which prompted Peter's negative reply as quoted at length above (pp. 148–149).

More specifically, Korobov had asked permission to go to France and Italy, "where the roots of architecture and the other arts are to be found," so that he might "inspect the local buildings and listen to skilled artists, whence I could obtain great benefit." He complained that during his time in Brabant he had not seen any "skilled architectural art in building" nor gained any practical experience. So now he most earnestly, indeed tearfully, entreated the tsar to be allowed to move on, and not be required to stay longer in the Netherlands, where "architecture as a fine art," he insisted, was not practiced. But Peter ordered Korobov to move from Brabant to Holland, there to study the "Dutch manner in architecture" and to learn in particular Dutch techniques in sluice making, foundation work, and landscaping. Korobov did as he was told, as a letter to Peter from him and Mordvinov sent from Amsterdam in January 1725 confirms.[53]

Soon after Peter's death Korobov and Mordvinov wrote to his widow and successor, Catherine I, asking to be relieved of their duty to investigate "sluice matters," which were "quite separate from architecture" and even "contrary to the principles of this science." They asked to be allowed to study, in Amsterdam, "only the Dutch manner in building and in decorating gardens and in foundation work," lest they lose what architectural training they had already acquired and meant to employ in Catherine's service. This request was also, apparently, denied; more than a year later Korobov and Mordvinov reported in a letter to the head of the empress's personal office that when not engaged in sluice making in Amsterdam they were left to their own devices, there being no architectural work available to them, "since all the houses in town are built from the ground up by carpenters, and not by architects in accordance with the rules we learned in Antwerp. . . ; but foundation work we frequently observe, and have seen sufficiently how to do it." They finally returned to St. Petersburg in 1727, when Korobov was certified as an architect and appointed to work at the Admiralty, which he did for the next fourteen years. Several of his sketches survive from this period to show his skill in drafting and his mastery of the St. Petersburg style in Russian architecture (fig. 83). The design of the church of St. Panteleimon in Leningrad (1735–1739) has been attributed to him (pl. 28).[54] He died in Moscow in 1747.

In all, at least seventeen young Russians were sent to Europe to study architecture in the later years of Peter I's reign, principally to Amsterdam and Rome. In every case, it seems, the objective was to complete the theoretical part of their training and to obtain as much practical experience as possible. Naturally, these students—or *pensionery*, as they came to be called—would also have learned languages while abroad and seen at first hand various masterpieces of European architecture. Returning to St. Petersburg after several years, they completed the practical side of their training in one of the commands administered by the Chancellery of Construction, where they were sooner or later certified to practice independently and then appointed to work on a royal residence or other major building project. The number of these Petrine *pensionery* included almost all of the first generation of native-born architects—*arkhitektory*—to work in Russia: I. F. Michurin, I. G. Ustinov, and M. A. Bashmakov were among them as well as Usov, Eropkin, Mordvinov, and Korobov. And thus was founded the tradition of architectural *pensionerstvo* in Russia, or the practice of sending young men abroad on state scholarships to study architecture in the leading centers of Europe.[55]

Figure 83   Design sketches for two palaces by I. K. Korobov, 1724.

It is clear that by the end of Peter I's reign young Russians trained abroad had absorbed both the principles of contemporary European architecture and the corresponding notion of the builder—the "architect [*arkhitektor*]"—as artist. Korobov's correspondence from Brabant and Amsterdam, or Kologrivov's Italian proposal of 1716, are proof enough of that. But more, the examinations administered at the St. Petersburg Chancellery of Construction for the rank of *arkhitektor* indicate that by this time, too, the contemporary European conception of architecture—*arkhitektura*—had been established in Russia itself.[56] The examinations proceeded first by posing questions of theory, to be answered orally, and then by setting practical problems of building, to be solved by designing a project; and plainly, throughout the proceedings, *arkhitektura* was understood as nothing less or other than the art or science of building—*iskusstvo* or *nauka*—in its most advanced and desirable form. More specifically, architecture was now understood to consist of a solid grounding in mathematics and in one or more European languages (Italian, French, Dutch, German, Latin), a knowledge of drawing including especially drawing to scale, a familiarity with the basic European works on architecture, notably Vignola's textbook, and an ability to put the principles it expounded into practice. Building at its best in Russia, in other words, had ceased being a craft acquired solely through practical experience in accordance with local traditions and was now a matter of theoretical knowledge and systematic training. It was an art or a science—an art based on science—acquired first by studying in a formal pedagogical setting imbued with universal (European, or Classical) norms and then by participating in one or more major building projects supervised by a certified architect. This new concept of what constituted building at its best informed the course of instruction established under the Chancellery of Construction by Trezzini, Michetti, Zemtsov, and others in the first years of St. Petersburg's existence: a course that by the end of Peter's reign was also regarded, in the training of the most promising students, as preparatory to several years' study in Europe.

To be sure, these changes in outlook and training affected in these early years only a tiny minority of patrons and builders, whose efforts were confined almost exclusively to St. Petersburg and its environs. But the break with tradition was to prove decisive. And a critical factor here was the continuity provided in the training of builders for the ruler's service. Zemtsov, just back from Reval and Stockholm, formed a command in 1723 on the model of those of his own teachers Trezzini and Michetti, and from which dozens of other native-born builders proceeded to their tasks. Korobov, just back from Antwerp and Amsterdam, organized a similar school in 1727 under the auspices of the Admiralty. His students included S. I. Chevakinskii, perhaps the most distinguished of the native architects to work in St. Petersburg in the middle decades of the eighteenth century and the creator, with others, of an authentic Russian version of the international Baroque (the earlier St. Petersburg style is best viewed as a variant of the northern Baroque). In short, the Petrine revolution in Russian building norms was perpetuated in the succession of architectural commands set up by leading architects, mainly under the St. Petersburg Chancellery of Construction, until the 1760s, when the formal training of Russian architects was institutionalized, reflecting a general European trend, in the new St. Petersburg Academy of Fine Arts.[57]

Nor did the crucial role played by European masters in the development of Russian architecture end with the training of the first generation of Russian architects. The single most important figure of the 1740s and 1750s, decades that witnessed the flowering of the Baroque in Russia, was Bartolomeo Francesco Rastrelli (1700–1771). Rastrelli's success was partly a matter of talent, partly of politics, and partly of luck—the luck in the first instance of having been born the son of the sculptor and architect Carlo Bartolomeo Rastrelli, his first teacher, who in 1716 had moved with his family from Paris to St. Petersburg at Peter I's invitation. It was also the luck of having come to maturity as an architect when trained Russian personnel were available to assist him in the realization of projects which in scale and even in finish are comparable to outstanding works of contemporary architecture in Europe. I. F. Michurin, for example, one of Peter I's *pensionery,* actually built the splendid church of St. Andrew in Kiev (pl. 29) according to plans by Rastrelli, a procedure that was not unusual in his career. For having received various commissions in the 1730s from Empress Anna and her favorites (from the notorious Count Biron, notably), Rastrelli survived the former's death (1740) and the latter's disgrace to become the favorite architect of Empress Elizabeth (1741–1762) and her court, by whom he was deluged with orders to build town residences, country houses, churches, and palaces: buildings that in turn engendered countless imitations throughout the Russian Empire.[58]

Another circumstance assisting Rastrelli's rise was that in spite of his European and especially Italian background and continuing connections (his marriage to an Italian woman, his travels and studies—and eventual retirement— in Europe), he knew Russian and was quite at home in St. Petersburg, where he had lived off and on from the age of sixteen. He was the first artist of any kind in Russia to become known beyond the confines of the court. Early in the twentieth century Grabar could still find "a naive, isolated country squire who will swear to you that his house and church, obvious products of the second half of the nineteenth century, are the work of Rastrelli!"[59]

The influence of Bernini and Borromini, on the one hand, and of Zemtsov, on the other, have been detected in Rastrelli's mature work in St. Petersburg, the most important examples of which include an elaborate Summer Palace built for Empress Elizabeth (pulled down in 1797) and, still standing, the Winter Palace (pls. 62A–C); it is the fourth such palace on the site, Rastrelli himself having built, between 1732 and 1735, the more modest third.[60] His main church of the Smolnyi convent (pl. 30) and the Stroganov (pl. 61) as well as Vorontsov palaces also survive.[61] And to these architectural monuments of Leningrad can be added the grandiose Catherine palace at suburban Tsarskoe selo, now Pushkino (fig. 84, pl. 60).[62] The Baroque splendor of these buildings, for all of their frequent and sometimes extensive restoration, excites admiration to this day.

Among the architects who worked in Rastrelli's shadow Pietro (or Piero) Antonio Trezzini should not be slighted, as historians, in highlighting the work of his Russian contemporaries, have tended to do. A relation—the son?—of Dominico Trezzini, by whom he was trained, P. A. Trezzini studied further in his family's native Switzerland before returning to Russia, where he worked

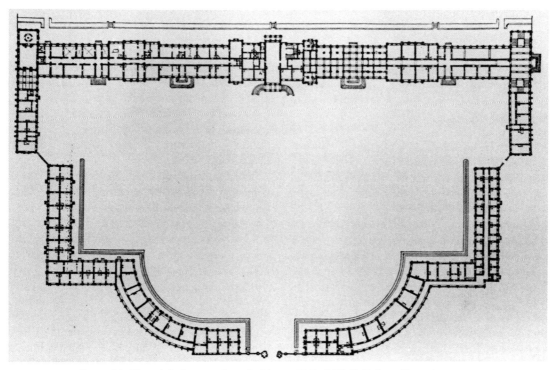

Figure 84   Plan of Catherine palace, Pushkino, 1742–1756; B. F. Rastrelli, architect.

between 1726 and 1751, when he went to Italy (perhaps in connection with Rastrelli's retirement there).[63] He was particularly active in St. Petersburg. By comparison with Rastrelli's work Trezzini's was more solidly in the Italian style, although local or localized features are also evident especially in his ecclesiastical projects, for example, in his cupolas, the handling of which reveals the influence again of Zemtsov (fig. 85; pl. 33). Yet it was precisely in his designs for churches particularly of the pentacupolar type that Trezzini in turn most strongly influenced his younger Russian collaborators, above all Chevakinskii, whose best surviving work is the pentacupolar St. Nicholas cathedral in Leningrad (pl. 31). Indeed, it has been suggested that together with Rastrelli P. A. Trezzini was largely responsible for the rapid spread in Russia in the 1740s and 1750s of major churches of this type.[64] Combining the traditional pentacupolar form with newly light and spacious interiors, lavish internal and external decoration, and an overall symmetry and refinement of design, Rastrelli's (and Michurin's) St. Andrew's church in Kiev (pl. 29) or Chevakinskii's St. Nicholas cathedral in Leningrad (pl. 31) represent perhaps the finest surviving examples of an architecture that was at once Russian and Baroque.

Figure 85 Church of the Transfiguration of the Savior, St. Petersburg, 1745–1754; P. A. Trezzini and M. G. Zemtsov, architects; contemporary drawing of the facade and plan.

REVOLUTION BY DECREE

St. Petersburg the military base, the shipyard and port, the administrative capital and royal residence, the principal site and then the embodiment of the
Petrine revolution in Russian architecture: St. Petersburg was built to order,
the order of one man, Peter I. His decision that it should become such a center
dates to soon after his forces conquered the site from the Swedes, in the spring
of 1703. But a less auspicious setting in which to found a city is difficult to
imagine.

In European urban history, it has been noted, "the choice of a site was probably the most significant single factor shaping a city's growth pattern and urban
picture." And

> traditionally the demands to be met included a healthy climate; a year-round
> fresh-water supply; a fertile surrounding countryside; accessibility to trade
> routes; safety from floods, avalanches, and landslides; and safety from enemies.
> The last consideration, although not always decisive, generally was of primary
> importance to city founders.[65]

In violation of virtually every one of these principles, the site chosen for St.
Petersburg was a marshy river delta, its maze of islands subject to frequent flooding,* its damp climate wearying if not downright insalubrious, its extreme
northern location—the northernmost of any major city in the world—unset-
tling in the prolonged darkness of its winter months and the extended day-
light—the "white nights"—of its short summer. The Neva itself, from the beginning the city's principal waterway, is free of ice, and therefore navigable, an
average of 218 days a year, or not much more than half the time. The soils of
the immediate area are poor, its vegetation sparse; under a natural economy it
never supported more than a few fishing hamlets. From a geopolitical perspective, moreover, its accessibility to major trade routes, and its defensibility, have
always been problematic.[66]

In 1703, to be sure, both the natural setting and the geographical position
of St. Petersburg's site offered certain strategic advantages to a commander bent
on controlling the area. Then too, under Swedish rule the fortified settlement
of Nyenskans (in Swedish) or Nienshants (in Russian; also Kantsy or Novyi
Kantsy in the Russian sources, Newaschanze in German, Skanz ter Nyen in
Dutch, Nevalinna in Finnish), located just to the south of the last big bend in
the Neva, where the river turns west to flow rapidly into its delta, had become
something of a regional trading center. Nyenskans/Nienshants, with its modern
fort and outworks (German *Schanze* = entrenchment, redoubt, earthworks), its

---

*In fact, 269 times (as of 1986) since the city's
founding, for an average of nearly one serious flood
a year. The problem of flooding remained so severe
that in 1980, finally, construction began on a gigantic sand, rock, and concrete barrier more than thirty
meters wide and twenty-four kilometers long across
the Gulf of Finland on a line with the island of Kotlin, which with various other islands is to be incorporated in the barrier. When completed (if ever),
the whole system will in effect seal off the city from
the rest of the Gulf and the Baltic Sea beyond it,
where the flooding is thought to originate. The barrier will be pierced by six locks or gates and two ship
canals, permitting sea traffic to and from Leningrad.

approximately 450 houses and Swedish, German, and Russian churches, was the nearest settlement of any size to the site where St. Petersburg would rise.

On or about May 2, 1703, Peter I renamed Nyenskans/Nienshants "Shlot-burg" (compare German *Schlot* or "neck," referring no doubt to the nearby neck of the Neva).[67] According to contemporary official sources, the tsar and his lieutenants then decided to look for a better place to fortify, which they soon found: a little island called "Lust-Eland" (in Swedish; "Janni-saari," or "Hare Island," in Finnish) located about four kilometers down river from Shlotburg, in the main channel of the Neva, roughly at the point where it separates into several branches, a spot accessible from the Finnish Gulf and Baltic Sea to the largest vessels then afloat (see fig. 92, Chap. 7). There, on May 16, 1703, the foundations of a fortress to be called "St. Petersburg"—*Sanktpeterburg* or *Sankt'-piterburkh* in Russian (or russified German)—were laid.[68]

There is some evidence that the new fortress only received this name on or about June 29, 1703, when its church was ceremoniously founded and dedicated to Sts. Peter and Paul, whose feast day it was.[69] Our first dated reference to St. Petersburg is a notation on a letter sent to the tsar by one of his officials in Moscow, which indicates that the letter was "received in Sant-Piterburkh" on June 30, 1703.[70] The Latin or Latin-based forms "Petropolis" and "Petro-pol' " are also to be found in documents of July 1703, and of later dates.[71] In any case, an edition of the Moscow *Vedomosti* (*Gazette*) published in August 1703 announced that "His Tsarish Majesty has ordered a fortified town [*gorod i krepost'*] to be built not far from Shlotburg, by the sea, so that henceforth all goods which arrive at Riga, Narva, and Shantsy should find a haven there, as should Persian and Chinese goods."[72] In a letter of September 1704 to A. D. Menshikov, Peter I wrote that "in three or four days we will be in the metropolis, St. Petersburg [*v stolitsu, Piterburkh*]."[73] That same autumn construction began on an "Admiralty [*Admiralteistvo*]" or fortified shipyard sited on the left or southern bank of the Neva, at a place just across and a little down river from the fortress.

A fortress and more, a fortified town; a harbor; shipyards; "the metropolis" (*stolitsa* could of course also be translated "capital" or "capital city"): within a year of choosing the site Peter I had obviously decided, for both strategic and commercial reasons, that a port city of some importance should rise on it and be called, in an oddly Germanic formulation, after his own patron saint. It is equally clear that for the next few years strategic considerations predominated in the city's development and that in this initial or outpost phase of its history it otherwise grew spontaneously—thus following, in these respects, traditional Russian norms.

By 1710 an up-to-date system of largely earthen defenses had been completed after Dominico Trezzini's designs, a system consisting mainly of the six-bas-tioned Peter-Paul fortress (as it came to be called, after its church) with extensive outworks (most notably the *Kronverk*, or "Crownwork," located just behind it); the ramparts of the Admiralty complex; and the round bastion on Kotlin

Island, out in the Finnish Gulf, protecting the seaward approach. By this time, too, a more or less permanent population of 8,000 laborers, soldiers, and others together with a seasonal population of that many again and more lived and worked and worshipped in some 16,000 houses, shops, and churches jurisdictionally divided into several *slobody*, again on the traditional pattern. Almost all of these buildings were small one-story wooden structures hastily and haphazardly erected by native builders along narrow crooked lanes, and were clustered in the vicinity of the fortress—on the large island immediately behind it—and on the left bank of the Neva, on either side of the Admiralty. The first masonry houses in St. Petersburg, belonging to Count G. I. Golovkin, Prince Menshikov, and the tsar (the Summer Palace), were begun only in 1710.[74]

Peter I's direct concern with the construction of St. Petersburg's defenses dates to the city's very beginnings, as indicated: to the spring of 1703, when the foundations of the first Peter-Paul fortress, to be built of earth and wood, were laid. His concern with the rest of the town's development dates to 1706. In Peter's correspondence with various officials of the second half of that year we find him issuing instructions on how to build wharves, observing with pleasure the completion of some masonry construction in the center of town, and insisting that new buildings outside the fortress should be uniform in size and face the street, whether it was straight or curved—this last instruction, as we know from the preceding chapter, a reflection of earlier directives to Moscow's residents.[75] It was also in 1706 that Peter founded, in a house belonging to Ulian Akimovich Seniavin and located very near his own, a Chancellery of Urban Affairs (*Kantseliariia gorodovykh del*) to coordinate all aspects of the building of St. Petersburg. Seniavin was named director of the chancellery, and Dominico Trezzini its chief architect. "Chancellery of Fortification Matters" might be a stricter translation of the Russian here, given the more limited meaning that the term *gorod* still generally bore; but "Urban Affairs" more accurately reflects the scope of the chancellery's activities, which in any case was renamed, in 1723, the Chancellery of Construction (*Kantseliariia ot stroenii*), the name historians use.[76]

The pedagogical role of the St. Petersburg Chancellery of Construction—the critical part played by its officials in training, examining, and certifying architects and other building specialists for the tsar's service—has already been discussed. The chancellery also oversaw the annual conscription and deployment of thousands of laborers, the administration of all moneys levied for the construction of the city, and the purchase if not the actual production of huge quantities of building materials. By 1721 the chancellery was spending annually sums of between 300,000 and 400,000 rubles, a figure approaching 5 percent of total state revenue.[77] Its architects and their assistants directed almost all of the principal works and drafted nearly all of the main projects; and anything of architectural significance undertaken elsewhere—at the Admiralty, for example—sooner or later required the chancellery's approval and cooperation.

Above all, it was the chief agent of Peter I, whose written and oral instructions regarding the building and beautifying of the new capital came, after 1714, in a flood.

In 1715 Siniavin was replaced as director by the higher ranking A. M. Cherkasskii, who knew nothing about the chancellery's business and in 1719 was named governor of Siberia; meanwhile, apparently, Trezzini assumed complete control, although he was nominally subordinate (until 1719) to Le Blond. In 1723, when Siniavin returned as director and Trezzini was confirmed as chief architect, the chancellery reported to Peter I's personal office that it had fifty "foreign masters" in its pay (including, with Trezzini, eight architects) and some 4,597 laborers currently at work on various projects in and around St. Petersburg (this was in May, before the building season was in full swing). In addition, according to other contemporary official sources, between 1724 and 1727 the chancellery had an administrative staff of fifty-four (the director, two subdirectors, nine "commissars," forty-two secretaries, interpreters, and guards), a further 1,650 craftsmen in its pay (366 of them "foreigners"), and a battalion of 669 soldiers at its disposal.[78]

In January 1725, when Peter I died, the Chancellery of Construction was under the immediate supervision of the emperor's personal office, a position it had been steadily attaining since 1711.[79] By 1732 the chancellery had become a kind of ministry of construction setting building standards for the whole country, and so large and cumbersome that some of its responsibilities were given to several other offices, one concerned with fortification, another with naval construction, and a third with the imperial residences; but everything else—"churches, colleges, covered markets, hospitals, and any other buildings," especially governmental buildings—remained in the chancellery's domain.[80] In the scope of its operations, as in the number of people it employed, the Chancellery of Construction had been without precedent in Russian history. It had served in effect as the chief administrative agency of the Petrine revolution in Russian architecture.

The annual conscriptions of laborers for the construction of St. Petersburg provide evidence of the scale both of the chancellery's operations and of the great project itself. According to the official Gazette (Vedomosti) of October 4, 1703, some 20,000 sappers had worked on the Peter-Paul fortress that first summer, a figure which did not include the thousands of workers felling trees up river of the fortress to be floated down to the site.[81] Beginning in 1704, decrees were issued requiring that provincial officials send annually to St. Petersburg a total of up to 44,000 construction workers in three shifts of two months' duration each, the first shift to start on March 25, the third to end on September 25 (soon the system was changed to two shifts of three months' duration each, beginning on April 1 and ending on October 1). Orders for the successive levies went out in November and December of the preceding year. In November 1706, for instance, Peter I directed that 15,000 workers be sent in two shifts from the regions around St. Petersburg itself, 9,000 of whom were to be put at Siniavin's disposal. At this time, however, the levies conflicted with those for the construction of Azov, as was reported to Peter in 1706. That year, he was told, Azov had not been sent the 26,000 workers and 3,000 craftsmen requested and without whom the business there could not proceed. Peter reiterated his order conscripting 15,000 workers for St. Petersburg, indicating that in any future competition for labor St. Petersburg took priority. It was in September 1706 that Peter referred to the place as his "paradise."[82]

Similarly, according to a decree of November 1707, two levies of 20,000 workers each were ordered for building in St. Petersburg during the upcoming season, with 8,000 men of each shift to be sent to General Bruce, in charge of fortification, and the rest to Siniavin at the Chancellery of Construction. In December 1709 a total of 40,000 construction workers were again conscripted for St. Petersburg, 4,000 men of the first shift to be sent to Bruce and 16,000 to Siniavin; and these figures do not include masons and bricklayers, who were to be separately recruited.[83] And so it went. In July 1710 a special levy in the Moscow government was to produce by September another 3,000 workers for St. Petersburg; in January 1712 it was the turn of the Kiev government to produce 3,000 men for the construction on Kotlin Island; in November 1713 a levy of 34,000 workers from all governments was announced for construction in St. Petersburg during the new building season.[84] Fifteen thousand workers; 20,000; 34,000; 40,000: by the standards of the time these were whole armies of men. *

We must not suppose that the continual levies of workers for the construction of St. Petersburg always reached the prescribed strength, however. Even more than in the case of Azov, the scarcity of free labor to hire, the administrative and other difficulties inherent in conscription (or forced labor), the distances workers had to travel from all over Russia to get to St. Petersburg, and the unattractive and even unsanitary conditions they had to endure, once there, all insured that the actual number of workers arriving in any one year fell short of the number conscripted. Thus in December 1709 Siniavin advised the tsar that out of the 8,000 men ordered to report to him by April 1 of that year, 1,569 had in fact shown up; in November 1711, again, the Senate complained that out of a levy of 15,800 workers imposed on the Moscow government in the previous year, only 12,064 men, or three-fourths of the prescribed number, were actually sent, the deficit including 1,365 critically needed masons.[85] Other figures show that more than a third of the laborers conscripted for construction in St. Petersburg in 1712 and again in 1714 did not report for work, and that in 1715 the proportion rose to more than 40 percent. Some of

*The yearly number of draftees for the army and navy during Peter I's reign ranged from a high of 51,912 in 1712 to a low of 500 in 1714, with an average annual conscription of about 27,000 men (L. G. Beskrovnyi, *Russkaia armiia i flot v XVIII veke* [M., 1958], pp. 23–29, 33–34). The Russian army that defeated the Swedes at Poltava in 1709, the major battle of the Russo-Swedish war, numbered about 42,000 men, while the army that campaigned in Finland in 1713 numbered about 15,000.

the shortage was made up by putting soldiers, convicted criminals, and prisoners of war to work. In 1712, for instance, more than 1,000 Swedish prisoners were sent from Moscow and Voronezh to St. Petersburg for building purposes. But such measures could not alleviate the chronic shortage of skilled craftsmen either available or willing to leave the Russian heartland to live and work in St. Petersburg. They had to be recruited, as best they could, by use of the carrot as well as the stick.[86]

Nevertheless, such figures as we have indicate that between 1703 and 1725 anywhere from 10,000 to 30,000 ordinary workers labored *annually* on the construction of St. Petersburg. These totals are the more impressive when set beside the maximum of a few thousand men known to have worked in any one season on any one project in pre-Petrine times (on the Belgorod defensive system, referred to in Chap. 3); or beside even the total of 30,000 workers said to have labored over two years (1707–1708), under what was thought to be a military emergency, building new defenses for Moscow (Chap. 5). At the same time, these figures tend to belie the allegations, originating in foreigners' travel accounts and acquiring thereafter the force of legend, that in these early years tens of thousands of workers—"60,000" in seven years, "100,000" in eight, "two-thirds" of the annual labor force—lost their lives in the construction of St. Petersburg. Luppov suggests reasonably enough that the total number of such deaths between 1703 and 1725 was in the thousands, and he points out that after 1710 if not before steps were taken to alleviate the situation by medical means.[87]

Equally impressive of the scale of St. Petersburg's construction under Peter I are figures relating to the production of building materials. Siniavin's reports to the tsar of 1709 and 1710, for example, indicate that 11,000,000 bricks had been manufactured in and around St. Petersburg for use in building in 1710.[88] This was an enormous sum for the time, greater by a factor of perhaps ten times than any comparable pre-Petrine figure; only the production in Moscow of 4,000,000 bricks over a period of two years (1702–1703) for use in the renovation of the Smolensk fortifications even approaches it; and that total was not to be reached again by Moscow's brickworks—soon subordinated to those in St. Petersburg—until the 1760s.[89] Moreover, after 1710 an annual production quota of 10,000,000 bricks was in force in St. Petersburg, a quota that the local brickmakers at first found hard to maintain. The Chancellery of Construction again took the lead, and by 1712 its brickworks employed several thousand craftsmen and laborers. In 1719 the latter were put under the direction of a foreign specialist, Timothy Fonarmus, and soon were producing to order 12,000,000 bricks and 3,000,000 tiles a year. In addition, by 1725 other governmental as well as private works were producing annually up to 3,000,000 bricks and 500,000 tiles in accordance with the chancellery's (with Dominico Trezzini's) specifications. And comparable advances had been made in the production of lumber, glass, lime, and cement *(tsement)*, which was now being manufactured in Russia for the first time.[90]

Yet for all of this remarkable progress the production of building materials fell far short of St. Petersburg's projected needs. What today is called "quality control" was one big problem, as contemporary European observers would notice (see Chap. 7). Wasteful construction methods meant that even with a total annual production of 15,000,000 bricks no more than thirty masonry houses of any size could be built in a year—and probably fewer, in view of the priority enjoyed by military construction (and of the universal need for brick stoves). The production of tiles was such that only official buildings and the mansions of grandees could be roofed with them; people of lesser means had to make do with wooden shingles, which following established methods were easier to manufacture; but even then there were shortages. Glass remained a rare and expensive commodity, so that windows were paned in mica even in the houses of grandees, while the mass of the population employed animal bladders or rags. Cut stone was used in considerable quantities in the building of St. Petersburg especially after 1714, and limestone and even marble were quarried nearby; but for years the finest stone needed for decorating in the "new style" had to be brought from afar, at great expense. And there is some evidence that even the most basic commodities—bricks, for instance—were also imported, either to augment the local supply or to improve on it. Thus in May 1720 Peter I ordered that three ships recently purchased in Holland were to be loaded with "English bricks" before sailing to Russia.[91]

Luppov considers it a "curious" yet "significant" fact, significant of the "success" in producing building materials which St. Petersburg had achieved, that fully 80 percent of the workers laboring under the Chancellery of Construction in 1709, and nearly 70 percent in 1714, were involved in the production and transport of building materials.[92] But surely these figures testify equally to the extravagance, if not the folly, of attempting to build, virtually overnight, a new-style metropolis in the wilderness.

Peter I's direct concern with the development of St. Petersburg beyond its fortifications dates, to repeat, to 1706. Over the next few years this concern was shared, however, by building projects at Azov or in Moscow and by, above all, the manifold tasks of his ongoing war against Sweden. Indeed, there is ample evidence that Peter regarded his decisive victory over the Swedes at Poltava in June 1709 as a turning point not only in the war but in the city's history as well: "Now with God's help the final stone in the foundation of St. Petersburg has been laid," he wrote to Admiral Apraksin on the day of the victory.[93] And after 1710 the city's rate of growth, as reflected in cadastral and other such records, sharply intensified. Its permanent population in 1710 of about 8,000 had tripled by 1717; and it had nearly doubled again—to approximately 40,000—by 1725.[94]

This rapid growth can be attributed directly to legislation by Peter I intended to enhance St. Petersburg's status as a commercial, industrial, administrative, and residential center. Beginning in 1712, for example, various ranks and categories of courtiers and administrators, members of the service nobility, and merchants were ordered to settle permanently in the city;[95] while another series of decrees redirected Archangel's foreign trade to the new port and otherwise favored St. Petersburg's commercial development.[96] In June 1714 a twice-weekly Moscow-St. Petersburg post was established; in 1718, Peter took steps to make St. Petersburg the ecclesiastical capital of his dominions; and in 1720, he ordered that its streets be cleared of unattended cattle.[97] The range if not the arbitrariness of these and numerous similar measures is remarkable. But of more direct interest here are Peter's regulations concerning the actual construction, planning, and beautifying of St. Petersburg in the years of its rapid initial growth.

This effort began in earnest in 1714 and drew both on his earlier legislation governing building in Moscow and on, more heavily than ever before, European models and expertise. The decree that houses be built in conformity with plans to be obtained from Dominico Trezzini has been mentioned. At the same time (April 1714), plain wooden construction was prohibited everywhere in St. Petersburg in favor of wattle and daub (*mazanka*), roofs were to be made of tiles or shingles, and houses alone—not fences, stables, or sheds—were to face the street, all under pain of severe fines. In October 1714 it was repeated that houses were to be built of wattle and daub—"in the Prussian manner"—with foundations of stone; in November, that houses were to face the street, that stables and sheds were to be kept to the rear of the lot, and that houses were to be built following the specified (Trezzini's) plans. It was also decreed that persons arriving in St. Petersburg, whether by land or water, were to bring with them a certain quantity of stones suitable for building purposes, there being a shortage of same in the vicinity of the new city. The decrees were printed to insure wide circulation.[98] It was in October 1714, and owing, it was said, to the shortage of skilled craftsmen available for work in St. Petersburg, that all further masonry construction was banned everywhere else in the tsar's dominions for an indefinite period of time.[99]

Peter I's regulations of 1714 governing building in St. Petersburg and elsewhere were reiterated, strengthened by the addition of penalties, and in some points augmented in the years that followed.[100] In fact, he would go much further. In 1715 and 1716, as noted earlier, he commissioned Trezzini and then Le Blond to draw up comprehensive plans for the city's development. Both plans focused on Vasilevskii Island, which at the time was largely unsettled:*

---

*According to a Dutch naval officer in Peter's service, Vasilevskii Island, uninhabited and nameless under the Swedes, was named after the Russian officer—Vasilii—who commanded the first battery emplaced on it. Messages then were sent "to Vasilii's island" (Staehlin, p. 193). But it is also thought that the island had been so named, in Russian, since 1500, possibly after a fourteenth-century local landowner, Vasilii Kazimer of Novgorod (*Russkii biograficheskii slovar'*, vol. 9 [SPb., 1903], pp. 294–95: entry "Vasilii Dmitrievich Korchmin").

in 1716 St. Petersburg's buildings were concentrated on Petersburg Island (behind the fortress), on the easternmost tip of Vasilevskii Island, and around the Admiralty complex, on the left bank of the Neva. Contrary, then, to the city's initial and natural pattern of growth—outward from the fortress and particularly from the Admiralty complex, where the progressively higher ground could afford protection against the continual flooding—Peter embraced the idea of making the desolate and exposed Vasilevskii Island the center of St. Petersburg; and for the rest of his life he issued numerous directives to that end.[101] The directives exude at times a maniacal air. For instance, a decree of April 9, 1719, ordered that from 700 to 1,000 large masonry houses were to be built on the Island along with 500 to 700 smaller ones, 300 to 500 smaller ones still, and so on; given the nexus of production quotas and building techniques mentioned above, whereby no more than thirty sizable masonry houses could be built annually, the order was exceedingly unrealistic. Yet it was issued again scarcely two years later, and equally without effect.[102]

As things turned out, Peter I's decision to develop Vasilevskii Island as the residential, commercial, and administrative center of St. Petersburg was to be largely frustrated. By the time of his death houses were finished on about a quarter of its assigned lots, and of these some 75 percent were wooden; while in the years immediately to follow the districts behind the Admiralty saw the most growth. Still, it is difficult not to admire the soaring ambition, the very impracticality of this legislation of Peter's last years. Gone is the preoccupation with fortification and fire prevention so characteristic of an earlier time. Instead, again and again we find an insistence on using "good builders," on following properly drawn plans, on building in a certain way not just to prevent fire but for the sake of "better construction"—on building, in what by the end of his reign had become a favorite phrase, "in accordance with architecture [*po arkhitekture*]." Build in St. Petersburg as it has been ordained, Peter commanded in April 1721, put up 595 streetlights, and do everything *po arkhitekture*.[103] Luppov is right to suggest that behind Peter's sometimes conflicting measures for the planning and construction of St. Petersburg can be detected a striving to create a capital in keeping with contemporary European notions of the ideal city, and that in doing so he was guided by several basic principles: (1) to create a well-built city of masonry structures fronting on straight streets and broad boulevards intersected at various points by an integrated system of canals; (2) to make the numerous waterways, natural and artificial, the city's principal means of communication and the city itself, as far as possible, a seaward or coastal town; (3) to subject all building both in and around the city to strict regulation; and (4) to settle categories of people—soldiers, tradesmen, merchants, artisans, officials—in specific districts of the city, which should provide it in turn with major functional zones or quarters.[104]

How far these objectives were achieved, during Peter I's life or at any time thereafter, is a question for the following chapter. But before addressing it one or two other matters need to be raised.

LANDSCAPES AND INTERIORS

St. Petersburg would not have been St. Petersburg—Leningrad would not be Leningrad—without its parks and gardens, both in town and in the suburbs. Before the reign of Peter I, however, the very concept of a large, artificially arranged space in the open air intended solely to provide pleasurable surroundings in which to relax and congregate, if not to dally, was virtually unknown in Russia.[105]

There is evidence from the later seventeenth century that some sort of terraced gardens existed within the Moscow Kremlin, that a pharmaceutical garden had been planted outside its walls, by the Main Pharmacy, and that a geometrically laid out garden with flowerbeds was to be found in the so-called *Tsaritsyn lug* or Royal Meadow stretching along the opposite bank of the Moscow river. Throughout the city, it seems, amid the abundance of trees and bushes, vegetables, herbs, and weeds, flowers grew in season. Suburban estate gardens were often extensive and might have included orchards and kitchen gardens, plantations of mulberry trees, junipers, and hop plants, stands of cedar, fir, and nut trees. The most extensive of these were at the royal estates of Kolomenskoe and especially Izmailovo, which was built up in the 1660s and 1670s and was celebrated for its vines from Astrakhan, its thirty-seven fish ponds, its apiaries, wild animal preserve, and numerous "German flowers and plants," in the words of a contemporary Russian source.[106]

Yet virtually all of this planting and gardening was at base an extension of the prevailing natural economy: was essentially utilitarian, or horticultural, in purpose, like the watermills that went with it; and was conceived within a tradition that in Europe went back to Roman times. For all of its expanse and occasional exotic touch, the estate at Izmailovo, centering on its wooden palace, was basically an Old-Russian *usad'ba* or farmstead. In 1702 the Dutch visitor Cornelis de Bruyn observed of Russian flowers generally that they were few and "feeble," that Russian gardens were "savage, without art or ornament," and that "fountains and water-jets," familiar in Europe since medieval times, were "unknown."* Only in the German Settlement, where a majority of the inhabitants kept gardens, were they "properly made." Bruyn did find one garden near a village belonging to a prominent figure at the tsar's court that was "quite large and very fine." It was the work of a gardener brought from Holland.[107]

The completely artificial garden or park designed exclusively to please the eye and perhaps also the ear and the nose, formal and elaborate, laid out along strict geometrical lines and animated by ornamental waterworks: a kind of outdoor theater of ideas and emotions expressed in statuary and peristyles, pavilions and grottos, lawns and measured walkways, hedges and enclosures, flowerbeds, trees, and shrubbery; this European concept, dating back to the Italian

---

*Indeed *any* sort of garden was rarely to be seen by peasant houses in Russia until the second half of the seventeenth century, and then only on suburban royal estates like Izmailovo (Ikonnikov, "Planirovochnye traditsii v narodnom zodchestve," p. 163).

Renaissance and much refined in France and Holland in the later seventeenth century, was implanted in Russia by Peter I. Already in 1702 Bruyn remarked that things had begun to change in Moscow in this regard, as they had with respect to building in general, "since the tsar has been in our country" (referring to Peter's lengthy stay in Holland in 1697).[108] It was not just an expression of Dutch pride. Although Peter had spent much of his youth on the royal estates near Moscow, including Izmailovo, there can be no doubt that in commissioning the parks and gardens of St. Petersburg and its suburbs he was inspired by what he had seen in Europe or knew from the European books, drawings, and prints that he collected.

His methods, again, were those of the Petrine architectural revolution more generally. Apart from acquiring countless books and graphics on the subject, Peter sent Russians abroad to study landscape gardening (especially Dutch, as we have seen), imported European masters to design parks and gardens, ordered the necessary materials and manpower, and oversaw both the planning and its execution.[109] In 1718 he supervised the publication in St. Petersburg of an album of engravings illustrating garden architecture in the French style (fig. 86); and in 1723 he ordered Zemtsov to copy the plates from LeClerc's popular

Figure 86 First page of *Kunshty sadov*, a book illustrating garden architecture, published St. Petersburg, 1718; engraving by A. Zubov.

work on the subject published at Paris in 1714.[110] In fact, the available evidence suggests that after shipbuilding and fortification Peter participated more closely in laying out the great parks and gardens of St. Petersburg and its environs than he did in any other aspect of his building program.[111]

The Summer Garden—at first it was called simply *Peterburgskii ogorod* or "Petersburg [kitchen] Garden," later *Letnyi sad* or "Summer Garden" after, presumably, the adjacent *Letnii dvorets* or "Summer Palace"—had been projected by Peter I as early as 1704; and he kept in close touch with its development for the remaining twenty years of his life.[112] Thus in 1708 and 1709 he supervised the work of Johannes van Blicklant, the "master of fountain affairs [*master fontannogo dela*]" who was in charge of laying out the Summer Garden, and corresponded with F. A. Vasilev, also a sometime engraver, who was designing galleries for it.[113] A letter of 1708 to Peter from a local official suggests the scale of the undertaking: 400 laborers were required to assist the gardeners and 100 carpenters, 60 masons, 16 plumbers, and another 60 workers were wanted to assist Blicklant with his fountains—although the official in question, A. V. Kikin, complained at the same time of having trouble finding the men.[114] In 1714 G. J. Mattarnowy arrived in St. Petersburg on Schlüter's recommendation bearing the splendid title of "grotto architect [*arkhitektor grotirnogo*] and master of fountain affairs," and proceeded to design among other projects a grotto and gallery for the Summer Garden. Peter himself is thought to have drawn up a plan for the Garden in 1717, while at Spa, perhaps with a view to guiding Le Blond, who was soon to take the matter in hand. At one time or another Dominico Trezzini, a certain Jan Roosen, and Zemtsov also took part in designing and constructing the Summer Garden. Early in the 1720s a series of Classical statues purchased in Italy (by Kologrivov) were installed; the statues are still to be seen in the Garden, except that then they included the famous Venus that is now on display in the Hermitage Museum.

Owing to later alterations, today's Summer Garden retains nearly nothing of its original aspect and layout, which to judge from contemporary engravings and descriptions (see Chap. 7) was in the Dutch rather than the French style, following Peter I's expressed preference. It is also much smaller than it once was. And of the many buildings originally standing within or along it, on either side, only the Summer Palace survives, having been restored, as closely as possible, to Trezzini's original design (pl. 54A).

Roughly the opposite is true of the palace and grounds at Peterhof (*Petergof;* russified to *Petrodvorets* in 1944), located about thirty kilometers from Leningrad on the southern shore of the Finnish Gulf.[115] Here the Upper and Lower Parks retain at least the general plan of Peter I's time, with many modifications and ornamental additions; but scarcely any of the main palace, its facade nearly 800 meters long (including jutties and wings, galleries and terminal pavilions), would have been recognizable to its first owner. As early as 1705 Peter had chosen the site as a convenient stopping place on his way from St. Petersburg to the fortress and naval base at Kronshtadt on the island of Kotlin, out in the gulf, and temporary wooden quarters were soon built for him. In May 1710 he initiated the planning of an elaborate park complete with grotto and fountains at Peterhof, as he had named the place. In 1714 the main palace was begun, also on Peter's orders and also, evidently, in conformity with his own rough sketches (fig. 76). In 1714 J. F. Braunstein was put in charge of constructing the palace while Le Blond, in 1716, was entrusted with planning the park. Michetti originally designed the latter's famous fountains and cascades.

Thanks to Le Blond the extensive grounds at Peterhof were completed largely in the French style, a style perfected in the later seventeenth century by his teacher Le Nôtre, who designed the gardens of Versailles and of the Tuilleries, both of which Peter I had seen during his visit to Paris in 1717. Drawing on Italian precedents, the style required that the garden be laid out along a well-defined axis with the main edifice—the palace—as the central pivot of the design; to these sixteenth-century fundamentals the seventeenth century had added a wealth of picturesque detail which Le Nôtre then simplified while expanding the overall composition. At Peterhof, as its various components came into being, the Upper Park spread out on a terrace behind the main palace and was comprised essentially of geometrically spaced plantings and strongly axial walkways bordered by trees, bushes, and fences. The Lower and far more complex Park radiated out in three directions from the great cascade beneath the front of the palace: directly ahead, by way of a large canal leading to the gulf, and slantwise to right and left, by way of two avenues leading to pavilions named Monplaisir and the Hermitage (*Monplezir* and *Ermitazh*: pls. 59B and 59D). These three rays were intersected by another avenue running west to east from a little house called Marly (the only surviving example of a Petrine country house: pl. 59C) and parallel to the gulf. At the points of intersection the so-called Adam and Eve fountains were located, and near each of the three pavilions another elaborate cascade was installed.

The main palace of Peterhof was finished by 1721 under the direction first of Braunstein and then of Le Blond. Judging from Zubov's engraved frontal elevation of 1717, which may be in part projectural (fig. 87), the palace was originally a tripartite structure of two stories, its central facade austerely decorated with a pediment and pilasters crowned by Corinthian capitals, and its adjacent facades covered with rusticated stonework and what looks like relief paneling. The most remarkable feature of the palace was located beneath its terrace, namely, the grotto and the great cascade, which formed a sort of socle for the building.

Already in 1721 work began on the first extension of the palace of Peterhof,

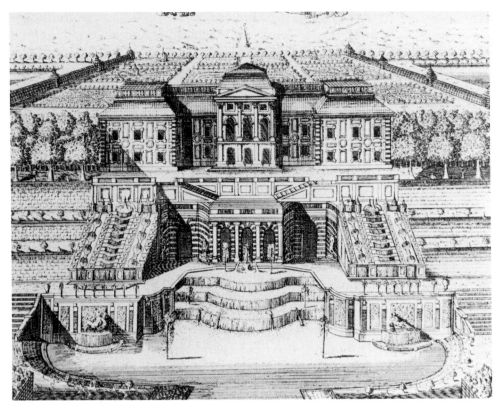

Figure 87   View of main palace at Peterhof with the Upper Park behind it and, beneath the terrace in front, the grotto and cascade; engraving by A. Zubov, 1717.

following plans by Michetti. Two lengthy galleries terminating in identical two-story wings were added to either side of the central structure, and the whole ensemble was freshly decorated in carved stone. Further renovations and extensions were undertaken later in the eighteenth century as well as in the nineteenth; and the entire structure, like the grounds and other buildings at Peterhof, was nearly obliterated in the Second World War. Since then it has been restored to something like its pre-War state (pl. 59A). Yet one of the palace's rooms, Peter I's oak-paneled study, preserves in the main its original aspect, as do the rooms in Monplaisir, in both cases the legacy of decorators brought from France by Le Blond. There is scarcely anything in the design, decoration, or furnishings of these rooms that is, or was, traditionally Russian (fig. 88). We have stepped into Europe.

Indeed, the Petrine revolution in interior decoration—in the decorative arts overall—was no less sweeping than in architecture itself. Between 1703 and 1707 a group of Swiss-Italian artisans who had come to Russia with Dominico Trezzini created for the interiors of three new churches in Moscow, as we noted in earlier chapters, a typically Baroque series of decorative sculptures that was

Figure 88   Catherine I as Minerva: carved wall panel after design by N. Pineau, ca. 1718; study of Peter I, main palace, Peterhof.

entirely new to Russia in both conception and execution (figs. 5, 41); and they thus inaugurated a trend that was to flower in the work of Rastrelli.[116] The Europeanization of the Russian iconostasis, begun in the later seventeenth century under Belorussian influence (fig. 51; pl. 20), was completed in the brilliant creation made to Trezzini's specifications for the Peter-Paul church in St. Petersburg by a team of fifty-six woodcarvers working in Moscow under I. P. Zarudnyi (pl. 25B; see also frontispiece).[117] Modeled to a considerable extent on the Baroque triumphal arch, which was of course also new to Russia, the iconostasis of the Peter-Paul church was thereafter widely imitated (pl. 32). The techniques of plaster and alabaster modeling, not alone in statuary but in interior decoration more generally, were brought to Russia in the Petrine period and first applied, by Italian and French masters, in the palaces of St. Petersburg (fig. 89).[118] Their decorative painting was another major aspect of the fundamentally new appearance that palace interiors assumed at this time.[119] Using a variety of techniques, French and Italian masters assisted by Russians painted the walls and *flat* ceilings of St. Petersburg palaces in an abundance of Baroque symbolic, allegorical, and mythological motives (fig. 90). Their work contrasts markedly with the elaborate vegetative ornamentation, animals, birds, and religious compositions that covered the walls and *vaulted* ceilings of seventeenth-century mansions and palaces in Moscow (fig. 91).

Still another Petrine innovation with respect to the interior of palaces was the picture gallery—and the practice itself of hanging easel paintings on walls. We noticed earlier in this chapter that in 1717 one of Peter I's officers, Kologrivov, purchased 117 paintings for him in Brussels and Antwerp. In Amsterdam that same year, according to a nearly contemporary report, Peter himself met a "dealer named Xsel, a Swiss, a good painter of history pieces and still life and, above all, an excellent connoisseur." Peter bought an entire lot of paintings, the report continues, and then hired Xsel "to attend to the preservation of his purchases and even to augment his collection." Xsel learned that Peter was particularly fond of the "Flemish and Brabantine schools" and of "Dutch sea pieces," especially those by Adam Silo, with specimens of which he "furnished the antechamber of his Summer Palace at Petersburg"; and "at Peterhof,

Figure 89   Allegory of Autumn sculpted in stucco after model by C. B. Rastrelli, 1716–1717; the Great Hall, palace of Monplaisir, Peterhof.

Figure 90 Allegory of Water (Neptune and Amphitrite) painted in tempera and gold leaf on stucco over plaster after design by P. Pillement, 1718; the Great Hall, palace of Monplaisir, Peterhof.

Figure 91 Interior of the Terem palace, Moscow Kremlin, 1630s, restored nineteenth century; view of arched passageway, staircase, vaulted ceiling.

where he formed the first gallery of paintings seen in Russia, in the palace called Monplaisir, the sea pieces of Silo were placed in the most conspicuous situations" (pl. 59B). The collection of seascapes, landscapes, portraits, still lifes, and genre paintings by Silo, Willem van de Velde II, Philips Wouwerman, and others which Peter hung at Monplaisir, a recent authority agrees, constituted "the ancestor of all other art galleries in Russia."[120]

Similarly, it was Peter I who gave the main impetus to the practice of decorating the interiors of Russian palaces and great houses with tapestries, first by acquiring for himself outstanding examples of the art, particularly at the Gobelins factory when he was in Paris (1717), and then by inviting several Gobelins masters to start up a factory in St. Petersburg. Soon Russian grandees as well as Peter's successors on the throne were buying tapestries abroad in large quantities, and within only a few years the St. Petersburg factory was producing good copies of French originals. By the end of the century the St. Petersburg "Tapestry Manufactory," in the judgment of a resident German, was producing "such excellent work—both hangings and carpeting—that better is not to be seen from the Gobelines [*sic*] at Paris." This observer was particularly impressed by the fact that "only native Russians are employed"; indeed, "nowhere perhaps is the progress of this nation in civilization more striking to the foreigner than in the spacious and extensive work-rooms of this manufactory."[121]

The eighteenth century in Russia, we read in the introduction to a major history of the country's decorative arts, was an age that

> lived under the magic spell of architecture. Architecture defined the very style of the age while decorative art, sculpture, and painting followed suit. Painting was filled with architectural details, with views of palaces, ruins, and cascades. Theatrical decoration was a continuous hymn to architecture. Triumphal processions and other public festivities were designed as architectural displays. Fireworks limned the outlines of a fantastical architecture.

A synthesis of the arts had come into being in which "decorative art played a huge role," a synthesis that was "defined in the first instance by architecture." Thus "to study eighteenth-century art is to witness not only the leading role of architecture among all the figurative arts, but the leading role of architecture in the creation of the synthesis." The assessment could not be clearer, and is amply borne out in the nearly 700 pages of text and 450 photographs that make up this collaborative work. Yet the crucial role played by European masters in this revolution in the decorative arts in Russia, the decisive nature of the underlying European and particularly French influences at work here, and the degree to which these Russian developments reflected a Europe-wide movement in interior decoration: none of this is brought out.[122]

Le Blond alone, to repeat, brought a train of specialists with him from France in 1716 who soon established nineteen workshops in St. Petersburg for producing the decorative and other finished materials needed to realize his designs.[123]

Nearly 300 Europeans—188 "foreigners" and 96 "newcomers from the conquered towns" of the Baltic region—were among the 1,455 registered tradesmen in St. Petersburg in the early 1720s, and by all indications they were concentrated in the building trades; other official figures indicate that of 1,650 craftsmen in the pay of the St. Petersburg Chancellery of Construction between 1724 and 1727, 366—nearly one-fourth—were "foreigners."[124] Of the approximately 250 artists and artisans identified as having decorated the Imperial palaces in and around St. Petersburg during the eighteenth century—the bulk of them (194) before 1760—some 49, or 1 in 5, were clearly European.[125] These figures may be contrasted with the 17 European names to be found among some 1,020 painters—scarcely 1 percent of the total—known to have worked for the tsars in the second half of the seventeenth century, primarily in decorating churches.[126]

Numbers, to be certain, cannot tell the whole story. C. B. Rastrelli, Philippe Pillement, Nicolas Pineau, François Pascal Wassoult, Bartolomeo Tarsia, Hans Conradt Ossner, Louis Caravaque: these were only the most prominent of the hundreds of painters and sculptors who decorated the palaces of St. Petersburg and its suburbs under Peter I while training countless Russians in their techniques. The designing, directing, training, fashion-setting role of the European decorative artists, like that of their compatriots the architects, must be stressed.

Nor can the whole story ever be told. Few enough buildings and gardens survive from the Petrine period in and around Leningrad, and fewer still interiors.[127] The immediate impact of the Petrine revolution on Russian architecture must therefore be traced in the surviving written and graphic memorials, lacunal though they are. That is the task of the next chapter.

The Revolution in Contemporary European Eyes

There reigns in this capital a kind of bastard architecture, one which partakes of the Italian, the French, and the Dutch.
—Francesco Algarotti, St. Petersburg, 1739[1]

By January 1725, when Peter I died, St. Petersburg had become the chief residence of the ruler of the Russian Empire, the principal seat of his government, and the administrative center of the Russian church. As measured by the monetary value of its imports and exports, it was now Russia's leading port as well, just as its thirty-two or more industrial enterprises made it one of the country's two or three major industrial zones. St. Petersburg's permanent population of about 40,000, second in size only to Moscow's in the Russian Empire, included some 4,000–5,000 industrial workers, another 2,000–3,000 people engaged in commerce, 1,500 registered tradesmen, up to 15,000 soldiers and sailors, a few hundred clergy, and any number of officials, idlers, and servants. The city was also the home of thousands of Europeans: artists, craftsmen, skilled laborers, and other technical or professional personnel; diplomats and their dependents, merchants and theirs; military, naval, or administrative officers in the Russian service; and countless domestics.* In fact, by 1725 St. Petersburg had become a city of international character and importance, outshining Moscow in both regards.

Since 1718 the new Russian capital had been divided administratively into five main districts: the St. Petersburg Island, with the adjacent Peter-Paul fortress; the larger Vasilevskii Island; the Admiralty Island, centering on the fortified Admiralty itself; the Moscow Section or Side, on the mainland behind the Admiralty Island; and the Vyborg or Finnish Side, east of the St. Petersburg Island, also on the mainland (fig. 92). In 1725 these five administrative districts were subdivided into the twenty-four *slobody*—"liberties" or special settlements—that had been established since 1703. Three of these settlements were reserved for European residents: the so-called Greek and German *slobody* in the Admiralty district, inhabited mainly by Italian, German, Dutch, and English craftsmen and sailors; and the "*sloboda* of the French master craftsmen" on Vasilevskii Island. By 1738 all of these *slobody* had disappeared as legal entities, having been merged with the more strictly functional subdivisions that prevailed by then; and within a few years the term *sloboda* itself, this relic of the Old-Russian town, would vanish from the St. Petersburg scene.

---

*Finns and Swedes from Finland were especially numerous among the craftsmen, skilled laborers, and domestics owing to their advantages in the St. Petersburg labor market, as compared to Russians, of personal freedom, ability to read, and proximity to the city (see M. Engman, *St. Petersburg och Finland. Migration och influens 1703–1917* [Helsinki, 1983], pp. 64–94).

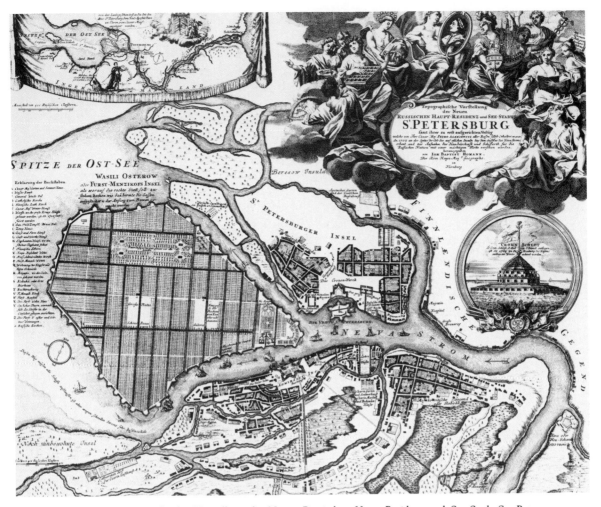

Figure 92 "Topographische Vorstellung der Neuen Russischen Haupt-Residenz und See-Stadt St. Peters-burg"; engraving by J. B. Homann of Nurenberg, ca. 1720, based evidently on a German original of 1718. St. Petersburg Island is at center, with the adjacent Peter-Paul fortress; Vasil'evskii Island is at center left; Admiralty Island, centering on the fortified Admiralty itself, is across the Neva from both, and behind it, on the mainland, is the Moscow Section or Side; the Vyborg or Finnish Side, across the river (going east) from St. Petersburg Island, is also on the mainland. Note the former settlement of Nyenskans/Nienshants (after 1703 the fortress of Shlotburg) lower right, near the bend of the river, and, inset right, the fortress of Kronshtadt (actually located off the plan to the left or west, in the Finnish Gulf).

In 1725 the new capital's population was concentrated in the three island districts and was housed in some 6,000 dwellings, the great bulk of which were built of wood or, at best, wattle and daub (*mazanka*). Figures from 1726 show that on Vasilevskii Island, which had enjoyed official priority in housing development for the past ten years or more, only 113 of 467 completed dwellings (nearly a fourth of the total) were of masonry construction. At the same time, St. Petersburg's official or public buildings—many constructed of brick and/or stone—included nineteen churches (three Lutheran, one Roman Catholic), fourteen Imperial palaces, eight episcopal residences, and various other great houses, most notably Prince Menshikov's establishment on Vasilevskii Island. Also prominent were eleven governmental office buildings as well as the Admiralty, a dozen barracks and magazines, the Arsenal and the Peter-Paul fortress, five major commercial buildings (warehouses, covered markets) and several large factories, two theaters and a military hospital, an almshouse, and a monastery named after the medieval warrior-prince, St. Alexander Nevskii ("of the Neva," near which he won a battle).[2]

In its overall plan and appearance St. Petersburg in 1725 stood in marked contrast to Moscow—or to any other Russian city. This was a matter of its free extension (unconstrained by fortified walls), of its straight streets and broad boulevards, of its canals, formal gardens, and numerous palaces, and of its regular rows of houses built facing the street. Yet in Leningrad today, as noted elsewhere in this book, few buildings survive from the first decades of the city's development, and scarcely any more survived into the age of photography. Nor has archaeological investigation been more than minimal. For a fuller and more exact sense of what St. Petersburg actually looked like in about 1725—or at any other point in the eighteenth century—we must turn once again to the written descriptions of contemporary European observers supplemented by what graphic depictions remain of the time. With their help we might judge how far Peter I succeeded, from an architectural point of view, in creating an entire city in the "new style."

INITIAL IMPRESSIONS

The first regular British ambassador to Russia, and the first to take up residence in St. Petersburg, was Charles Whitworth. His special report on conditions in the country as of 1710 affords a chilly glimpse of Peter I's "favorite town and haven" in its initial or outpost phase:

> Built on the river Neva, which is there large and deep enough to receive sixty-gun ships close to the walls of the [Peter-Paul] fortress, the foundations of this new town were laid in hopes it might one day prove a second Amsterdam or Venice. To people it the nobility have been ordered to remove hither from the farthest parts of the country, though with no small difficulty, since the climate is too cold and the ground too marshy to furnish the conveniences of life, which are all brought from the neighbouring countries. However the Tsar is charmed with his new production and would lose the best of his provinces sooner than this barren corner. The [Peter-Paul] fortress is built on a separate island, with good stone bastions laid on piles, but of much too narrow an extent to make any considerable defense in case of attack. The floods in autumn are very inconvenient, sometimes rising in the night to the first floors, so that the cattle are often swept away and the inhabitants scarce saved by their upper story; on which account they can have no magazines or cellars; nor is the ground practicable for digging, the water coming in at two foot depth. The river is seldom or never clear of ice before the middle of May, and the ships cannot hold the sea any longer than the end of September without greater danger.[3]

A more detailed description of St. Petersburg as it appeared at this time was published in German at Leipzig in 1713, the work evidently of Heinrich von (or van) Huyssen, an official in the tsar's service whose duties included projecting a more favorable image of Russia in Europe.[4] This work formed the basis in turn of a second description of the new Russian city published in German at Frankfurt and Leipzig in 1718, its observations updated to account for developments between 1710 and 1717.[5] The anonymous as well as the lacunal and official if not propagandistic character of these works precludes their use here. But the second of the two did provide the Hanoverian representative in Russia, F. C. Weber, with material for the much more detailed description of St. Petersburg that he wrote in 1720 and then published, in an authorized English edition, in 1723.[6] Weber's work also included a "plan" of the city which had been published with the German description of 1718 (cf. fig. 92).

Weber's "Description of the City of St. Petersbourg" as it appeared in about 1720 is by far the best to have survived from the last years of its founder's reign, and so will be quoted or paraphrased here at some length. Its observations are supplemented moreover by others to be found in the accompanying journal of Weber's stay in Russia. The latter provide a rare glimpse of the city's development between 1714 and 1719.

Thus in October and November 1714 Weber noted intense activity

> especially about the [Peter-Paul] fortress and other edifices [figs. 93A–B], as also the building of ships, in which several works the Tsar caused more than forty thousand men to be employed; which number not being sufficient, the Finlandish peasants and Swedish prisoners [of war] were obliged to help. Six hundred of the latter were sent for.

In November he went to see what was left of the former Swedish fortified settlement of Nyenskans, a few kilometers up river from St. Petersburg, and found only "some ruins, the deep ditch, wells, and cellars; all the materials of the houses having been removed to Petersburg and employed in the building of that city." At this time, too, Weber visited the suburban residences of Peter I at Peterhof and Strelna, and noticed with respect to the former that "the ablest architects and some thousands of workmen have been employed about it for these ten years past, which will give a sufficient idea of the magnificence of that work; as also of another at Strelna, where I saw last year [1719] ten thousand men daily employed, who are like to make another Versailles of that place."[7]

The analogue or model of Versailles, which Weber repeats, was a recurrent one at the time. Indeed, a Polish visitor in the summer of 1720 heard Peter I himself say, "If I live three more years, I will have a garden [at Strelna or Peterhof, it was not clear] better than the French king's at Versailles." From the Summer Palace to the area around the Admiralty, this same visitor wrote,

Figures 93A–B A, The original Peter-Paul fortress, St. Petersburg; mid-eighteenth-century Russian engraving. B, The original timber church of Sts. Peter and Paul, Peter-Paul fortress, St. Petersburg, showing clearly how the exterior was painted to resemble masonry; mid-eighteenth-century Russian engraving.

St. Petersburg itself "already has the appearance of a city." On the island behind the Peter-Paul fortress he saw "many artisans—French, English, Dutch—and manufacturers of other nations whom the tsar has hired to teach the Russians." On Vasilevskii Island, behind Menshikov's palace, he found the "French street, where live only artisans such as sculptors, carpenters, fountain-masters, and those who make things from pewter and other metals, all for the tsar."[8]

This visitor's remarks confirm and in part amplify the legislative record of St. Petersburg's rise that was cited in the preceding chapter. The same is true of Weber's observations—both those just quoted, and these:

> Strict orders were issued to all the inhabitants of Petersburg who had houses but one story high to put another story upon them. As for the rest, a late mandate was confirmed by virtue of which the great number of wooden houses were permitted to stand; but it was forbid to build any more, other than with roofs of tiles and walls of stone-work.

That was in 1714. In October 1715 "orders were sent into Russia for twelve thousand families more to come and settle at Petersburg, whither they are also at great pains and expence endeavouring to draw the whole commerce of Archangel." And in 1716, Weber noted that "above one thousand Swedish prisoners are employed on the works at Petersburg, where they have a daily allowance of meal, salt, etc. and for the rest have liberty to beg."[9]

As for building materials,

> The many brick kilns provide Petersburg with a sufficient number of bricks and tiles for the building of new houses; however, they prove not very durable, and as their mortar is likewise none of the best or at least is mostly prepared and used in winter (building going on all the year round), it is no wonder that the new houses and palaces want to be repaired every second or third year. The streets of that vast place are at present all paved, which indeed causes a great expence to the inhabitants, because there are but few stones found in the marshy ground of that neighbourhood; however, it has added very much to the embellishing of that city, where every housekeeper besides is obliged to plant lime-trees before his house.

In October 1718 Weber recorded in his journal that a fire broke out in the German *sloboda,* where he was staying; but it was

> soon extinguished through the admirable regulations the like of which are hardly to be met with any where else in the world. The building of Petersburg having cost the Tsar such immense sums, and his heart being so much set on the preservation of that place, and yet the greatest part of the houses being at present built only of wood, his Majesty takes all imaginable care to prevent dangers arising from fire; and with this view has assigned to all his officers, military and civil of all degrees, certain employments and functions in case of fire to which is annexed a monthly salary. The Tsar not only has taken upon himself such a function for which he receives his monthly pay, but even goes to work in person in such emergencies, climbing with the most imminent danger of life on the tops of the houses which are on fire, to encourage his Russians by his example to follow and assist him. It is owing to these good regulations that all the fires that have hitherto happened [in St. Petersburg], how dangerous soever, were always extinguished before four or five houses could be burnt down.[10]

Weber would not tire his reader by relating the other regulations introduced by Peter I "for keeping his new city in good order, the great encouragements given to architects, mechanics, and all other imaginable sorts of artificers, and the like." Instead, he contented himself with observing that

> the improvements which the Tsar has made in his dominions were not merely calculated for profit, but for delight also. He has built splendid pleasure houses, raised noble gardens and adorned them with greenhouses, aviaries and menag-

eries, grottos, cascades, and all other sorts of water-works. He has placed in the steeple of the [Peter-Paul] church a chime made in Holland. He has ordered assemblies to be kept in the winter; operas, plays, and concerts of music are to be set up for the diversion of his court; and in order to engage foreigners to frequent it, draughts have already been made and proper places marked out to build houses for those purposes.[11]

This was to invoke not only the image of Peter I as the visionary builder of a new city, but also the theme of cultural Europeanization in Petrine Russia more generally, which remains the overall theme of this study and one that is encapsulated in Weber's reference to the "chime made in Holland" for the Peter-Paul church. In the words of an authoritative history of bells in Russia, "few eighteenth-century monuments in St. Petersburg reveal the extent of Peter the Great's uncompromising [Europeanization] more than the Dutch carillon and clock that he had installed in the still unfinished tower of the cathedral of Saints Peter and Paul in 1720. European bell music, Peter thus decreed, would crown the new Baltic capital of Russia."[12]

Weber once heard Prince Menshikov boast that someday St. Petersburg would be "another Venice, to see which foreigners would travel thither purely out of curiosity." Reflecting on his nearly six years of living in the city and of watching it grow—from a "heap of villages linked together, like some plantation in the West Indies," to a "wonder of the world, considering its magnificent palaces, thousands of houses, and the short time employed in the building of it"—Weber did not think that Menshikov's boast was idle. On the contrary,

> Setting aside the perpetual objection of the raw climate of the place, it is possible his saying might prove true in time—if the Russians would be less refractory to the Tsar's intentions and use strangers better than they do at present, as likewise if passengers were allowed more liberty than hitherto in going thither and returning from thence, and if care was taken to provide against the excessive dearness of all necessities of life at Petersburg.[13]

"If": in the eyes of this acute observer St. Petersburg in 1720 was still a city in the process of becoming, more than a city in being—and a city whose future was far from certain. The point is fleshed out considerably in Weber's detailed "Description" of the new capital as it looked in about 1720, our best such memorial, as mentioned, from the last years of Peter I's reign.

F. C. Weber's "Description"

Weber began his tour of St. Petersburg at the Peter-Paul fortress, an "oblong and irregular hexagon" with four bastions, three of them sporting one and the other, two, oreillons (pl. 47).

At first the fortress was only raised of earth, but in the year 1710 the Tsar began to have it changed into strong and thick walls; that side which looks [north] is quite finished, but towards the river people are still at work. The wall from the ground to the parapet is thirty foot [nine meters] high; in the flanks, which are somewhat short, there are strong casements one above the other arched within and without but not vaulted, instead of which they are only covered with strong beams against bombs. . . . The fortress has two gates; that which looks down the river is not yet finished, but that above is now brought to perfection and is of fine statuary work. On the outside is a statue of St. Peter with two keys in his hand, very well contrived. There is also an inscription marking the foundation of the fortress and the year 1703. [Pl. 48]

Weber provides some further details of the fortifications and notes that "on one of the bastions they hoist every day, after the Dutch manner, the great flag of the fortress." The permanent church of Sts. Peter and Paul, within the walls, was "near finished": its high steeple of stone with columns and arches, "contrived by the Italian architect Tressini [Trezzini]," contained (as we have noted) a "chime which the Tsar caused to be made in Holland with great expence." Apart from it and the "Dispensary, one of the finest that can be seen anywhere," there was as yet "nothing else remarkable in the fortress; a few wooden houses, which are in but an indifferent condition."[14]

Crossing the river, Weber next described the Summer Palace and Garden. The former was "built of stone, small indeed but well contrived" (pl. 54A). A canal had been dug around the Garden and on all sides "arbours" facing walkways had been created with "fine statues of white marble placed in them"—a reference, no doubt, to the Classical sculptures purchased by Kologrivov in Italy and still to be seen in the Summer Garden. "A plantation or nursery of oaks" caught Weber's eye "because not only the neighbouring country, but all the northern Russia does not produce that sort of trees." Elsewhere in the Garden he found "a green-house, water-works, and particularly a grotto, which when finished will yield to no other whatsoever": a promising start, all in all.

Weber proceeded down river to the district where "most of the Germans live," the Post Office and "several fine houses" were located, and the "Finlandish corner . . . inhabited for the greater part by Finlandish and Swedish exiles" was found. Here too were situated the Finnish Lutheran and Roman Catholic churches, both simple structures of wood, which prompted the reflection that "if one excepts two or three hundred houses in this place, the rest are but poor huts crowded together, more like cages than houses." Moreover, "not one street of Petersburg has a name. If one asks for another's house, they give him direction by describing the place or naming some person that lives thereabouts, till they hit upon one that he knows, and then he may go thither and inquire further." For a European visitor of the time this was a "remarkable" holdover,

Figure 94 Facade of the first Winter Palace, St. Petersburg, 1711; D. Trezzini, architect; engraving by A. Zubov, 1717.

in Peter I's new capital city, of an ancient (and once universal) custom.

Further along the river, in the neighborhood of the Winter Palace—"a stone building two stories high" (fig. 94)—Weber passed more streets full of houses owned by Germans as well as the German Lutheran church, which was also a "wooden structure in the form of a cross." In back of these were located the "habitations of the great officers of the Admiralty," five of which were "large and built of stone; the others, which are as yet of wood, are likewise to be transferred into stone buildings, for which [purpose] the materials lie ready." Behind and beyond the Admiralty in turn dwelled "none but Russians; the houses are small and placed at random, without any regularity." Thus too did the old Russia live on, as yet, in the new capital.

The great yard or "wharf" of the Admiralty itself, where large warships were built, "commonly seven or eight at once upon the stocks," was surrounded by a ditch and rampart with parapet and contained two large wooden storehouses (fig. 95). Nearby stood the Admiralty church, as Weber called it, "wither the court goes to divine service". It was small, built of wood, and soon to be replaced. Next to it stood a would-be hotel which housed, for the moment, "some German and French manufacturers and artificers"; behind it was the rope yard, the shops of the coppersmiths, and the great Admiralty forge, with its "thirty odd furnaces." The further or western end of the Admiralty district was taken up with slaughterhouses, storehouses, yards for building galleys, and then, facing the river, the houses and gardens of various grandees. Last of all came the "garden and pleasure-house" of Peter's wife, Catherine, which was called "Catherinehof" (*Ekateringof*). The garden was "not much advanced" because of frequent flooding, while the palace was "but of wood and the apartments, small and very low" (fig. 96).

Yet on looking back at the whole length of the south or left bank of the Neva, past the Admiralty and as far up river as the Summer Garden, Weber declared himself favorably impressed by what he had seen and had heard was to come:

> All along this side of the river, as far as there are any houses, the banks are lined with thousands of piles and stakes driven into the ground, behind which all is filled up with rubbish and earth, upon which the houses are to be built down to the water and the foundations of them raised, the ground there being low and very much exposed to high water. On this key stand actually above thirty large stone palaces. That of the Great Admiral Apraxin [Apraksin; palace designed by Le Blond] is the most splendid, and contains above thirty apartments; the others belong to . . . other great officers of the court, and give that side of the city a fine aspect from the water.

Weber then turned his gaze to Vasilevskii Island, which was dominated by the establishment of Peter I's leading favorite, Prince Menshikov, the governor-general of the St. Petersburg region. Menshikov's palace surpassed them all, having been

> built of stone after the Italian manner, three stories high and covered [roofed] with large iron plates painted red. It has wings behind and before, is all vaulted underneath, and provided with everything that is requisite in a fine house. It has a great number of apartments furnished with rich household goods. In the middlemost story is a spacious hall, in which are usually kept all great entertainments. [Fig. 97]

Nearby was Menshikov's church, also "neatly contrived" of masonry "with a pretty steeple and a gallery going round on the outside." But more remarkable in some respects was the church's interior, with "figures carved of wood and

Figure 95   The Admiralty, St. Petersburg; engraving by Ia. Rostovtsev, 1717.

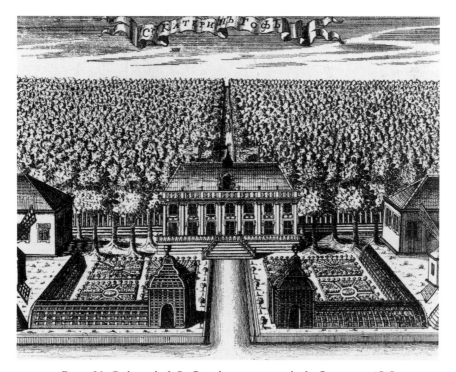

Figure 96   Catherinehof, St. Petersburg; engraving by Ia. Rostovtsev, 1717.

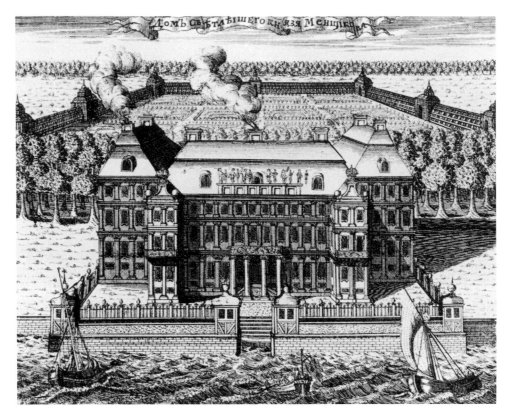

Figure 97 "House of the Most Illustrious Prince Menshikov," Vasil'evskii Island, St. Petersburg; engraving by A. Zubov, 1717.

another sort of gallery," neither "very customary in Russia," and "a pulpit, a thing very extraordinary in this country." And close to his church stood the house of Menshikov's "chief groom" (administrator of his vast personal domain), which was also of masonry construction and roofed with iron plates. It was the "finest house in Petersburg" after Menshikov's own and that of Admiral Apraksin, across the river on the new "key."

As Weber understood it, having virtually given Vasilevskii Island to Menshikov Peter I "afterwards took a particular fancy" to it, "resolved that the true city of Petersburg should be built upon it in a regular order," and commissioned "several draughts" to that end (all as documented in Chap. 6). Moreover, "pursuant to this resolution" substandard housing near Menshikov's palace was to be pulled down "to make room for the persons of distinction to whom places have been assigned here"; two rows of houses "built after the manner of Holland" were to be left standing; and work was to begin on Menshikov's garden, where a "pleasure-house" had already been built of wood "after the Italian manner, with noble apartments." Beginning in 1716, Weber continued, "streets and canals were laid out and marked with poles" on the Island and orders to settle it had been issued.

These orders have had so much effect that many persons have made a beginning: [one] street is actually built on both sides and other streets laid out, the
houses of which, though only of wood, are for the greater part [roofed] with
tiles and of better condition than those that stand in other parts of the town.
Many persons of quality have already built their stone palaces there and others
have sent the materials for theirs thither, pursuant to the Tsar's orders.

Indeed, as Weber saw it, Vasilevskii Island would in time become "a considerable town, and render Petersburg one of the largest cities in Europe." For if the
"greater part" of the Island was "still covered with a thick wood and bushes,"
this would prove no obstacle to Peter I, "at whose simple command so many
thousands of people must be ready to put his designs into execution."

So much for F. C. Weber's depiction of St. Petersburg proper as it appeared in
about 1720. The overall impression it conveys, however, rests on two further
points, both of which are the subject of lengthy additional comment by Weber:
the unsuitability of the site for the construction of a major city, if not for
human habitation; and the extent to which St. Petersburg in his time was still
constructed of wood, much of it roughly so, in compliance with tradition as
well as economic necessity.

Weber himself put the first point succinctly: "The whole city is as it were
sunk in a morass, and everywhere surrounded with wilderness and bushes. . . .
Hence it is that the whole town is exposed to great danger of inundation."
Turning to the effect of its situation and climate on the area's food supply, he
observed that it was

> so cold that there is seldom a good harvest to be expected, particularly in a
> wet year, when nothing at all comes to ripen. Turnips, white cabbage of an
> indifferent sort, cucumbers and grass for cattle is the chief product of those
> parts. Yet all sorts of cattle, particularly sheep and swine, are very thin; for
> this war [against Sweden] and bad times have destroyed the greater part of
> them, and the prodigious consumption occasioned by the vast number of in-
> habitants of Petersburg hinders the propagation of the few that remain.

For these reasons, Weber noted, the city was largely provisioned by shipments
from the interior, which were "carried to Petersburg in winter on thousands of
sleds, and in summer by water on the rivers and lakes." St. Petersburg, in short,
could not even begin to feed itself.

Weber was particularly depressed by the state of the countryside around the
new capital, which was "the reverse of other great towns in this respect." For
in the latter case, "one meets sometimes with large forests, sometimes open
fields again, with towns and villages within sight of each other, and roads on
all sides for communication between them"; while surrounding St. Petersburg,
on the contrary, one saw only

vast and horrid forests, and deserts, but not above one or two roads in all the country; if one should happen to miss his way, he will pass his time very ill among bushes and morasses till he finds the road again; nor must he expect to meet with open fields or villages. There are indeed here and there some poor farms in the midst of the woods, but without regular roads or paths leading to them, and the peasant endeavours to creep through the bushes as well as he can.

Still, Weber did think that with industry and good husbandry the land around St. Petersburg could be cleared, drained, and cultivated and thus "improved as well as in Germany, a great part of which, according to History, was much like these parts in ancient times." In fact, much was already being done within the city itself, both in the "German liberty," where the "Dutch and Germans have taken great pains in planting gardens," and on Vasilevskii Island, where Prince Menshikov's people were beginning to do the same.

Weber also alluded to the psychological effects of St. Petersburg's extreme northern latitude, especially in winter, when

> the days are so short that one has but little comfort during the three hours that the sun appears, which besides is but seldom seen at all by reason of the thick fogs with which the air is filled and darkened; such that one may justly say that the winter with them is a long and tedious night, and what they then call day is but a dawn. In August it begins to grow cold and from that time till May nobody is ashamed to wear a good fur coat and fur boots. In winter it freezes so hard that the beams of their wooden houses crack and give a report like small arms. The ice in the rivers and other waters is commonly five and a half feet thick.

And while noting that there was "plenty of wood" around St. Petersburg, Weber estimated that the "greater part" of the wood was "good for nothing, as it has neither a right sap nor pith, and is not near so good as that in Germany." The forests of the area were composed of "fir, pine, alder, birch, asp, and elm, but all very short, wry, and knobbly stuff, so that their woods may rather be called bushes than forests"; the timber derived from them "usually rots in ten to twelve years time, which makes the houses very soon decay and stand in need of props and repair."

The last remark led Weber to expand on the second of his more general points about the St. Petersburg he knew, namely, the ubiquitous use of wood in building.

> The houses generally speaking are all built of wood, beam upon beam, rough without and smoothed within by the help of a hatchet. The roofs are made of thin splinters of fir ten or twelve foot long laid one near the other, and laths nailed across over them. Those who will have a better fence against the rain lay large pieces of very thin bark of birch under the splinters, which never rot and keep out the water tolerably well but are dangerous by reason of their

easily taking fire. Others cover their roofs with large square turfs laid over the said splinters, which as long as they are fresh remain green and keep the house pretty dry within.

These were the "common houses" of the city in about 1720, among which "many" were "poor and small ones, which in two hours' time may be taken to pieces and put up again in another place." Indeed, the technique by which such houses were built was remarkable:

> The carpenter takes the fir trees unhewn as they are and piles them up into a square figure, fastening them on the corners with dents or notches without much minding whether one tree juts out and another runs in. Such a wooden box being raised to a sufficient height, he gets into it by the help of a ladder and cuts his way out again with a hatchet in the place where the door is to be; the windows he forms in the same manner. Next, to make the inside smooth he planes the walls with the hatchet, and leaves the outside as it is. Then the roof-timber is set up and the thin splinters nailed upon it; and so the house is finished. The floor is laid with planks three inches thick close to one another yet without fastening them to the ground, so that commonly they move up and down when people walk on them. The planks that make the ceiling are covered with a great deal of sand to keep the room warm. The whole architecture wants no other tool but a hatchet, which their carpenters understand to handle with more skill than those of any nation whatsoever.

The doorway of the finished house was "seldom three foot high," so that "nobody can go in without stooping very low." At the same time, the "threshold is raised from the ground two feet at least," so that one entered with "one foot very high" while simultaneously "stooping very low," a maneuver "no less comical than that of Harlequin when he appears upon the stage; and often those who are not used to it come tumbling into the house with their heads foremost." The interior of the house usually consisted of one room dominated by a "large square oven or stove," which was "flat above and in which they not only boil, bake, and roast their victuals winter and summer but even sleep—in it as well as on top of it." The windows had shutters and some had sashes "over which they paste paper, rags of linen, hogs' bladders and the like to keep out the air; but people who think themselves above the common sort have some small window or other of isinglass, about a foot square."

Weber's uniquely detailed description of St. Petersburg's basic "wooden box" instantly brings to mind the Old-Russian *izba,* which he, like every European visitor before him, was struck to see in Moscow, Novgorod, indeed everywhere he traveled in the country. At this basic level of architecture, one which needed "no other tool but a hatchet," the Petrine revolution had as yet hardly penetrated. But Weber did find that in St. Petersburg the consequent threat of devastation by fire had been brought under control by means of the regulations referred to in his journal, which were "so strict and well observed that, though there scarcely passes a week without a fire breaking out in some part of the town, there is seldom above a couple of houses burnt down, how great soever the danger may appear." It was done in this way:

> There are watchmen appointed who keep guard on the steeples day and night, and as soon as one observes any fire he tolls a bell after a particular manner, in which he is immediately followed by the rest all over town, and the drummers go up and down beating the alarm. Upon this notice there appear thousands of *plotnicks* [*plotniki*] or carpenters' boys, of whom all sections of the town are full, with hatchets in their hands running at full speed to the fire; and all soldiers of whatever rank soever are obliged on severe penalties to repair to the place. The Tsar himself when in town is usually one of the first, or Prince Menshikov or the governor of the fortress and other generals and superior officers. It is a common thing to see the Tsar among the workmen with a hatchet in his hand climbing to the top of the houses that are all in flame with such danger that the spectators tremble at the sight of it. Considering therefore that a good command in such cases is of more effect than hundreds of hands, there is a speedy stop put to the raging element by pulling down in a minute the two houses standing next to the [house on] fire; and as the engines arrive in the meantime, the flame is soon quite extinguished.

Thus was that curse of the Old-Russian town, the devastating fire, to be banished from the new capital—a matter of vigorous leadership, effective organization, and the introduction of the fire engine.

Weber also left detailed descriptions of the principal building projects in St. Petersburg's environs (fig. 98). He began with the "barren" island of Kotlin out in the Finnish Gulf, which owing to its location was "justly called the key" to the city. Formerly uninhabited "except by a few fishermen," Peter I realized its "advantageous situation, made it the port of his fleet, and not only fortified it with a strong castle called *Kronslot* or *Kronshloss* (crown-castle), but also caused a pretty large town to be built upon it which commonly goes by the name of the castle." The "spacious and deep" harbor at Kronslot (later Kronshtadt) was protected by the castle, which stood in the sea "about a cannon shot from the island, on a sand bank." The castle's foundations were "boxes formed of strong timber and filled with stone on which the rest was afterwards built of earth and timber" in the form of a "round tower with three galleries around, one above the other, well furnished with cannon from top to bottom" (fig. 99; see also fig. 92). But this design (Dominico Trezzini's) prevented its garrison from firing more than three or four guns at any one time against a warship attempting to run past it; and so Peter I planned to have it pulled down, Weber had learned, and a triangular bastion built in its place. At any rate, with the batteries on the island itself, the provision for more guns to be mounted at various points in the harbor, and the firepower of the tsar's warships usually at anchor there, Weber judged the seaward approach to St. Petersburg "sufficiently covered and guarded against any insult."[15]

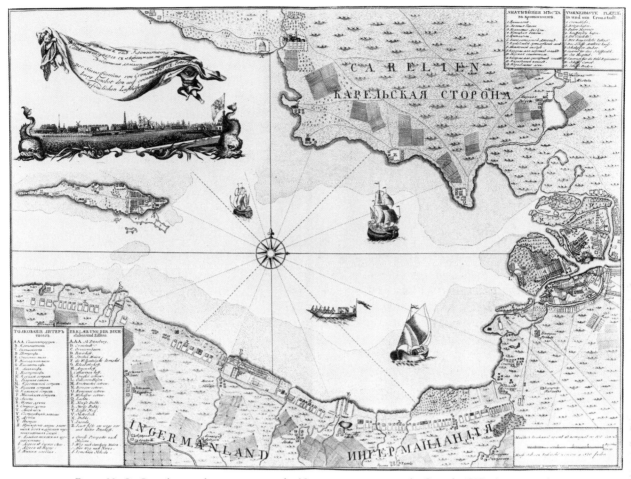

Figure 98 St. Petersburg and its environs in the Neva estuary; engraving by Grimel, 1737. A—center, far right—marks St. Petersburg proper with Vasil'evskii Island; B—center, extreme left—marks the settlement of Kronshtadt on Kotlin Island; C = Prince Menshikov's palace and grounds of Oranienbaum; D = Peterhof; E = Strelna.

Figure 99 View of the fortress (offshore) of Kronshtadt; engraving of ca. 1720.

As for the town of Kronslot, it was "pretty large" only in consideration of the "short time since it was begun to be built." The houses, "which are all of wood, lie dispersed; nor is there so much as a ditch or even a hedge around the place." Weber had also learned that Peter planned to upgrade the town by having "all those wooden houses changed into stone buildings, built in regular streets, through which canals were to be cut after the way of Holland." Yet so far there were only half a dozen masonry structures worthy of mention: a church, finished in 1718; four warehouses, soon to be let to merchants; and a "large stone building raised by Prince Menshikov, with two wings, the ground floor of which is adapted for trade and the two remaining stories are designed for a palace." Kronslot in about 1720, inhabited by a "medley of nations," suffered from "exorbitant" prices; but "every day people go to settle there," urged on, as always, by the tsar.

From Kronslot Weber crossed to the southern shore of the gulf, there to find the road to Petersburg "full of country houses and farms" belonging to various senior officials, which made a "very agreeable" sight. He confined himself to describing three of these country estates: Oranienbaum, directly opposite Kronslot, which belonged to Prince Menshikov; Peterhof, "the Tsar's favourite place"; and Strelna, "another garden and palace newly raised by the Tsar," who was "resolved to make a royal seat of it that might vie with that of Versailles." But Weber's relatively sparse depictions of these major architectural undertakings in the environs of St. Petersburg are superceded for our purposes by the nearly contemporary observations of other European visitors, especially F. W. von Bergholtz.

In leaving Weber, the provisional nature of his overall description might be stressed: his recurrent suggestion that in 1720 the future of St. Petersburg, and therefore of the Petrine architectural revolution, was in some doubt.

OTHER VIEWS

Friedrich Wilhelm von Bergholtz, born in 1699, was the son of a Holstein nobleman who served as a general in the Russian army under Peter I, for which reason he spent much of his childhood and youth in Russia. In 1717, on his father's death, he returned to Germany, where he became first a page to the duke of Mecklenburg and then a gentleman-attendant to the duke of Holstein, Karl Friedrich, whom he accompanied on trips to Stockholm and Paris. In 1721 Duke Karl Friedrich came to St. Petersburg, seeking marriage with Anna, daughter of Peter I. Bergholtz came, too, and was appointed gentleman-usher to the duke, who finally won his suit in 1726. Meanwhile, from 1721 until the end of 1725, Bergholtz kept a copiously detailed diary of their movements in St. Petersburg and Moscow. It remains the single best source of information on the life of the court in Peter I's last years.[16]

Interspersed among the entries in Bergholtz's diary, particularly of the first few months of 1721, are his comments on architecture in St. Petersburg and its environs; he has comparatively little to say about architecture in Moscow, significantly, and that in the largely critical vein of the European visitors quoted in Chapter 2. It is the view of a man in his early twenties, considerably younger than F. C. Weber and less experienced of the world, although he had already lived and traveled in north Germany, Sweden, and France. It is also clear from his diary, as from his later architectural drawings, that Bergholtz took a keen interest in the buildings that he saw.[17]

Bergholtz arrived in St. Petersburg one evening in June 1721 and found the city "changed so much since I left it [in 1717] that I scarcely recognized it." He provides the first known description of the Nevskii Prospekt (fig. 100):

> We entered down a long, wide avenue paved in stone and called, rightly, the Prospect, since its end is almost invisible. It was built only in the last few years and exclusively by Swedish prisoners. Notwithstanding that the three or four rows of trees on either side of it are still not large, it is extraordinarily beautiful by reason of its enormous extent and state of cleanliness (Swedish prisoners must clean it every Saturday). It makes a more wonderful sight than any I have ever beheld anywhere.

At the lower end of the Nevskii Prospekt (so called because it runs from the city center out to the Alexander-Nevskii monastery) Bergholtz passed the Ad-

Figure 100   The Nevskii Prospekt, St. Petersburg; engraving after drawing by M. I. Makhaev, ca. 1750.

Figure 101   The Bourse *(Birzha)*, St. Petersburg; engraving after drawing by M. I. Makhaev, ca. 1750.

miralty ("a huge and beautiful building"), crossed a pontoon bridge to Vasilev-skii Island, where the new *Birzha* (Bourse or Commodities Exchange) now stood ("a regular building that is also very beautiful") (fig. 101), and eventually reached his lodgings not far from the Summer Palace.

Soon, like everybody else in fine weather, he was strolling in the Summer Garden, of which he was concerned to "relate in turn everything that is remarkable," having explained that it was oblong in form and "on the east abuts the Tsar's Summer Palace, on the south, an orangery, on the west, a large and beautiful meadow, and on the north, the Neva, which at this point is quite wide." He begins at the northern end, by the main entrance and the three long open galleries used for serving refreshments on festive occasions, in the middle one of which he saw the famous marble statue of Venus brought from Italy (and now in the Hermitage Museum), "which the Tsar so values that he has posted a guard to watch over it: she is in fact magnificent, if slightly damaged from lying so long in the ground." In front of this gallery began the Garden's main alley, along which "several fine and quite tall fountains" had been installed (fig. 102).

Bergholtz goes on to describe birdhouses with numerous and rare birds, a dovecote with "rare and lovely pigeons," and the small pavilion standing in a "clump of trees surrounded on all sides by water" where Peter I would go to be alone or to speak privately with someone, "since it can only be reached by a little boat that is kept by." Elsewhere he found a "beautiful fountain of gilded marble built in the form of a cascade, with many gilded ornaments," a grotto

Figure 102 View of the Summer Garden, St. Petersburg, ca. 1725; contemporary—Dutch?—engraving.

that when finished would be "very splendid" indeed, still more fountains and shrubs and trees—"in a word, everything that could be wanted in a pleasure garden." But "especially decorative" were its "fountains of precious marble and the statue of Venus, which must be 2,000 years old and was bought from the Pope." We are reminded of the Russian visitor's joyful description, only twenty years before, of the papal garden in Rome (Chap. 5).

And the admiration to be sensed thus far is characteristic of Bergholtz's further comments on architecture in St. Petersburg. The Admiralty (fig. 95) is described in positive detail and "nearby a fine masonry church is being built"— the second church of St. Isaac, replacing the small wooden structure mentioned by Weber. If most churches in the city were "poorly built of wood," the churches of the Holy Trinity on St. Petersburg Island (fig. 103) and of Prince Menshikov on Vasilevskii Island were among the "most beautiful." The latter particularly had a "small but beautiful steeple with a sizable chime," and its interior was "handsomely painted and gilded." But Bergholtz's fullest praise was reserved for Trezzini's Peter-Paul church in the fortress (pl. 25A), the "largest and most beautiful church" in St. Petersburg.

> Above it rises a high steeple in the new style, covered in brightly gilded copper plates which look extraordinarily fine in the sunlight. The chimes in its steeple are as large and fine as those at the Admiralty. . . . This fine church is entirely of masonry construction, and not in the Byzantine but in the new taste, adorned with prominent arches and columns and, front and side, a splendid portico.

Figure 103 Original church of the Holy Trinity, St. Petersburg; mid-eighteenth-century engraving.

It was from the steeple of the Peter-Paul church, the highest in St. Petersburg, that Bergholtz and the duke took a panoramic view of the city at noon one day in August 1721:

> When we got to the top, under the bell, we were given a large telescope with the aid of which we could see Peterhof, Kronslot, and Oranienbaum. Petersburg has the shape of an oval and is of enormous extent. In many places it is still meagerly built, but these gaps will not be slow to fill up if the Tsar lives longer. The fortress has several thick and high masonry bastions fitted with a large number of cannon. They say that its very rapid construction cost countless lives. . . . From the landward side it is not so fine a sight and is far from as well-fortified as on the river side, being enclosed only by a rampart and ditch; still, it could be defended for quite some time.

Viewed from this vantage point Vasilevskii Island, where "many large buildings have already been erected," constituted a town in itself, although it was built up only along its southern and eastern shores. Over on the left or south bank of the river, around the Admiralty, the city was intersected by numerous canals, making travel there, Bergholtz calculated, as well as from there to other parts of town, more convenient by boat. Lastly, the steeple of the Peter-Paul church afforded a splendid view of the Nevskii Prospekt, receding in a straight line far into the distance.

As a member of the court Bergholtz inevitably traveled to the surburban royal residences, which he found more or less attractive and more or less finished. Strelna was

> a large place, still abuilding, on a very high and fine site. In front of it flows the [Finnish Gulf], along which spreads a wonderful stand of trees. Three terraces of extraordinary length descend by stages from the hill to the garden, where the pipes have already been laid for numerous fountains. In the middle of the upper terrace (which, like the other two, is as long as the garden is wide), the foundations of a huge palace have already been laid; they say it will be scarcely less splendid than Versailles [fig. 104]. From the main part of the building a large, wide cascade descends through the terraces to the garden; it will have an internal vault something like a grotto. Water for it and for the numerous fountains on the terraces and elsewhere will be brought from distant heights by means of a costly canal, thus enabling them to run day and night. Directly in front of the cascade begins another, very wide canal.

Oranienbaum, Menshikov's country residence, situated some thirty-five kilometers from St. Petersburg, was also built on a hill, and from which there

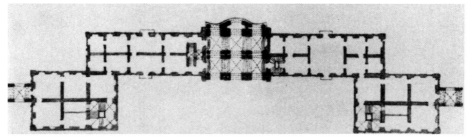

Figure 104 The palace of Strelna as projected by N. Michetti, ca. 1719; section and plan.

was a "magnificent view." Bergholtz had little to say concerning the exterior of the palace, beyond the fact that it was a three-story masonry affair with long, semioval wings on either side. Below the palace was an extensive garden, "still far from finished," and beyond that a fine stand of trees through which a wide alley and canal had been cut, providing a "fine view of the sea." The rooms in the palace were "small but beautiful, and decorated with fine paintings and furniture." Elsewhere he discovered a "glorious bath with a rounded glass roof" such as "I had never seen." Nearby was a long building to house Menshikov's servants, which also served as the palace's gate house, and over the gate a large tower was being raised—much to Bergholtz's annoyance.

> It destroys the symmetry of the whole complex. They say the Tsar has already told the Prince that he must either pull it down or move it to the other side of the palace. It is thought the Prince will do the latter, and build another wing, since he has already built everything here by bits and pieces. First he ordered only the main building put up; then, to augment that, the galleries were added and finally, to them, the [semioval] wings. His large house in Petersburg was built in the same way. It is a very poor way to build; nothing considerable can ever come of it, especially if as many different architects are employed as have been in building Oranienbaum.

Bergholtz's criticisms here, no doubt well taken, are largely absent in his description of Peterhof, which was reached by a "rocky road that is very tiring." He and the duke made a private visit and were pleased to discover that a Swedish former prisoner of war was in charge of the estate, and invited them to stay in his house. They began their tour with Monplaisir, a "small but very nice house, decorated most notably with many choice Dutch paintings." The main palace on its hill comprised two stories, the lower for the servants, the upper for the tsar's family (fig. 87).

> Below are large and fine hallways with pretty columns, and above there is a splendid hall whence one has a wonderful view of the sea and, in the distance, of Petersburg to the right and Kronslot to the left. The rooms in general are small but not bad, and are hung with fine paintings and provided with beautiful furniture. Especially remarkable is the cabinet containing a small library belonging to the Tsar made up of various Dutch and Russian books; it was done by a French craftsman and is distinguished by its excellent carved decoration. [Fig. 88]

Behind the palace was a large garden—"very beautifully laid out"—and an extensive animal preserve, which was not yet finished. In front of and below the palace Bergholtz spied the "magnificent cascade, as wide as the palace itself, made of natural stone and decorated with gilded lead figures in relief against a green background." The canal connecting the cascade with the open Gulf of Finland was impressively wide as well as long, with "fine dikes on either side; at its end is a small harbor surrounded by strong walls where small boats can tie up without danger in time of storm: one can proceed up this canal by boat to the cascade itself, beneath the palace, which is very agreeable and convenient."

As for the Lower Park, spread out beneath the palace on either side of the cascade and canal, it was

> intersected by many fine and pleasant alleys shaded by groves of trees. The two principal alleys lead from the two sides of the Park through a grove of trees to two pleasure houses located exactly the same distance from the palace and the Gulf. To the right is Monplaisir, in whose garden, also surrounded by trees, grow many beautiful bushes, plants, and flowers; here there are also a large pond with swans and other fowl swimming in it, a little house for them, and various other structures built for fun. At the opposite end of the alley from Monplaisir a similar garden and house [Marly], already begun, will be completed.

Bergholtz's overall impression of the grounds at Peterhof was one of "gardens, pleasant places, groves of trees, and water, all in harmony with one another." And this was consistent with his generally favorable assessment of the architecture to be seen in St. Petersburg and its environs in the early 1720s. He was certainly less exacting in his descriptions than Weber had been and more sanguine, evidently, with regard to the city's future. No doubt it was a matter, at least in part, of his youth and, still more, of his close association with the Russian court.

In the autumn of 1726, nearly two years after the death of Peter I, a physician and botanist named Pierre Deschisaux spent five weeks in St. Petersburg. He described the experience in a long letter to a friend back in France. The letter, soon published, but entirely ignored by historians, contains various passages of direct interest here.[18]

"Cronstat" was Deschisaux's port of entry, and it continued to show signs of extensive construction, particularly on the great canal that would bisect the main square. Several new houses had been "coated with a plaster or cement that preserves its whiteness, which can be seen from afar and gives the town a beautiful aspect." The palace at suburban Peterhof Deschisaux found "unremarkable" but not its grounds, which were quite "agreeable." The Alexander-Nevskii monastery, in town, though not yet finished, was "magnificent," its church "superb." Vasilevskii Island would in time become the "Faubourg St. Germain of Petersburg" owing to the palaces of the "seigneurs" that were rapidly going up there. Deschisaux was favorably taken by the Academy of Sciences' new building (the future *Kunstkamera*) and by Menshikov's palace and garden, "the most considerable on the Island" (pl. 55); but the Admiralty ensemble took pride of place because of the "good order by which its canals, yards, storerooms, lodgings, roperies, and other parts are distinguished." By contrast, the Winter and Summer Palaces were scarcely mentionable, while the

Summer Garden, which Bergholtz had so much admired, was found to be "divided up, in the Dutch manner, into various compartments, bowers, arbors of one sort or another, fenced enclosures, and such other bits and pieces as are called, vulgarly, *les colifichets* [gew-gaws]."

Nor was Deschisaux's enthusiasm for the new Russian capital dampened solely by his French (Neoclassical) taste in architecture. The strongest impression conveyed by his letter is a horrified reaction to the flood that occurred during his time in St. Petersburg (November 1726), when the various tributaries of the Neva "joined together to form one great sea, on the surface of which the city seemed to float." The streets became canals; the square by the Admiralty was completely inundated; Deschisaux himself had to seek refuge from the water in the attic of his house. "The particular disasters caused by this flood," he remarked in sum, "would fill a volume much larger than the work I intend." And it was the same, he was told, every year at this time.

Deschisaux was primarily concerned while in St. Petersburg to secure a position in the Russian service, a quest in which he failed. Another French visitor of that year, Aubry de LaMottraye, evidently only a tourist, left a more detailed as well as more positive record of what he had seen.[19] In fact, apart from the poverty of its natural setting—"if there is a tolerable piece or spot of ground that can be called pleasant or fertile it is entirely owed to Art"—and the still extensive use of wood in building, this visitor found much to admire. In particular, the Alexander-Nevskii monastery, when finished, would be the "best built, the most magnificent, and the largest in all of Russia; it should suffice to say, to give some good idea of it, that Signor Tressini [Dominico Trezzini] designed it and that various other good architects have been employed in it." LaMottraye noted that construction of the monastery's central church of the Holy Trinity was well under way and that the church on the right of his plan, although "built for the most part of wood," was "very pretty" (figs. 105A–B). Moreover, Trezzini's church of the Annunciation, on the left of his plan, was "an architectural jewel" (pl. 26). In short, what was finished of the ensemble— about half of that pictured in the plan—was "extremely well-ordered and executed."

The Alexander-Nevskii monastery, as LaMottraye pointed out, was connected to the city by a "fine, broad, well-paved road"; he referred to the Nevskii Prospekt, on either side of which, every fifty paces or so, "lanterns on posts, after the English manner," were now in place. The city itself, he discovered, was dominated by the Peter-Paul fortress, whose high walls were "very thick and good, having been built out of the materials of Nienschantz." The Peter-Paul church within the fortress was a "very fine church," having been constructed "on the designs and by the direction of the ingenious Signor Tressini [Trezzini]." Indeed "everything therein" was

> worthy of his good taste. The body of the edifice is of brick, except the pillars, the corners, and the shoulderings. All the ornaments of Architecture and Sculpture are distributed and disposed with great judgement and elegance. Its

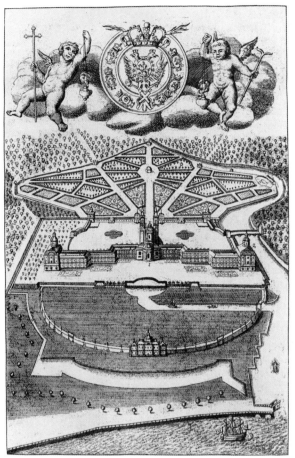

A

B

Figures 105A–B A, Plan of the Alexander-Nevskii monastery, St. Petersburg; engraving in A. de LaMottraye, *Voyages en divers provinces* (The Hague, 1732). B, Model for the church of the Holy Trinity, Alexander-Nevskii monastery, 1720–1723, by D. Trezzini and T. Schwertfeger.

steeple is all of stone save the spire, which is of wood covered with copper and gilded towards its point: this is set upon four rows of pillars each above another with great arches; two are of the Ionic, and the two other of the Corinthian, order. Inside is a good chime. The portico of the church is noble, its columns made of hard free stone and of the Tuscan order. [Pl. 25A].

Behind the Peter-Paul fortress, on St. Petersburg Island, LaMottraye saw little that he considered memorable: churches and offices and houses built mostly of wood, some "pretty well," and "several much finer houses" constructed of brick. But the decaying condition of one of the latter prompted a remark that Weber had also made: bricks produced in St. Petersburg were "so bad that the houses which are built thereof want to be repaired at least every three years"— although some people, for sure, attributed the problem to the practice of "building in winter." LaMottraye was the earliest of these witnesses to notice that the first house built in St. Petersburg—"if one can call such a hall of planks and joists a house"—had become a shrine, "preserved for memory by enclosing it with a gallery erected on a wall three or four foot high" (fig. 106). This was the so-called *domik* of Peter I, which even today remains, after several restorations, a major tourist attraction (pl. 39).

Taking note of the "great market" on St. Petersburg Island, a "vast square building" of wood "enclosing an empty yard with four gates and regularly built," LaMottraye crossed to the mainland, to the neighborhood of the Summer Palace and Garden. Like his compatriot, Deschisaux, he was not much impressed by the late Emperor Peter's beloved "Dutch" retreat. But like Weber a few years earlier he noted with pleasure that just beyond, "on a key above 800 paces long and 30 broad," a whole "row of palaces" had been built; and that behind these were to be found "streets well and evenly paved, regular and broad: I measured several which were 20 to 30 feet across." A new Winter Palace was being built "wholly of brick, except some ornaments" (fig. 107), and the row terminated in a "pretty large, well-paved square with the Post-House, which is a good convenient building." But nearby again everything was constructed "for the most part of timber"; apart from the "college and church of the Jesuits, pretty neat and finely adorned," and the Imperial Stable—"a vast square building enclosing an empty yard, and very regular"—the rest of this part of town was a jumble of warehouses, shops and factories, wooden houses, and covered markets. To be sure, the house of an English merchant was also "neat and pretty well built . . . after the Dutch fashion, as are so many others here and there on all the different canals."

The Admiralty, next, was a "vast body or pile of magnificent and regular structures not unlike the Arsenal of Venice," while the new St. Isaac's church going up nearby promised to be "one of the most magnificent of St. Petersburg." Like Weber and Deschisaux before him, LaMottraye thought that Menshikov's palace on Vasilevskii Island "eclipses all the rest, not excepting the Imperial palaces." Of the latter, Empress Catherine's in particular, situated near the mouth of the Neva, was "pleasant" enough but "wholly built of timber, the apartments low and narrow, the garden much neglected": all as observed by Weber. And LaMottraye agreed with Weber that the prospect afforded by the great houses facing each other across the Neva, as one looked back, up river, was "stately" (figs. 108A–C).

Similarly, the Imperial residence at suburban Strelna, for all of its potential "magnificence," was "already threatening ruin," while the main palace at Peterhof was "an ordinary sort of mansion which, if it deserves the name of palace, does so because of the great prince who built it." But it was "most agreeably situated on an eminence" and, with one reasonably good garden behind it, looked out on another—the Lower Park—that was "much more richly adorned," an ensemble indeed of "columns, statues, busts, paintings, temples, salons, bowers." LaMottraye's account is more specific than Bergholtz's, and refers at times to other things: to a fountain "in the midst of a bed of flowers near the grotto that throws up water from more than a hundred pipes, forming a most agreeable pyramid"; to an "Orangery well and quite richly furnished with

Figure 106 Peter I's *domik* (little house) and, below, its protective gallery, St. Petersburg; mid-eighteenth-century Russian engravings.

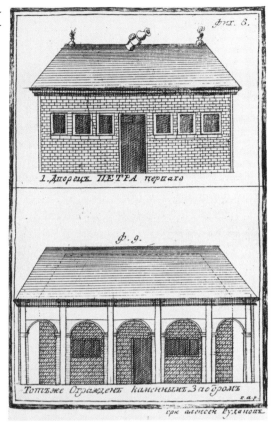

Figure 107 View of the second Winter Palace, St. Petersburg, built 1719–1721 after designs by G. J. Mattarnowy, expanded 1726–1727 (under D. Trezzini?); engraving from drawing by M. I. Makhaev, ca. 1750.

Figures 108A–C View of the left bank of the Neva, St. Petersburg. A, Various grandees' houses terminating (extreme left) at the Summer Garden and (foreground) lumber being moved into the city by raft; engraving of ca. 1730 attributed to O. Elliger. B, Various grandees' houses including (extreme left) the second Winter Palace (cf. fig. 107) and (extreme right) the palace of Admiral Apraksin; engraving of ca. 1730 attributed to O. Elliger. C, The Admiralty and (extreme right) the second church of St. Isaac (1717; G. J. Mattarnowy, architect); engraving of ca. 1730 attributed to O. Elliger.

plants and trees from foreign countries"; and to Montplaisir and Marly (pls. 59B–C), which he considered to be "among the finest works of architecture." Monplaisir especially was

> very neat, and comprises a fine hall on either side of which a gallery terminates in finely proportioned apartments. The ceilings of the hall, galleries, and some of the apartments are well painted in *fresco* and adorned besides with some of Mr. Pilman's [Pillement] best scenes [fig. 90]. Before this palace, as they call it, is a terrace where one can take an agreeable stroll, looking out on the Gulf; it terminates in balconies which form a kind of gallery around a flower bed.

LaMottraye also inspected Prince Menshikov's country estate of Oranienbaum, with its "magnificent pleasure house or rather stately palace," which was decorated across the front with a "fine colonnade" and complemented by an "extensive garden where the Useful and the Agreeable abound" (fig. 109). Like Bergholtz, he judged the palace's rooms to be "perfectly disposed, adorned with numerous fine paintings, mostly of historical subjects, and richly furnished." The prince's house at Kronshtadt was the best on the island: "built magnificently . . . all of brick and stone . . . with two fine wings." LaMottraye was soon back in St. Petersburg and admiring, once again, Menshikov's establishment on Vasilevskii Island. The facade of its palace was "superb, the two-staged entry-way, majestic; the architectural ornaments and paintings are in fine taste, and most pleasing; the halls, antechambers, rooms, and galleries are perfectly disposed: everything is grand and well-proportioned, the furniture exquisite." Again like Weber, some six years before, LaMottraye found Menshikov's church "very beautiful" and was similarly surprised to find statues and a pulpit inside. He walked through "spacious courtyards" and "beautifully laid out gardens adorned with everything that could flatter the taste and please the eye." The house of Menshikov's "chief groom" was "among the finest palaces of Petersburg, if it does not surpass them; it is roofed with iron plates, is three stories high, like his, and yields nothing to his in the richness and grandeur of its furnishing." Menshikov, Peter I's great favorite, was now, in the brief reign of Peter's wife, Catherine I (1725–1727), at the height of his power.

The last major building in St. Petersburg mentioned by LaMottraye, later named the *Kunstkamera,* was designed by G. J. Mattarnowy to house the Imperial (Peter I's) Library, meetings of the St. Petersburg Academy of Sciences (founded by Peter I, active from 1726), and an observatory (figs. 110A–B, 111). One of the city's few original buildings to have survived to this day, even then, in 1726, it was something to see. "If this edifice, which is already well advanced, is ever finished," declared LaMottraye, "it will be one of the most magnificent of its kind in Europe" (pl. 57).

Figure 109 View of the palace of Oranienbaum, 1711–1725; G. M. Fontana and G. Schädel, architects; engraving after drawing by M. I. Makhaev, 1761.

Figures 110A–B A, "East Front of the Imperial Library and *Kunstkamera*," St. Petersburg, 1718–1734; G. J. Mattarnowy, architect; engraving by G. Kachalov, 1741. B, Section of building in fig. 110A showing (right) the Imperial Library and (left) the *Kunstkamera*, or Peter I's collection of anatomical exhibits and artifacts of anthropological or historical interest; the central tower housed an anatomy theater, globe, and observatory— all the first of their kind in Russia; engraving by G. Kachalov, 1741.

A

(*Figure 109 continued*)

(*Figure 110 continued*)

B

Figure 111   View of the interior of the Imperial Library, St. Petersburg; engraving by C. A. Wortman, 1744.

REVOLUTION TRIUMPHANT

During the reign of Peter I's grandson, Peter II (1727–1730), when the court moved back to Moscow, St. Petersburg's development slowed to a snail's pace. Menshikov had fallen from power and lived in distant exile, never to return; and the "party" so to speak of Peter I, the party of rapid and intensive Europeanization, was in disarray. Indeed, in these years St. Petersburg assumed in some degree the appearance of a ghost town, its imperial pretense a complete sham. Such is the picture conveyed by the straightforward comments of the wife of the newly appointed British consul-general, Mrs. Thomas Ward.

St. Petersburg, she wrote to a friend back in England not long after arriving in 1729,

> is pleasantly situated on a fine river called the Neva. It consists of three islands; on one stands the Admiralty, from which it takes its name. The second is called Petersburg-island, in which are the citadel and a fine [the Peter-Paul] church, wherein is interred the body of Peter the First. The third is called Basil's [Vasilevskii] island, on which are the exchange, the market, and the courts of justice and trade (called here colleges) and other public buildings. Here the merchants were designed to live; but though the houses and streets are very handsome, they are uninhabited. . . . The [second] Winter Palace is small, built round a court, is far from handsome, has a great number of rooms ill-contrived, and nothing remarkable either in architecture, painting, or furniture. The Summer Palace is still smaller, and in all respects mean, except

the gardens, which are pretty (for this country, fine), with a good deal of shade and water. . . . A mile from the town is the monastery of St. Alexander Newski begun by Peter the First, and will be very fine if ever it is finished. . . . There are many fine houses in the town belonging to the nobility, but now, in the absence of the court, quite empty; most of them have pretty gardens.

Mrs. Ward also visited Peterhof, with similar reactions, noting for instance that while "some good pictures" hung in the palace there, they were "much spoiled for want of care." And with that she left for Moscow.[20]

A detailed description of St. Petersburg as it appeared in 1733, during the reign of Empress Anna Ivanovna (1730–1740), when it had again become the capital, was compiled by Sir Francis Dashwood. His diary of a three-week visit in June of that year reveals a city that in many respects remained, in spite of the court's return, a raw, unfinished place. Dashwood had traveled in Italy and France, and in approaching St. Petersburg had stopped in both Copenhagen and Danzig; and his diary, in its editor's words, "shows him as a serious-minded traveller, observant, intelligent and enquiring."[21]

Arriving by sea, Dashwood noted that Kronshtadt—"Crownstad"—was a "prodigious work very regularly laid out." The entrance to the harbor was "excessive strong, there being seven hundred piece of cannon," and "large canals, well lined with stone," brought "ships or large vessels into the town." An "exceeding large fine windmill built by a Dutchmen" sawed wood as well as helped maintain the water level in the canals. But from "want of proper repair and through the violence of the cold" as well as "bad workmanship," the "large brick houses" of the town had gone "very much to decay." Dashwood understood that Kronshtadt had been "designed by Peter the Great for the residence of all merchants and his own navy, but his plans have been faintly put into execution since his decease," and his ships, in particular, were in poor condition; still, "they continually keep going, there being actually at work five hundred people under the inspection and direction of Vice-Admiral Saunders," an Englishman in the Russian service.

From Kronshtadt Dashwood crossed to Oranienbaum, which he found "very fine and grand, but going the way of their other buildings," a matter, again, of the climate, human neglect, and faulty building techniques and materials. He conveys a similarly melancholy impression of St. Petersburg itself, various individual buildings of merit excepted. The fortress was "very regular and well built, though not quite finished," and the Peter-Paul church within it was the "richest and finest by much of any whereabouts." Trezzini's plan for the Alexander-Nevskii monastery was "exceeding grand and fine" but remained uncompleted, while the Imperial stable was a "very regular piece of work, although of wood." The city's streets were "pretty well paved, straight, and of a good breadth," and Empress Anna's new wooden summer palace (by Zemtsov) "looks very well for the season," having been built in a mere six weeks. "But they think nothing here of employing two thousand men at work upon the same building; I have been credibly and by several informed that in building or rather laying the foundation of this town and Crownstad, there were three hundred thousand men perished by hunger and the air." Thus had the story, sad enough to begin with, grown (the best historical estimate, as noted earlier, puts the actual total of deaths in the thousands).[22]

From the "Isle of the Admiralty," where the Empress and her court lived as well as the foreign diplomats and merchants, Dashwood crossed by a "good handsome bridge upon boats" to Vasilevskii Island. This was the "real town of St. Petersburg, where the exchange is, where the merchants daily resort though not reside, as also the greatest part of the shops for retail commodities." Indeed it was the "real town" only by day, for its "long rows of large houses that look well on the outside" were "almost all unfurnished, and most uninhabited." Dashwood went out to Peterhof: "The house is of no consideration, but the gardens that go down to the sea are worthy of notice." Moreover, Monplaisir and Marly were the "prettiest things I have seen in these parts, and both worthy of a place in any garden in Italy," the latter especially being "a very exact piece of Architecture." Dashwood was further surprised to find "so many fine pictures" at Peterhof, although, like Mrs. Ward, he observed that they were "taken no sort of care of, and several are spoiled and all aspoiling."

Leaving St. Petersburg for home, Dashwood thought it "very much worth any curious man's while going to see, and to stay there three weeks or a month." But "once curiosity is satisfied," he concluded, "one could amuse oneself better in more southern climes."

In 1733, when Dashwood visited St. Petersburg, it had only just begun to grow again, reaching a population of about 75,000 by the end of the decade (up from about 40,000 in 1725). The growth was largely uncontrolled, however, and in 1736 and 1737 the city suffered extensive damage from fire. A master plan for its continued development was then drawn up and its future as the Empire's capital was confirmed. Count Francesco Algarotti, like Dashwood a "curious man," came to see it in the summer of 1739.

Algarotti was born in Venice, the son of a rich merchant, and was educated in Rome, Venice, and Bologna. He went on to acquire a reputation as both a scientist and a man of letters, and to correspond with a wide circle of notables in England, France, and Germany, including Frederick the Great, Voltaire, and Lord Hervey, to the last of whom he sent several letters from St. Petersburg describing what he saw. The letters make it clear that Algarotti was attracted to the new Russian capital purely out of curiosity, to discover for himself "this new city" created by Peter I, "this great window recently opened in the north through which Russia looks on Europe."[23]

Algarotti was suitably impressed by Kronshtadt's fortifications and particularly by the "magnificent canal" that was now nearing completion on a scale "worthy of the Romans." The thirty or forty warships at anchor or in drydock in and around the harbor produced the "most picturesque effect in the world"; one of the warships, in the later stages of construction under the direction of an Englishman, was of "enormous size, perhaps the largest now afloat." It had emplacements for 114 guns and was called the "Anna" after the empress.

Sailing up the channel toward the city, Algarotti observed that "this triumphal way, this sacred way of the Neva, is not adorned with either arches or temples" but rather was "flanked by forest to both right and left—and that not of majestic oaks or tufted elms or evergreen laurels, but of the most wretched species of trees on which the sun shines." Here is an echo of Weber. Similarly, Algarotti "listened in vain for the melodious singing of the birds with which [Peter I] had wished to populate this wild and gloomy forest; in vain had he had numerous colonies of them brought from the southern provinces of his empire; they all perished in a short while." But his first glimpse of St. Petersburg made up for "sailing several hours through these frightful and silent woods," for

> all of a sudden the river bends; the scene instantly changes, as in an opera, and we behold before us the Imperial city. On either bank groups of sumptuous edifices, towers topped by gilded spires, ships with banners flying . . . such is the brilliant spectacle that greets us. Here, they tell us, is the Admiralty, there the Arsenal; here the fortress, there the Academy; ahead, the Winter Palace. [Fig. 112]

When Algarotti's party actually set foot in the city, however, "we no longer found it as superb as it appeared from a distance, perhaps because the gloominess of the forest no longer brightened our perspective." On the one hand, "the situation of a city located on the banks of a large river and made up of various islands, providing different vantage points and optical effects, could only be beautiful"; and "when one recalls the cabins of Reval and of the other cities in these parts, one cannot but be content with the houses and buildings of St. Petersburg." On the other hand, "the ground on which it is founded is low and marshy, the forest amidst which it is located is both immense and frightful, the materials of which it is constructed are of little value, and the designs of the buildings are not by an Inigo Jones or a Palladio." Indeed, "there reigns in this capital a kind of bastard architecture, one which partakes of the Italian, the French, and the Dutch" (figs. 113, 114).

"Dutch" architecture predominated in the St. Petersburg of 1739, Algarotti suggested, owing to the background and tastes of its founder, Peter I. Thus "it was solely in memory of Holland," for example, "that he planted rows of trees along the streets and bisected them with canals, which certainly do not serve the same purpose here as do those of Amsterdam and Utrecht"—a remark which plainly implies that Peter's adoption of elements of Dutch town planning, in Algarotti's view, was more imitative than practical. Nor did the suburban villas of the grandees, in the eyes of this critic, fare any better. On the contrary, "one sees clearly that they were built more in obedience than by choice. Their walls are all cracked, out of plumb, and remain standing with difficulty." This provoked the witticism that "elsewhere ruins make themselves, while in St. Petersburg they are built"; for it was "necessary in this new capital constantly to rebuild, because of the instability of the ground and the poor quality of the materials used."

Figure 112 Panoramic view of St. Petersburg from the Neva; engraving by E. Vinogradov after drawing by M. I. Makhaev, 1753. Prominent on the right is the third Winter Palace, built 1732–1735 after designs by B. F. Rastrelli incorporating the former Apraksin palace (cf. fig. 108B); prominent on the left are the Academy of Sciences (fig. 113) and the Peter-Paul fortress and church.

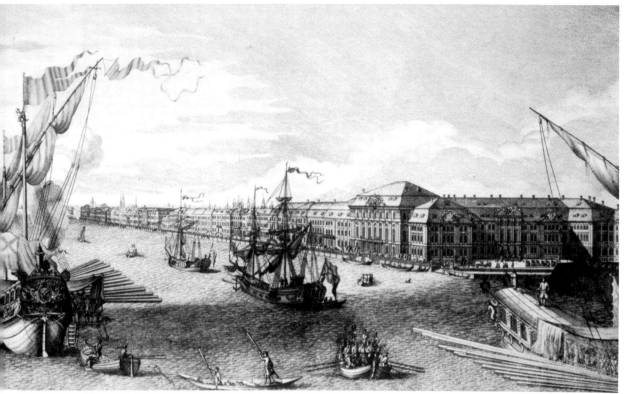

(Figure 112 continued)

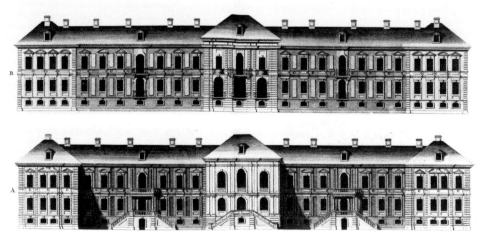

Figure 113 Front (river) and back facades of the building housing the St. Petersburg Academy of Sciences from its founding in 1726 until the 1780s, when a new structure was built on the site (pl. 66); engraving by C. A. Wortman, 1741.

Figure 114 Building of the Twelve Colleges, St. Petersburg, 1724–1732; D. Trezzini, architect; engraving by E. Vnukov after drawing by M. I. Makhaev, 1753.

Yet the city had survived. The necessities of life were brought from the Novgorod region, as Algarotti reported, and oak for shipbuilding was floated up the waterways from Kazan (a procedure that took two summers). If food was occasionally in short supply, it happened only in summer, owing to navigational difficulties; in winter everything was there in abundance, easily brought by sled. Algarotti put St. Petersburg's permanent population (around 1739) at 120,000, in fact a gross exaggeration (the population was, as mentioned, more like 70,000). But his figure reflects an impression of bustling density.

And in the 1740s this impression would give way to one of outright prosperity. "Though so lately a morass," observed a British merchant around 1745, St. Petersburg was "now an elegant and superb city, very beautiful, and abounding in all the necessities, and many of the pleasures, of life. It was formerly built of wood," Jonas Hanway continued, "but now the use of this material is permitted only in the suburbs." Hanway was witnessing the building boom in St. Petersburg that followed the accession in 1741 of Empress Elizabeth, daughter of Peter I, a boom in which "the taste of Italy is adopted in almost all their houses" thanks to the efforts of "an Italian architect some years since established in Russia."[24] He referred, of course, to Rastrelli and to what in Chapter 6 was described as the flowering, under Empress Elizabeth's patronage and Rastrelli's overall direction, of the Russian Baroque (figs. 115, 116; pls. 60–62).

Figure 115 View of the Nevskii Prospekt, St. Petersburg, crossing the Fontanka with, left, the Anichkov palace, built 1740s on commission from Empress Elizabeth by M. G. Zemtsov and G. D. Dmitriev, architects; engraving by Ia. Vasiliev after drawing by M. I. Makhaev, 1753.

From the Baroque of Rastrelli and Elizabeth architectural taste in St. Petersburg passed to the Neoclassical favored by Catherine II (1762–1796), under whom the city experienced another building boom. The best contemporary account of these developments is contained in the detailed and authoritative "Picture of Petersburg" compiled in the 1790s by Henry (Heinrich?) Storch, a German in Russian service who drew on the work of two other resident Germans, both members of the St. Petersburg Academy of Sciences, as well as on his own observations. A few highlights from Storch's "Picture" will round out these contemporary European views of the course of the Petrine architectural revolution in eighteenth-century Russia.[25]

By the 1790s St. Petersburg had surpassed Moscow as the Empire's largest metropolis and was indisputably its biggest port as well as greatest single market.[26] Its appearance, moreover, reflected its status. In Storch's words:

> Straight, broad and generally long streets, frequently intersecting each other in abrupt and sharp corners—spacious open squares—variety in the architecture of the houses—in short, the numerous canals and the beautiful river Neva, with their substantial and elegant embankations [built under Catherine II], render the general view brilliant and inchanting. In regard to regularity and capacity for embellishment, but few capital cities in Europe can be compared with it.

Figure 116 View of Peterhof; engraving after drawing by M. I. Makhaev, 1761. The central portion of the main palace, begun in 1714 and designed by J. B. A. Le Blond and J. F. Braunstein, was augmented with galleries designed by N. Michetti in 1721. Between 1746 and 1755 B. F. Rastrelli greatly enlarged and redecorated the structure, as can be seen here, producing an outstanding example of the Russian Baroque.

(*Figure 116 continued*)

Thus if, in Berlin, that other new capital city,

> the eye is less frequently hurt with large vacant spaces or mean wooden build-
> ings, here it is recreated with more palaces and grand private structures, wider
> streets and a number of fine canals. The view of Petersburg delights us less by
> what it is than by the idea of what it will be when compleated by its vast and
> grand dispositions; an idea which is very naturally excited by the buildings
> constantly going up with surprising rapidity.

The Admiralty district of the city was "the most elegant and completest," and
"what the Quartier du Palais Royal is to Paris, this quarter is to St. Petersburg."
It was "the heart of the city, in which luxury and wealth have established their
seat . . . the centre of amusement and business, the brilliant resort of pleasure
and fashion." Here, Storch declared, there were "three and twenty structures
of the first magnitude, of which the Imperial Winter Palace is the most conspicuous" (fig. 117).

Indeed Rastrelli's Winter Palace, owing to its "colossal size, the magnificence
which reigns within and around it, the treasures of costly works and curiosities
of every kind that are here collected," was the "most striking object of the
city." Its Baroque design offended Storch's Neoclassical sensibilities, to be sure:
"imposing by its huge mass," it was "not remarkable for any elegance of architecture; the style and the exuberance of decoration sufficiently betray the period
in which it came into being." Yet the attached "Hermitage," built by J. B. M.

Figure 117 The Winter Palace, Leningrad, river facade, much as it would have appeared at the end of the
eighteenth century. The granite embankment was built under Catherine II.

Vallin de la Mothe and G. F. Veldten between 1764 and 1787, was composed of two "superb buildings" housing a library, picture gallery, and other artistic and scientific collections (pls. 64A–B). Equally, the "sumptuous exterior" of the attached Court Theater by Giacomo Quarenghi (1783–1787) was "ornamented with columns and colossal statues of the Grecian, Roman, and Russian dramatists," while in its "inner disposition an elegant simplicity prevails" (pl. 65). Again, the Taurida Palace of Prince Potemkin, Catherine II's great favorite, which had been built to commemorate Potemkin's conquest of the Crimea ("Taurida") by I. E. Starov between 1783 and 1789 (Starov had studied in St. Petersburg under De la Mothe and then in Paris and Italy), was a "superb edifice," with its "large cupola," its "wings extending to the street," and its "grand portal supported on columns" (pl. 67). Finally, De la Mothe's severely Neoclassical Academy of Fine Arts (1764–1788), to Storch's mind, was "one of the most elegant structures in all Petersburg" (pl. 63).

Storch accounted more than half of St. Petersburg's houses in 1787 to be made of brick, and "entirely in brick, not timber and brick." These houses were built

> with great taste and a proper regard to convenience, if not with equal solidity. Most are on the Italian plan of architecture, having a basement story rising but little above the pavement and generally built of granite, producing a very noble and substantial effect. The fronts of the houses are in excellent style and display uncommon taste, only at times overloaded with ornaments. . . . The taste at present runs upon columns, and as long as that lasts it will be carried to excess like every other reigning mode. These structures being always of brick covered with stucco, the outside is washed with some particular colour; formerly the favorite was yellow or pink, at present it seems to be green and café au lait. The coverings [roofs] are sometimes of sheet iron, sometimes of cast iron, occasionally of sheet copper, which, besides their duration and security, present an agreeable view when, as is now frequently done, they are painted green or red. Tiles are only used for out-houses and the meaner sort of buildings. The roofs according to the best rules of architecture are nearly flat.

And in the "internal construction and accommodation of the houses," Storch emphasized, "convenience and luxury are as much consulted as in any city of Europe."

Storch also pointed out that many of the timber houses still being built in St. Petersburg had "brick foundations," and that "to give them a somewhat better appearance" their exteriors were "often cased with boards and painted according to the fancy of the owner." These practices were to become widespread in nineteenth-century Russia, as would the technique of covering timber houses—always designed now in the "new" or "modern" style—with plaster and/or stucco (figs. 118A–B). Yet in the 1790s such "improved" timber houses stood out sharply from the mass of "huts" or "rural huts" still to be found even

A

Figures 118A–B A, House in Little Mokhanovka Street, Moscow, ca. 1820. Typical period log construction covered with stucco and plaster, and with a framed pedimental roof. B, Russian wooden houses, Khabarovsk (Soviet Far East), late nineteenth century. Note brick foundations, log walls "cased with boards" or planed flat with cased corners, and framed pedimental roof.

B

in elegant St. Petersburg—in the "remoter lines [streets]" of Vasilevskii Island, for instance, which were "mostly built with wooden huts gradually becoming worse and meaner in their appearance."

Storch provides data in his "Picture" of St. Petersburg indicating that in about 1790 over 32,000 foreigners lived in the city (more than half of them Germans, with large contingents of Swedish, French, and English people), together making up about one-seventh of its total population, and among whom were a sizable number of builders and decorators. He also gives evidence that if Europeans were still dominant in some of the building arts, Russians had mastered most of them.

> Among the trades carried on almost exclusively by the Russians are those of bricklayer and carpenter. Besides the bricklayers and masons that live constantly at Petersburg, above six thousand of them come annually from the provinces to work during the short summer. Spacious and handsome buildings are usually constructed after the plans of an architect, of whom the court has some of the first eminence in its service, and under the inspection of a surveyor; but all the rest is performed by Russian builders. It is impossible to refrain from surprise at the talent for imitation that forms the prominent feature in the character of this nation, on seeing how quickly these clownish people, destitute of all idea of art, attain to the utmost dexterity and the nicest judgement in the execution of such works.

Like other European observers before him, Storch was particularly struck by the dexterity of the native carpenters, whose "axe, though so simple in its construction, supplies with them the place of the hammer, the plane, the saw, and the chisel; with this compendium of all tools they build houses, make tables, chairs, carts—in short, all the common necessaries of life that can be made of wood." But the "cabinet-maker's art, in which the price of ingenuity far exceeds the value of the materials, is at present solely confined to foreigners, amongst whom the Germans distinguish themselves." Similarly, if Russians were the "only gardeners," growing "everything that can come up in their soil and climate," landscape architecture or "artificial gardening" remained the province of foreigners, "mostly Dutchmen."

POSTSCRIPT

The importance of these contemporary European descriptions of St. Petersburg in the eighteenth century, like that of the contemporary European views of seventeenth-century Russian architecture quoted in Chapter 2, lies first of all in their evaluative aspect. In both cases, at base, the criteria were the same: the standards of contemporary European architecture ruled without question. Yet now, equally obviously, the reaction was as positive as it had once been negative. By the 1720s, if somewhat tentatively, and certainly by the 1740s,

Europeans visiting St. Petersburg considered the architecture of the city and its environs essentially European—"a kind of bastard architecture," in Algarotti's exacting phrase, but "one which partakes of the Italian, the French, and the Dutch." A palace said to rival that of Versailles, houses and gardens in "the Dutch fashion" or "the taste of Italy," streetlights "after the English manner," a district that suggested the Faubourg St. Germain, an Admiralty "not unlike the Arsenal of Venice": the choice of words matters less than the consensus conveyed. And the praise: structures were "regularly built" or "well contrived," a church was "an architectural jewel" and an Imperial retreat, "a very exact piece of architecture." Here was a "splendid portico," a "superb facade," or a "fine colonnade," there a "stately prospect" or "brilliant spectacle," "sumptuous edifices" or a "magnificent cascade." Among ecclesiastical buildings the Peter-Paul church was judged surpassing: built "not in the Byzantine but in the new taste," in it "all the ornaments of Architecture and Sculpture" were displayed with "great judgement and elegance." Palace interiors were also found worthy, to say the least: "noble" or "finely proportioned" apartments were now to be seen, as were "excellent carved decoration," "fine paintings," and "exquisite furniture." "Beautiful," "magnificent," "superb," "elegant," "most agreeable," "majestic": the adjectives echo those of contemporary Russians traveling in Europe (Chap. 5). Kronstadt was a "prodigious work," the building called the *Kunstkamera* "one of the most magnificent of its kind in Europe." Indeed, the language of these witnesses—two Germans, a Pole, two Frenchmen, four English people, an Italian (excluding Henry Storch for the moment)—provides some of the best evidence available that within little more than a generation a revolution in Russian architecture had taken place.

Secondly, these contemporary descriptions of St. Petersburg amplify, at times greatly, the evidence derived from official sources. The observations of Bergholtz and particularly of Weber convey pointedly, for example, the rapid and forced character of the city's development in Peter I's last years and the utter grandiosity of some of his architectural projects. Their accounts are the more impressive in view of St. Petersburg's bleak and generally unpromising natural setting, which Weber especially was at pains to describe and which helps to explain, perhaps, why foreigners were so ready to exaggerate the number of fatalities suffered in the early construction of the city. Equally notable are their reports of the "admirable regulations" introduced in St. Petersburg to control the age-old curse of the Russian town, periodic destruction by fire. Nor do we miss, in Weber and Bergholtz, or in remarks by Deschisaux and LaMottraye, the raw, unfinished quality the city retained at its founder's death; "in many places," as one of them said, "still meagerly built."

Further, the comments of the two French observers, and then of Mrs. Ward and Sir Francis Dashwood, clarify starkly the degree to which St. Petersburg's rapid development had depended on the driving presence of Peter I. It was as if following his death in 1725 the city was to be left to the elements, except perhaps for its commercial—and military—sections. Yet survive St. Petersburg most certainly did. Even Sir Francis, writing in 1733, reckoned it "very much worth any curious man's while going to see"—thus vindicating Prince Menshikov's prediction, as recorded by Weber scarcely a dozen years before, that in time the city would become "another Venice, to see which foreigners would travel thither purely out of curiosity."

It was another such "curious" visitor, Count Algarotti in 1739, who launched the famous description of St. Petersburg as a "great window recently opened in the north through which Russia looks on Europe." But the metaphor is too passive. For the new capital had also become a channel through which countless Europeans, bearing their values and their ways, poured into Russia, working transformations in the culture unimaginable in an earlier age. As Henry Storch put it, writing from St. Petersburg in the 1790s:

> Allured by the numerous wants of a great city, and the profusion of a court, many thousands of industrious and ingenious foreigners [like himself] have been induced to settle here; by the continual influx of whom, and the communication of their talents, this Imperial city is become not only the seat of all ingenious trades, but likewise a source of industry which flows from hence in beneficial streams through all the adjacent provinces.[27]

The flow was particularly marked in architecture, as will be seen in Chapter 8.

8
Conclusion

As for architecture [*arkhitektura*], what can be said about the
building that was and the building we now see? That which was
scarcely answered our greatest needs, could scarcely protect us
from the aerial injuries of rain and wind and flying refuse; while
that which now is, beyond its most commodious convenience,
shines forth in beauty and splendor. As for military and naval
architecture: these, before, our artists could not even properly
depict.

—Feofan Prokopovich, eulogy of Peter I,
St. Petersburg, June 29, 1725[1]

The Petrine revolution in Russian architecture affected every aspect of the
building art and sooner or later reached into every part of the Russian Empire,
producing transformations in the built environment that would give it a more
or less European—or "modern"—appearance. Initially a matter of necessity
with respect to fortification and shipbuilding but essentially one of taste with
regard to "civil" architecture, the revolution can be viewed as a process
whereby the values and techniques of contemporary European architecture were
deliberately brought to Russia, there to be so firmly implanted in the first decades of the eighteenth century that they determined the subsequent course of
Russian architectural history. Ordinary domestic housing, parks and gardens,
warehouses and wharves all came within the revolution's purview as did
churches and palaces, official buildings of every variety, fortresses and other
military structures, and ships—overwhelmingly naval ships—of every known
kind. The Petrine architectural revolution was responsible for bringing to Russia everything from the idea of large-scale and detailed town planning to the
art of applying plaster and alabaster modeling in the interior decoration of
buildings. Scarcely any building or ensemble of buildings of any social importance would ever again be the same.

To recapitulate briefly, the revolution involved several distinct if interrelated
steps. European architectural books and prints were collected in huge, entirely
unprecedented numbers; Russian editions of various European architectural
works—notably, Vignola's textbook—were produced for the first time, as were
engravings of Russian buildings in the "new style," engravings that were designed now by Russian as well as foreign artists;[2] at least seventeen Russians
were dispatched to Europe—mainly to Amsterdam and Rome—for the express
purpose of studying architecture, something that had never been done before;
and, most decisively, thousands of European experts were imported both to
supervise or assist in the work of designing and building and to train, by precept
and by example, their Russian pupils and assistants. Regular training in architectural theory as well as practice was established in Russia; and Russian build-

ers, absorbing a whole new technical vocabulary of Dutch, Italian, English, German, French, and Latin terms, went on to apply their new knowledge in the construction of numerous buildings in what came to be called the St. Petersburg style—a new, local variant of the northern Baroque.

This concluding chapter attempts to show how the Petrine architectural revolution then took root in Russia in the decades after Peter I's death (1725). In doing so, the obviously crucial matter of architectural training will be considered first.

THE REVOLUTION INSTITUTIONALIZED

Academies of art in Europe go back to sixteenth-century Italy and particularly to Florence, where in about 1560 the Academy of Design was formed by the grand duke Cosimo d'Medici for the purpose of uniting under his protection the best architects, painters, and sculptors of the day—"best" meaning those artists who shared to an exemplary degree an interest in Classical "design." Duke Cosimo's artists were thus freed from the restrictions of the medieval guild system and able to disregard the economic aspect of their art, which was now being thought of less as a handicraft or manual skill to be learned at the master's elbow and more as a science or spiritual expression, like poetry or physics, requiring considerable theoretical study. The Academy in Florence was followed by the Academy of St. Luke in Rome, established in 1593; by numerous lesser, often private academies founded elsewhere in Italy in the seventeenth century; and by the Royal Academy of Painting and Sculpture in Paris (1648) and its offshoot, the Academy of Architecture (1671). The operations of the French academy reflected the centralizing and authoritarian methods and aims of the French monarchy, and it soon developed the now familiar panoply of publications, prizes, exhibitions, and traveling scholarships while closely regulating the teaching and other work of its members. It was the model for the German and various other art academies which sprang up in seventeenth- and eighteenth-century Europe and in which teaching the Classical tenets of the three "fine arts" remained a fundamental purpose—the *arts nobles* or *beaux arts* as they were called, to distinguish them from the humble *arts mécaniques* or *moindres métiers* with which architecture, painting, and sculpture had once been confused.[3]

The notion of founding a St. Petersburg academy of fine arts goes back to the time of Peter I, too. Leaving aside various minor precedents, it was first formally proposed to him in 1721 by M. P. Avramov, a senior official and amateur painter who had spent five years on mission in Holland and who as head (from 1712) of the St. Petersburg Printing House (*Tipografiia*) had been instrumental in establishing a school of drawing under its auspices; it was the "first regular art school in Russia."[4] In an earlier report to Peter, Avramov had invoked the tsar's order to found a "small Academy [*Akademiia*]" for the purpose of "proper training in drawing . . . and the other arts . . . following the custom of the European realms"; and he now requested permission from Peter to implement his scheme, which expressly provided for training in architectural draftsmanship. Peter's response to the proposal was positive, as a document of January 1724 found among his private papers clearly indicates.[5] The proposal was in essence repeated in December 1724 by A. K. Nartov, a skilled turner and all-around craftsman who also had studied in Europe (1718–1720) and who now urged the creation of a central arts academy that would provide training in "civil architecture" among other subjects—a proposal which he revived in 1743.[6]

That nothing came of these schemes while Peter I lived (to January 1725) was evidently only a matter of time. His last years were marked by a flurry of proposals for creating institutions of higher education and specialized or technical training in Russia, some of which—like those for an ecclesiastical academy in St. Petersburg or for the Academy of Sciences—were well on their way to fruition at the time of his death. Meanwhile, of course, training in both painting and draftsmanship proceeded apace in St. Petersburg in the "commands" set up by the Chancellery of Construction (Chap. 6), at the Naval Academy (since 1715) and the Military Hospital (1716), and at Avramov's drawing school.

On arriving in St. Petersburg the French painter Louis Caravaque, hired by Peter I in 1724, proposed the foundation of an "academy of painting like that in Paris"; he even administered some such school located in the Post Office until 1727, when he renewed his earlier proposal, this time to see it accepted by the Chancellery of Construction. But again nothing actually came of the scheme—nor of his new proposal of 1731, when V. N. Tatishchev, later to be famous as a historian but now in charge of Empress Anna's coronation, joined him in pushing for an academy of arts that Tatishchev would head.[7] The difficulties seem to have been rooted in court politics, in funding, and in the shortage of suitable Russian candidates for membership. Meanwhile, to repeat, architectural training in the "new style" progressed in the commands run by Zemtsov, Korobov (under the Admiralty), and B. F. Rastrelli (figs. 119, 120). In 1727 it was reported that some 133 students of architecture and painting were being supported by the Chancellery of Construction.[8]

The 1730s and the 1740s experienced new pressures for the creation of a European-style academy of art in St. Petersburg, but it was only in 1757 that the founding of such an institution was finally announced.[9] The announcement proved to be somewhat premature, however, for it was only in 1764 that an Imperial charter was issued, by Catherine II, and a permanent president named (I. I. Betskoi, who had lived for a time in Paris and was a devoted favorite of the new empress). Catherine's charter noted that under her predecessor, Empress Elizabeth (daughter of Peter I), an "Academy of the Three Finest Arts"—architecture, painting, and sculpture—had been founded but not properly provided for, an omission she hereby repaired while granting the new academy the right to open a junior school and to set up a press, all at Imperial expense; its graduates were also to have priority of appointment in all official and public

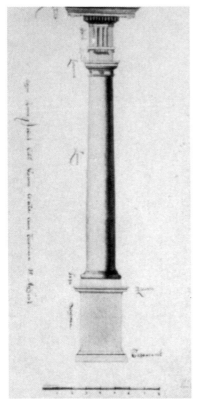

Figure 119 Architectural drawings from a Russian student's sketchbook, St. Petersburg, 1741.

works throughout the Russian Empire (fig. 121).[10] In 1765 a building for the new Academy was begun following plans drawn up by J. B. M. Vallin de la Mothe, who had come from France in 1759 to be the academy's senior professor of architecture. The building, still standing and still the Academy's home, exudes the principles of Neoclassicism, which, owing to the influence of the Academy, were then to dominate Russian architecture until the end of the century (figs. 122A–B, pl. 63).[11]

Figure 120 Model for the Smol'nyi church, St. Petersburg, ca. 1747, in two sections; studio of B. F. Rastrelli.

Figure 121 "Seal of the Imperial Academy of Painting, Sculpture and Architecture," St. Petersburg; engraving of 1765. Double-headed eagle with cipher of Catherine II denotes Imperial patronage.

A

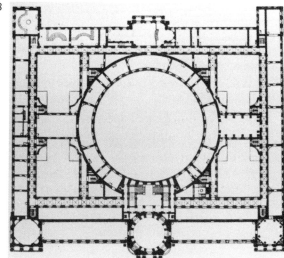

B

Figures 122A–B Academy of Fine Arts, Leningrad, 1765–1788; J. B. M. Vallin de la Mothe and A. Kokorinov, architects. A, Upper vestibule. B, Plan of the second floor.

With the foundation in St. Petersburg of the Imperial Academy of Fine Arts (*Akademiia khudozhestv*), as it soon came to be called, training in architectural theory and draftsmanship was definitively separated from the workshop or building site and given a central, authoritative, and privileged position in the preparation of builders in Russia. Not coincidentally, the profession of architect in Russia was acquiring new prestige, as it had elsewhere. Of students enrolled at the Academy already in 1758, nearly a third—eleven of thirty-eight—gave their social status (*chin*) as "of the nobility [*iz dvorian*]."[12] Builders, like painters, were no longer drawn exclusively from the peasantry and townsfolk.

In 1764 the first class of the new junior school of the Imperial Academy of Fine Arts was enrolled: sixty boys, all six years of age. The idea was that if after nine years in the school any of its pupils was not judged sufficiently talented to move up to the Academy, he would remain to prepare for a trade such as metalworking or cabinetry. The architectural historian Pevsner thus finds two features of the St. Petersburg Academy that make it unique in the history of such institutions: one, the combination of secondary school, trade school, and art academy under one roof, suggesting "a country where public education of all kinds was still undeveloped"; and two, the amount of state control exercised, which can be explained, in Pevsner's view, "only by the particular coincidence of a nation grown up outside Western civilization being suddenly forced into it with an epoch in Western history in which absolutism and its commercial corollary, mercantilism, were ruling."[13] Be that as it may, with respect to architecture and the decorative arts the St. Petersburg Academy of Fine Arts, like the 100 or more public schools of art established everywhere in Europe by 1790, served to disseminate, initially, the tenets of Neoclassicism (figs. 123, 124; pls. 34, 63–69). And in this way the Academy brought Russia firmly into the European mainstream.

The advance of Russian architecture under Catherine II (reigned 1762–1796) was the culmination of an extraordinary convergence of power and taste, one that had begun under Peter I and whose effects would reach still further into the future. For by the end of Catherine's reign, to take only the most obvious instance, the Russian government had directed the planning or replanning and renovation of more than 400 cities and towns, producing a deliberate uniformity of urban design throughout the Russian Empire. The purpose of this gigantic enterprise, it will be seen shortly, was to give the Russian built environment a "more European appearance." The words are Catherine II's, about whom it is always helpful to remember that she was born and raised in Germany (as Sophia of Anhalt Zerbst), spoke French as her second language, arrived in Russia at the age of fifteen to become the wife of the heir to the throne (whom she eventually supplanted), and spent most of the rest of her life in St. Petersburg.[14]

Figure 123 Model of the Trinity Church, Alexander-Nevskii monastery, St. Petersburg, ca. 1776; I. E. Starov, architect (cf. pl. 34).

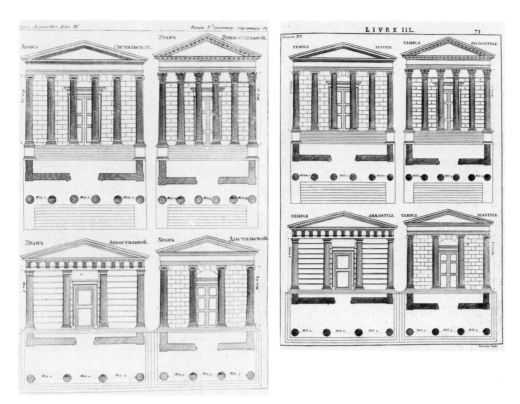

Figure 124 Extracts from (left) the Russian edition of Vitruvius's *Ten Books on Architecture* published 1790–1797 by the St. Petersburg Academy of Fine Arts, and (right) the 1694 French edition of same from which the text of the Russian edition was translated and its illustrations copied. The French edition in turn is a critical and much expanded version of the Latin original of Claude Perrault, member of the Royal Academy in Paris and a leading proponent of French Neoclassicism (architect, e.g., of the east front of the Louvre). The Russian translation "with further explanatory notes for the benefit of Architectural students" was done by Vasilii Bazhenov, member of the St. Petersburg Academy of Fine Arts and a leading Russian proponent of Neoclassicism in architecture (cf. fig. 128). A comparison of these two works provides excellent evidence of the actual transfer of European architectural norms, here Neoclassical, to Russia.

FROM ST. PETERSBURG TO MOSCOW

The Petrine revolution in Russian architecture actually began in and around Moscow, as we saw, only to be interrupted there by Peter I's growing and then nearly exclusive concern with the building of St. Petersburg, a concern made manifest by his ban of 1714 on masonry construction everywhere else in his dominions for an indefinite time. St. Petersburg thus became the principal site, and then the embodiment, of the Petrine revolution in Russian building norms. Yet the revolution itself, worked out in St. Petersburg, would eventually reach the old capital, where it produced startling contrasts of old and new.

Sytin observes, in his detailed history of the planning and construction of Moscow, that Peter I's legislation did not make Moscow into a modern well-built city even in externals. But it served as a program for the later activities of the local authorities—although even then, it is true, it was not always followed. Only at the end of the eighteenth century was the center of town more or less rebuilt, with masonry structures standing in straight rows. As in much else, so in the construction of Moscow did Peter provide the impetus for many decades to come.

In fact, in the years immediately following Peter's death, as Sytin goes on to say, things were done that intensified rather than altered Moscow's traditional development, contributing nothing to the making of the "genuine city that Peter I had wanted."[15]

The problem was primarily one of patronage. With the court and central government removed to St. Petersburg together with many of the merchants and the leaders of the church, Moscow lacked permanently resident patrons with either the taste or the means to build extensively in the "new style." Nor would there have been, in the later 1720s and the 1730s, enough trained architects to go around. Moreover, the drain over the years of the best or better craftsmen to St. Petersburg, as well as the ban on masonry construction in the old capital, which was only lifted in 1728,[16] left Moscow bereft of builders. It would take a generation or more of practice in building, and the revival of Moscow as a political and social center, to make good the loss.

Kadashevskaia sloboda or Kadashi, the flourishing weavers' district across the Moscow river from the Kremlin, provides a case study in point.[17] This and two smaller adjoining districts—the three forming *Zamoskvorech'e* or the town "Across the Moscow river"—witnessed extensive construction in the earlier eighteenth century: two-thirds of its parish churches, for example, underwent greater or lesser alterations, everything from replacing an entire wooden structure with a masonry one to simply adding a bell tower. Yet all of the eighteen newly built churches that have been identified preserved their seventeenth-century plan, while the new bell towers, exhibiting rusticalized Petrine forms, served only to muddle the contrast between old and new. At the same time, practically all of the domestic construction in *Zamoskvorech'e* in the first half of the eighteenth century preserved far more of tradition than it reflected the new. It was only in the 1730s that renewed attempts were made, here as elsewhere in Moscow, to "regularize" the city by widening and straightening streets, eliminating dead-ends, limiting wooden construction, embanking the rivers, and so forth.

One notable and at least partial exception to this general rule was the renovation of the Golovin estate located just outside Moscow, across the Iauza river from the German Settlement, beginning in 1722. An expression of Peter I's late interest in the scenes of his youth, the new St. Petersburg principles in palatial and landscape architecture were applied here and then elsewhere around the old capital in ways that represented a drastic break in Muscovite estate architecture.[18] But it was Rastrelli and his followers, as mentioned earlier, who brought the new architecture to Moscow in the 1740s and 1750s in all of its major manifestations, whether in nobiliar townhouses or suburban estates, the occasional church or Imperial residence (fig. 125).

The work of Rastrelli and his followers was facilitated and carried forward, in turn, by the efforts of a number of talented local architects, especially D. V. Ukhtomskii (1719–1774?) and his school, who also enjoyed the patronage of Empress Elizabeth and her court (figs. 126, 127).[19] Still, it was only under Catherine II that serious attempts were made to replan the old capital and to control its growth (in the 1760s, as her reign began, its population numbered as many as 250,000 as compared with about 150,000 for St. Petersburg). In the words of one historian, "Catherine deplored Moscow's sprawling layout and teeming streets, its Eurasian architecture and disorderly appearance," and so dreamed of renovating it "after the fashion of the new, European-style, planned Imperial capital of St. Petersburg."[20]

Figure 125 Facade of "Winter Palace" erected in Moscow for Empress Elizabeth, 1742; school of B. F. Rastrelli. Contemporary engraving by I. Sokolov.

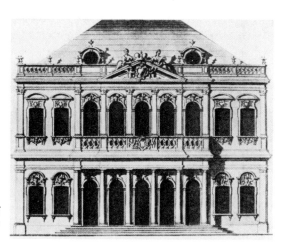

Figure 126 Design of main facade of house of N. Iu. Trubetskoi, suburban Moscow, by D. V. Ukhtomskii.

Figure 127 Bell tower, Trinity–St. Sergius monastery, Zagorsk, 1741–1769; D. V. Ukhtomskii and I. Michurin, architects.

Fire remained a major hazard. Its housing still constructed overwhelmingly of wood, between 1770 and 1775 roughly a third of Moscow's timber dwellings and their outbuildings were consumed by fires, many of which had been deliberately set to counter the plague. Brick buildings—in 1775 perhaps one-sixth of Moscow's remaining houses were built of brick—were concentrated in the city's center and were often of inferior construction as well as conspicuous, still, for their wooden appurtenances. In 1775 a special commission for rebuilding both Moscow and St. Petersburg established by Catherine II produced a grandiose plan for the old capital of predictably Classical pretensions.[21] Catherine also commissioned the architect V. I. Bazhenov (1737–1799) to transform the Kremlin into a kind of Neoclassical showpiece, at whatever cost. The work of clearing the site and laying the foundations began in 1770. The Kremlin was to become a "regular" structure, one that should reflect the principles of "order, perspective, and proportion [*order, perspektiva i proportional'nost*]" as the historian Loktev says, using terms that in Russian go directly back to the Petrine revolution. Several buildings, towers, and a part of the Kremlin wall were razed to make way for Bazhenov's Grand Palace, which was to be the masterpiece of his plan, before Catherine ordered the project brought to a halt (fig. 128). It was never resumed.[22]

But the overall plan of 1775 for Moscow itself was to be partly realized between then and the great fire of 1812.[23] Industries were moved from the city's center, where the proportion of masonry structures steadily grew, a large number of Neoclassical mansions went up (pl. 68), squares began to take shape, the rivers were cleaned and canalized or embanked, and streetlights were installed. Here is how William Coxe, an English scholar who toured the city in 1778–1779 and again in 1785, described it:

> I was all astonishment at the immensity and variety of Moscow: a city so irregular, so uncommon, so extraordinary, and so contrasted never before claimed my attention [Coxe had traveled extensively in Europe]. The streets are in general exceedingly long and broad: some are paved; others, particularly those in the suburbs, formed with trunks of trees, or boarded with planks like the floor of a room; wretched hovels are blended with large palaces; cottages of one story stand next to the most stately mansions. Many brick structures are covered with wooden tops; some of the timber houses are painted, others have iron doors and roofs. Numerous churches present themselves in every quarter, built in the oriental style of architecture: some with domes of copper, others of tin, gilt or painted green, and many roofed with wood. In a word, some parts of this vast city have the appearance of a sequestered desert, other quarters, of a populous town; some of a contemptible village, others of a great capital. Moscow may be considered as a town built upon the Asiatic model, but gradually becoming more and more European; and exhibiting in its present state a motley mixture of discordant architecture.[24]

Figure 128 Project for Grand Kremlin Palace, Moscow, ca. 1770, by V. I. Bazhenov, architect.

For our purposes now this description could not be more apt. And here is another, from a letter of 1788 sent by a young Englishman of much less worldly experience than Coxe to his sister back in London. The writer, James Brogden, found that in Moscow

> the palaces of the nobility are in general built in the highest style of magnif-
> icence and elegance. Many of them are superior both in size and elegance to
> anything I ever saw in England. They are all built of brick plastered over in
> imitation of stone, ornamented with pillars and every other embellishment of
> Grecian or Italian architecture. They are in general grand and simple, forming
> a very striking contrast with the convents and churches, which are in general
> the most tawdry tempery structures you can form an idea of. They are con-
> structed of the same materials but the ornaments are truly grotesque. They are
> painted all the colours of the rainbow, many ornamented with paintings which
> I suppose are meant to represent saints and virgins; but a man must have the
> intelligence of a saint to know by the pictures what beings they are meant to
> represent. I believe the Egyptians were never here or I should suppose they
> were hieroglyphics. . . . Everything within the churches is in the same taw-
> dry style.[25]

Thus the striking contrasts between the "oriental" or "Asiatic" elements in

(*Figure 128 continued*)

architecture and the "European" that the progress of the Petrine revolution had produced in Moscow by the end of the eighteenth century.[*]

TO THE PROVINCES AND BEYOND

A process of architectural change similar to that which produced St. Petersburg and transformed old Moscow in the eighteenth century gradually invaded the vast and remote provinces of the Russian Empire, and with similar results. The process is easiest to trace in fortification and town planning.

For Russian historians the key term here—and a term that in Russian, again, goes directly back to the Petrine revolution—is *reguliarnost'* ("regularity"). Sytina observes that in the first half of the eighteenth century the "planning

---

[*]And the basic impression abides, as in these remarks by a resident British journalist in 1985, comparing Moscow to Leningrad: "Moscow is a city altogether more crude, more blunt, more Asian [in appearance]. Parts of it are the classic dirty concrete of 1960s Western architectural fashion, but in the old [center] you can still find the remnants of a city that grew up looking eastwards. Moscow's streets teem with Asian, Mongol, and Moslem faces. Parts of it, in the jumble of new high rises, muddy streets and broken pavements, have a Third World feel. Even the Kremlin feels non-European, a walled city that makes you think of Peking or the fortress palace of Bangkok" (Martin Walker, in *The Guardian* newspaper, October 19, 1985, p. 8).

[*planirovka*] of towns was carried out to a large extent on the basis of *reguliar-nost'*," this to be explained by the "striving to envision a rationally organized and impressive urban center that would correspond with the growing power and importance of the young Russian Empire." The political and strategic motives that continued to guide Russian town planning are thus underlined. The "principle of *reguliarnost'*," Sytina goes on to say, was first applied to the residential districts of new military and industrial towns, which were laid out in accordance with one or other variant of a "rectangular-rectilinear plan." The main streets were straight and connected with thoroughfares that were also built in a line. Outbuildings and gardens were located behind the houses, which stood flush with the street. Streets uniformly lined with residential buildings led to the main industrial enterprise or to the fortress, which had its own regular layout with main entrance and gates.[26] In Shkvarikov's account, similarly, the "regular planning and construction" of Russian towns, that is to say, the "formation of modern urban layouts in Russia," an idea "first posed in the Petrine period," was realized by stages in the eighteenth century, particularly under Catherine II; until by the first quarter of the nineteenth century "ensembles of squares, streets, embankments, parks, and so on had been created in numerous cities in Russia."[27] In fact, Peter I himself personally set the precedent when he ordered, in May 1723, that in certain burnt-out areas of old Novgorod new houses were to be built "regularly [*reguliarno*], as in St. Petersburg, in one and the same style, and with the streets [laid out] according to a set plan [*plan*]"—orders that were to be carried out by a certain "Architectural Student Okhlopokov" who was being sent to the scene.[28]

Reguliarnost' in architecture, then, was a matter of right angles and straight lines, of order and uniformity, of the "rational" organization of space: virtues that were to infuse both the design of individual buildings and the layout of whole towns; and St. Petersburg was the "great laboratory in which the new principles of town planning and new types of construction, unknown to the architecture of pre-Petrine Russia, were developed and then disseminated over the entire country."[29] The historical literature affords numerous examples of the process. Between 1723 and 1726 Ekaterinburg was built as the administrative and commercial center of the Urals industrial region, to become in turn a model town for the entire area. Sharply divided into industrial and residential districts, and enclosed by rectangular walls with arrowhead bastions, the plan of Ekaterinburg drawn up in 1726 (fig. 129) reveals how completely it was to embody the principles of *reguliarnost'*.[30] The layout of Orenburg, founded in 1743, was similarly distinguished from the layouts of pre-Petrine Russian towns by being based on the new tendencies in Russian urban planning, "tendencies which consisted in the application of the principles of *reguliarnost'* "; and Orenburg, too, both its overall layout and its individual buildings, was to serve as a model for the new towns of its region (fig. 130).[31] It should be noted, however, that in every other way Orenburg, like Ekaterinburg, perpetuated the Old-Russian tradition of building fortified administrative centers with only limited industrial and commercial facilities and inhabited by a highly stratified

Figure 129 Plan of Ekaterinburg as projected in 1726: *1* = workers' houses; *2* = workshops; *3* = a dam; *4* = administrative offices; *5* = the school; *6* = masters' houses; *7* = a hospital; *8* = the church; *9* = shops; *10* = fortifications; *11* = a mill pond.

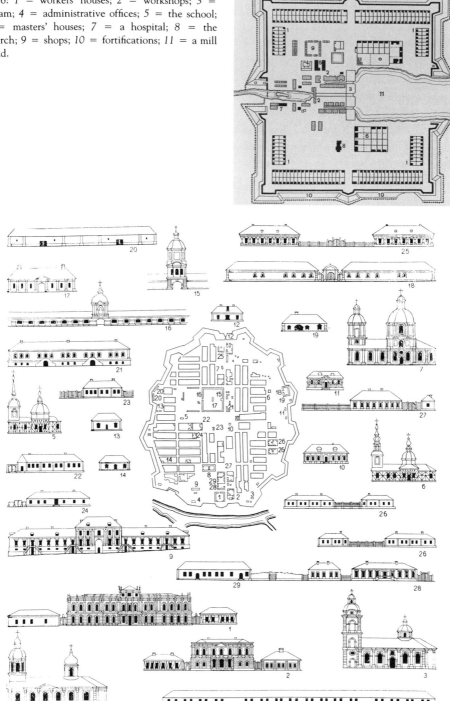

Figure 130 Reconstruction of plan and buildings of Orenburg, 1740s–1790s: *1* = the governor's palace; *2* = his chancellery; *3* = the church of the Transfiguration; *7* = the church of Sts. Peter and Paul; other official and residential buildings, churches, etc.

permanent population. Socially and economically this was the Old-Russian *gorod*, now more strictly regulated than ever before by the central government, in new architectural form.[32]

In general, the fortification of the southeastern and Siberian frontiers in the eighteenth century and the construction of associated new towns directly reflected the Petrine revolution in architecture, which was both facilitated and spread by the use of "model projects" (figs. 131, 132).[33] The degree to which old forms held on and the new prevailed was a matter of local circumstances, distance from a main town, extent of previous settlement, and the strategic and/or administrative importance attached to a particular fortress, settlement, or town by the central government. Rusticalization especially in the decoration and design of churches also occurred, naturally enough, the result no doubt of ignorance and technical deficiency as much as conscious design (figs. 133A–B).[34] And the new norms in composition and decoration were particularly slow to appear, again not surprisingly, in wooden architecture (pls. 37, 38, 40, 41). Yet as Teltevskii says, referring to domestic architecture in the eastern provinces, "the techniques of composition and decoration were close in the first half of the eighteenth century to the norms of the capital"; it was only that "the new always penetrated the provinces with some delay."[35]

The contrast between the old and the new in Russian architecture as the century wore on is a recurrent theme of the contemporary European travel literature, as we saw in the case of Moscow. Here again is William Coxe, this time on the Novgorod that he discovered in 1778, not long after entering the country from the west:

> One of the most antient cities in Russia, the present town is surrounded by a rampart of earth, with a range of old towers at regular distances, forming a circumference of scarcely a mile and a half; and even this inconsiderable circle includes much open space, and many houses which are not inhabited. As Novgorod was built after the manner of the antient towns of this country, in the Asiatic style, this rampart probably enclosed several interior circles: without it was a vast extensive suburb. . . . The Trading Part [of the city] is, excepting the governor's house, only a rude cluster of wooden habitations, and in no other respect distinguished from the common villages than by a vast number of brick churches and convents, which stand melancholy monuments of its former magnificence. . . . Towards its extremity a brick edifice and several detached structures of the same materials, erected at the empress's [Catherine II's] expence for a manufacture of ropes and sails, exhibited a most splendid figure when contrasted with the surrounding wooden hovels in the town.

Similarly, Coxe compared the huge medieval walls of Smolensk with the surrounding "regular covered way with traverses, glacis, and redoubts of earth according to the modern style of fortification." Here, too, "one long broad street, which is paved, intersects the whole length of the town in a straight line" while "the other streets generally wind in circular directions, and are floored with planks." Altogether Smolensk presented a "most singular and contrasted scene."[36]

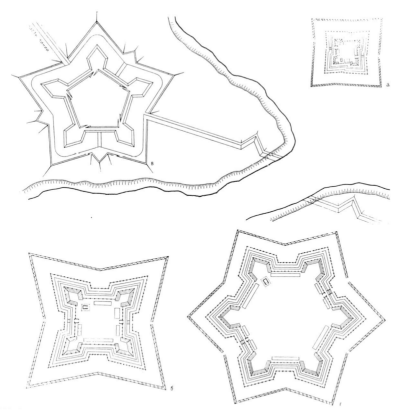

...theastern defensive line, mid-eighteenth century.

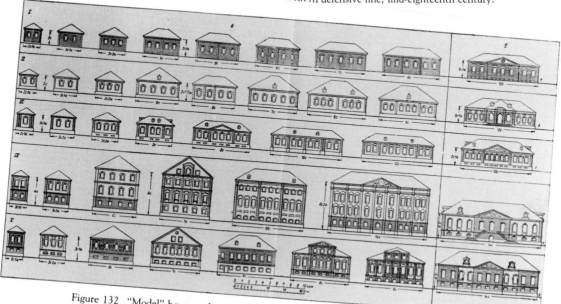

Figure 132 "Model" houses taken from official St. Petersburg publications, 1737–1768.

A

Figures 133A–B A, Church of the Savior, Irkutsk, 1706–1758. B, Church of the Epiphany, Irkutsk, 1718–ca. 1750; main entrance.

B

On the other hand, Hans Jakob Fries, in a letter to his parents in Zurich describing a journey through Siberia in 1774–1776, had this to say about Omsk, "the principal fortress and the headquarters of the general staff of the Siberian [defensive] line." He found it

> a neat fortress; even its location on the right bank of the Irtysh where the Om flows into it, is unforgettable; and the general staff makes this fortress even more impressive, for everything which is demanded by the rules of war and policy is given here the minutest attention. The newly built local stone church is so well constructed that as a masterpiece of architecture it could challenge for first place the most beautiful buildings even in splendid Petersburg. Among other excellent things I ought to mention the local army school. . . . A beautiful hospital is under construction and a pharmacy is being built.

Fries later remarked that Omsk had become "very dear to me, as if I were at home." Considering its architecture and mixed German and Russian population, he did not doubt that Omsk was an outpost of Europe in the "Siberian Asiatic region of the earth." Nor did he confuse Omsk with Tomsk, where

> I saw nothing other than what one finds or sees in most old Russian cities. Nothing but wooden houses and narrow irregular alleys covered with bridges of wooden planks. It is for this reason that in this large Siberian trading city so many conflagrations originate which occasionally consume several hundred houses and more. During the last fire, in 1773, half of the city, which consisted of two thousand houses, was reduced to ashes.[37]

We have read such reports before (Chap. 2).

The practice of comprehensive, detailed, and "regular" town planning introduced in St. Petersburg under Peter I was made universal, as indicated above, by Catherine II, Peter's self-appointed successor in this as in other endeavors. Disliking Moscow as much as she did and devoted to St. Petersburg, Catherine responded to the devastation by fire of the old city of Tver in May 1763 by ordering the planning or replanning of all the cities and towns of the Russian Empire.[38] In another official document dating to about the same time, Catherine denounced the traditional "confusion" in Russian town building whereby "the plan of the ground was not regularly marked out before the people began to build" but instead "everyone fixes upon a spot which he thinks most convenient, without the least regard to the symmetry or extent of the place he had selected: whence a heap of edifices are huddled together which can hardly ever be brought into a regular form by the efforts and careful attention of whole ages."[39] Catherine's writings show that she thought of towns first as administrative centers, then as centers of health care, education, and general welfare, then as "safe havens" for industry and commerce, and then as the home of a kind of middle class, neither noble nor peasant, which was to engage in the arts and sciences, business and trade. Yet nothing like full self-government was to be extended to the towns and particularly not in their planning, which was to be strictly centralized and in every instance approved, ultimately, by the empress herself.[40]

In 1762 Catherine established a Commission on the Building of St. Petersburg and Moscow, which shortly also became the central planning agency for the rest of the Russian Empire. In addition to the razing and renovation of perhaps 200 older towns, the commission went on to direct the planning of 216 new towns founded between 1775 and 1785. Under its regime towns could not exceed a certain geographical limit and were to be laid out as a unified whole unless naturally divided by a river, in which case each side would have its own plan. As Jones says,

> Except for Moscow, the concentric pattern of old Russian cities was completely abandoned. Walls between sections were pulled down, the streets were laid out so as to unite rather than separate the various parts of the town, and often settlements on the edges of the old towns were incorporated and integrated into the new one. . . . The street plans were invariably of a radial or a grid-like design, resembling the radial plan of the Admiralty district of St. Petersburg or the gridlike plan of Vasilevskii Island.

Under a radial plan, the town's focal point was usually the kremlin, a monastery, or the largest church, which often meant that monuments of Old-Russian architecture became more prominent than before.[41] Squares with major public buildings grouped around them became common in towns; streets were now generally wide, both to please the eye and facilitate traffic as well as to limit the spread of fire. Catherine's numerous planning regulations also ordained that construction in town centers was to be, again quoting Jones,

Figure 134 Row of model houses built in the center of Tver' shortly after the fire of 1763.

compact, expensive, and as magnificent as possible [figs. 134, 135A–B]. Public buildings, administrative offices, churches, the nobles' meeting hall, and the homes of the officials formed the nucleus of the town, and the remaining plots were to be filled with private residences of comparable size and quality. Known as "dwellings of the first class," houses in the center were to be two stories in height and built of stone or brick. Anyone who agreed to build such a house would have no taxes to pay on it for five years and in some instances could obtain an interest-free loan from the state to defray the costs of construction. . . . If the taker of a lot in the center did not build a stone house within five years, the property was to be reclaimed by the state. The streets adjacent to the center were reserved for "dwellings of the second class," one-story wooden houses built on stone foundations and covered with stucco. . . . Fountains, water pipes, drainage ditches, and canals were regularly provided for in the plans of the later eighteenth century, and the government passed strict laws against unsanitary practices such as dumping garbage and waste in the streets.[42]

Figures 135A–B A, The White House (former governor's palace), Irkutsk, 1800–1804. B, Town Hall, Iaroslavl', 1781–1784, reconstructed 1820s; Pankov, architect.

A

B

In these and other ways, following Petrine initiatives, Catherine II determined the appearance and character of the modern Russian urban environment. Moreover, as the rich quarries of Russian Siberia, Finland, and the Ukraine were increasingly exploited in the eighteenth century, variegated marble, fine-grained granite, glistening labradorites, malachites, and porphyries came to be used with dazzling effect in the construction and interior decoration of cathedrals and palaces, thus setting a standard of material magnificence that also came to typify modern Russian architecture.

Nor was it only a matter of cities and towns, or of architecture at the upper levels of society. More slowly than in the urban centers, to be sure, and by a process that is far more difficult to trace, the Petrine architectural revolution reached into the villages of rural Russia, where a necessarily preliminary process of nucleation appears to have been in progress since well before the eighteenth century. As recently as 1550, it seems, some 90 percent of agricultural settlements were composed of fewer than five households, with about 70 percent of the total containing no more than one or two.[43] But steadily in the later sixteenth and the seventeenth centuries, and on into the eighteenth, these tens of thousands of tiny isolated agricultural settlements were consolidating into larger villages—villages whose layout did not reflect, we can be sure, any fixed or "regular" plan. The mass of new or newly consolidated settlements had no centers, no streets worthy of the name, usually not even a church, and no masonry structures; while the relatively few villages of some administrative and commercial significance, and comprising perhaps 100 to 150 households, were architecturally little better off. We might recall here the clustered heaps of wooden boxes described in Chapter 2.

In August 1722 Peter I decreed that to control the spread of fire and "for the sake of better construction" villages were to be built (or rebuilt, after a fire) in accordance with a prescribed plan (fig. 136). The plan specified that houses and yards were to be standard in size and to maintain a set distance between them, and that the houses themselves were to face forward, in a straight line, flush with a would-be street.[44] *Reguliarnost'* had come to the countryside. Compliance with Peter's decree was not widespread until, once again, the time of Catherine II, whose government converted the largest villages into towns, as mentioned, and vigorously enforced the planning and rebuilding of the rest. By the end of the eighteenth century the linear village plan prevailed throughout Russia, with houses—or cottages—and sheds positioned flush with the street, in straight rows, and with the church and any other public buildings grouped in and around a central square (figs. 137–140). Only in a few villages, situated far from the main roads and regional centers, did the random "circular plan" survive.[45]

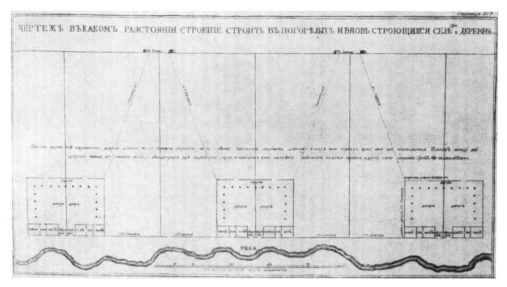

ЧЕРТЕЖЪ ВЪ КАКОМЪ РАЗСТОЯНИИ СТРОЕНІЕ СТРОИТЬ ВЪ ПОГОРѢЛЫХЪ И ВНОВЬ СТРОЮЩИХСЯ СЕЛѢХЪ, ДЕРЕВНѢ.

Figure 136 Fragment of plan accompanying printed decree of August 1722 on the building or rebuilding (after a fire) of villages in Russia.

Figure 137 "A Russian Village," ca. 1790, as drawn and etched by J. A. Atkinson. One of a series of drawings done by Atkinson in Russia in the 1780s and 1790s, this one is captioned by him: "The villages in Russia are generally composed of one street with houses on each side; their length, in consequence of this plan of building, is sometimes very considerable; nor is the uniform shape of their houses less remarkable, all of them having the same roofs and facade."

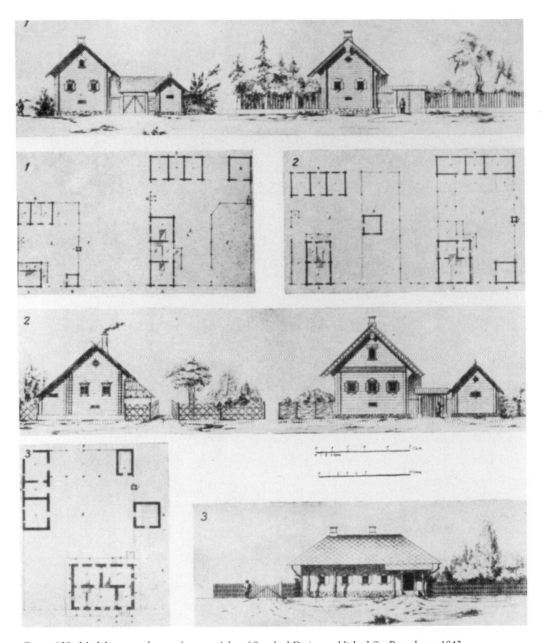

Figure 138 Model peasant houses from an *Atlas of Standard Designs* published St. Petersburg, 1842.

Figure 139 House of a rich peasant, first half of the nineteenth century, now at the open-air Museum of Old-Russian Architecture near Irkutsk.

Figure 140 A Russian village in 1930.

The Petrine revolution in Russian architecture had proved irreversible. From St. Petersburg to the village the "new" style or the "modern" in building (in Russian the word is the same, *novyi*) increasingly held sway. Beginning with the revolutionary transitions of the turn of the eighteenth century, and culminating in Catherine II's grand *pereplanirovka* near its end, the Russian built world had been radically transformed. Moreover, by 1800 or so, if not earlier, Russians possessed individual buildings and ensembles of buildings, parks and gardens, squares and other public spaces, whole townscapes and landscapes that could stand comparison with the best of architecture anywhere in the European world. Indeed, the success of the revolution was such that by 1800 or so Russia had become, at least in architecture, an integral part of that world.

At the most important level of building the Neoclassicism of Catherine II, having succeeded the Baroque of Peter I and his daughter, Empress Elizabeth, was succeeded in turn by the Empire style of Catherine's grandson, Alexander I (reigned 1801–1825), a style that represented yet another enactment of the European Classical heritage (pls. 35, 70–75). Again measures were taken by the central government to impose architectural uniformity throughout the Russian Empire; and the reign of Alexander, especially after the victorious conclusion of the Napoleonic wars, witnessed another great boom in building.[46] Then, following a phase of Romantic or Muscovite revivalist architecture in the middle and later decades of the nineteenth century, and of uncontrolled industrial expansion at its end, both classicism and rigorous town planning made a comeback in the early twentieth—to be given widespread application in the Soviet Union by the Stalin regime after the defeat of the local avant-garde.[47] But the larger historical point to be registered is that at every stage advances in European architecture were more or less immediately reflected in Russia, where fully formed variants of the successive international styles were produced and major technical innovations more or less readily absorbed.

We have traced this momentous development to the reign of Peter I. Yet even then, it deserves stressing, it was perceived by contemporaries as having begun (fig. 141). In the words of Peter's favorite prelate, Feofan Prokopovich, whose eulogy of the first Russian emperor was quoted at the outset of this chapter, thanks to him the defenses of the state had been greatly strengthened, Russians were much better protected than formerly against the elements, and they now had buildings of which they could justly be proud: buildings of a "most commodious convenience, shining forth in beauty and splendor." In this as in other respects, Prokopovich proclaimed to the assembled Russian elite, Russia under "Peter the Great" had been reborn.

Figure 141 Allegory of Peter I endowing a grateful Russia—woman in traditional dress—with "Truth, Religion, and the Arts"; engraving by F. Ottens, 1725. Prominent among Peter's gifts are symbols of his architectural revolution.

Plate 1 Church of the Savior, Andronikov monastery, Moscow, 1420s; east view.

Plate 2 Cathedral of the Dormition, Moscow Kremlin, 1475–1479; Aristotele Fieravanti (Fioravanti), architect; south facade.

Plate 3 Cathedral of the Archangel Michael, Moscow Kremlin, 1505–1509; Aloisio Novi (Alevisio Novy), architect; north and west facades.

Plate 4   Bell tower of Ivan the Great (Ivan Velikii), Moscow Kremlin, 1505–1508; top tier and cupola added in 1600. Structure to the left, dating to the sixteenth century, was converted to a bell tower in the seventeenth century, blown up by Napoleon in 1812, and rebuilt with modifications in 1814–1815.

Plate 5   Church of the Ascension, Kolomenskoe (now in Moscow), 1530–1532; southeast view.

A

B

Plates 6A–B Church of the Intercession on the Moat (also Basil the Blessed), Red Square, Moscow, 1555–1560/1588. A, Southwest view. B, Detail of the exterior decoration, sixteenth and seventeenth centuries.

Plate 7 Church of the Crucifixion, Aleksandrov, 1570s; northeast view.

Plate 8 Church of the Mother of God, Monastery of the Don, Moscow, 1591–1593; apses and other additions, 1677–1678; bell tower, 1679; southeast view.

A

B

Plates 9A–B Church of the Trinity in Nikitniki,
Moscow, 1634–ca.1654. A, West view. B, Detail of
the exterior decoration.

Plate 10 Church of the Nativity of the Mother of God in Putinki, Moscow, 1649–1652; southwest view.

Plate 11 Church of the Trinity, Ostankino (now in Moscow), 1678–1683; Pavel Potekhin, architect; east end.

Plate 12 Church of St. Nicholas in Khamovniki, Moscow, 1679–1682; south view.

Plate 13 Refectory with church of St. Sergius, Trinity–St. Sergius monastery, Zagorsk, 1686–1692.

Plate 14 Church of the Resurrection in Kadashi, Moscow, 1687–1695; south view of the main portion.

Plate 15 Gate church of the Transfiguration, Novodevichii convent, Moscow, 1687–1689; south view.

Plate 16   Bell tower, Novodevichii convent, Moscow, 1690.

Plate 17 Church of the Sign of the Most Holy Mother of God, Dubrovitsy (near Moscow), 1690–1697/1704(?); southwest view.

Plate 18 Church of the Intercession of the Mother of God, Fili (now in Moscow), 1690–1693; south view.

Plate 19 Entrance to the Krutitskii complex (church and residence of the metropolitan [senior bishop] of Krutitskii), Moscow, 1693–1694. Note details of the decoration, with ceramic work by Osip and Ivan Startsev. North view.

Plate 20 Iconostasis of the Great Church, Monastery of the Don, Moscow, 1695–1699; detail. Executed by local artists working under the influence of Belorussian masters and "German" or "Italian" graphic models, as is clear from the work itself and related documentary evidence (see Arenkova and Mekhova, *Donskoi monastyr'*, pp. 26–28).

A

B

Plates 21A–B Cathedral of the Dormition, Riazan',
1690s; Ia. Bukhvostov, architect. A, West facade,
with the five cupolas under restoration (1984). B,
Detail of the exterior decoration.

Plate 22 Church of the Trinity, Troitskoe-Lykovo, 1698–1704; detail of the exterior decoration.

Plate 23 Church of the Archangel Gabriel (Menshikov Tower), Moscow, begun 1701(?), restored 1770s; I. P. Zarudnyi(?) and/or G. M. Fontana(?), architects; west facade.

Plate 24 Church of St. John the Warrior, Moscow, 1709–1714; northwest view of the main tower church and attached refectory.

A

B

Plates 25A–B Church of Sts. Peter and Paul, Peter-Paul fortress, Leningrad, 1712–1732; D. Trezzini, architect. A, Southwest View. The church was restored after a fire in 1756 by B. F. Rastrelli, S. I. Chevakinskii, and G. Trezzini (son of D. Trezzini), architects. B, Detail (top portion) of the iconostasis, 1722–1726; designed by D. Trezzini, executed by I. P. Zarudnyi and others (see also frontispiece).

Plate 26 Church of the Annunciation, Alexander-Nevskii monastery, Leningrad, 1717–1722; D. Trezzini, architect; northwest view. Structure to the right, housing a grand stairway, was added in 1764–1765.

Plate 27 Church of Sts. Simeon and Anna, Leningrad, 1731–1734; M. G. Zemtsov, architect; south facade.

Plate 28 Church of St. Panteleimon, Leningrad, 1735–1739; I. K. Korobov(?), architect; southeast view.

Plate 29   Church of St. Andrew, Kiev, 1747–1767; B. F. Rastrelli, architect; southwest view.

Plate 30 Church of the Resurrection, Smol'nyi convent, Leningrad, 1748–1764; B. F. Rastrelli, architect; west front.

Plate 31 Cathedral of St. Nicholas, Leningrad, 1753–1762; S. I. Chevakinskii, architect; west front.

Plate 32 Iconostasis, church of the Dormition, Goritskii monastery, Pereslavl'-Zalesskii, 1750s.

Plate 33   Church of St. Clement, Moscow, 1762–1770(?); P. A. Trezzini(?), architect.

Plate 34 Church of the Trinity, Alexander-Nevskii monastery, Leningrad, 1776–1790; I. E. Starov, architect.

Plate 35 Cathedral of the Mother of God of Kazan', Leningrad, 1801–1811; A. N. Voronikhin, architect.

Plate 36 Church of the Nativity of the Mother of God, village of Peredki, now at Vitoslavitsy open-air museum near Novgorod. Presumed to have been built before 1539, the church is known to have been rebuilt in 1699, 1886, 1891, 1894, 1897, and ca. 1900; it was moved to its present site and restored in 1967–1971. South view.

Plate 37 Church of the Transfiguration, village of Kozliatevo, 1756, now at the Suzdal'
open-air museum; west view.

Plate 38 Church of the Resurrection, village of Potakino, 1776, now at the Suzdal' open-air museum; south view.

Plate 39 *Domik* of Peter I, Leningrad, 1703. Note the large, mullioned windows and planed log walls with traces of paint applied to resemble brickwork.

Plate 40 House of Ekimovaia (a rich peasant), village of Ryshevo, second half of the nineteenth century, now at the Vitoslavlitsy open-air museum near Novgorod.

Plate 41 Rich peasant's house from the village of Lug, mid-nineteenth century, now at the Suzdal' open-air museum.

Plate 42 Kremlin walls and towers, Moscow, late fifteenth century; turrets and steeply pitched roofs added in the seventeenth century. In the foreground, the Beklemishev Tower, 1487–1488; Marco Ruffo (or Marco "Friazin," i.e., "the Italian"), architect. Further along, the Constantine and Helen Tower and the Spasskaia Tower, 1490–1491; Pietro Antonio Solari, architect. Southeast view.

A

B

Plates 43A–B Spaso-Evfimyi monastery, Suzdal'. A, Walls and towers, later seventeenth/eighteenth centuries; west view. B, Wall tower, 1660–1664; view from within the monastery walls.

Plate 44 Main gates to the royal residence at Kolomenskoe (now in Moscow), 1672–1673; west view.

Plate 45 Siuiumbeki Tower, kremlin of the city of Kazan', late seventeenth century; southeast view.

Plate 46 (*top left*) Trinity–St. Sergius monastery, Zagorsk. Walls and gates to the right date to the sixteenth and seventeenth centuries; bastion with pyramidal roof, center, to 1640. The large pentacupolar Dormition church (1559–1585) is clearly visible center right and, rising behind it, the great bell tower (1741–1770; B. F. Rastrelli and D. V. Ukhtomskii, architects). Visible above the wall to the left, with its single cupola, is the refectory and church of St. Sergius (1686–1692; cf. pl. 13). Southeast view.

Plate 47 (*bottom left*) Peter-Paul fortress, Leningrad, with the church of Sts. Peter and Paul (cf. pl. 25A). Domed structure to the right is the former burial vault of the grand dukes, built in 1908 and now, like the rest of the fortress complex, a museum. Construction of the masonry fortress, to replace the original earth and timber fortifications, began in 1706 and continued with interruptions until 1740; D. Trezzini, architect. Visible here, center lower left, is the arrowhead bastion of Peter I (formerly, Sovereign's bastion), begun in 1717, with its two oreillons; also, lower right, across a moat (filled in, nineteenth century), part of a contemporary ravelin, the two structures connected by a masonry bridge with sentry post. Walls, bastions, and outworks faced with granite in 1779–1787. Southeast view.

Plate 48 (*below*) Petrovskie gates, Peter-Paul fortress, Leningrad, 1717–1718; D. Trezzini, architect. The central panels, depicting the overthrow of Simon Magus by St. Peter (allegory of the defeat of Charles XII of Sweden by Peter I), were sculpted by H. C. Ossner, ca. 1720; the carved two-headed eagle of Peter I, with scepter and orb, over the arch, is by F. P. Wassoult, 1722; the statues in niches to the left (Minerva, goddess of handicrafts) and right (Bellona, goddess of war) are after designs by C. B. Rastrelli and/or N. Pineau.

IV

Plate 49 *(top left) Granovitaia palata* (Faceted Chamber), Moscow Kremlin, 1487–1491; Marco Ruffo "Friazin" and Pietro Antonio Solario, architects. "Faceted" refers to the rusticated stone of the eastern facade, as seen here, which inspired numerous imitations in painted *trompe-l'oeil* (e.g., pl. 13). Original small windows with late-Gothic decoration were replaced by larger windows with typically "Moscow Baroque" decoration in 1685, when the corner columns with their spiral motive were also added.

Plate 50 *(bottom left)* English Residence *(Angliiskoe podvor'e)*, Moscow (near Red Square), sixteenth/seventeenth centuries. The building was originally a hostel for English merchants and was only recently rediscovered and restored.

Plate 51 *(below) Mariinskie palaty* (Chambers of Tsarevna Maria Alekseevna, sister of Peter I), Novodevichii convent, Moscow, 1683–1688.

Plate 52 Sukharev Tower, Moscow, 1692–1701; fragment of the decorative program as preserved at the Museum of Russian Architecture, Monastery of the Don, Moscow.

Plates 53A–B *Palaty* of Averkii Kirillov, Moscow.
A, Part of the original building, second half of the
seventeenth century. B, Remodeled central portion,
with new facade, 1705–1709. Kirillov (died 1682)
was a *dumnyi d'iak,* one of the four highest ranks of
the Muscovite nobility.

A
B

319

A

B

Plates 54A–B Summer Palace, Leningrad, 1710–1712; D. Trezzini, architect. A, North facade. B, Detail of the exterior decoration, by A. Schlüter, 1713–1714.

Plate 55 Menshikov Palace, Leningrad, 1711–1716; G. M. Fontana and G. Schädel, architects.

Plate 56 *Palaty* of A. V. Kikin, Leningrad, 1714–1720; architect unknown. After Kikin, a senior naval officer and close associate of Peter I, was cashiered in 1718, the mansion housed Peter's collection of "curiosities" and library until 1727, when they were moved to the *Kunstkamera* (pl. 57). Considerably altered later in the eighteenth century, the mansion was badly damaged in 1941–1944 but restored to its original appearance in 1952–1953.

Plate 57 *Kunstkamera*, Leningrad, 1718–1734; G. J. Mattarnowy, architect.

A   B

Plates 58A–B Building of the Twelve Colleges,
Leningrad, 1724–1732; D. Trezzini, architect. A,
East facade. B, Detail of the east facade.

A

B

324

C

D

Plates 59A–D Peterhof (*Petrodvorets*), near Leningrad. A, Main palace, 1714–1755; J. B. A. Le Blond, N. Michetti, and B. F. Rastrelli, architects. Grotto and cascade, 1715–1722; Le Blond and J. F. Braunstein, architects. Sculptures and bas-reliefs, 1721–1723, by C. B. Rastrelli, F. P. Wassoult, H. C. Ossner, and others. B, Palace of Monplaisir, 1714–1723; J. F. Braunstein, J. B. A. Le Blond, and N. Michetti, architects. The view is of the southern or garden facade, with the Psyche Cloche fountain (after Michetti's design, 1721–1723) in the foreground. The central building, behind the statue-fountain, built low in the Dutch style with a high mansard roof, houses the Great Hall, kitchen, pantry, study and bedroom of Peter I, etc.; it is flanked by glazed arcades with balustraded roofs terminating in miniature pavilions. Inside, the arcades serve as picture galleries (here, the Western Gallery); note their mullioned windows, rusticated pilasters, and other typically Dutch features. C, Palace of Marly, 1720–1723; J. F. Braunstein, architect. D, Hermitage pavilion, 1721–1725; J. F. Braunstein, architect.

Plate 60 Catherine Palace, Pushkino, near Leningrad, 1742–1756; B. F. Rastrelli, architect; park facade.

Plate 61 Stroganov palace, Leningrad, 1752–1754; B. F. Rastrelli, architect; Moika (canal) facade.

A

B

C

Plates 62A–C Winter Palace, Leningrad, 1754–1762; B. F. Rastrelli, architect. A, Portion of the south facade. B, Jordan Staircase, 1757–1761; B. F. Rastrelli, architect (destroyed by fire in 1837, restored in 1838 by V. P. Stasov, architect). C, Rastrelli Gallery, 1757–1761; B. F. Rastrelli, architect.

Plate 63 Academy of Fine Arts, Leningrad, 1764–1788; J. B. M. Vallin de la Mothe and Alexander Kokorinov, architects; Neva facade.

A

B

Plates 64A–B The Small Hermitage, flanking the Winter Palace, Leningrad. A, Neva facade, 1764–1775; J. B. M. Vallin de la Mothe, architect.

B, South Pavilion, 1771–1787; G. F. Veldten, architect.

328

Plate 65 The Court (or Hermitage) Theater, Leningrad, 1783–1787; G. Quarenghi, architect.

Plate 66   Academy of Sciences, Leningrad, 1783–1789; G. Quarenghi, architect; Neva facade.

Plate 67   Taurida Palace, Leningrad, 1783–1789; I. E. Starov, architect; main entrance.

Plate 68 Pashkov mansion (now part of the Lenin Library), Moscow, 1784–1786; V. I. Bazhenov, architect; street facade.

Plate 69 Sheremetev palace, Ostankino (now in Moscow), 1792–1798; F. Camporesi, G. Quarenghi, and P. Argunov, architects; street facade.

Plate 70 The former Bourse (now Naval Museum), Leningrad, 1805–1810; T. de Thomon, architect; southeast view.

Plate 71 The Admiralty, Leningrad, 1806–1823; A. Zakharov, architect. Main (park) facade, with Zakharov's recreation of the "needle" spire of Peter I's original Admiralty.

Plate 72 Krushchev mansion, Moscow, 1814; A. Grigorev, architect; side facade. The building is constructed of stuccoed wood on stone foundations.

Plate 73 Lopukhin mansion, Moscow, 1817–1822; A. Grigorev, architect; street facade. The building is constructed of stuccoed wood on stone foundations.

Plate 74 Moscow University, 1782–1793; M. Kazakov, architect. Rebuilt 1817–1819; D. Gilardi, architect. Street facade.

Plate 75 General Staff Building, Palace Square, Leningrad, 1819–1829; C. Rossi , architect. Alexander Column, by A. R. Montferrand, 1830–1834.

Notes

Chapter 1

1. B. LeBouvier de Fontenelle, *Éloge du Czar Pierre Ier . . . Prononcé à l'Assemblée Publique de l'Académie des Sciences, le 14 Novemb. 1725* (Paris, 1727), p. 5. See also A. Galitzin, "Pierre Ier, membre de l'Académie des Sciences," *Bulletin du Bibliophile,* ser. 14 (September 1859), pp. 611–17.

2. G. Livet and R. Mousnier, *Histoire générale de l'Europe,* vol. 2 (Paris, 1980), pp. 404–5. Cf. M.-A Chabin, "La curiosité des savants français pour la Russie dans la première moitié du XVIIIe siècle," *Revue des études slaves* 67, no. 4 (1985), pp. 565–76; and G. Stökl, "Russland und Europa vor Peter dem Grossen," in Stökl, *Der Russische Staatim im Mittelalter und Früher Neuzeit* (Wiesbaden, 1981), pp. 294–317.

3. *Encyclopaedia Britannica; or a Dictionary of Arts, Sciences, and Miscellaneous Literature . . . ,* vol. 2 (Dublin, 1791), pp. 217–56, with twenty full-page plates; *A New and Complete Dictionary of Arts and Sciences, Comprehending all the Branches of Useful Knowledge,* 2d ed., vol. 1 (London, 1763), pp. 183–84; and the *Encyclopédie, ou Dictionnaire raisonné des sciences, des arts et des métiers,* vol. 3 (Lausanne and Berne, 1778), pp. 252–59.

4. Cf. J. Rykwert, *The First Moderns: The Architects of the Eighteenth Century* (Cambridge, Mass., 1980), pp. 5–6; or, making the same general point, the standard H. A. Miller and A. Frazer, *Key Monuments of the History of Architecture* (New York [1965]), p. lxvii. The view extends beyond scholarship; in the words of an architectural journalist, "The history of European architecture can be generalized as a series of 'returns' to its Classical beginnings. Alternately, it is viewable as a Classical continuum with ups and downs but only one major interruption—Gothic. And while Gothic, which got its name from its Renaissance critics, lasted four centuries, it was largely confined to Northern Europe. After two millennia, Classicism remains a force to be reckoned with" (V. Raynor, "Paestum Views Classicism of the 1700's," *New York Times,* March 1, 1986, p. 14).

5. See I. M. Shanskii, *Etimologicheskii slovar' rus-* *skogo iazyka,* vol. 1, pt. 1 (M., 1963), pp. 155–56; R. I. Afanesov et al., eds., *Slovar' russkogo iazyka XI–XVII vv.,* vol. 1 (M., 1975), p. 53; G. Huttl-Worth, *Foreign Words in Russian: A Historical Sketch, 1550–1800* (Berkeley and Los Angeles, 1963); and numerous examples cited below, particularly in Chapters 5, 6, and 8.

6. M. S. Briggs, "Building Construction," in C. Singer et al., eds., *A History of Technology,* vol. 3 (Oxford, 1957), p. 250; and, more generally, "Vitruvius," *Encyclopedia of World Art,* vol. 14 (New York, 1967), cols. 805–11.

7. T. K. Derry and T. I. Williams, *A Short History of Technology* (Oxford, 1960), pp. 180–81; Briggs, "Building Construction" and "Town-Planning from the Ancient World to the Renaissance," in Singer et al., pp. 247–52, 285 ff.; and J. S. Ackerman, "The Planning of Renaissance Rome, 1450–1580," in P. A. Ramsey, ed., *Rome in the Renaissance: The City and the Myth* (Binghamton, N.Y., 1982), pp. 3–17 and figs. 1–11. See also R. Krautheimer, *The Rome of Alexander VII, 1655–1667* (Princeton, 1985); and, for the rise of the new architect, L. D. Ettlinger, "The Emergence of the Italian Architect during the Fifteenth Century," and C. Wilkinson, "The New Professionalism in the Renaissance," both in S. Kostof, ed., *The Architect: Chapters in the History of the Profession* (Oxford, 1977), pp. 96–123, 124–60.

8. D. Knoop and G. P. Jones, *The Medieval Mason: An Economic History of English Stone Building in the Later Middle Ages and Early Modern Times,* 3d ed. (Manchester and New York, 1967), p. 175.

9. On Wren, see K. Downes, *Sir Christopher Wren* (London, 1982), and Downes, *The Architecture of Wren* (London, 1983); also, for "our English Vitruvius," see G. Beard, *The World of Christopher Wren* (Edinburgh, 1982), pp. 16 ff.

10. H. Bagger, *Ruslands alliance-politik efter freden i Nystad (1721–1732)* (Copenhagen, 1974), with English summary; and review of same by R. M. Hatton, *English Historical Review* 92, no. 362 (1977), pp. 150–51. See also D. McKay and H. M. Scott, *The Rise of the Great Powers, 1648–1815* (London and

New York, 1983), especially pp. 80–93, 124–34, and, for a useful chapter on "Diplomacy and the European States [sic] System," pp. 201–14.

11. C. Peterson, *Peter the Great's Administrative and Judicial Reforms: Swedish Antecedents and the Process of Reception*, trans. M. Metcalf (Stockholm, 1979); E. V. Anisimov, *Podatnaia reforma Petra I. Vvedenie podushnoi podati v Rossii 1719–1728 gg.* (L., 1982). On the development of the Russian navy in the eighteenth century—a task begun by Peter I, continued under Catherine II, and crucial to the goals of linking Muscovy with Europe and of making Russia a great power—see Andreas Bode, *Die Flottenpolitik Katharinas II und die Konflikte mit Schweden und der Türkei (1768–1792)* (Wiesbaden, 1979); and on economic developments, A. Kahan, *The Plow, the Hammer, and the Knout: An Economic History of Eighteenth-Century Russia*, ed. R. Hellie (Chicago, 1985).

12. Quoted in G. von Rauch, "Political Preconditions for East-West Cultural Relations in the Eighteenth Century," *Canadian-American Slavic Studies* 13, no. 4 (1979), p. 394 (trans. K. and D. Griffiths).

13. M. Raeff, "The Well-Ordered Police State and the Development of Modernity in Seventeenth and Eighteenth-Century Europe: An Attempt at a Comparative Approach," *American Historical Review* 80, no. 5 (1975), pp. 1221–43.

14. The historical literature devoted to the life and times of Peter I is vast. Apart from works already cited, see the survey with bibliography by J. Cracraft in *The Modern Encyclopedia of Russian and Soviet History*, ed. J. L. Wieczynski, vol. 27 (Gulf Breeze, Fla., 1982), pp. 224–35. See further R. Wittram, *Peter I. Czar und Kaiser. Zur Geschichte Peters des Grossen in seiner Zeit*, 2 vols. (Göttingen, 1964); N. V. Riasanovsky, *The Image of Peter the Great in Russian History and Thought* (Oxford, 1985); and, on Europe at this time, *The New Cambridge History*, vol. 6: *The Rise of Great Britain and Russia, 1688–1715/1725*, ed. J. S. Bromley (Cambridge, 1970), or, more broadly, W. H. McNeill, *The Rise of the West: A History of the Human Community* (Chicago, 1963). A still more ambitious analysis of the emergence by the end of the eighteenth century of "a competitive, diplomatically regulated, European multistate civilization" (or system of "permanent war states") is Michael Mann, *The Sources of Social Power*, vol. 1: *A History of Power from the Beginning to A.D. 1760* (Cambridge and New York, 1986), pp. 373–517.

15. V. I. Baldin, "Role and Functions of Museums of Architecture" (paper prepared for the First International Conference of Architectural Museums, August 20–25, 1979, Helsinki); G. M. Martynov and K. F. Kniazev, *Planirovka i blagoustroistvo kolkhoznogo sela* (M., 1963); A. G. Khalturin, introduc-

tion to A. Il'f and N. Nedbaeva, eds., *Okhrana pamiatnikov istorii i kul'tury v SSSR* (M., 1978).

16. Cf. R. Daniloff, "Restoring a Russian Heritage," *Smithsonian* 13, no. 12 (1983), pp. 64–73, and W. C. Brumfield, "Saint Basil's and Other Curiosities," *Harvard Magazine* (July–August 1982), pp. 42–48; also Brumfield, "Russia's Glorious Churches," *Historic Preservation* (February 1985), pp. 42–46. See further P. M. White's comprehensive *Soviet Regional and Urban Planning: A Bibliography with Abstracts* (New York, 1980), with scarcely a reference to historic preservation; A. I. Tselikov, *Okhrana, restavratsiia i konservatsiia pamiatnikov russkoi arkhitektury (1917–1968); bibliograficheskii ukazatel' literatury* (M., 1970), and A. V. Ikonnikov et al., *Pamiatniki arkhitektury v strukture gorodov SSSR* (M., 1978) for evidence of serious Soviet interest in the problem; and Il'f and Nedbaeva, which prints the text of a comprehensive law protecting architectural monuments enacted by the Supreme Soviet in October 1976, the first such legislation in Soviet history. A rare glimpse of high-level official concern is found in the remarks of the head of the Moscow City Communist Party Committee to a meeting of party workers in April 1986. Complaining that under his predecessors "the historical face of Moscow has been disfigured," Boris Yeltsin, at the time also a Candidate member of the national party Politburo, admitted that "since 1935, 2,200 important architectural monuments have been obliterated. Many others are in a pitiful condition and are being used for purposes other than those for which they were designed. The church in which Pushkin was married has been turned into offices used by the Ministry of Energy." Remedial action was promised as well as a new effort to preserve Moscow's "unique architectural character" (Yeltsin's speech, leaked to a Western correspondent, is printed in English translation in *Detente*, no. 7 [Autumn 1986], pp. 2–5).

17. See Daniloff, p. 66; Berton, *Moscow*, pp. 198 ff.; Anon., *Razrushennye khramy*; or Anon., *Moskva zlatoglavaia*. The extensive destruction of architectural monuments particularly of the seventeenth and eighteenth centuries in Belorussia and the Ukraine is touched on in Čarniauskja, *Arkhitektura Mahilova*, passim, and in Tsapenko, *Arkhitektura Ukrainy*, p. 6; see also Hewryk, *Lost Architecture*, with details of numerous architectural landmarks—including thirty-two churches and bell towers—demolished in Kiev alone in the 1930s.

18. See observations by Chiniakov, "O nekotorykh osobennostiakh," pp. 3–22; and below, Chapter 8.

19. See A. A. Sidorov, "Arkhitektura," in B. P. Vipper and T. V. Livanova, eds., *Istoriia evropeiskogo iskusstvoznaniia vtoroi poloviny XIX veka—nachalo XX veka (1871–1917)*, vol. 2 (M., 1969), pp. 48–75, for

the beginnings of Russian architectural historiography. Cf. brief comments on "the discovery of Old Russian art" in R. Milner-Gulland, "Art and Architecture of Old Russia," in Auty and Obolensky, *Art and Architecture*, pp. 5–6, 18; Milner-Gulland notes (p. 6) that the original ground plan of so major a medieval monument as the St. Sophia cathedral in Novgorod was only established in the 1960s, in connection with the installation of central heating.

20. P. Anker, *The Art of Scandinavia*, vol. 1 (New York, 1970), pp. 201–447, with numerous photographs.

21. H. M. Taylor, *Anglo-Saxon Architecture*, vol. 3 (Cambridge, 1978); A. Clifton-Taylor, *English Parish Churches as Works of Art* (London, 1974).

22. Cf. Il'in, "O professional'nykh navykakh," pp. 129–32.

23. See M. W. Thompson, *Novgorod the Great: Excavations at the Medieval City Directed by A. V. Artsikhovsky and B. A. Kolchin* (London, 1967), for an introduction to the subject.

24. Compare the wealth of primary material in R. A. Goldthwaite, *The Building of Renaissance Florence: An Economic and Social History* (Baltimore, 1980), or in the relevant volumes (3 and 4) of H. M. Colvin et al., *The History of the King's Works*, 6 vols. (London 1963–76). In both cases, of course, in fifteenth-century Florence or in sixteenth- and seventeenth-century England, the extent of durable masonry construction was no doubt far greater than in contemporary Moscow or Russia—not to mention comparative levels of literacy, learning, record keeping, etc.

25. Grabar' et al., *Istoriia* [1909], 2:269–70, 274.

26. See I. Bondarenko, "Zdanie Posol'skogo Prikaza," in D. N. Anuchin et al., *Sbornik statei v chest' P. S. Uvarovoi* (M., 1916), pp. 98–101.

27. N. A. Baklanovoi, "Obstanovka moskovskikh prikazov v XVII veke," *Trudy gos. Istoricheskogo muzeia*, vol. 3 (1926), pp. 54–57.

28. Bondarenko, pp. 102, 104; Baklanovoi.

29. E.g., Evsina, *Arkhitekturnaia teoriia* (1975), who again prints (p. 165) the Palmquist drawing (fig. 2 here), captions it "the Posol'skii Prikaz in the Kremlin in the second half of the seventeenth century," and elsewhere (p. 17) remarks: "Erich Palmquist in his drawings obviously transformed Muscovite architecture in the spirit of European buildings; the Posol'skii Prikaz, for example, reminded him of an Italian palazzo." The works of Bondarenko and Baklanovoi, cited above, appear not to have been known to Evsina.

30. Cf. Grabar' et al., *Istoriia* [1909], 4:43, and photographs on pp. 45, 47, 49, 51, with Grabar' et al., *Russkaia arkhitektura* (1954), pp. 40 ff., with fourteen illustrations.

31. G. I. Vzdornov, "Zametki o pamiatnikakh russkoi arkhitektury kontsa XVII–nachala XVIII v.," in Alekseeva, *Russkoe iskusstvo* (1973), pp. 25–30.

32. Cf. Grabar' et al., *Russkaia arkhitektura*, pp. 49, 61, 88, and photographs on pp. 51–55, with T. A. Gatova, "Iz istorii dekorativnoi skul'ptury Moskvy nachala XVIII v.," in Alekseeva, *Russkoe iskusstvo* (1973), pp. 31–44.

33. Tel'tevskii, *Bukhvostov*, pp. 77–82.

34. S. V. Bezsonov, *Krepostnye arkhitektory* (M., 1938), is an obvious instance of the scholarship under criticism; but Tel'tevskii's own work, just cited, offers another, if less egregious, example.

35. A Mikhailov, "O nekotorykh zadachakh izucheniia russkogo arkhitekturnogo nasledstva," *AN*, no. 1 (1953), pp. 3–8.

36. N. N. Kovalenskaia, in Grabar' et al., *Russkaia arkhitektura*, pp. 5–14.

37. Cf. Grabar' et al., *Istoriia* [1909], vol. 3, chap. 2, or Grabar', "Arkhitektory-inostrantsy" (1911), pp. 132–50, with Grabar' et al., *Russkaia arkhitektura* (1954), p. 116.

38. Sidorov complains of an "absence of clarity on questions of periodization" in pre-Revolutionary Russian architectural scholarship which "led to an illogical mixing of the typological distribution of material with the territorial, stylistic, and chronological principles of grouping same" (Sidorov, p. 68). In fact, the lack of a clear and consistent, generally accepted scheme of periodization is equally characteristic of Soviet work in this field, work which is further confused by the injection of Marxist, Leninist, and/or Stalinist categories.

Chapter 2

1. See n. 15 below, this chapter.

2. A Mayerberg, *Iter in Moschoviam Augustini Liberi Baronis de Mayerberg . . . ad Tzarem et Magnum Ducem Alexium Mihalowicz* (n.p., n.d. [Vienna? Frankfurt? 1680?]): I quote from the French edition of same, *Voyage de Moscovie . . .* (Leiden, 1688), pp. 221–22.

3. A. Olearius (Oelschlager), *Travels in Seventeenth-Century Russia*, trans. and ed. S. H. Baron (Stanford, 1967), p. 113. Baron's edition is based on the Schleswig 1656 edition, revised by the author, and now available in facsimile: Olearius, *Vermehrte Newe Beschreibung der Muscowitischen und Persischen Reyse*, ed. D. Lohmeier (Tübingen, 1971).

4. S. Collins, *The Present State of Russia: In a Letter to a Friend at London* (London, 1671), p. 61.

5. J. Struys, *Voyages en Moscovie, en Tartarie, en Perse, aux Indes*, 2 vols. (Lyons, 1684), 1:339.

6. P. Avril, *Voyage en divers états d'Europe et d'Asie* (Paris, 1692), p. 158.

7. Struys, p. 347.

8. J. Reutenfels, *De rebus Moschoviticus ad . . . Cosmum Tertium* (Padua, 1680), trans. and ed. A.

Stankevich, *Skazaniia svet. Gertsogu toskanskomu Kozme tretemu O Moskvii* (M., 1905), p. 92.

9. G. David, *Status Modernus Magnae Russiae seu Moscoviae (1690)*, ed. A. V. Florovskij (The Hague, 1965), p. 87.

10. F. de la Neuville, *Rélation curieuse et nouvelle de Moscovie* (The Hague, 1699), pp. 185, 202, 178.

11. J. G. Korb, *Diary of an Austrian Secretary of Legation at the Court of Czar Peter the Great*, 2 vols., ed. and trans. from the original Latin by the Count MacDonnell (London, 1863; facsimile reprint, London, 1968), 2:168.

12. Collins, p. 64; Struys, pp. 347–48; Reutenfels, pp. 92–93; David, pp. 77, 88–89. Neuville also observed that Moscow's churches were "very dark" (p. 202).

13. Quotations from Olearius, pp. 112–17.

14. From the anonymous journal printed in John Harris, *Navigantium atque Itinerantium Bibliotheca; or, A Compleat Collection of Voyages and Travels*, 2 vols. (London, 1705), 2:23.

15. G. A. Schleussing (or Schleussinger), "Die gantze Beschreibung Russlants . . .": manuscript in the library of the Czechoslovak Academy of Sciences, Prague; I quote from the Russian translation by L. P. Lapteva, "Rasskaz ocheviditsa o zhizni Moskvy kontsa XVII veka," *Voprosy istorii*, 1970, no. 1, pp. 103–26.

16. *A Relation of Three Embassies from his Sacred Majestie Charles II to the Great Duke [Tsar] of Muscovie . . . Performed by the Earl of Carlisle in the Years 1663 to 1664: Written by an Attendant [Guy Miege] on the Embassies* (London, 1669), pp. 112, 95.

17. *Passages from the Diary of General Patrick Gordon of Auchleuchries, 1635–1699*, ed. J. Robertson (Aberdeen, 1859), pp. 43–44.

18. Struys, pp. 307–8, 312, 318, 319, 326.

19. Olearius, p. 89; F. C. Weber, *The Present State of Russia*, 2 vols. (London, 1722–23), 1:117.

20. Olearius, pp. 43, 110–11.

21. "Zapiski Airmanna o Pribaltike i Moskovii 1666–1670 gg.," ed. and trans. N. R. Levenson, *Istoricheskie zapiski*, vol. 17 (1945; reprinted 1968), p. 284. For the original German text, see "Hans Moritz Ayrmanns Reisen durch Livland und Russland in den Jahren 1666–1670," in *Acta et Commentationes Universitatis Tartuensis (Dorpatensis)* (B Humaniora) 40, no. 5 (1937), pp. 16–61; and editor's introduction (K. Schreinert), pp. 1–16.

22. Reutenfels, p. 194.

23. Miege, pp. 33–34, 135–36, 88–89.

24. [Balthasar Coyet,] *Posol'stvo Kunraada fan-Klenka k tsariam Alekseiu Mikhailovichu i Fedoru Alekseevichu*, ed. and trans. anon. (SPb., 1900), pp. 323, 330, 350, 357. This excellent edition includes the original Dutch text of Coyet's account of the embassy of Koenraad van Klenk as published at Amsterdam in 1677.

25. C. de Bruyn, *Travels into Muscovy, Persia, and Part of the East Indies . . .*, 2 vols. (London, 1737; 1st ed., Amsterdam, 1711, in Dutch), 1:15.

26. Coyet, pp. 372, 393, 472, 474, 476, 519, 523–25.

27. Poul Heins to the king, Moscow, July 23, 1697: Rigsarkivet (Copenhagen), TKUA, Special Del, Rusland A III, 42; Neuville, p. 4.

28. Bruyn, 1:58. Also Collins, p. 65; Struys, pp. 343–51; David, p. 88; Neuville, pp. 175, 179–80, 178.

29. Coyet, pp. 315, 516, 464–65, 524; David, pp. 89–90; Gordon, p. 49 and passim; Neuville, p. 187.

30. Bruyn, pp. 58, 77, 86–88; Avril, p. 97.

31. Weber, pp. 124–26.

32. Korb, 1:102, 121, 123, 125, 150, etc.; 2:167, etc.

33. BL Additional MSS. 31, 128, ff. 108–9.

34. Struys, p. 345; Bruyn, 1:41; Olearius, pp. 11, 116; Neuville, p. 189; Weber, 1:126.

35. J. Perry, *The State of Russia under the Present Czar* (London, 1716; facsimile reprint, London, 1967), pp. 14, 22–24, 263–67.

Chapter 3

1. N. Brunov, *Geschichte der Altrussischen Baukunst* (= vol. 1 of Alpatov and Brunov, *Geschichte der Altrussischen Kunst*), pp. 197 ff.

2. Suslov, *Ocherki*, p. 19.

3. Cf. Grabar' et al., *Istoriia* [1909], 1:341–92; Loukomski, *L'Architecture religieuse russe*, p. 57; Zabello, *Russkoe dereviannoe zodchestvo*, especially pp. 8–9; M. A. Il'in et al., "Shatrovoe zodchestvo XVI veka," in Grabar' et al., *Istoriia* (1955), 3:409 ff.; Rappoport, *Drevnerusskaia arkhitektura*, pp. 90–91; or Faensen and Ivanov, *Early Russian Architecture*, pp. 39–47. The last work is a generally informative discussion that nevertheless offers such utterly unprovable statments—indicative of our problem here—as these: "The ancestral cell from which all wooden architecture in Eastern Europe is descended is the north Russian log-built peasant house" (p. 39); "The pyramidal structure of the first Cathedral of St. Sophia in Novgorod, built of oak in 989 with thirteen domes, was already a model for the stone cathedral of the same name in Kiev. . . . The Byzantine type of the domed cruciform church was transformed from the very start by the innate Russian preference for tall, many-domed, pyramidal massing, by the accumulated experience of centuries of timber construction" (pp. 40, 45). Such non-Russian students as have written on the subject tend to follow, uncritically, the nationalist view, e.g., Berton, *Moscow*, p.

66, which refers to "an indigenous development of purely Russian origin, the *shatrovy* or pyramid-shaped towers, built of stone in the sixteenth and seventeenth centuries but known from time immemorial in Russian wooden architecture."

4. Chap. 14, "Wooden Church Architecture," in Hamilton, *Architecture of Russia*, illustrates what perambulations a reluctant acceptance of this fact can lead to. See also the hypothetical discussion of "Wooden Architecture Up to the Sixteenth Century" and its supposed influence on Muscovite architecture of the seventeenth, in Buxton, *Russian Medieval Architecture*, pp. 33–39, 45–46. Buxton has more recently modified his views in line with the direction taken here. See his handsome *Wooden Churches*, pp. 1–16, and particularly his remarks on the problem of dating (pp. 34, 44, 48, 55) and on the "artificiality" of the open-air museum (p. 43). For some critical Soviet discussion of the problem, see Vilkov, *Istoriko-arkhitekturnyi muzei* and review of same, by Iu. V. Kurskov, in *Istoriia SSSR*, 1982, no. 4, pp. 176–78; and the vigorous critique of the restoration, under way for the last thirty years, of the famous wooden church of the Transfiguration of the Savior on the island of Kizhi, by G. Sorokin, "Groza nad Kizhami," *Literaturnaia gazeta*, 1986, no. 15, p. 12.

5. For relevant examples of Romanesque architecture, see Z. Swiechowski, *Budownictvo Romańskie w Polsce* (Warsaw, 1963) and, more generally, K. J. Conant, *Carolingian and Romanesque Architecture 800–1200* (2d ed., New York, 1978); and for the medieval Scandinavian or "stave" churches, P. Anker, *The Art of Scandinavia*, vol. 1 (New York, 1970), pp. 201–447. On Romanesque and Gothic influence in early Muscovite church architecture, see summary remarks by M. A. Il'in in his *Moskva* (1973), pp. 13–14; here (if not elsewhere) Il'in also decisively rejects the notion of important wooden architectural influence on the development of high Muscovite architecture (pp. 42–45). On German Gothic influence, via Novgorod, in north Russian timber architecture, see Buxton (citing the little known work of the Finnish scholar Lars Pettersson), *Wooden Churches*, pp. 81–82, 84.

6. Cf. Voronin, *Ocherki*, pp. 98 ff.

7. M. A. Il'in, "Dereviannoe zodchestvo pervoi poloviny XVIII veka," in Grabar' et al., *Istoriia* (1960), 5:276–78 and, for the Kizhi/Vytegorsk churches, p. 272.

8. Nekrasov, *Ocherki*, pp. 338–40, 379. See also Buxton, *Wooden Churches*, pp. 42, 84–86, for three major adaptations in eighteenth-century timber construction of previous developments in masonry church architecture.

9. Cf., arguing similarly, Nekrasov, *Ocherki*, pp.

309–10; I. E. Grabar', in Grabar' et al., *Russkaia arkhitektura*, p. 39; P. N. Maksimov, "Dereviannaia arkhitektura XVII veka," in Grabar' et al., *Istoriia* (1959), 4:91–120; Voronin, *Zodchestvo*, 2:170–71; Iu. P. Spegal'skii, "K voprosu o vzaimovliianii dereviannogo i kamennogo zodchestva v drevnei Rusi," *AN*, no. 19 (1972), pp. 66–75; Buxton, *Wooden Churches*, p. 86; and Faensen and Ivanov, *Early Russian Architecture*, pp. 45, 47.

10. Cf. Zabello, *Russkoe dereviannoe zodchestvo*, pp. 8, 21, 41, 49–52, with numerous illustrations; Makovetskii, *Pamiatniki narodnogo zodchestva*, with 161 photographs and drawings; Fiodorov, *Architecture of the Russian North*, especially plates 102–212; Opolovnikov, *Russkii sever*, also with numerous photographs; and, on building techniques, Faensen and Ivanov, *Early Russian Architecture*, pp. 40, 46, 505–6, and Buxton, *Wooden Churches*, pp. 19–32 (well illustrated).

11. A. A. Tits, "Russkoe zhiloe zodchestvo XVIv.," pp. 32–87, is a pioneering work based on both documentary evidence and onsite inspection of some 100 masonry domestic buildings of the period; it was more recently published in book form (Tits, *Russkoe kamennoe zodchestvo*). On this subject see also articles by Tits and P. A. Tel'tevskii in *Pamiatniki kul'tury: issledovaniia i restavratsiia*, no. 3 (1961), pp. 142–48, and no. 4 (1963), pp. 44–55; Spegal'skii, *Pskov*, especially pp. 157 ff.; and Gol'denberg, *Planirovka zhilogo kvartala Moskvy*, pp. 19–62.

12. Cf. A. N. Petrov, "Palaty v Moskve," pp. 138 ff.

13. Tits, "Russkoe zhiloe zodchestvo XVIIv.," p. 74.

14. Rappoport, *Drevnerusskaia arkhitektura*, pp. 86–87. Other estimates cited here are based on figures in I. Smolitsch, *Geschichte der Russischen Kirche 1700–1917* (Leiden, 1964), p. 709, and V. I. Pluzhnikov, "Sootnoshenie ob"emnykh form v russkom kul'tovom zodchestve nachala XVII veka," in Alekseeva, *Russkoe iskusstvo* (1974), pp. 81–108.

15. Information gathered by the author in Moscow in 1979. For Bruyn's figure, see his *Travels into Muscovy* (London, 1737), 1:41.

16. For Muscovite ecclesiastical architecture, see F. Gornostaev, "Kamennoe zodchestvo epokhi rastsveta Moskvy," in Grabar' et al., *Istoriia* (1909), 2:5–224; Krasovskii, *Ocherk istorii tserkovnago zodchestva*; Il'in et al., "Kamennoe zodchestvo epokhi rastsveta Moskvy," in Grabar' et al., *Istoriia* (1955), 3:282–371, 409–81; Brunov, *Istoriia arkhitektury*, pp. 78–110, 135–59; B. A. Ognev, "Nekotorye problemy rannemoskovskogo zodchestva," *AN*, no. 12 (1960), pp. 45–62; Rappoport, *Drevnerusskaia arkhitektura*, pp. 72–97; Il'in, *Moskva* (1973), pp. 2–58; and the more specialized works cited below.

17. *Polnoe sobranie russkikh letopisei*, vol. 6 (SPb., 1904), p. 199.

18. See especially Snegirev, *Fioravanti*; also Lo-Gatto, *Gli artisti*, 1:44–45, 191. Faensen and Ivanov, *Early Russian Architecture*, pp. 399–402, is a useful summary in English.

19. Voronin, *Ocherki*, pp. 91, 97.

20. Logatto, *Gli artisti*, 1:55–73, 189; also Pod"iapol'skii, "Venetsianskie istoki Arkhangel'skogo sobora," pp. 252–79.

21. See Krasovskii, *Ocherk istorii tserkovnago zodchestva*, pp. 191–428; Nekrasov, *Ocherki*, pp. 297–350; Brunov, *Istoriia arkhitektury*, pp. 173–80, 197–213; Il'in et al., "Kamennoe zodchestvo . . . XVII veka," in Grabar' et al., *Istoriia* (1959), 4:121–278; Gulianitskii, "Tserkov' Pokrova . . . i russkoe zodchestvo XVI–XVII vv.," pp. 52–64.

22. Nekrasov, *Ocherki*, p. 313.

23. Il'in, "O professional'nykh navykakh," pp. 131–32.

24. Il'in, "Zodchestvo XVII veka," in Grabar' et al., *Istoriia* (1959), 4:60–61.

25. Kostochkin, "Dereviannyi 'gorod' Koly,"pp. 200–246; cf. Fride, "Russkie dereviannye ukrepleniia," pp. 113–43.

26. Alferova, "Gosudarstvennaia sistema," pp. 3–11; Iakovliev, *Zasechnaia cherta*; Nikitin, "Oboronitel'nye sooruzheniia," pp. 116–213; V. I. Buganov, "Zasechnaia kniga 1638 g.," *Zapiski Otdela rukopisei, Gos. Biblioteka SSSR im. Lenina*, no. 23 (1960), pp. 181–252; S. M. Kashtanov, "Izvestie o Zasechnom prikaze XVI veka," *Voprosy istorii*, 1968, no. 7, p. 204; Kashtanov, "Eshche raz o Gorodovym prikaze XVIv.," ibid., 1963, no. 11, pp. 211–13; and Buganov, "O Gorodovym prikaze v Rossii XVI veka," ibid., 1962, no. 11, p. 213. For a general study in English, see Shaw, "Southern Frontiers," pp. 117–42.

27. Zagorovskii, *Belgorodskaia cherta*.

28. In addition to the works by Kostochkin listed in the Bibliography, see Kostochkin, "Krepost' Ivangorod [1492–1507]," *MiIA SSSR*, no. 31 (1952), pp. 224–317; Kostochkin, "K kharakteristike pamiatnikov voennogo zodchestva Moskovskoi Rusi kontsa XV-nachala XVI vekov (Korpor'e, Orekhov i Iam)," ibid., no. 77 (1958), pp. 101–42; Kostochkin, "Russkoe krepostnoe zodchestvo XIV-XVII vv.," *Sovetskaia arkhitektura*, 1957, no. 8, pp. 91–101; and Kostochkin, "O 'reguliarnoi' planirovke v krepostnoi arkhitekture russkogo gosudarstva (K voprosu ob evoliutsii russkogo oboronnogo zodchestva v sviazi s razvitiem artillerii)," *Ezhegodnik III 1957* (M., 1958), pp. 83–137. See also P. A. Rappoport, "Ocherki po istorii voennogo zodchestva severovostochnoi i severo-zapadnoi Rusi X–XV vv.," *MiIA SSSR*, no. 105 (1961), pp. 5–247, which continues Rappoport, "Ocherki po istorii russkogo voennogo zodchestva X–XIII vv.," ibid., no. 52 (1956), pp. 5–184; and Rappoport, "Iz istorii voenno-inzhenernogo iskusstva drevnei Rusi (Staraia Ladoga, Porkhov, Izborsk, Ostrov)," ibid., no. 31 (1952), pp. 133–201.

29. Kostochkin, "K kharakteristike," p. 101; Kostochkin, *Oboronnoe zodchestvo*, p. 8.

30. Kostochkin, "O 'reguliarnoi' planirovke," p. 136. An isolationist approach also marks Epifanov, "Kreposti," pp. 284–96, which is otherwise a useful survey. Cf. Iu. A. Nel'govskii, "Nekotorye osobennosti zamkov podol'skikh zemel' Ukrainy XVI–nachala XVII vv.," *AN*, no. 27 (1979), pp. 89 ff., where the issue of European, ultimately Italian Renaissance influence in local fortress modernization is openly admitted.

31. Cf. Bartenev, *Moskovskii kreml'*, 1:35; Rappoport, *Drevnerusskaia arkhitektura*, p. 134; Chiniakov, "O nekotorykh osobennostiakh," pp. 3–22; Duffy, *Siege Warfare*, p. 170; L. V. Trofimov and I. A. Kir'ianov, "Materialy k issledovaniiu Nizhegorodskogo kremlia," *MiIA SSSR*, no. 31 (1952), pp. 320–46; T. N. Sergeeva-Kozina, "Mozhaiskii kreml' 1624–1626 gg. (opyt rekonstruktsii)," ibid., pp. 347–75; Kirpichnikov and Khlopin, "Krepost' Kirillo-Belozerskogo monastyria," pp. 143–99.

32. H. de la Croix, *Military Considerations in City Planning: Fortifications* (New York, 1972), pp. 32 ff.; also Duffy, *Siege Warfare*, pp. 2 ff.

33. Nekrasov, *Ocherki*, pp. 324–30.

34. Duffy, *Siege Warfare*, p. 173. Cf. Rappoport, *Drevnerusskaia arkhitektura*, pp. 134–36; Epifanov, "Kreposti," p. 285.

35. A. V. Petrov, *Gorod Narva. Ego proshloe i dostopriemechatel'nosti* (SPb., 1901), pp. 183 ff.; also Kostochkin, "Krepost' Ivangorod."

36. Figures from Eaton, "Russian Cities 1500–1700," pp. 225–27; and Rozman, *Urban Networks*, pp. 60, 69, 72. On the Old-Russian town, see also French, "Early and Medieval Russian Town," pp. 249–77; chapters by L. N. Langer and D. H. Miller in Hamm, *The City in Russian History*, pp. 11–33; remarks by R. Hellie, reviewing Hittle, *The Service City in Russia 1600–1800*, in *Journal of Modern History* (April 1982), pp. 197–201, with further references; Shaw, "Southern Frontiers"; and the stimulating discussion of the Old-Russian town in a comparative European framework, in R. Pipes, *Russia Under the Old Regime* (New York, 1974), pp. 192–203.

37. Tverskoi, *Russkoe gradostroitel'stvo*; Lavrov, *Razvitie planirovochnoi struktury*, pp. 7–47; Proskuriakova, "Planirovochnye kompozitsii gorodovkrepostei," pp. 58–63; Alferova, "Gosudarstvennaia sistema," pp. 5 ff.; and Alferova, "K voprosu o stroitel'stve gorodov," pp. 20–28.

38. Chiniakov, "O nekotorykh osobenostiakh," pp. 3–22.

39. Rozman, *Urban Networks*, pp. 56–57.

40. R. Hellie, "The Stratification of Muscovite Society: The Townsmen," *Russian History* 5, pt. 1 (1978), p. 160. It might be noted that the relevant parts of Shkvarikov, *Gradostroitel'stvo* (pp. 107–29, 204–37), emphasize that the Petrine period was a "revolutionary stage in the history of Russian town planning," a point reiterated in Shkvarikov, *Ocherki istorii planirovki*, p. 63. Cf. Duffy, *Siege Warfare*, which insists (p. 264) that the "wandering, irregular patterns" of pre-Petrine Russian towns "reveal no evidence of deliberate design" and that "there is no sign of any continuity with the layouts which were adopted under Western influence" in the eighteenth century.

41. See Speranskii, *Ocherki po istorii Prikaza kamennykh del*, and especially Voronin, *Ocherki*, which is intended to supplement Speranskii.

42. Voronin, *Ocherki*, pp. 64–71; Kostochkin, "K voprosu o traditsiiakh i novatorstve," pp. 29–30. Cf. J. Harvey, *The Medieval Architect* (London, 1972), pp. 101–19, which indicates that such architectural drawing as was practiced in medieval (1200–1500) western Europe was considerably in advance of anything known in pre-Petrine Russia. Cf. also Tits, "Dva chertezha XVII veka," pp. 5–16: Tits, like other Soviet scholars, appears reluctant to accept the implications of his own findings with respect to the state of seventeenth-century Russian architectural drawing, and thus speculates that the fact that very few such drawings survive may be attributed to the builders' practice of discarding them when done with a project or even of deliberately destroying them to protect their "professional secrets"; he later suggests that the high cost of paper in Russia was at fault, leaving builders no choice but to draw their plans on birchbark or the ground.

43. Voronin, *Ocherki*, pp. 78–97; Voronov, "Dokumenty o kirpichnom proizvodstve," pp. 7–114; and for figures illustrating extensive purchases of bricks from outside manufacturers by the Department of Masonry Affairs in, e.g., 1683, A. Viktorov, *Opisanie zapisnykh knig i bumag starinykh dvortsovykh prikazov 1584–1725 gg.*, vol. 2 (M., 1883), p. 545.

44. Speranskii, *Ocherki po istorii Prikaza kamennykh del*, p. 127; Voronin, *Ocherki*, pp. 33–36.

45. Kirpichnikov and Khlopin, "Krepost' Kirillo-Belozerskogo monastyria," pp. 161–62; Voronin, *Ocherki*, p. 36.

46. On this question, see especially Afanas'ev, *Postroenie arkhitekturnoi formy drevnerusskimi zodchimi*, and Il'in, "O professional'nykh navykakh," pp. 129–32.

47. Cf. N. A. Evsina, "Iz istorii arkhitekturnykh vzgliadov i teorii nachala XVIII veka," in Alekseeva, *Russkoe iskusstvo* (1974), pp. 11–12.

48. Voronin, *Ocherki*, pp. 62–63; Leo Bagrov, *History of Cartography*, ed. R. A. Skelton, trans. D. L. Paisey (Cambridge, Mass., 1964), pp. 170 ff. See also, in much greater detail, Bagrov, *History of Russian Cartography*; and P. D. A. Harvey, *The History of Topographical Maps: Symbols, Pictures and Surveys* (London, 1980). The now standard Russian word for map, *karta*, from Latin/French, perhaps via German or Polish, dates to Peter I's time.

49. Kostochkin, "K voprosu o traditsiiakh i novatorstve," p. 34; also, but much more forthrightly, Afanas'ev, *Postroenie arkhitekturnoi formy drevnerusskimi zodchimi*, p. 11.

50. E.g., Braitseva, "Novye konstruktivnye priemy," pp. 133–52.

51. Voronin, *Ocherki*, pp. 122–29.

52. Cf. Grabar' et al., *Istoriia* (1909), 2:117.

53. See W. Harvey, *Church of the Holy Sepulchre, Jerusalem: Structural Survey, Final Report* (London, 1935); and, for Bernardino and his treatise, the English edition of the 1620 Florence edition of same by T. Bellorini, E. Hoade, and B. Bagatti, *Publications of the Studium Biblicum Franciscanum*, no. 10 (Jerusalem, 1953), with reproductions of the original drawings.

54. Alferova, "O stroitel'noi deiatel'nosti Nikona," pp. 30–44.

55. Il'in, "Dereviannoe zodchestvo," in Grabar, et al., *Istoriia* (1960), 5: 280, n. 1. For the New Jerusalem monastery and its church, see Il'in et al., "Kamennoe zodchestvo," in Grabar' et al., *Istoriia* (1955), 3:173–79; Il'in, "Problema 'Moskovskogo barokko'," pp. 335–38; and Hughes, "Byelorussian craftsmen," pp. 327–41. V. Ia. Libson, *Po beregam Istry i ee pritokov* (M., 1974), is a practical guide to the architecture of the monastery among neighboring monuments.

56. Tel'tevskii, *Bukhvostov*, pp. 15 ff.

57. Kopylova, *Kamennoe stroitel'stvo v Sibiri*, pp. 18 ff., 86 ff.

58. Kirillov, "Postroiki Remezova," pp. 109–24 (illustrated); Kirillov, "Metody Remezova," pp. 53–62; and Kirillov, "Ansambl' Tobol'skogo kremlia (Opyt sozdaniia obshchegorodskogo publichnogo tsentra rannepetrovskogo vremeni)," in Alekseeva, *Russkoe iskusstvo* (1974), pp. 53–67 and figs. 19–38. See also Kopylova, *Kamennoe stroitel'stvo v Sibiri*, pp. 28 ff.; and, for Remezov the mapmaker, L. Bagrov, "Semyon Remezov—a Siberian Cartographer," *Imago mundi* 9 (1954), pp. 111–25, and Bagrov, ed., *S. U. Remezov: The Atlas of Siberia* (The Hague, 1958).

59. Cf. Kirillov, "Metody Remezova," pp. 55, 61–62; also Tverskoi, *Russkoe gradostroitel'stvo*, passim and conclusion; Lavrov, *Razvitie planirovochnoi struktury*, pp. 27–47; and Proskuriakova, "Planirovochnye kompozitsii gorodov-krepostei," pp. 58–63.

60. Beletskaia, *"Obraztsovye" proekty*, p. 11; cf. Kirillov, "Proekty 'obraztsovykh domov'," pp. 153–68.

61. Vorob'ev, "Voevodskii dvor v Novgorode," pp. 95–106, which is based on newly uncovered documentary as well as archaeological evidence.

62. Vagner, "Cherty traditsii i novatorstva v Riazanskoi arkhitekture," pp. 108–9.

Chapter 4

1. Vipper, *Arkhitektura russkogo barokko*, p. 33.

2. Ilyin (Il'in), *Moscow*, pp. 64–65; Il'in, *Moskva* (1973), pp. 82–84.

3. See V. I. Pluzhnikov, "Sootnoshenie ob"emnykh form v russkom kul'tovom zodchestve nachala XVIII veka," in Alekseeva, *Russkoe iskusstvo* (1974), pp. 81–108 passim; also Vagner, "Cherty traditsii i novatorstva v Riazanskoi arkhitekture," pp. 107–18; P. A. Tel'tevskii, "Troitskii sobor v Verkhotur'e," *AN*, no. 12 (1960), pp. 169–78; I. Untilov, "Neizvestnyi pamiatnik russkoi arkhitektury nachala XVIII veka," *AN*, no. 6 (1956), pp. 147–49; Braitseva, "Nekotorye osobennosti," pp. 45–60; Braitseva, "Tvorcheskii metod," pp. 45–59; and Braitseva, "Novoe i traditsionnoe v khramovom zodchestve," pp. 31–40. G. K. Lukomskii, *Pamiatniki starinnoi arkhitektury Rossii*, vol. 1: *Russkaia provintsiia* (Petrograd, 1916), provides photographs (pp. 89–96) of provincial examples of "Moscow Baroque" which do not survive.

4. C. Norberg-Schulz, *Baroque Architecture* (New York, 1972), pp. 26, 10. See also R. Wittkower, *Art and Architecture in Italy, 1600 to 1750* (rev. ed., Baltimore, 1973); T. H. Fokker, *Roman Baroque Art: A History of a Style* (New York, 1972); and A. Blunt et al., *Baroque and Rococo Architecture and Decoration* (New York, 1978), for illustrated summaries as well as, most recently, J. Varriano, *Italian Baroque and Rococo Architecture* (Oxford, 1986). Varriano offers an exceptionally concise definition of Baroque architecture: "The more progressive seventeenth- and early eighteenth-century buildings do share some features that differ, sometimes superficially, but at times radically from more conservative [Renaissance] works: a fondness for complex, often centralized ground plans; an increasing tendency toward greater height, eventually establishing the dome rather than the high altar as the physical and spiritual focus; the love of curved wall planes, of projecting columns rather than flat pilasters, and of rhythmic bay arrangements; controlled illumination; a fusion of sculpture with architecture; a sensitivity to site and location; and a coextensive space that actively engages the sensory perceptions of the spectator" (p. 4).

5. C. Norberg-Schulz, *Late Baroque and Rococo Architecture* (New York, 1974); N. Powell, *From Baroque to Rococo: An Introduction to Austrian and German Architecture from 1580 to 1790* (New York, 1959); E. Hempel, *Baroque Art and Architecture in Central Europe* (Baltimore, 1965); K. Downes, *English Baroque Architecture* (London, 1966); Y. Bottineau, *Baroque ibérique* (Fribourg, 1969) or A. Sancho Corbacho, *Arquitectura Barroca Sevillana del Siglo XVIII* (Madrid, 1952); P. Kelemen, *Baroque and Rococo in Latin America*, 2 vols. (2d ed., New York, 1967); etc.

6. See Grabar' et al., *Istoriia* [1909], 1:16–18, and 4:7–26, for summaries. For the details, see ibid., especially 2:337–416 ("Barokko Ukrainy," by Grabar' and G. Pavlutskii), and 2:417–468 ("Barokko Moskvy," by F. Gornostaev).

7. Grabar' et al., *Istoriia* [1909], 3:173–80.

8. Ibid., 3:175, n. 1; cf. A. Blunt, *Some Uses and Misuses of the Terms Baroque and Rococo as Applied to Architecture* (London, 1973), pp. 5 ff.

9. Nekrasov, ed., *Barokko v Rossii*, pp. 13–42 (Zgura) and pp. 43–55 (Brunov).

10. F. I. Shmit, " 'Barokko' kak istoricheskaia kategoriia," in Shmit, ed., *Russkoe iskusstvo XVII veka*, pp. 7–26.

11. Nekrasov, *Ocherki*, pp. 307–93; also Nekrasov, *Barokko v Rossii*, pp. 7–9, 56–78.

12. B. R. Vipper, 'Russkaia arkhitektura XVII veka i ee istoricheskoe mesto," in Vipper, *Arkhitektura russkogo barokko*, pp. 9–28. On Vipper and his career, see the extended review of this book by J. Cracraft in *Kritika: A Review of Current Soviet Books on Russian History* 17, no. 1 (1981), pp. 18–28.

13. B. Vipers (B. R. Vipper), *Baroque Art in Latvia* (Riga, 1939; Latvian ed. published Riga, 1937), pp. 8–9, 25 ff., 120–77.

14. Vipper, *Arkhitektura russkogo barokko*, pp. 18–23.

15. Ibid., pp. 23–24.

16. Ibid., pp. 25–27.

17. Rzianin, *Pamiatniki*, pp. 73, 67, 92 ff.

18. Mikhailov, *Arkhitektor Ukhtomskii*, pp. 9–10.

19. Tel'tevskii, *Zodchii Bukhvostov*, p. 10.

20. Il'in, "Problema 'Moskovskogo barokko'," pp. 324–39. See also Il'in in Grabar' et al., *Istoriia* (1959), 4:57–68 and 217–78, and in Lazarev et al., *Drevnerusskoe iskusstvo* (1964), pp. 232–35; Ilyin (Il'in), *Moscow* (1968), pp. 64–65; Il'in, *Moskva* (1973), pp. 75–89; and Il'in, "Arkhitektura" (1979), pp. 170–207.

21. Il'in, "Problema 'Moskovskogo barokko'," pp. 331–37.

22. Il'in, in Lazarev et al., *Drevnerusskoe iskusstvo*, pp. 232–35. Similarly, Il'in in Grabar' et al., *Istoriia* (1959), 4: 65–67, 218–21; and, affirming Dutch influence on the "Moscow Baroque," Il'in, *Kamennaia letopis'*, p. 241, as well as Il'in, *Moskva* (1975), p. 9.

23. Il'in, "Arkhitektura," pp. 170, 183, 207.

24. Grabar' et al., *Istoriia* [1909], 2:383–408. G. Pavlutskii in a short companion essay (ibid., pp. 409–16) discussed the few secular masonry buildings surviving from the same period, and concluded that their development in the Ukraine paralleled that of church architecture, with "forms worked out within the Baroque style being transferred to domestic architecture."

25. Pavlutskii in Grabar' et al., *Istoriia* [1909], 2:337–59.

26. Lukomskii, "Ukrainskii Barokko" (1911), pp. 5–13. See also, at greater length, and emphasizing the European significance of the whole "Ukrainian Baroque," Zalozieckyj, "Die Barockarchitektur" (1929), pp. 65–116.

27. G. K. Loukomski (Lukomskii), *La Ville sainte de Russie: Kiev* (Paris, 1929), p. 80.

28. Tsapenko, *Arkhitektura Ukrainy*, pp. 7, 45, 180. Cf. Bezsonov, "Rassvet ukrainskoi arkhitektury," pp. 25–48; chapters by Tsapenko and P. H. Iurchenko in Iurchenko et al., *Istoriia ukrains'koho mystetstva*, pp. 21–125; and Tsapenko, "Arkhitektura Ukrainy," p. 383–402. See also, covering much of the same ground, A. T. Hall, "The Royal Gates of the Pechersk Lavra: The Evolution of the Kievan Baroque and Rococo" (Ph.D. diss., University of Southern California, 1984), pp. 16 ff.

29. Chanturiia, *Istoriia arkhitektury Belorussii*, p. 81 and chap. 4.

30. Hughes, "Byelorussian craftsmen," pp. 327–41.

31. On the last point, cf. Braitseva, "Novoe v kompozitsii vkhodov," pp. 37–51. For the role of Belorussian masters (not identified as such but as the "Nikonian tile masters" or the "tilers from Istra") in the development of Russian ceramic decoration, see N. V. Voronov and I. G. Sakharova, "O datirovke i rasprostvanenii nekotorykh vidov Moskovskikh izraztsov," in *MiIA SSSR*, no. 44 (1955), pp. 77–115.

32. Hughes, "Graphic Material," pp. 433–43.

33. G. K. Vagner, "O proiskhozhdenii tsentricheskikh kompozitsii v russkom zodchestve kontsa XVII veka," in *Pamiatniki kultury: issledovanie i restavratsiia*, no. 3 (1961), pp. 123–33; see also Vagner, "Cherty novatorstva v Riazanskoi arkhitekture," p. 116.

34. E. H. Ter Kuile, "Architecture," in J. Rosenberg et al., *Dutch Art and Architecture 1600 to 1800* (Baltimore, 1966), especially pp. 221–29 and pls. 183(B), 184, 185, 187(B), 189, etc.

35. V. V. Stech, "Rustikalisierung als Faktor Stilentwickelung," *XIIIe Congrès international d'histoire de l'art: Résumés des communications présentées au congrès* (Stockholm, 1933), pp. 210–13.

36. Ter Kuile, p. 225.

37. E.g., Rappoport, *Drevnerusskaia arkhitektura*, p. 110, or M. A. Il'in in Grabar' et al., *Istoriia* (1959), 4:63.

38. Tel'tevskii, *Bukhvostov*, especially pp. 11, 76.

On Startsev, see G. Karpinskii, "Novye dannye k biografii zodchikh Startsevykh," *AN*, no. 10 (1958), p. 205; and N. Soshina, "Krutitskii teremok v Moskve," *AN*, no. 6 (1956), pp. 136–37. On Zarudnyi, see Grabar' et al., *Istoriia* [1909], 4:43–58; Grabar', "Zarudnyi," in Grabar' et al., *Russkaia arkhitektura* (1954), pp. 39–92; and Grabar' et al., *Istoriia* (1959), 4:25 ff.

39. Grabar', "Zarudnyi" (see n. 38, above), pp. 50, 56.

40. Ibid., especially pp. 40, 84, 88, 89–90.

41. G. I. Vzdornov, "Zametki o pamiatnikakh russkoi arkhitektury kontsa XVII–nachala XVIII v.," in Alekseeva, *Russkoe iskusstvo* (1973), pp. 20–30; cf. Makovskii, "Dve podmoskovnyia," pp. 32–36.

42. T. A. Gatova, "Iz istorii dekorativnoi skul'ptury Moskvy nachala XVIII v.," in Alekseeva, *Russkoe iskusstvo* (1973), pp. 31–44.

43. Cf. Mikhailov, *Arkhitektor Ukhtomskii*, who points out (pp. 16–18) that there is no documentary evidence of Zarudnyi's participation in any major building project of the time and that, in particular, it is "impossible to consider it proven that he was the author of the [Menshikov Tower]"; indeed, that on the evidence of Zarudnyi's own accounts of his career, in petitions to the government of 1725, where he omits any mention of the Menshikov Tower or of any other major architectural work, "his creative activity took place mainly in the realm of decorative art." Il'in, in 1975, while still maintaining that Zarudnyi built the Menshikov Tower, concedes that its decoration "owes much to the Italian masters working here" and finds it "impossible not to connect the architectural character of the Menshikov Tower with the victories of young Petrine Russia" (*Moskva* [1975], pp. 10–12). Evsina, citing the relevant literature, observes discreetly (1978) that "Zarudnyi remains one of the most enigmatic figures in eighteenth-century Russian art" (Vipper, *Arkhitektura russkogo barokko*, p. 103, n. 23.)

44. Most notably Hughes, "Byelorussian craftsmen," with numerous references; and Hughes, "Graphic Material."

45. Hall, in the dissertation cited above (n. 28, this chapter), adduces further evidence of seventeenth-century Ukrainian architectural influence in Russia in the form of albums of both European (especially German) and locally produced engravings and drawings that were assembled in Kiev precisely for this purpose (and for distribution in the Ukraine itself)—material that at the same time documents the existence of a "direct line of artistic communication between Kiev and the West." Although many such albums are to be found in the Central State Library in Kiev, according to Hall, they have yet to be properly organized and inventoried, let alone critically or systematically studied (see especially pp. 57–58).

51. TsGADA, F. 181, op. 1, d. 268/474a, d. 269/474b, and d. 270/474c.

52. *Pravilo o piati chinekh Arkhitektury Iakova Barotsiia devignola . . .* (M., 1709, 1712, 1722); for further details, see *Opis. I,* nos. 29, 61, 720.

53. *Opis. I,* nos. 14–19, 24, 28; for both earlier and later editions of some of these works, see ibid., nos. 1, 5, 6, 10, 11, 33, 34, 44. For details of the translation of Bouillet's treatise in French on rendering rivers navigable (Amsterdam, 1696) published Moscow 1708, see ibid., no. 4. Manuscript—printers'—copies of three of these translations are at TsGADA: F. 381, op. 1, No. 999, No. 1001, and No. 1202.

54. *Opis. I,* nos. 49, 786. A contemporary manuscript copy of the Vauban is at TsGADA, F. 381, op. 1, No. 1003.

55. V. Shilkov, "Russkii perevod Vitruviia nachala XVIII veka," *AN,* no. 7 (1955), pp. 89–92.

56. *Opis. I,* appendix 4 (pp. 524–27); also Evsina, *Arkhitekturnaia teoriia,* pp. 57–60. For details of the "Petrovskii al'bom" of some 130 architectural graphics now in the State Hemitage Museum, Leningrad, see Voronikhina, *Peterburg v chertezhakh,* pp. 5 ff., and A. I. Andreev, ed., *Istoricheskii ocherk i obzor fondov rukopisnogo otdela Biblioteki akademii nauk,* vol. 2: *XVIII vek: Karty, plany, chertezhi, risunki i graviury Sobraniia Petra I* (M./L., 1961), passim.

57. Evsina, *Arkhitekturnaia teoriia,* chap. 2; Andreev; and Hughes, "Architectural Books," pp. 101–8. Archival records show, e.g., that in Piermont in June 1716 Peter purchased various architectural prints and books from one Nicolaus Forster, including (in Forster's invoice) bound volumes of "Sturms Bau Kunst" and "Deckers Fürstliche Baukunst" (TsGADA, F. 396, op. 2, d. 1082, 1. 28).

58. Cf. Evsina, p. 16; also Evsina, *Arkhitekturnaia teoriia,* p. 37.

59. N. V. Kliazina, "Dvorets A. D. Menshikova v Peterburge," in Gessen, pp. 8–9; also Vipper, *Arkhitektura russkogo barokko,* p. 105, n. 32 (note by Evsina).

60. *PSZ,* vol. 3, nos. 1579, 1548, 1585, 1594, 1595, 1560. The last measure, concerning masonry construction, had some precedent in official exhortations of 1681, 1685, and 1688 to residents of central Moscow to build in brick so as to prevent the spread of fire: see vol. 2, nos. 892, 1133, 1314.

61. Ibid., vol. 4, no. 1825.

62. Ibid., no. 1963. Contemporary figures for the number and distribution of Muscovite households or lots—*dvory*—are printed in Sytin, *Istoriia Moskvy,* 1:190.

63. *PSZ,* vol. 4, nos. 2051, 2052.

64. *PiB,* vol. 6, note to no. 2112 (pp. 563–64).

65. Sytin, *Istoriia Moskvy,* 1:186–87 and 196–97,

indicates the range of legislation involved. It has been suggested that the requirement to build houses facing the street itself had a fiscal motive—to eliminate the practice of householders joining together behind one gate so as to pay only one household tax (Sytina, "Arkhitekturnoe zakonodatel'stvo," p. 68).

66. Sytin, *Istoriia Moskvy,* 1:185.

67. *PSZ,* vol. 4, nos. 2072, 2109, 2225, 3147, 4017. For the new street-cleaning regulations, *PSZ,* vol. 3, no. 1684; ibid., vol. 4, nos. 2225, 2504; and Sytin, *Istoriia Moskvy,* 1:193.

68. *PSZ,* vol. 4, no. 2232.

69. Ibid., no. 2265.

70. Ibid., no. 2306.

71. Ibid., no. 2534.

72. Sytin, *Istoriia Moskvy,* 1:200.

73. *PSZ,* vol. 4, no. 2531; decree confirmed and strengthened with new penalties in September 1712: ibid., no. 2591.

74. Ibid., nos. 2534, 2552.

75. Sytin, *Istoriia Moskvy,* 1:202.

76. *PSZ,* vol. 5, no. 2848; *Opis. I,* no. 118.

77. *Opis. I,* nos. 287, 356, 785.

78. *PSZ,* vol. 5, nos. 2868, 2972.

79. Ibid., no. 3147; also Mikhailov, *Arkhitektor Ukhtomskii,* pp. 12–15 and nn. 16–18 (p. 334).

80. *PSZ,* vol. 5, no. 3147; *Opis. I,* no. 268, also nos. 356 and 785 for later issues.

81. *PSZ,* vol. 5, no. 3750; vol. 6, no. 3885; *Opis. I,* no. 667.

82. *PSZ,* vol. 6, no. 4047.

Chapter 6

1. *PiB* vol. 4, pt. I, no. 1349: letter of Sept. 11, 1706.

2. For the Russian literature on the early history of St. Petersburg and its architecture, see the comprehensive bibliography by Piliavskii and Gorshkova, *Russkaia arkhitektura,* especially nos. 430–537; the most important works are cited in the notes below and/or in the Bibliography. For manuscript collections of relevance at the State Public Library, Leningrad, see A. I. Andreev, ed., *Istoriia Leningrada: katalog rukopisei* (L., 1954); and, for the relevant graphic material at the same place, the detailed commentary by L. K. Koshkarova in Ostroi, *Fond graviur kak istochnik izucheniia arkhitektury,* pp. 8–102. Relevant works in English, etc., tend to be superficial, ill-informed, and/or anecdotal; exceptions include those by Bater, Egorov, Geyer, Rebas, and Zernack as listed in the Bibliography; but see also E. Amburger, *Ingermanland: Eine junge Provinz Russlands im Wirkungsbereich der Residenz und Weltstadt St. Petersburg-Leningrad,* 2 vols. (Cologne and Vienna, 1980), passim.

3. Cf. P. Pekarskii, *Nauka i literatura pri Petre Velikom,* vol. 1 (SPb., 1862), p. 10; V. P. Adrianova-

Peretts, ed., *Istoricheskii ocherk i obzor fondov rukopisnogo otdela Biblioteki akademii nauk*, pt. 1: *XVIII vek*
(M./L., 1956), p. 374; and E. I. Bobrova, *Biblioteka
Petra I: Ukazatel'-spravochnik* (L., 1978), no. 1496.
On Schijnvoet, see U. Thieme et al., *Allgemeines
Lexikon der Bildenden Künstler*, vol. 30 (Leipzig,
1936), p. 393; and on Peter first learning the basics
of "naval architecture [*korabel'naia arkhitektura*]" in
Amsterdam, see his preface to the Naval Statute of
1720, as printed in M. G. Ustrialov, *Istoriia tsarstvovaniia Petra Velikago*, vol. 2 (SPb., 1858), p. 400.

4. Peter's own draft of the letter is at TsGADA:
F. 9, otd. I, kn. 53, 1. 635. The letter is quoted in
Grabar' et al., *Russkaia arkhitektura*, p. 178. See also
Vipper, *Arkhitektura russkogo barokko*, pp. 32–33 and
no. 9 (p. 102).

5. TsGADA, F. 9, otd. I, kn. 53, 1. 637.

6. Ibid., 1. 570.

7. I. Semevskii, ed., *Arkhiv kn. F. A. Kurakina*,
vol. 1 (SPb., 1890), nos. 30 (letter dated July 8,
1720) and 51 (January 15, 1724); also nos. 9, 10,
11, 14, etc.

8. ZAP, no. 174.

9. M. M. Bogoslovskii, *Petr I: Materialy dlia biografii*, vol. 2 (M., 1941), pp. 530 ff.

10. TsGADA, F. 9, otd. I, kn. 53, 1. 481.

11. See Vipper, *Arkhitektura russkogo barokko*,
p. 46 and n. 39 (p. 106).

12. TsGADA, F. 9, otd. II, kn. 64, 11. 200–201.

13. *PiB*, vol. 4, no. 1374; *PiB*, vol. 4, pt. II, p.
1110; *PiB*, vol. 4, pt. I, no. 1453; *PiB*, vol. 5, nos.
1544, 1545, 1778, and pp. 414, 681, 713.

14. E.g., TsGADA, F. 396, op. 2, d. 1082,
1. 28, showing that in Piermont (Pyrmont) in June
1716 Peter purchased various architectural books and
prints from a Nicolaus Forster, including (this is
Forster's invoice) bound volumes of "Sturms Bau
Kunst" and "Deckers Fürstliche Baukunst"—volumes
that were then added to Peter's library (see Bobrova,
nos. 1064–66, 1537, 1542).

15. Bobrova, nos. 14, 135, 147, 290, 302, 327,
333, 342, 343, 513.

16. See *Opis. I*, no. 19, with further citations (to
which add *PiB*, vol. 8, nos. 2525, 2902; *PiB*, vol. 9,
pt. I, no. 2994; and Bobrova, nos. 290, 1543).

17. *PiB*, vol. 9, pt. I, no. 3412.

18. *Opis. I*, nos. 29, 61, 720, with further citations (add *PiB*, vol. 9, pt. II, pp. 1236–37, and Bobrova, nos. 14, 896–902); Evsina, *Arkhitekturnaia teoriia*, p. 37.

19. ZAP, nos. 147, 149; cf. *PiB*, vol. 1, no. 291,
and *PSZ*, vol. 4, no. 1751.

20. See *Opis. I*, nos. 24, 44, with further citations (add *PiB*, vol. 5, no. 1544; *PiB*, vol. 8, pt. I,
no. 2525; *PiB*, vol. 8, pt. II, pp. 537–39; and Bobrova, nos. 1225–29); also *Opis. II*, p. 347 (nos.
24, 44).

21. *Opis. I*, no. 49, with further citations (add
PiB, vol. 8, pt. II, p. 565; *PiB*, vol. 9, pt. I, no.
3095; *PiB*, vol. 9, pt. II, p. 728; ZAP, no. 7; and
Bobrova, nos. 327, 939); also *Opis. II*, p. 348
(no. 49).

22. ZAP, no. 187.

23. *Opis. I*, no. 28, with further citations (add
Bobrova, nos. 302, 870).

24. *Opis. I*, no. 201, with further citations (add
Bobrova, no. 513).

25. *Opis. I*, no. 4 (add Bobrova, nos. 342, 960,
961); *Opis. I*, no. 72.

26. Bobrova, no. 163.

27. Peter's ship diagram is reproduced in Semevskii, p. 17. See further V. Shilkov, "Chetyre risunka
Petra I po planirovke Petergofa," *AN*, no. 4 (1953),
pp. 35–38; Grabar' et al., *Russkaia arkhitektura*, pp.
108, 109, 115; Voronikhina, *Peterburg v chertezhakh*,
nos. 42, 43, and (possibly) nos. 9, 19; and M. N.
Murzanova et al., *Istoricheskii ocherk i obzor fondov
Rukopisnogo otdela Biblioteki Akademii nauk: karty,
plany, chertezhi, risunki i graviury sobraniia Petra I*
(M./L., 1961), pp. 61–258, which refers in detail to
the vast collection of graphics that Peter I left behind, including hundreds of architectural drawings of
both European and local provenance. Among the
latter are various items annotated by Peter himself as
well as rough sketches done wholly or in part by
him.

28. Grabar', *O russkoi arkhitekture*, p. 282.

29. For details of the work of European builders
in Russia and especially St. Petersburg from 1703 to
about 1725, see the chapters by I. E. Grabar', V. F.
Shilkov, and S. S. Bronshtein in Grabar' et al., *Russkaia arkhitektura*, pp. 93–117, 118–66, and 181–238
(shortened versions of same in Grabar' et al., *Istoriia*
[1960], 5:65–84, 84–115, 122–50); Grabar', "Arkhitektory-inostrantsy," pp. 132–50 (reprinted in Grabar', *O russkoi arkhitekture*, pp. 264–83 and 410–14);
Vipper, *Arkhitektura russkogo barokko*, pp. 29 ff. and
notes (pp. 110 ff.); and further references below.

30. The search went back to 1711, if not earlier:
see *PiB*, vol. 10, pt. II, no. 4787 and p. 477; also,
more generally, Hällstrom, *Architector Schlüter*, and
Voinov, "Andreas Shliuter," pp. 367–77.

31. TsGADA, F. 9, otd. II, kn. 64, 1. 200.

32. On Michetti, see E. Gavrilova, "Arkhitekturnyi proekt N. Miketti po planu F. Prokopovicha 'Sad
Petrov' 1721 goda," *Soobshcheniia gos. Ermitazha* 34
(1972), pp. 50–53; Iogansen, *Zemtsov*, p. 26; and
J. Pinto, "An Early Design by Nicola Michetti,"
Journal of the Society of Architectural Historians 38,
no. 4 (1979), pp. 375–81.

33. Cf. essays by Shilkov and by Bronshtein just
cited (n. 29 above); Grabar' et al., *Russkaia arkhitektura*, p. 116; or the introduction to the latter by
N. N. Kovalenskaia, which is reprinted with some

modifications in Grabar' et al., *Istoriia* (1960), 5:7 ff.

34. On Trezzini, the best work is now Lisaevich, *Pervyi arkhitektor Peterburga*. But see also N. Krasheninnikova and V. Shilkov, "Proekty obraztsovykh zagorodnykh domov D. Trezini i zastroika beregov Fontanki," *AN*, no. 7 (1955), pp. 5–12; M. V. Iogansen, "Raboty Domeniko Trezini po planirovke i zastroike Strelki Vasil'evskogo ostrova v Peterburge," in Alekseeva, *Russkoe iskusstvo* (1973), pp. 45–55; Vipper, *Arkhitektura russkogo barokko*, pp. 43–46; LoGatto, *Gli Artisti*, 2:21–52 and 2:121–24; J. Ehret, "Tessiner Künstler in Moskau," *Die Garbe, Schweizerisches Familienblatt* 31 (1947), especially pp. 109–10; Ehret, "Domenico Trezzini aus Astano," pp. 97–115 (with thanks for the last two references to Professor L. Schelbert); and Korol'kov, "Arkhitekty Trezini," pp. 17–36.

35. Cf. J. Bourke, *Baroque Churches of Central Europe* (London, 1958), pp. 32 ff.

36. See Lisaevich, *Pervyi arkhitektor*, pp. 95–104, indicating that only the church's spire, originally in wood but replaced in metal in the nineteenth century, raising the overall height of bell tower and spire from 106 to 122.5 meters, has changed. Cf. E. Timofeevna, "Pervonachal'nyi oblik Petropavlovskogo sobora," *AN*, no. 7 (1955), pp. 93–108.

37. *PSZ*, vol. 5, nos. 2792, 2932; *Opis. I*, nos. 86, 162.

38. Lisaevich, *Pervyi arkhitektor*, p. 39; also Vipper, *Arkhitektura russkogo barokko*, p. 105, n. 31.

39. Letter in I. I. Golikov, *Deianiia Petra Velikago, Dopoleniia*, vol. 11 (M., 1797), p. 245. See also Lossky, *Le Blond, Architecte de Pierre le Grand*.

40. On Le Blond in St. Petersburg, see Evsina, *Arkhitekturnaia teoriia*, pp. 56–57, 84, 90, 99; Egorov, *Planning of St. Petersburg*, pp. 11–26, 62, 78–79; Vipper, *Arkhitektura russkogo barokko*, p. 104, n. 27; N. V. Kaliazina, "Proekt dvortsa v Strel'ne Arkhitektora Zh.-B. Leblona," *Soobshcheniia gos. Ermitazha* 34 (1972), pp. 53–56; and Kaliazina, "O dvortse admirala F. M. Apraksina v Peterburge," *Trudy gos. Ermitazha* 11 (1970), pp. 131–40. A complete copy of Le Blond's projected scheme for St. Petersburg, in the form of three reports to Menshikov, is among Menshikov's papers at TsGADA: F. 138, op. 1, d. 696, 11. 70–79, 100–109, 209–99.

41. E. A. Borisova, "Arkhitekturnye ucheniki petrovskogo vremeni i ikh obuchenie v komandakh zodchikh-inostrantsev v Peterburge," in Alekseeva, *Russkoe iskusstvo* (1974), pp. 68–80.

42. Iogansen, *Zemtsov*, p. 22.

43. Iogansen, *Zemtsov*, is the essential work. For Zemstov as teacher, see also Borisova, "Arkhitekturnoe obrazovanie, " pp. 97–109.

44. TsGIA, F. 467, op. 63/187, 1. 247.

45. Iogansen, *Zemtsov*, pp. 45–46; also TsGADA, F. 9, otd. II, kn. 64, 11. 196, 200–201.

46. Iogansen, *Zemtsov*, pp. 47 ff., 57–59; also Iogansen, "K istorii stroitel'stva Ital'ianskogo dvortsa v Peterburge," in Alekseeva, *Russkoe iskusstvo* (1977), pp. 212–15; and S. S. Bronshtein and S. M. Grozmani, "Neizvestnyi proekt M. G. Zemtsova," *Soobshchen. III*, no. 7 (1956), pp. 70–79. On the derivation of Zemtsov's church of Sts. Simeon and Anna from, in particular, Trezzini's Peter-Paul church, see Lisaevich, *Pervyi arkhitektor*, p. 102.

47. TsGADA, F. 9, otd. II, kn. 30, 1. 441.

48. A. G. Kaminskaia, "Odin iz pervykh pensionerov Petra I," in Gesen, pp. 11–12; V. N. Stroev et al., *200-letie Kabineta Ego Imperatorskago Velichestva, 1704–1904: Istoricheskie issledovaniia* (SPb., 1911), pp. 109–19.

49. TsGIA, F. 470, d. 19, 11. 91–93.

50. Shilkov, "Zodchii Usov," pp. 63–65; Arkin, " 'Dolzhnost' Arkhitekturnoi Ekspeditsii': traktat-kodeks 1737–1740 godov," pp. 7–20 (this is followed by the text of the "codex," pp. 21–99).

51. See especially Podol'skii, "Korobov," pp. 105–16, and Piliavskii, "Korobov," pp. 41–62.

52. TsGADA, F. 9, otd. II, kn. 37, 1. 20.

53. Piliavskii, "Korobov," p. 54.

54. Petrov, *Pamiatniki Leningrada*, p. 267.

55. Cf. I. E. Grabar', "Obuchenie russkikh masterov za granitsei," in Grabar' et al., *Russkaia arkhitektura*, pp. 167–80 (shortened version in Grabar' et al., *Istoriia* [1960], 5:115–21); Evsina, *Arkhitekturnaia teoriia*, pp. 53–54; and Vipper, *Arkhitektura russkogo barokko*, pp. 57–62.

56. Cf. Borisova, pp. 78–79.

57. Borisova; also Borisova, "Arkhitekturnoe obrazovanie"; Borisova, "S. I. Chevakinskii i arkhitekturnoe obrazovanie pervoi poloviny XVIII veka," in Alekseeva, *Russkoe iskusstvo* (1968), pp. 96–109; and Evsina, *Arkhitekturnaia teoriia*, chaps. 2, 3, and 4.

58. For Rastrelli and his followers in Russia, see Grabar' et al., *Istoriia* (1909), vol. 3, chaps. 13 and 14; Denisov and Petrov, *Zodchii Rastrelli*; B. R. Vipper, "V. Rastrellil i arkhitektura russkogo barokko," in Grabar' et al., *Russkaia arkhitektura*, pp. 279–310 (see also essays here by A. N. Petrov and by Grabar' on Chevakinskii [pp. 311–68] and Ukhtomskii [pp. 369–411]: shortened versions of all three essays are in Grabar' et al., *Istoriia* [1960], 5:174–209, 209–243, 244–271; Vipper's essay also reprinted in Vipper, *Arkhitektura russkogo barokko*, pp. 65–85); Mikhailov, *Arkhitektor Ukhtomskii*, especially pp. 33 ff.; N. F. Gulianitskii, "O maloissledovannoi storone tvorcheskogo metoda V. Rastrelli—gradostroitel'stvo," *AN*, no. 21 (1973), pp. 24–43; and further references below. On Rastrelli's activities in what is now Latvia (annexed to Russia under Peter I), see also Vipers (Vipper), *Baroque Art in Latvia*, pp. 164–77 and Vipper, *Arkhitektura russkogo barokko*, pp. 86–94, 112. For Rastrelli's father in Rus-

sia, see Arkhipov and Raskin, *Bartolomeo Karlo Rastrelli*. Note that father's and son's actual names, the confused Russian usage notwithstanding, are Carlo Bartolomeo and Bartolomeo Francesco.

59. Grabar' et al., *Istoriia* [1909], 3:192.

60. S. B. Alekseeva, "Arkhitektura i dekorativnaia plastika Zimnego dvortsa," in Alekseeva, *Russkoe iskusstvo* (1977), pp. 128–58; Piliavskii, *Ermitazh*, pp. 39–63.

61. See Petrov, *Pamiatniki Leningrada*, pp. 23, 135, 201, for details of the three buildings mentioned; also, Piliavskii, *Smol'nyi*.

62. See Bronshtein, *Arkhitektura goroda Pushkina*, with numerous photographs taken before the destruction of World War II, and the lavish A. Benua (Benois), *Tsarskoe selo*.

63. Ehret, "Piero Antonio," pp. 83–102; G. I. Vzdornov, "Arkhitektor P'etro Antonio Trezini i ego postroika," in Alekseeva, *Russkoe iskusstvo* (1968), pp. 139–56. Lisaevich (*Pervyi arkhitektor*, pp. 34, 95) disputes Vzdornov's contention that P. A. Trezzini was not Dominico's son, as would Ehret.

64. Vzdornov, p. 143. See also T. P. Fedotova, "K probleme piatiglaviia v arkhitekture barokko pervoi poloviny XVIII veka," in Alekseeva, *Russkoe iskusstvo* (1977), pp. 70–87.

65. H. de la Croix, *Military Considerations in City Planning* (New York, 1972), p. 9.

66. See K. N. Serbina, "Istoriko-geograficheskii ocherk raiona Peterburga do osnovaniia goroda," in Viatkin, *Ocherki istorii Leningrada*, pp. 11 ff., and Amburger, 1:13–17 (with notes in 2:680–81). See also, stressing the natural obstacles to the city's economic development, R. E. Jones, "Getting the Goods to St. Petersburg: Water Transport from the Interior 1703–1811," *Slavic Review* 43, no. 3 (1984), pp. 413–33.

67. *PiB*, vol. 2, nos. 517–21.

68. M. Shcherbatov, ed., *Zhurnal ili podennaia zapiska Imperatora Petra Velikago*, vol. 1 (SPb., 1770), p. 69; *PiB*, vol. 2, p. 560.

69. See Predtechenskii, *Peterburg*, pp. 18–20; *PiB*, vol. 2 p. 561.

70. *PiB*, 2:565; see also Peter I's letter of July 1, 1703, "from Sanktpiterburkh" (ibid., no. 548).

71. *PiB*, vol. 2, no. 559 and p. 600; also Predtechenskii, *Peterburg*, pp. 18–20 and Luppov, *Istoriia stroitel'stva*, pp. 15–16.

72. As quoted in Luppov, *Istoriia stroitel'stva*, pp. 16–17.

73. *PiB*, vol. 3, no. 725.

74. See Lisaevich, *Pervyi arkhitektor*, pp. 16–17, 22 ff., and Petrov, "Peterburgskii zhiloi dom," pp. 133–34. Luppov, *Istoriia stroitel'stva*, is the basic account of the initial construction of St. Petersburg.

75. *PiB*, vol. 4, nos. 1284, 1349, 1460, etc.

76. For the chancellery's activities, see especially Borisova; Borisova, "Arkhitekturnoe obrazovanie"; Lisaevich, *Pervyi arkhitektor*, pp. 32, 52, 54, 84, 86, and passim; Iogansen, *Zemtsov*, pp. 11, 44, and passim; and Luppov, *Istoriia stroitel'stva*, pp. 18, 62–66, and passim.

77. Until 1717 yearly expenditures for civilian construction in St. Petersburg were fixed at 242,700 rubles; between 1717 and 1721, at 266,700 rubles, and from 1721, at 300,000 rubles; although actual expenditures in 1720 were 316,484 rubles and in subsequent years ran 80,000–100,000 rubles over budget: see A. Kahan, "Continuity in Economic Activity and Policy during the Post-Petrine Period in Russia," in M. Cherniavsky, ed., *The Structure of Russian History: Interpretive Essays* (New York, 1970), p. 204, n. 12. Total state revenue in 1724 was 8,713,000 rubles (see E. V. Anisimov, *Podatnaia reforma Petra I* [L., 1982], p. 278). Elsewhere Kahan judged the construction of St. Petersburg to be "the single most massive Russian investment of the [eighteenth] century" (see his *The Plow, the Hammer, and the Knout: An Economic History of Eighteenth-Century Russia* [Chicago, 1985], p. 247 and passim).

78. TsGADA, F. 9, otd. II, kn. 64, ll. 200–201, 167–72; I. K. Kirilov, *Tsvetushchee sostoianie vserossiiskogo gosudarstva*, ed. Iu. A. Tikhonov (M., 1977), pp. 44–45, 61–62. Kirilov was an official of the time.

79. Stroev, pp. 67–70, 106–26.

80. *PSZ*, vol. 8, no. 5969.

81. Luppov, *Istoriia stroitel'stva*, p. 78.

82. *PiB*, vol. 4, pt. I, nos. 1425, 1426, 1428, and—for the reference to "paradise"—no. 1349. Drawing on other official sources, Miliukov calculated that, in 1706, 7,272 workers were actually employed in construction at Azov and about 20,000 at St. Petersburg; and that by 1709 the figures were 405 and 10,734, respectively (P. N. Miliukov, *Gosudarstvennoe khoziaistvo Rossii v pervoi chetverti XVIII stoletiia i reforma Petra Velikago*, 2d ed. [SPb., 1905], p. 269).

83. *PiB*, vol. 6, no. 2069 (1707); *PSZ*, vol. 4, no. 2240; and *PiB*, vol. 9, pt. I, no. 3555 (1709).

84. *PSZ*, vol. 4, nos. 2282, 2467; vol. 5, no. 2744. See also *PiB*, vol. 10, nos. 3568, 3640, 3932–34, 3936, 3991, 3992, 4046, and 4047, for like measures in 1710.

85. *PiB*, vol. 9, pt. I, no. 3538; *PSZ*, vol. 4, no. 2448.

86. Luppov, *Istoriia stroitel'stva*, pp. 81, 84–88.

87. *Istoriia stroitel'stva*, pp. 94 ff.

88. *PiB*, vol. 9, no. 3538; also Luppov, *Istoriia stroitel'stva*, p. 99.

89. Cf. Voronov, "Dokumenty o kirpichnom proizvodstve," p. 11. Voronov estimates (p. 13) that 25 percent of the men conscripted in Moscow and the provinces for work in St. Petersburg were brickmakers.

90. Luppov, *Istoriia stroitel'stva*, pp. 99–113.

91. Semevskii, no. 26. Drawing on the records of the Customs House at Archangel, the British ambassador informed London early in 1707 that Russian imports in 1706 included "9,041 staves of iron," "190 boxes window glasses," and "54 barrels of steele" (BL Addl. MS. 37, 355, ff. 302–5). A similar source indicates that in 1714 Russian imports via Riga included quantities of steel, iron, tin, lead, and "13 chests" of glass (Public Record Office, London, SP 91/107: report of George Mackenzie, ff. 26–27).

92. *Istoriia stroitel'stva*, pp. 112–13.

93. *PiB*, vol. 9, pt. I, no. 3259.

94. G. E. Kochin, "Naselenie Peterburga do 60-kh godov XVIII v.," in Viatkin, *Ocherki istorii Leningrada*, pp. 94–102; also Luppov, *Istoriia stroitel'stva*, pp. 23, 26, 28–30, 45.

95. *PSZ*, vol. 4, nos. 2536, 2540, 2563; vol. 5, nos. 2747, 2788, 2817, 3016, 3118; vol. 6, no. 3339; vol. 7, no. 4474; etc. As early as 1708 less formal orders were summoning Moscow's leading citizens to St. Petersburg, as the British ambassador reported to London in April of that year (Bl. Addl. Ms. 31,128, f. 132). Forced settlement of workers had taken place since 1703, of course.

96. *PSZ*, vol. 5, nos. 2732, 2737, 2760, 2766, 2784, 3051, 3115; vol. 6, nos. 3620, 3672, 3959; vol. 7, no. 4475; etc. See further I. I. Liubimenko, "Torgovlia v Peterburge," in Predtechenskii, *Peterburg*, especially pp. 75–80.

97. *PSZ*, vol. 5, nos. 2830, 2972; *PSZ*, vol. 6, no. 3589. See also J. Cracraft, *The Church Reform of Peter the Great* (Stanford, 1971), pp. 147–48, 157–62, 165 ff.

98. *PSZ*, vol. 5, nos. 2972, 2850, 2855, 2852; *Opis. I*, nos. 86, 119, 122, 121.

99. *PSZ*, vol. 5, no. 2848; *Opis. I*, no. 118. The ban was lifted—but only with regard to churches that in 1714 had already begun to be built—in 1721 (*PSZ*, vol. 6, no. 3706); it was lifted completely, with regard to Moscow, only in 1728 (*PSZ*, vol. 8, no. 5233).

100. E.g., *PSZ*, vol. 5, nos. 2932, 3192 (decrees of September 1715 and April 1718); or vol. 6, nos. 3777, 3799, 3822 (decrees of April, June, August 1721).

101. E.g., *PSZ*, vol. 5, nos. 3305, 3348; vol. 6, nos. 3505, 3538, 3766; vol. 7, no. 4405, 4439, 4505.

102. Ibid., vol. 5, no. 3348; vol. 6, no. 3766.

103. Ibid., vol. 6, no. 3777.

104. Luppov, *Istoriia stroitel'stva*, pp. 23–24, with modifications by me. See also Sytina, "Arkhitekturnoe zakonodatel'stvo," especially pp. 69 ff.

105. See Dubiago, *Sady i parki*, and Evangulova, *Dvortsovo-parkovye ansambli*; and cf. M. Laurie, *An Introduction to Landscape Architecture* (New York,

1977), pp. 13 ff., and especially C. Thacker, *The History of Gardens* (Berkeley, 1979), pp. 81 ff.

106. Palentreer, "Sady v Izmailove," pp. 80–103.

107. C. Le Brun (C. de Bruyn), *Voyages en Moscovie*, vol. 2 (Amsterdam, 1718), p. 37.

108. Ibid.

109. The records of his personal office show, e.g., that between 1711 and 1715 several European gardeners—notably Denis Brouquet—were in Peter's pay working with the assistance of hundreds of laborers on projects in St. Petersburg (TsGADA, F. 396, kn. 1080 passim).

110. *Opis. I*, appendix 4 (pp. 524–27); Iogansen, *Zemtsov*, p. 38.

111. Much of Peter's own graphic legacy is so connected; see again works cited in n. 27, this chapter, especially Shilkov, "Chetyre risunka"; Voronkhina, *Peterburg v chertezhakh*, nos. 9, 19; and Murzanova, no. 59 and p. 253.

112. Dubiago, *Letnii sad*, pp. 74–77; Egorova, *Leningrad*, pp. 7–12, figs. 10–89.

113. *PiB*, vol. 7, no. 2323, and pp. 511–12; vol. 8, pt. II, p. 576; vol. 9, pt. I, no 2979.

114. Ibid., vol. 7, pt. I, p. 512.

115. The standard work is Arkhipov and Raskin, *Petrodvorets*, with documents. See also Gurevich, *Bol'shoi Petergofskii dvorets;* and the splendid Raskin, *Petrodvorets (Peterhof)*, with 236 photographs and text in English.

116. T. A. Gatova, "Iz istorii dekorativnoi skulptury Moskvy nachala XVIII v.," in Alekseeva, *Russkoe iskusstvo* (1973), pp. 31–44.

117. Lisaevich, *Pervyi arkhitektor*, p. 100.

118. N. V. Kaliazina, "Lepnoi dekor v zhilom inter'ere Peterburga pervoi chetverti XVIII v.," in Alekseeva, *Russkoe iskusstvo* (1974), pp. 109–18.

119. N. V. Kaliazina, "Monumental'no-dekorativnaia zhivopis' v dvortsovom inter'ere pervoi chetverti XVIII v.," in Alekseeva, *Russkoe iskusstvo* (1977), pp. 55–69; Kaliazina, "Ob inter'ere paradnogo zala vtorogo Zimnego dvortsa," *Soobshcheniia gos. Ermitazha* 35 (1972), pp. 30–33; and, more generally, Bartenev and Batazhkova, *Russkii inter'er*, especially pp. 5–19, stressing the sharp break in the history of Russian interior design and decoration that occurred under Peter I.

120. Raskin, *Petrodvorets (Peterhof)*, p. 302. For the nearly contemporary report quoted, see Staehlin, pp. 69–70, 383.

121. Henry Storch, *The Picture of Petersburg* (London, 1801), p. 274. See further N. Iu. Biriukova, "Western European Tapestries in the Hermitage," *Burlington Magazine* 57, no. 749 (1963), pp. 415–16 and pls. 19–22; V. K. Makarov, "Sud'ba odnogo khudozhestvennogo zamysla Petra I," *Trudy gos. Ermitazha* 11 (1970), pp. 122–30; and T. T. Korshunova, "Novye materialy o sozdanii shpaler

'Poltavskaia bataliia'," in Komelova, *Kul'tura petrovskogo vremeni*, pp. 163–73.

122. Quoting A. I. Leonov, "Russkoe dekorativnoe iskusstvo XVIII veka," in Leonov, *Russkoe dekorativnoe iskusstvo*, 2:8. Cf. P. Thornton, *Seventeenth-Century Interior Decoration in England, France and Holland* (New Haven and London, 1978), with numerous illustrations and further references.

123. L. Réau, *Pierre le Grand* (Paris, 1960), pp. 128–33, 138–47; also Vipper, *Arkhitektura russkogo barokko*, p. 49.

124. Kochin, pp. 101–2; also TsGADA, F. 9, otd. II, kn. 64, ll. 200–201, 167–72; and Kirilov, pp. 44–45, 61–62, as cited above (n. 78, this chapter).

125. Figures drawn from Uspenskii, *Imperatorskie dvortsy*, 1:1–182; see also names listed in Lo Gatto, *Gli artisti*, 2:131–33.

126. Figures drawn from A. I. Uspenskii, *Tsarskie ikonopistsy i zhivopistsy XVII v.*, vol. 1: *Slovar'* (M., 1910), passim.

127. The point is made repeatedly by Kaliazina, in the works cited above (n. 119, this chapter); also by I. M. Sukhanova, "Sadovo-parkovaia skul'ptura i fontany," in Leonov, *Russkoe dekorativnoe iskusstvo*, 2:183, n. 1; and by Dubiago, "Usad'by petrovskogo vremeni," pp. 125–40.

Chapter 7

1. *Lettres du comte Algarotti sur la Russie* (London and Paris, 1769), p. 69.

2. Details from Luppov, *Istoriia stroitel'stva*, pp. 42, 45, 150, 155–56, 160–61, 166; Bater, *St. Petersburg*, pp. 42 ff.; Predtechenskii, *Peterburg*, pp. 75–92; Viatkin, *Ocherki istorii Leningrada*, 1:101–2; and N. I. Tsylov, *Plany S. Peterburga v 1700 . . . i 1849 godakh* (SPb., 1853), passim.

3. BL Addl. MS. 37,359, ff. 240–41; see also the published version of same, C. Whitworth, *An Account of Russia as it was in the Year 1710* (Strawberry Hill, 1758), pp. 128–29.

4. *Exacte Relation von der von Sr. Szaarschen Majestät Petro Alexiowitz . . . an dem grossen Newa Strohm und der Ost-See neu erbauten Festung und Stadt St. Petersburg* (Leipzig, 1713); Russian translation published in *Russkaia starina* 36 (1882), pp. 33–60, 293–312. For Baron Huyssen, see P. Petschauer, "In Search of Competent Aides: Heinrich van Huyssen and Peter the Great," *JGO* 36, no. 4 (1978), pp. 481–502.

5. *Eigentliche Beschreibung der an der Spitz der Ost-See neuerbaueten Residentz-Stadt St.-Petersburg* (Frankfurt and Leipzig, 1718).

6. "A Description of the City of St. Petersbourg," in F. C. Weber, *The Present State of Russia*, vol. 1 (London, 1723), pp. 297–344; also the related "Description of Cronslot," ibid., pp. 345–52. On the

relation to one another of these and the two German descriptions just cited, see Luppov, *Istoriia stroitel'stva*, pp. 8–9; also, the "Translator's Preface" to Weber's book, which indicates that the translation was done in consultation with Weber himself and that his description of St. Petersburg was taken from one "published before by M. Schutz in High-Dutch [German], though our author [Weber] has adapted it to his own observations" (Weber, p. A3).

7. Weber, pp. 41–42.

8. S. L. Ptashitskii, ed. and trans., "Peterburg v 1720 godu. Zapiska poliak-ochevidtsa," *Russkaia starina* 25 (1879), pp. 26–27.

9. Weber, pp. 43–44, 102, 167.

10. Ibid., pp. 182–83, 238–39.

11. Ibid., pp. 184–85.

12. E. V. Williams, *The Bells of Russia: History and Technology* (Princeton, 1985), pp. 82–84. Here we also learn that the carillon, the first in Russia, cost 45,000 rubles—an enormous sum at the time—and that its clock mechanism struck the quarters and the half hours and played the bells automatically every hour; also, that at noon each day one Johann Christian Förster performed selections on the bells while the technician responsible for maintaining the instrument was a man named Drunk *(sic)* Miller.

13. Weber, pp. 4, 190.

14. These and the following quotations are all from Weber's "Description of the City of St. Petersbourg" as cited above (n. 6, this chapter).

15. These and the following quotations are from Weber's "Description of Cronslot" as cited above (n. 6, this chapter).

16. Bergholtz's diary was first published in successive issues of *Buschings Magazin für die neue Histoire und Geographie* printed at Halle between 1785 and 1787 (Bergholtz had met Busching in Wismar, where he lived from 1746 until his death in 1771). A Russian translation of this German edition of the diary by I. F. Ammon was published in four parts in Moscow between 1857 and 1860 and again between 1859 and 1862. In 1902–3 a third Russian edition of the Ammon translation, by P. Bartenev, was published in Moscow, still with the title *Dnevnik Kameriunkera F. V. Berkhgol'tsa, 1721–1725*. See further N. Pavlov-Sil'vanskii, "Berkhgol'ts, F. V.," *Russkii biograficheskii slovar'*, vol. 2 (SPb., 1900), pp. 755–57.

17. All subsequent quotations are from the third Russian edition (1902–3) of Bergholtz's diary, in my translation. For the architectural drawings referred to, which were collected by Bergholtz during a later stay in Russia (1742–46) as tutor to the future Emperor Peter III, see Hallstrom, *Architectural Drawings*.

18. P. Deschisaux, *Déscription d'un voyage fait à Saint Petersbourg* (Paris, 1728), especially pp. 16–24. For Deschisaux and his interest in St. Petersburg, see also his *Mémoire pour servir à l'instruction de l'histoire*

naturelle des plantes de Russie et à l'établissement d'un jardin botanique à Saint-Petersbourg (Paris, 1725).

19. Aubry de LaMottraye, *Voyages en divers provinces* (The Hague, 1732), pp. 224–74, with parallel texts in French and English (the latter, not always faithful to the former, is sometimes corrected here).

20. *Letters from a Lady, who resided some years in Russia, to her friend in England,* 2d ed. (London, 1777; facsimile reprint, New York, 1970; 1st ed., London, 1775), pp. 2–6, 7–8. The lady of the title is Jane, Mrs. Thomas Ward, later Lady Rondeau and then, at the time of publication, Mrs. William Vigor (see A. G. Cross, *Russia under Western Eyes, 1517–1825* [New York, 1971], p. 385).

21. B. Kemp, ed., "Sir Francis Dashwood's Diary of His Visit to St. Petersburg in 1733," *Slavonic and East European Review* 38 (1959–60), pp. 194–213.

22. See Luppov, *Istoriia stroitel'stva,* pp. 94 ff.

23. F. Algarotti, pp. 43–109. For the celebrated words just quoted, see p. 64.

24. J. Hanway, *An Historical Account of the British Trades over the Caspian Sea,* 4 vols. (London, 1753), 1:82; 2:131, 135–36.

25. *The Picture of Petersburg: From the German of Henry Storch* (London, 1801; German edition, *Gemähldе von Sanct Petersburg,* published Riga, 1794). Storch's preface is dated St. Petersburg, 1792; but it is clear from internal references that the work was brought up to date for the English edition. The quotations from Storch that follow are found, in this order, on pp. 9–10, 29, 30–32, 48, 53, 24–26, 24, 53, 87–89, 279–80, 287, 281, 291.

26. Cf. H. H. Kaplan, "Observations on the Value of Russia's Overseas Commerce with Great Britain during the Second Half of the Eighteenth Century," *Slavic Review* 45, no. 1 (1986), pp. 88, 85–94 passim.

27. Storch, p. 277.

Chapter 8

1. I. P. Eremin, ed., *Feofan Prokopovich: sochineniia* (M./L., 1961), p. 136.

2. See Komelova, " 'Panorama Peterburga'—graviura raboty A. F. Zubova," in Komelova, *Kul'tura petrovskogo vremeni,* pp. 111–43.

3. N. Pevsner, *Academies of Art Past and Present* (Cambridge, 1940; reprinted New York, 1973); also G. Scavizzi, "Art Academies from the 16th to the 18th Century," *Encyclopedia of World Art,* vol. 8 (New York, 1963), cols. 150–58.

4. Moleva and Beliutin, *Pedagogicheskaia sistema Akademii khudozhestv XVIII veka,* p. 15. This is a major work, rich in documentation and illustrative material.

5. TsGADA, F. 9, otd. I, kn. 53, 1. 570.

6. Moleva and Beliutin, *Pedagogicheskaia sistema,* pp. 19–22; E. I. Gavrilova, "O pervykh proektakh

Akademii khudozhestv v Rossii," in Alekseeva, *Russkoe iskusstvo* (1971), pp. 220–23. The original of Avramov's 1721 proposal is at TsGADA, F. 9, otd. II, d. 57, 11. 48–50.

7. Moleva and Beliutin, *Pedagogicheskaia sistema,* pp. 223–27; also E. I. Gavrilova, "Istoki i predposylki akademicheskoi shkoly risunka v Rossii XVIII veka," Kand. diss. (M., 1970), with texts of the various projects appended.

8. TsGIA, F. 467, op. 4/401, 1727 g.; Borisova, "Arkhitekturnoe obrazovanie," pp. 97–131.

9. Moleva and Beliutin, *Pedagogicheskaia sistema,* pp. 29–65.

10. *Privilegiia i ustav Imperatorskoi Akademii trekh znateishikh khudozhestv, Zhivopisi, Skulptury i Arkhitektury, s vospitatel'nym pri onoi akademii uchililishchem* (SPb., 1765).

11. Moleva and Beliutin, *Pedagogicheskaia sistema,* pp. 66 ff.; Lisovskii, *Akademiia khudozhestv;* Petrov, *Sbornik materialov.* See also I. A. Pronina, "Nikola Fransua Zhilli—pedagog i master dekorativnoi skul'ptury," and V. V. Antonov, "Zhivopistsy-dekoratory Skotti v Rossii," both in Alekseeva, *Russkoe iskusstvo* (1979), pp. 137–44 and 69–107, for studies of important French and Italian decorative artists active in later eighteenth-century Russia under the Academy's auspices; and M. V. Iogansen, "Raboty Kvarengi na Strelke Vasil'evskogo ostrova v Peterburge," in ibid., pp. 7–17, which concentrates on little-studied works in St. Petersburg by the Academy's Giacomo Quarenghi, a leading exponent in the 1780s and 1790s of Neoclassicism.

12. Petrov, *Sbornik materialov,* pp. 9–10.

13. Pevsner, pp. 181–83.

14. The best work in English on Catherine II is I. de Madariaga, *Russia in the Age of Catherine the Great* (New Haven and London, 1981), although, strangely, it has nothing to say about architecture. For Catherine's words, just quoted, see Shkvarikov, *Ocherki istorii planirovki,* p. 83.

15. Sytin, *Istoriia Moskvy,* 1:232–33.

16. PSZ, vol. 8, no. 5233.

17. Kudriavtseva, "Kadashevskaia sloboda," pp. 38–48.

18. Evangulova, *Dvortsovo-parkovye ansambli Moskvy,* pp. 35–98. See also Il'ch, "O russkikh usad'-bakh," pp. 157–73, and, for a well-illustrated study of a prominent example, Seminova, *Ostankino.*

19. Mikhailov, *Arkhitektor Ukhtomskii;* also Evangulova, "O nekotorykh osobennostiakh Moskovskoi arkhitekturnoi shkoly serediny XVIII v.," pp. 259–69, and Gulianitskii, "Gradostroitel'nye osobennosti Peterburga i cherty russkoi arkhitektury serediny XVIII v.," pp. 12–21.

20. J. T. Alexander, *Bubonic Plague in Early Modern Russia: Public Health and Urban Disaster* (Baltimore, 1980), p. 62. This fine study of the Moscow

plague of 1770–72 includes a detailed description of the city (pp. 61–97).

21. Ibid., pp. 78–79; also Zombe, "Proekt plana Moskvy," pp. 53–96.

22. Loktev, "O Bazhenovskom proekte," pp. 356–77; also Chernov and Shishko, *Bazhenov*, and Grabar', *Neizvestnye postroiki Bazhenova.*

23. Cf. Schmidt, "Restoration of Moscow," pp. 37–48.

24. W. Coxe, *Travels in Poland, Russia, Sweden, and Denmark*, vol. 1, 5th ed. (London, 1802), pp. 283–84. Coxe recokoned Moscow's population at roughly 250,000 "within the ramparts" and another 50,000 "in the adjacent villages" (pp. 282–83).

25. J. Cracraft, ed., "James Brogden in Russia, 1787–1788," *Slavonic and East European Review* 47, no. 108 (1969), p. 241.

26. Sytina, "Arkhitektura russkoi provintsii," p. 139.

27. Shkvarikov, *Ocherki istorii planirovki*, p. 63; also Shkvarikov, *Planirovka gorodov Rossii* and Shkvarikov, *Gradostroitel'stvo*, pp. 204–37; and A. A. Maksimov, "Torgovye tsentry v planirovkakh russkikh gorodov vtoroi poloviny XVIII–nachala XIX v.," in Vygolov, *Pamiatniki russkoi arkhitektury*, pp. 126–39.

28. *PSZ*, vol. 7, no. 4224; also Kargar, *Novgorod Velikii*, p. 55.

29. S. S. Bronshtein, "Peterburgskaia arkhitektura 20-30-kh godov XVIII veka," in Grabar' et al., *Russkaia arkhitektura*, p. 181. The "concept of *reguliarnost'*" permeates the first extensive work on architecture produced in Russia, the "treatise-codex" prepared by the Commission for the Construction of St. Petersburg in 1737–40: see Arkin, " 'Dolzhnost' Arkhitekturnoi Ekspeditsii': traktat-kodeks 1737–1740 godov," noting especially Arkin's comments on pp. 1, 13 ff. (complete text of the work on pp. 21–99). Proskuriakova points out that in eighteenth-century Russia, beginning with Peter I, the term *reguliarnost'* and its adjective, *reguliarnyi*, acquired beyond its more strictly architectural meanings such aesthetic and moral connotations as "respectable" or "decent," "durable" or "permanent," "proper," "beautiful," "correct," and "good" (Proskuriakova, "O Reguliarnosti," pp. 37–46).

30. Sytina, "Arkhitektura russkoi provintsii," pp. 141–44.

31. See Krasheninnikova's detailed studies of Orenburg in the eighteenth century: "Printsipy reguliarnoi planirovki," pp. 14–23; "Oblik russkogo goroda," pp. 72–75; "K voprosu planirovki," pp. 140–46.

32. See further J. H. Bater's introduction to Bater and R. A. French, eds., *Studies in Russian Historical Geography*, vol. 2 (New York, 1983), pp. 243–44; Hittle, *Service City*; Klokman, *Istoriia russkogo*

goroda, especially pp. 31–52; Klokman, "Gorod v zakonodatel'stve," pp. 320–54; and B. Knabe, *Die struktur der russischen Posadgemeinden und der Beschwerden und Forderungen der Kaufmannschaft (1762–1767)* (Berlin, 1975).

33. In addition to works by Krasheninnikova cited above (n. 31, this chapter), see her "Stroitel'stvo po 'obraztsovym' proektam," pp. 72–78; also Proskuriakova, "Planirovochnye kompozitsii gorodov-krepostei Sibiri," pp. 57–71, and Proskuriakova, "Staroe i novoe v gradostroitel'stve Sibiri," pp. 53–66.

34. See Proskuriakova, "Osobennosti Sibirskogo barokko," pp. 147–60; V. I. Pluzhnikov, "Organizatsiia fasada v arkhitekture russkogo barokko," in Alekseeva, *Russkoe iskusstvo* (1977), pp. 88–127; and V. P. Vygolov, "Arkhitektura barokko v Tot'me," in Vygolov, *Pamiatniki russkoi arkhitektury*, pp. 103–25 for studies in the rusticalization of Russian Baroque architecture. Baklanov, "Evoliutsiia arkhitekturnykh form v russkom provintsial'nom tserkovnom zodchestve XVIII v.," as its title indicates, is a more general study of the problem.

35. Tel'tevskii, "Zhilye doma," p. 148.

36. Coxe, pp. 218–19, 291–92.

37. Hans Jakob Fries, *A Siberian Journey*, ed. and trans. W. Kirchner (London, 1974), pp. 104–5, 111, 139.

38. *PSZ*, vol. 16, no. 11,883. See also A. S. Shchenkov, "Opyt rekonstruktsii plana Tvery kontsa XVII v.," *AN*, no. 28 (1980), pp. 29–36.

39. Quoted in Jones, "Urban Planning," p. 326.

40. Cf. J. Hartley, "Town Government in Saint Petersburg Guberniya after the Charter to the Towns of 1785," *Slavonic and East European Review* 62, no. 1 (1984), pp. 61–84; also H. D. Hudson, "Urban Estate Engineering in Eighteenth-Century Russia: Catherine the Great and the Elusive *Meshchanstvo*," *Canadian-American Slavic Studies* 18, no. 4 (1984), pp. 393–410.

41. Cf. Gulianitskii, "Cherty preemstvennosti," pp. 3–17, and Gulianitski, "Russkii reguliarnyi gorod," pp. 3–13, which stress this and other features of continuity, as well as rusticalization (without using the word), in eighteenth-century Russian town planning; similarly, Proskuriakova, "O preemstvennosti," pp. 40–51.

42. Jones, "Urban Planning," pp. 338–40. See also Lavrov, *Razvitie planirovochnoi struktury*, especially pp. 143 ff.; Beletskaia, *"Obraztsovye" proekty*, pp. 59 ff.; works by Shkvarikov cited above (e.g., n. 27, this chapter), passim; and articles by V. Shilkov, B. Vasil'ev, and D. Arkin on the planning of St. Petersburg and other Russian towns in the eighteenth century, in *AN*, no. 4 (1953), pp. 7–13, 14–29, 30–38 and no. 7 (1955), pp. 13–38.

43. Degtiarev, *Russkaia derevnia*; A. A. Shennik-

ov, "Poseleniia," in A. V. Artsikhovskii, ed., *Ocherki russkoi kul'tury XVII veka,* vol. 1 (M, 1979), pp. 165–83.

44. *PSZ,* vol. 6, no. 4070; also *Opis. I,* no. 697, reproducing part of the illustrative plan attached to the printed decree (see fig. 136).

45. Cf. Ikonnikov, "Planirovochnye traditsii v narodnom zodchestve," pp. 159–84.

46. See Nekrasov, *Russkii ampir;* Grimm, *Arkhitektura klassitsizma,* with 193 plates; Nikolaev, *Klassicheskaia Moskva;* R. M. Baiburova, "Russki usadebnyi inter'er epokhi klassitsizma," in Vygolov, *Pamiatniki russkoi arkhitektury,* pp. 140–61; Gulianitskii, "Tvorcheskie metody klassitsizma," pp. 30–52; Lossky, "Thomas, dit de Thomon," pp. 591–604; Grabar' et al., *Istoriia* (1961), 6:411 ff.; and Schmidt, "Restoration of Moscow," pp. 37–48.

47. Cf. Brumfield, *Gold in Azure,* pp. 325 ff. See further Schmidt, "Architecture in Nineteenth-Century Russia," pp. 172–93; J. Bowlt, "Art and Architecture in Soviet Russia, 1917–1972," in Auty and Obolensky, *Introduction,* pp. 164–72; V. S. Terekhov, *Russkaia natsional'naia arkhitektura/Russian National Architecture* (Frankfurt/Main, 1983); S. F. Starr, *Melnikov: Solo Architect in a Mass Society* (Princeton, 1978); E. Dluhosch, "The Failure of the Soviet Avantgarde," *Oppositions: A Journal for Ideas and Criticism in Architecture,* no. 10 (1977), pp. 31–55; El Lissitzky, *Russia: An Architecture for World Revolution,* trans. E. Dluhosch (Cambridge, Mass. 1984); A. Kopp, *Constructivist Architecture in the USSR* (London and New York, 1985); and Kopp, *L'Architecture de la période stalinienne* (Grenoble, 1978).

Bibliography

The following list includes the most important works consulted in writing this book as well as all known works of relevance published in English. It does not include documentary sources, printed or manuscript, or highly specialized studies in Russian (or languages other than English) of strictly limited interest here; in all such cases full citations are provided in the appropriate notes to the text. Nor does the list include standard reference works, cited or uncited, or even major scholarly works of only peripheral or general interest. The list is meant to serve as a basic bibliography of Russian architectural history of the period 1650–1800.

Afanas'ev, K. N. *Postroenie arkhitekturnoi formy drevnerusskimi zodchimi.* M., 1961.

Alekseeva, T. V., ed. *Russkoe iskusstvo barokko: materialy i issledovaniia.* M., 1977.

———, ed. *Russkoe iskusstvo XVIII-pervoi poloviny XIX veka: materialy i issledovaniia.* M., 1971.

———, ed. *Russkoe iskusstvo XVIII veka: materialy i issledovaniia.* M., 1968.

———, ed. *Russkoe isskustvo XVIII veka: materialy i issledovaniia.* M., 1973.

———, ed. *Russkoe iskusstvo pervoi chetverti XVIII veka: materialy i issledovaniia.* M., 1974.

———, ed. *Russkoe iskusstvo vtoroi poloviny XVIII-pervoi poloviny XIX v.: materialy i issledovaniia.* M., 1979.

Alferova, G. V. "Gosudarstvennaia sistema stroitel'stva gorodov i osvoenie novykh zemel' v XVI–XVII vv. (na primere g. Kozlova i ego uezda)." *AN*, no. 27 (1979).

———. "K voprosu o stroitel'noi deiatel'nosti Patriarkha Nikona." *AN*, no. 18 (1969).

———. "K voprosu o stroitel'stve gorodov v Moskovskom gosudarstve v XVI–XVII vv." *AN*, no. 28 (1980).

———. *Pamiatnik russkogo zodchestva v Kadashakh.* M., 1974.

Alpatov, M., and N. Brunov. *Geschichte der Altrussischen Kunst.* 2 vols. Augsberg, 1932.

Anon. *Moskva zlatoglavaia: Pamiatniki religioznogo zodchestva Moskvy v proshlom i nastoiaschem.* Paris, 1980.

Anon. *Razrushennye i oskvernennye khramy: Moskva i Srednaia Rossiia s poslesloviem "Peredely vandalizma."* Frankfurt/Main, 1980.

Anuchin, D. N., et al. *Moskva v eia proshlom i nastoiashchem.* 10 vols. M. [1909].

Arenkova, Iu. I., and G. I. Mekhova. *Donskoi monastyr'.* M., 1970.

Arkhipov, N. I., and A. G. Raskin. *Bartolomeo Karlo Rastrelli, 1675–1744.* L./M., 1964.

Arkin, D. " 'Dolzhnost' Arkhitekturnoi Ekspeditsii': traktat-kodeks 1737–1740 godov." *Arkhitekturnyi arkhiv* 1 (M., 1946).

Auty, R., and D. Obolensky, eds. *An Introduction to Russian Art and Architecture.* Cambridge, 1980.

Bagrov, L. *A History of Russian Cartography up to 1800.* Edited by H. W. Castner. Wolfe Island, Ontario, 1975.

Baklanov, N. B. "Evoliutsiia arkhitekturnykh form v russkom provintsial'nom tserkovnom zodchestve XVIII v." *Izvestiia Rossiiskoi Akademii Istorii material'noi kul'tury* 2 (1922).

Bartenev, S. P. *Moskovskii kreml' v starinu i teper'.* M., 1912.

Bater, J. H. *St. Petersburg, Industrialization and Change.* London, 1976.

Beletskaia, E., et al. *"Obraztsovye" proekty v zhiloi zastroike russkikh gorodov XVIII–XIX vv.* M., 1961.

Benua (Benois), A. *Tsarskoe selo v tsarstvovaniia Imp. Elizavety Petrovny.* SPb., 1910.

Berton, K. *Moscow: An Architectural History.* New York, 1977.

Bezsonov, S. V. "Rassvet ukrainskoi arkhitektury v period vossoedineniia Ukrainy s Rossiei." *AN,* no. 8 (1957).

Bogdanov, G. *Istoricheskoe, geograficheskoe i topograficheskoe opisanie Sanktpeterburga, ot nachala zavedeniia ego, s 1703 po 1751 god.* Edited by V. Ruban. SPb., 1779. (With numerous plates from Bogdanov's original [1751] edition.)

Borisova, E. A. "Arkhitekturnoe obrazovanie v Kantseliarii ot stroenii vo vtoroi chetverti XVIII veka." *Ezhegodnik III 1960.* M., 1961.

Bozherianov, I. N. *Nevskii prospekt: kul'turno-istoricheskii ocherk dvukhvekovoi zhizni S.-Peterburga.* SPb., 1901.

———. *S.-Peterburg v Petrovo vremia.* SPb., 1901.

Braitseva, O. I. "Nekotorye osobennosti ordernykh kompositsii v russkoi arkhitekture rubezha XVII–XVIII vv." *AN,* no. 18 (1969).

———. "Novoe i traditsionnoe v khramovom zodchestve Moskvy kontsa XVII v." *AN,* no. 26 (1978).

———. "Novoe v kompozitsii vkhodov russkikh khramov kontsa XVII v." *AN,* no. 23 (1975).

———. "Novye konstruktivnye priemy v russkoi arkhitekture kontsa XVII-nachala XVIII veka." *AN,* no. 12 (1960).

———. "Tvorcheskii metod zodchikh nachala XVIII v." *AN,* no. 21 (1973).

Bronshtein, S. S. *Arkhitektura goroda Pushkina.* M., 1940.

Brumfield, W. C. *Gold in Azure: One Thousand Years of Russian Architecture.* Boston, 1983.

Brunov, N. I., et al. *Istoriia russkoi arkhitektury.* 2d ed. M., 1956.

Bunin, A. W. *Geschichte des Russischen Stadtebaues bis zum 19. Jahrhundert.* Berlin, 1961.

Buxton, D. R. *Russian Medieval Architecture.* Cambridge, 1934.

———. *The Wooden Churches of Eastern Europe: An Introductory Survey.* Cambridge, 1981.

Čarniauskaja (Charniavskaia), T. I. *Arkhitektura Mahilova.* Minsk, 1973.

Chanturiia, V. A. *Arkhitekturnye pamiatniki Belorussii.* Minsk, 1982.

———. *Istoriia arkhitektury Belorussii: dooktiabr'skii period.* 2d ed. Minsk, 1977.

Chernov, E. G., and A. V. Shishko. *Bazhenov.* M., 1949.

Chiniakov, A. G. "O nekotorykh osobennostiakh drevne-russkogo gradostroitel'stva." *AN,* no. 12 (1960).

Degtiarev, A. Ia. *Russkaia derevia v XV–XVII vekakh: ocherki istorii sel'skogo rasseleniia.* L., 1980.

Denisov, Iu. M., and A. N. Petrov. *Zodchii Rastrelli: Novye materialy i issledovaniia.* L., 1963.

Dubiago, T. B. *Letnii sad.* M./L., 1951.

———. *Russkie reguliarnye sady i parki.* M., 1963.

———. "Usad'by petrovskogo vremeni v okrestnostiakh Peterburga." *AN,* no. 4 (1953).

Duffy, L. *Siege Warfare: The Fortress in the Early Modern World, 1494–1660.* Boston, 1979.

Dyshlenko, B., et al. *Kuskovo: Gosudarstvennyi muzei keramiki i usad'ba XVIII veka.* L., 1983.

Eaton, H. L. "Decline and Recovery of the Russian Cities from 1500 to 1700." *Canadian-American Slavic Studies* 11, no. 2 (1977).

Egorov, Iu. A. *Ansambl' v gradostroitel'stve SSSR: Ocherki.* M., 1961.

———. *The Architectural Planning of St. Petersburg.* Edited and translated by E. Dluhosch. Athens, Ohio, 1969.

Egorova, K. M. *Leningrad: House of Peter I, Summer Garden and Palace of Peter I.* Translated by L. Barnes and J. Monroe. L., 1975.

Ehret, J. "Domenico Trezzini aus Astano. Der erste Erbauer von St. Petersburg." *Zeitschrift für schweizerische Archäologie und Kunstgeschichte* 12 (1951).

———. "Piero Antonio und Carlo Guiseppe Trezzini, Domenico Trezzinis Nachfolger in St. Petersburg." *Zeitschrift für schweizerische Archäologie und Kunstgeschichte* 12, (1952).

Epifanov, P. P. "Kreposti." In A. V. Artsikhovskii, ed., *Ocherki russkoi kul'tury XVII veka*, vol. 1. M., 1979.

Evangulova, O. S. *Dvortsovo-parkovye ansambli Moskvy pervoi poloviny XVIII veka*. M., 1969.

⸻. "O nekotorykh osobennostiakh Moskovskoi arkhitekturnoi shkoly serediny XVIII v." In V. L. Ianin, ed., *Russkii gorod (istoriko-metodologicheskii sbornik)*. M., 1976.

Evsina, N. A. *Arkhitekturnaia teoriia v Rossii XVIII v.* M., 1975.

Faensen, H., and V. Ivanov. *Early Russian Architecture*. Translated by M. Whittall. London, 1975.

Fal'kovskii, N. I. *Moskva v istorii tekhniki*. M., 1950.

Filippova, L. A. *"Vitoslavlitsy"—Muzei dereviannogo zodchestva*. L., 1979.

Fiodorov, B. *Architecture of the Russian North*. L., 1976.

French, R. A. "The Early and Medieval Russian Town." In J. H. Bater and R. A. French, eds., *Studies in Russian Historical Geography*, vol. 2. New York, 1983.

Fride, M. A. "Russkie dereviannye ukrepleniia po drevnim literaturnym istochnikam." *Izvestiia Rossiiskoi akademii istorii Material'noi kul'tury* 3 (1924).

Geyer, D. "Peter und St. Petersburg." JGO 10, no. 2 (1962).

Gol'denberg, P. and B. *Planirovka zhilogo kvartala Moskvy XVII, XVIII i XIX vv.* M./L., 1935.

Grabar', I. [E.] "Arkhitektory-inostrantsy pri Petre Velikom." *Starye gody* (July–September 1911).

⸻. *Neizvestnye i predpologaemye postroiki V. I. Bazhenova*. M., 1951.

⸻. *O russkoi arkhitekture*. M., 1969.

Grabar', I. [E.], et al. *Istoriia russkago iskusstva*. 4 vols. M. [1909–14].

⸻. *Istoriia russkogo iskusstva*. 13 vols. M., 1953–69.

⸻. *Russkaia arkhitektura pervoi poloviny XVIII veka: issledovaniia i materialy*. M., 1954.

Grimm, G. G. *Arkhitektura perekrytii russkogo klassitsizma*. L., 1939.

Grozmani, M. V. "Stroitel'stvo i pervonachal'nyi oblik zdanii 12 Kollegii." *Vestnik Leningradskogo universiteta*, ser. obshchest. nauk, 1953, no. 6, pt. II.

Gulianitskii, N. F. "Cherty preemstvennosti v kompozitsii tsentrov russkikh gorodov, pereplanirovannykh v XVIII v." *AN*, no. 29 (1981).

⸻. "Gradostroitel'nye osobennosti Peterburga v cherty russkoi arkhitektury serediny XVIII v." *AN*, no. 27 (1979).

⸻. "Russkii reguliarnyi gorod na traditsionnoi osnove." *AN*, no. 33 (1985).

⸻. "Tserkov' Pokrova v Medvedkove i russkoe zodchestvo XVI–XVII vv." *AN*, no. 28 (1980).

⸻. "Tvorcheskie metody arkhitektorov russkogo klassitsizma pri razrabotke ordernykh kompozitsii." *AN*, no. 22 (1974).

Gurevich, I. M., et al. *Bol'shoi Petergofskii dvorets*. L., 1979.

Gutkind. E. A., et al. *Urban Development in East-Central Europe: Poland, Czechoslovakia, and Hungary*. New York, 1972.

⸻. *Urban Development in Eastern Europe: Bulgaria, Romania, and the USSR*. New York, 1972.

Hall, A. T. "The Royal Gates of the Pechersk Lavra: The Evolution of the Kievan Baroque and Rococo." Ph.D. diss., University of Southern California, 1984.

Hällstrom, B. *Der Architector A. Schlüter in Petersburg*. Stockholm, 1961.

⸻. *Russian Architectural Drawings in the National Museum*. Stockholm, 1963.

Hamilton, G. H. *The Art and Architecture of Russia*. 2d ed. Baltimore, 1975.

Hamm, M. F., ed. *The City in Russian History*. Lexington, Ky., 1976.

Hewryk, T. D. *The Lost Architecture of Kiev*. New York, 1982.

Hittle, J. M. *The Service City: State and Townsmen in Russia, 1600–1800*. Cambridge, Mass., 1979.

Hughes, L. A. J. "Architectural Books in Petrine Russia." In A. G. Cross, ed., *Russia and the West in the Eighteenth Century*. Newtonville, Mass., 1983.

⸻. "Byelorussian Craftsmen in Late Seventeenth-Century Russia and Their Influence on Muscovite Architecture." *Journal of Byelorussian Studies* 3, no. 4 (1976).

————. "Moscow Baroque—a Controversial Style." *Transactions of the Association of Russian-American Scholars in the USA* 15 (1982).

————. "Moscow Baroque Architecture: A Study of One Aspect of Westernization in Late Seventeenth-Century Russia." Ph.D. diss., Cambridge University, 1975.

————. "Western European Graphic Material as a Source for Moscow Baroque Architecture." *Slavonic and East European Review* 55, no. 4 (1977).

Iakovlev, A. *Zasechnaia cherta Moskovskago gosudarstva v XVII veke.* M., 1916.

Ikonnikov, A. V. "Planirovochnye traditsii v narodnom zodchestve." *AN*, no. 14 (1962).

Il'ch, M. A. "K voprosu o russkikh usad'bakh XVIII v." In V. L. Ianin, ed., *Russkii gorod: Moskva i podmoskov'e.* M., 1981.

Il'in, M. A. "Arkhitektura." In A. V. Artsikhovskii, ed., *Ocherki russkoi kul'tury XVII veka,* vol. 1. M., 1979.

————. *Kamennaia letopis' moskovskoi Rusi. Svetskie osnovy kamennogo zodchestva XV–XVII vv.* M., 1966.

————. *Moskva: pamiatniki arkhitektury XIV–XVII vekov.* M., 1973.

————. *Moskva: pamiatniki arkhitektury XVIII–pervoi treti XIX vekov.* 2 vols. M., 1975.

————. "O professional'nyak navykakh drevnerusskikh zodchikh." *Soobshchen. III,* no. 12 (1958).

————. "Problem Moskovskogo barokko' XVII veka." *Ezhegodnik III 1956.* M., 1957.

Ilyin, M. (M. A. Il'in). *Moscow: Architecture and Monuments.* Translated by B. Meares. M., 1968.

Iogansen, M. V. *Mikhail Zemtsov.* L., 1975.

Iurchenko, P. H., et al., eds. *Istoriia ukrains'koho mystetstva,* vol. 3. Kiev, 1968.

Jones, R. E. "Urban Planning and the Development of Provincial Towns in Russia during the Reign of Catherine II." In J. G. Garrard, ed., *The Eighteenth Century in Russia.* Oxford, 1973.

Kaliazina, N. V., et al. *Dvorets Menshikova.* M., 1986.

Karavasva, E. M., and A. A. Shennikov. "Suzdal' v 1700 godu (po izobrazheniiu na ikone)." *AN,* no. 18 (1969).

Karger, M. K. *Novgorod Velikii.* L., 1961.

Kennett, A. *The Palaces of Leningrad.* New York, 1973.

Kerblay, B.H. *L'Isba d'hier et d'aujourd'hui: l'évolution de l'habitation rurale en U.R.S.S.* Lausanne, 1973.

Kirillov, V. V. "Metody proektirovaniia Semena Remezova." *AN,* no. 22 (1974).

————. "Postroiki Semena Remezova v Tobol'ske." *AN,* no. 14 (1962).

————. "Proekty 'obraztsovykh domov' razrabotannye S. Remezovym dlia Tobol'ska." *AN,* no. 12 (1960).

Kirpichnikov, A. N., and I. I. Khlopin. "Krepost' Kirillo-Belozerskogo monastyria i ee vooruzhenie v XVI–XVIII vekakh." *MilA SSSR,* no. 77 (1958).

Klokman, Iu. P. "Gorod v zakonadatel'stve russkogo absoliutizma v vtoroi polovine XVII–XVIII vv." In N. M. Druzhinin et al., *Absoliutizm v Rossii (XVII–XVIII vv.).* M., 1964.

————. *Sotsial'no-ekonomicheskaia istoriia russkogo goroda: vtoraia polovina XVIII veka.* M., 1967.

Kniazev, G. A. "Akademicheskii plan S.-Peterburga 1753 goda." *Izvestiia Vsesoiuznogo geograficheskogo obshchestva* 85, no. 3 (1953).

Komech, A. I., and V. I. Pluzhnikov, eds. *Pamiatniki arkhitektury Moskvy: Kreml', Kitai-gorod, tsentral'nye ploshchadi.* M., 1982.

Komelova, G. N. "K istorii sozdanii gravirovannykh vidov Peterburga i ego okrestnostei M. I. Makhaevym." *Trudy gos. Ermitazha* 11 (1970).

————, ed. *Kul'tura i iskusstvo petrovskogo vremeni: publikatsii i issledovaniia.* L., 1977.

Kopylova, S. V. *Kamennoe stroitel'stvo v Sibiri konets XVII–XVIIIv.* Novosibirsk, 1979.

Korol'kov, M. "Arkhitekty Treziny." *Starye gody* (April 1911).

Kostochkin, V. V. "Dereviannyi 'gorod' Koly (Iz istorii russkogo oboronnogo zodchestva kontsa XVI–nachala XVIII vv.)." *MiIA SSSR,* no. 77 (1958).

———. *Drevnie russkie kreposti.* M., 1964.

———. *Fedor Kon': Gosudarev master.* M., 1964.

———. *Krepostnoe zodchestvo drevnei Rusi.* M., 1969.

———. "K voprosu o traditsiiakh i novatorstve v russkom zodchestve XVI–XVII vv." *AN,* no. 27 (1979).

———. *Russkoe oboronnoe zodchestvo kontsa XIII–nachala XVI vekov.* M., 1962.

Krasheninnikova, N. L. "K voprosu planirovki gorodov Orenburgskikh linii (na primere g. Troitska)." *AN,* no. 27 (1979).

———. "Oblik russkogo goroda XVIII v. na primere Orenburga." *AN,* no. 24 (1976).

———. "Printsipy reguliarnoi planirovki gorodov-krepostei Rossii XVIII v. na primere Orenburga." *AN,* no. 21 (1973).

———. "Stroitel'stvo russkikh krepostei XVIII v. po 'obraztsovym' proektam." *AN,* no. 25 (1976).

Krasovskii, M. *Ocherk istorii moskovskago perioda drevnerusskago tserkovnago zodchsetva.* M., 1911.

Kudriavtsev, F. *Zolotoe kol'tso.* L., 1974.

Kudriavtseva, T. N. "Kadashevskaia sloboda v Moskve i ee razvitie v kontse XVII–XVIII vv. (gradostroitel'nyi analiz)." *AN,* no. 27 (1979).

Lavrov, V. A. *Razvitie planirovochnoi struktury istoricheski slozhivshikhsia gorodov.* M., 1977.

Lazarev, V. N., et al., eds. *Drevnerusskoe iskusstvo: XVII vek.* M., 1964.

Leonov, A. I., et al. *Russkoe dekorativnoe iskusstvo.* 2 vols. M., 1963.

Lisaevich, I. *Domeniko Trezini.* L., 1986.

———. *Pervyi arkhitektor Peterburga.* L., 1971.

Lisovskii, V. G. *Akademiia khudozhestv.* L., 1972.

LoGatto, E. *Gli artisti italiani in Russia.* 3 vols. Rome, 1934–1943.

Loktev, V. "O Bazhenovskom proekte rekonstruktsii Moskovskogo kremlia." In A. N. Barnov, ed., *Khudozhestvennaia kul'tura XVIII veka: materialy nauchnoi konferentsii (1973).* M., 1974.

Lossky, B. *J. B. A. LeBlond, architecte de Pierre le Grand, son oeuvre en France.* Prague, 1936.

———. "Un architecte français en Russie à l'aube du XIXe siècle: J. P. Thomas, dit de Thomon." *Revue des études slaves* 57, no. 4 (1985).

Loukomski (Lukomskii), G. K. *L'Architecture réligieuse russe du XIe siècle au XVIIIe siècle.* Paris, 1929.

Lukomskii, G. K. "Ukrainskii Barokko." *Apollon,* 1911, no. 2.

Luppov, S. P. *Istoriia stroitel'stva Peterburga v pervoi chetverti XVIII veka.* M./L., 1957.

Makovetskii, I. V. *Pamiatniki narodnogo zodchestva russkogo severa.* M., 1955.

Makovskii, S. "Dve podmoskovnyia Kn. S. M. Golitsyna." *Starye gody* (January 1910).

Mikhailov, A. *Arkhitektor D. V. Ukhtomskii i ego shkola.* M., 1954.

Moleva, N., and E. Beliutin. *Pedagogicheskaia sistema Akademii khudozhestv XVIII veka.* M., 1956.

Nekrasov, A. I., ed. *Barokko v Rossii.* M., 1926.

———. *Ocherki po istorii drevnerusskogo zodchestva.* M., 1936.

———. *Russkii ampir.* M., 1935.

Nickel, H. L. *Medieval Architecture in Eastern Europe.* New York, 1983. (Originally published as *Osteuropäische Baukunst des Mittelalters.* Leipzig, 1981.)

Nikitin, A. V. "Oboronitel'nye sooruzheniia zasechnoi cherti XVI–XVII v." *MiIA SSSR* no. 44 (1955).

Nikolaev, E. V. *Klassicheskaia Moskva.* M., 1975.

Olgy, B. I. "Arkhitekturnye pamiatniki Irkutska XVIII–nachala XIX vv." *AN,* no. 27 (1979).

Opolovnikov, A. V. *Russkii Sever.* M., 1977.

Ostroi, O. S., ed. *Fond graviur kak istochnik izucheniia arkhitektury russkikh gorodov.* L., 1978.

Ovchinnikova, E. S. *Tserkov' Troitsy v Nikitnikakh (XVII veka).* M., 1970.

Ovsiannikov, Iu. *Novo-Devichii monastyr'*. M., 1968.

Palentreer, S. N. "Sady XVII veka v Izmailove." *Soobshchen. III*, no. 7 (1956).

Petrov, A. N. "Palaty fel'dmarshala B. P. Sheremeteva i F. M. Apraksina v Moskve." *AN*, no. 6 (1956).

———. "Peterburgskii zhiloi dom 30–40-kh godov XVIII stoletia." *Ezhegodnik III 1960*. M., 1961.

Petrov, A. N., et al. *Pamiatniki arkhitektury Leningrada*. L., 1971.

Petrov, P. N. *Istoriia Sankt-Peterburga s osnovaniia goroda do 1782*. SPb., 1873.

———, ed. *Sbornik materialov dlia istorii S-Peterburgskoi Akademii khudozhestv za sto let eia sushchestvovaniia*, vol. 1. SPb., 1864.

Piliavskii, V. I. "Ivan Kuz'mich Korobov (materialy k izucheniiu tvorchestva)." *AN*, no. 4 (1953).

———. *Smol'nyi*. L., 1970.

Piliavskii, V. I., and N. Ia. Gorshkova. *Russkaia arkhitektura XI–nachala XX v*. L., 1978.

Piliavskii, V. I., et al. *Ermitazh: istoriia i arkhitektura zdanii*. L., 1974.

Pod"iapol'skii, S. S. "Venetsianskie istoki arkhitektury moskovskogo Arkhangel'skogo sobora." In G. V. Popov, ed., *Drevnerusskoe iskusstvo: zarubezhnye sviazi*. M., 1975.

Podol'skii, R. "Ivan Korobov." *Sovetskaia arkhitektura*, no. 3 (1952).

———. "Petrovskii dvorets na Iauze." *AN*, no. 1 (1951).

Popov, I. G. *Vvedenie v istoriiu g. S.-Peterburga*. M., 1903.

Predtechenskii, A. V., et al. *Peterburg petrovskogo vremeni*. L., 1948.

Proskuriakova, T. S. "O preemstvennosti v russkom gradostroitel'stve vtoroi poloviny XVIII v." *AN*, no. 33 (1985).

———. "O reguliarnosti v russkom gradostroitel'stve XVII–XVIII vv." *AN*, no. 28 (1980).

———. "Osobenosti Sibirskogo barokko." *AN*, no. 27 (1979).

———. "Planirovochnye kompozitsii gorodov-krepostei Sibiri (vtoroi poloviny XVII—60-e XVIII v.)." *AN*, no. 25 (1976).

———. "Staroe i novoe v gradostroitel'stve Sibiri (vtoraia polovina XVII–XVIII vv.)." *AN*, no. 26 (1978).

Rappoport, P. A. *Drevnerusskaia arkhitektura*. M., 1970.

Raskin, A. *Petrodvorets (Peterhof)*. 2d ed. L., 1979.

Rebas, H. "Von Landskrone bis St. Petersburg: zur Frage der Besiedlung der Neuwandung bis 1703." *Journal of Baltic Studies* 14, no. 3 (1983).

Rozman, G. *Urban Networks in Russia, 1750–1800, and Premodern Periodization*. Princeton, 1976.

Rzianin, M. I. *Pamiatniki russkogo zodchestva*. M., 1950.

Sakharova, I. G. "O datirovke i rasprostvanenii nekotorykh vidov Moskovskikh izraztsov." *MIA SSSR*, no. 44 (1955).

Savkov, V. M. "Issledovanie krepostnykh soruzhenii Oreshka-Shlissel'burga." In R. E. Krupnova et al., eds., *Iz istorii restavratsii pamiatnikov kul'tury*. M., 1974.

Schmidt, A. J. "Architecture in Nineteenth-Century Russia: The Enduring Classic." In T. G. Stavrou, ed., *Art and Culture in Nineteenth-Century Russia*. Bloomington, Ind., 1983.

———. "The Restoration of Moscow after 1812." *Slavic Review* 40, no. 1 (1981).

Semionova, I. *Ostankino: Eighteenth-Century Country Estate*. Translated by V. Friedman. L., 1981.

Shaw, D. J. B. "Southern Frontiers of Muscovy, 1550–1700." In J. H. Bater and R. A. French, eds., *Studies in Russian Historical Geography*, vol. 1. New York, 1983.

Shilkov, V. "Proekty obraztsovykh zagorodnykh domov D. Trezini i zastroika beregov Fontanki." *AN*, no. 7 (1955).

———. "Proekty planirovki Peterburga 1737–1740 godov." *AN*, no. 4 (1953).

———. "Roboty A. V. Kvasova i I. E. Starova po planirovke russkikh gorodov." *AN*, no. 4 (1953).

———. "Zodchii Timofei Usov." *AN*, no. 4 (1953).

Shkvarikov, V. A. *Ocherki istorii planirovki i zastroiki russkikh gorodov.* M., 1954.

——. *Planirovka gorodov Rossii XVIII i nachala XIX veka.* M., 1939.

Shkvarikov, V. A., et al. *Gradostroitel'stvo.* M., 1954.

Shmit, F. I., ed. *Russkoe iskusstvo XVII veka: sbornik statei po istorii russkogo iskusstva do-Petrovskogo perioda.* L., 1929.

Simonov, A. G., and M. G. Lukashevich. *Rus' belokamennaia.* L., 1969.

Snegirev, V. *Aristotel' Fioravanti i perestroika moskovskogo kremlia.* M., 1935.

Spegal'skii, Iu. P. "K voprosu o vzaimovliianii dereviannogo i kamennogo zodchestva v drevnei Rusi." *AN,* no. 19 (1972).

——. *Pskov: khudozhestvennye pamiatniki.* 2d ed. L., 1972.

Speranskii, A. N. *Ocherki po istorii Prikaza kamennykh del Moskovskogo gosudarstva.* M., 1930.

Suslov, V. *Ocherki po istorii drevne-russkago zodchestva.* SPb., 1889.

Sytin, P. V. *Istoriia planirovki i zastroiki Moskvy: materialy i issledovaniia.* 2 vols. M., 1950–54.

Sytina, T. M. "Arkhitektura russkoi provintsii pervoi poloviny XVIII veka." *Ezhegodnik III 1957.* M., 1958.

——. "Russkoe arkhitekturnoe zakonodatel'stvo pervoi chetverti XVIII v." *AN,* no. 18 (1969).

Tel'tevskii, P. A. "Zhilye doma XVII–XVIII vekov v Cheboksarakh." *Pamiatniki kul'tury: issledovanie i revstavratsiia,* no. 3 (1961).

——. *Zodchii Bukhvostov.* M., 1960.

Terekhov, V. S. *Russkaia natsional'naia arkhitektura/Russian National Architecture.* Frankfurt/Main, 1983. (Text in Russian and English.)

Thompson, M. W. *Novgorod the Great: Excavations at the Medieval City Directed by A. V. Artsikhovsky and B. A. Kolchin.* London, 1967.

Tits, A. A. "Dva drevnerusskikh proektnykh chertezha XVII veka." *Ezhegodnik III 1960.* M., 1961.

——. *Russkoe kamennoe zhiloe zodchestvo XVII veka.* M., 1966.

——. "Russkoe zhiloe zodchestvo XVII v. (Opyt izucheniia osnovnykh etapov razvitiia i kompozitsionnykh priemov)." *Soobshchen. III,* no. 12 (1958).

Trubinov, Iu. V. "Letnii dvorets Menshikova v Peterburge." *AN,* no. 29 (1981).

Tsapenko, M. P. *Arkhitektura Levoberezhnoi Ukrainy XVII–XVIII vekov.* M., 1967.

——. "Arkhitektura Ukrainy vtoroi poloviny XVII—20-e gg. XVIII v." In N. Ia. Kolli et al., eds., *Vseobshchaia istoriia arkhitektury,* vol. 6. M., 1968.

Tverskoi, L. M. *Russkoe gradostroitel'stvo do kontsa XVII veka: planirovka i zastroika russkikh gorodov.* L./M., 1953.

Uspenskii, A. I. *Imperatorskie dvortsy.* 2 vols. M., 1913.

Vagner, G. K. "Cherty traditsii i novatorstva v Riazanskoi arkhitekture kontsa XVII-nachala XVIII vekov." *AN,* no. 12 (1960).

Vasil'ev, B. "K istorii planirovki Peterburga vo vtoroi polovine XVIII veka." *AN,* no. 4 (1953).

Viatkin, M. P., ed. *Ocherki istorii Leningrada,* vol. 1. M./L., 1955.

Vilkov, O. N., et al. *Istoriko-arkhitekturnyi muzei pod otkrytym nebom. Printsipy i metodika organizatsii.* Novosibirsk, 1980.

Vipers, B. (B. R. Vipper). *Baroque Art in Latvia.* Riga, 1939.

Vipper, B. R. *Arkhitektura russkogo barokko.* Edited by N. Ia. Libman and N. A. Evsina. M., 1978.

Voinov, V. S. "Andreas Shliuter—arkhitektor Petra (K voprosu o formirovanii stilia 'Petrovskoe barokko')." *Sovetskoe iskusstvoznanie,* 1976, no. 1.

Vorob'ev, A. V. "Voevodskii dvor v Novgorode." *AN,* no. 12 (1960).

Voronikhina, A. N. *Peterburg i ego okrestnosti v chertezhakh i risunkakh arkhitektorov pervoi treti XVIII veka: katalog vystavki.* L., 1972.

Voronin, N. N. "Ocherki po istorii russkogo zodchestva XVI–XVII vv." *Izvestiia gos. Akademii istorii material'noi kul'tury,* no. 92. M./L., 1934.

————. *Zodchestvo severo-vostochnoi Rusi XII–XV vekov.* 2 vols. M., 1960–62.

Voronov, N. V. "Dokumenty o kirpichnom proizvodstve XVII–XVIII vv." In A. A. Novosel'skii et al., *Materialy po istorii SSSR,* vol. 5. M., 1957.

Voyce, A. *The Art and Architecture of Medieval Russia.* Norman, Okla., 1967.

Vygolov, V. P., ed. *Pamiatniki russkoi arkhitektury i monumental'nogo iskusstva: materialy i issledovaniia.* M., 1980.

Zabello, S., V. Ivanov, and P. Maksimov. *Russkoe dereviannoe zodchestvo.* M., 1942.

Zagorovskii, V. P. *Belgorodskaia cherta.* Voronezh, 1969.

Zalozieckyj, V. R. "Die Barockarchitektur Osteuropas mit besonderer Berucksichtigung der Ukraine." *Abhandelungen des Ukrainischen Wissenschaftlichen Institutes in Berlin* 2 (1929).

Zernack, K. "Zu den regionalgeschichtlichen Voraussetzungen der Anfange Petersburgs." *Forschungen zur osteuropäischen Geschichte* 25 (1978).

Zombe, S. A. "Proekt plana Moskvy 1775 goda i ego gradostroitel'noe znachenie." *Ezhegodnik III 1960.* M., 1961.

Index